171 ANSWERS to the Most-Asked College Admission Questions

MARK STUCKER

171 ANSWERS to the Most-Asked College Admission Questions

Illustrations courtesy of Alin Aguilar

Interior layout and design by www.writingnights.org

Cover design by Nyasha Wooling
Cover design by Panagiotis Lampridis

Book preparation by Chad Robertson and Mark Stucker

Library of Congress Cataloging-in-Publication Data is available at loc.gov

ISBN 978-069-295-347-1 (paperback)

Manufactured in the United States of America

Dedication

This book is dedicated to all of the students and parents I have worked with at Westtown School, KIPP, and at School Match 4U.

You have made admissions, placement, and college coaching a constant source of joy and even exhilaration. It is you who inspired me to write *171 Answers.*

Contents

Section 1 – Selecting the Right Career

Section 2 – Building the Right College List

Section 3 – Getting Accepted Where You Apply

Section 4 – Paying for College Without Going Broke

Section 5 – Staying in and Graduating

SECTION 6 – RECOMMENDED RESOURCES

Ten of My Favorite Admission Quotes

1. "For too many parents and their children, getting into a highly selective school isn't just another challenge, just another goal. A yes or no from Amherst or Dartmouth or Duke or Northwestern is seen as the conclusive measure of a young person's worth, a binding verdict on the life that he or she has led up until that point, an incontestable harbinger of the successes or disappointments to come. Winner or loser: This is when the judgment is made. This is the great, brutal culling. What madness. And what nonsense." (Frank Bruni, author of *Where You'll Go Is Not Who You'll Be*)
2. "The commercialization of college admissions has created a crisis by undermining educational values, and the commercialization has been led by the Ranksters, the Rankings ... The rankings imply a degree of precision and authority that is simply not supported by educational data. Their influence on education in this country has grown way beyond any educational jurisdiction. They have dictated the way education is perceived and pursued." (Lloyd Thacker, Founder of the Education Conservancy)
3. "I actually thought at times at Stanford that having a perfect SAT hurt you. It represented a commitment to a standardized test that we really didn't think measured much." (Martin Walsh, Former Assistant Dean of Admission, Stanford University)
4. "College is a match to be made and not a prize to be won." (Frank Sachs, former president of the National Association for College Admission Counseling)
5. "Even more than impressive test scores or great transcripts or fantastic essays, colleges are looking for authenticity, not the appearance of authenticity, not the packaging of authenticity, not the strategy of authenticity. Just authenticity, plain and simple ... so why is that? If they detect exaggeration or pretense or packaging, how do they know which parts of the application are real?" (Robin Mamlet, Former Dean of Admissions, Stanford University)

6. "I mean, the most common test we had at Stanford was not how smart are they, and what have they invented, but it was actually, would you want to share a dorm with this person for a year?"(Martin Walsh, Former Assistant Dean of Admission, Stanford University)
7. "Economist Robert Reich, who was the country's labor secretary during Bill Clinton's administration, wrote a blistering attack on the *U.S News Rankings* in September 2015, after the latest installment was published. He complained that the rankings were analogous to a restaurant guide that gives top rankings to the most expensive establishments that are backed and frequented by the wealthiest gourmands and much lower rankings to the restaurants with the best food at lower prices that attracts a wide range of diners. He was making a point about diversity." (Frank Bruni, author of *Where You'll Go Is Not Who You'll Be*)
8. "Nobody cares what your activities are, at all. All they care is that you care what your activities are!" (Arun Ponnusamy, former admissions officer, University of Chicago)
9. "Personality is something people think is not a factor, but it is really hard in these environments for an admissions officer—because remember, they are people, and this is a selective process—to give an offer to someone they don't like." (Christopher LaBounty, Former Admissions Officer, MIT)
10. "Everything you do isn't about how it looks on a college application ... High school is all about getting into the right college. Your undergraduate program is all about getting into the right MBA or JD or medical school. And then you wind up in your adulthood working, or you have a family, and you look back and you're like, 'I didn't really have fun, I didn't really get to be a kid.'" (Gary Clark, Director of Undergraduate Admissions, UCLA)

Acknowledgments

Some wise sage aptly said, "If you see a turtle sitting on top of a fence post, it didn't get there by accident." My name may be on the book, but this truly was a team project.

- ✓ Special thanks to Alin Aguilar for your creative illustrations, but also for your sense of humor and upbeat disposition. It was when you joined our team that I thought, "This book has a chance to be special."
- ✓ Kasey Phifer-Byrne, this is the second project we have worked on together. Thanks for your skilled copywriting, and for telling me what I need to hear. You did all this while moving across the country and then moving again, all while getting ready to have your first child.
- ✓ Margarita Martinez, I cannot imagine hiring a better proofreader and line editor. I need a lot of your business cards because I will be telling everyone who asks me that your line editing and proofreading took our book to the next level.
- ✓ Panagiotis Lampridis, my first draft cover designer, thanks for being so patient with all of my revisions; you persevered even when an earthquake destroyed where you grew up.
- ✓ Nyasha Wooling, thanks for taking Panagiotis' initial cover design and bringing it to the next level. Thanks for designing the website for 171answers.com. Your commitment to excellence keeps me coming back and hiring you over and over again.
- ✓ Kimberly Blas, I am extremely pleased with your design work for all of our postcards, flyers, and our fair banner.
- ✓ Chad Robertson, you proved to be more than a book designer, but also a wise strategist.
- ✓ To Anika Madden, Marion Henderson, and Angela Campbell, thanks for always being there for me when I wanted to bounce an idea off of you.
- ✓ To my good friend, Dr. Dave Williams. We have known each other our whole lives. You were the one who challenged me to write this book. Thanks for your inspiration, encouragement, and persistence. You wouldn't take no for an answer, and I am grateful.

- ✓ To my wife Anitra, thanks for being so supportive and so patient with me not only for the 27 years we have been married, but because when I went into hibernation to dedicate myself to completing this book, you never complained one single time.
- ✓ To Karis and Joy, you were kind enough to not complain when I used your stories over and over throughout the book. I know I am biased, but I feel I have the best two daughters in the world.
- ✓ To my parents, Alfred and Norma Stucker, both lifetime educators. You gave me my passion for education but more importantly, you modeled putting Jesus Christ first in your lives.
- ✓ To all of the students and parents I have worked with over the years who have brought me so much joy.
- ✓ To Westtown School, the nine years (2001-2009) I did boarding school holistic admissions while simultaneously doing college counseling could not have been better training.
- ✓ To Angie Lyons, Jondre Pryor, Charmaine Lau, Dr. Lisa Shannon, Katie Rigby, and Siobhan Gardner, the six leaders at KIPP who have supported me 100 percent in my nine years at KIPP.
- ✓ To Daisy Abdur-Rahman, for her advice about the test prep questions in Section 2.

To the Lord Jesus Christ, for giving me the idea for this book; for giving me the health, the motivation, the discipline, the finances, and my amazing team.

Introduction

I know what you are thinking: how is this admission book different from the others? I would be thinking the same thing. There are a lot of outstanding college admissions books, and I'll let you know at the end of this book which ones I think are the best. But this one is different.

There are four things that are very unique about *171 Answers*, and one other thing that is rare:

1) *171 Answers* is a reference book; you don't have to read a 500-page book to get the answers to your most pressing questions. The 171 chapters take you right to the page that you need to get the answer to your urgent or curious college admission questions.

From 2012-2014, I poured my heart into developing a college admissions video series that was designed to be "your counselor in a box." When the *Game Changer* series was released in 2014, I was ecstatic. The response to the content was outstanding from those who watched the series, but I heard over and over, "Mark, I just don't have ten hours to watch DVDs." I learned my lesson! You may be working a second job just to make ends meet, and then you come home to children and other responsibilities. You have questions about this complex process, and you don't want to flip through 500 pages to get your answers.

It isn't just that we are busy, but also that our minds have changed. Microsoft found that since the year 2000 (or about when the mobile revolution began) the average attention span has dropped from 12 seconds to eight seconds.

2) We all nod our head in agreement when someone says, "a picture is worth a thousand words," but if we really believe that, why are there so few pictures in most nonfiction books? This book believes that personal stories coupled with images and illustrations are how we enjoy learning, and how we remember what we are exposed to. Our minds are a picture gallery, not an encyclopedia of facts. This book has detailed content, but it also has over two hundred true, fun, personal admissions stories from my experience. The stories are all masterfully illustrated with hand-drawn images that are insightful and witty, making *171 Answers* an enjoyable and memorable read.

3) This is a book your teenage child, who really needs this information, will read—even if they are a non-reader. Every college admission counselor will tell parents, "we want the student driving the bus and the parent in the passenger seat," but how can you trust your child if they don't have any college knowledge?

I sat down with Liz and her son Chris at a bookstore in Exton, Pennsylvania, while I was writing this book.

Liz said, "I'll buy that book and read it, but my son is not a reader." Chris spoke up and said, "I'll read the stories and look at the pictures."

You may be thinking, "Okay, great. But what good are 200 stories and illustrations going to do?" I was ecstatic, though, because the 200 stories and 200 illustrations teach powerful content. They aren't just fluff. This is a book that the non-reader will read.

4) *171 Answers* is written so that someone who knows nothing about the admission process can benefit immensely from it, but it is also written with such a level of depth and substance that even a college admission veteran will learn something. I wrote *171 Answers* in a way that really puts some meat on the bones.

Finally, so much has changed in college admissions since 2016, with Early FAFSA, the New SAT, and the ACT jettisoning the Plan and Aspire and replacing it with the PreACT. The Common App is letting juniors roll their information over, and using a whole new application, "The Coalition" is now here. Rates have changed for PLUS loans and Stafford Loans, and at the time I'm writing this introduction, the fate of DACA is now in the hands of Congress. There are a lot of great college admissions books, but if they came out before 2016, they may not be current enough; there have been many very important new developments in college admissions recently. Such a current comprehensive book is rare.

I encourage you to read the chapter titles very closely, and if we scratch where you are itching, take the plunge and go for it. I will be flattered if you read the book cover to cover, but it was written for you to use as a reference book.

Caveats

This is not a book about graduate school, medical school, for-profit colleges, or law school admissions. This is also not a book about admission to international colleges and universities.

I use the term *college* throughout the book. It is important to know that the word *college* is being used to represent colleges and universities. I realize that some parts of the world (including Canada, where I was born) believe a college is a non-selective institution that is not a first-choice option for academically talented students. However, in the United States, *college* and *university* are used interchangeably, and besides, college is two syllables, and university is five syllables, so it was just easier to use the word college throughout the book to speak for both college and universities.

The word *admission* and *admissions* are also used interchangeably throughout the book, as they are in the industry.

When I say "171 Answers to the Most-Asked Questions," I don't presume to speak for every college counselor. I am sharing my perspective. The truth is, sometimes I included some questions I *should* be asked more frequently.

Sometimes I refer to admission professionals as admission counselors, other times as admissions officers, and still other times as admission reps. These terms are all synonyms.

I also use private college coach (my preferred term), educational consultant, and independent counselor interchangeably.

The personal stories that you read are true. When a student or family wanted their names included and gave permission, we used their true names, but in other cases, we changed their names to protect their privacy.

We know that parents will buy this book and read it and we encourage that 100 percent, but in an attempt to really appeal to students, it is written directly to them.

Section 1

Selecting the Right Career

1

WHAT DOES IT REALLY MEAN TO BE SUCCESSFUL?

Our society often defines success in two words: "fame" and "fortune." Here's the thing, though. Many of the most successful people are neither well-known (fame) nor wealthy (fortune).

I define success differently. Success is to improve the lives of others in a way that utilizes your talents, and in a way that is also personally fulfilling for you. The more you do this, the more successful you are. Think of people like Oprah Winfrey, Bill Gates, Michelle Obama, Warren Buffett, and Lebron James. But think also of people like Bernie Madoff, who is famous for launching a 50-billion-dollar enterprise, but whose life has been an abysmal failure.

All components of this definition must be in place to achieve success. God gave you gifts to be used. God desires your life to be lived out doing something that fulfills you, and your life cannot be only about yourself.

As you read this book, keep this definition of success in mind. As students, we need to learn this early, and as parents, we must model it for our children.

I was a tenth grader sitting at our round kitchen table when my mom opened her mail to find a newspaper copy of Jack's college graduation photo. Mom had lost touch with Jack, a former student; he lived over four hours away, but someone who knew Mom had sent the clipping to her. Jack had room for four lines under his name, and this is what he said: "I attribute my success to my second grade teacher, Norma Stucker, who inspired me and taught me to believe in myself." Mom loved to teach, she was good at it, and she impacted lives. This is the embodiment of success.

2

WHAT FREE RESOURCES ARE THERE TO HELP ME IDENTIFY MY AREAS OF PASSION?

Try these online tests and note when their projections are similar.

http://yourfreecareertest.com This one is ideal for middle school, high school, or college students. It takes five minutes, and after answering about 50 questions, you'll have your answers immediately. Make sure to email the results to yourself and save the report.

http://mymajors.com This test uses your grades and passions to generate a list of majors where your strongest skills overlap with your interests.

Another fun and worthwhile endeavor is to have a parent, sibling, or someone else who knows you very well take the test as if they were you. Compare their results with the test you took by yourself.

Benjamin did not learn about these major and career tests until he had already graduated from Morehouse College. When he learned about them, he realized he could have saved himself $30,000 by starting out with the right major for him, instead of starting off with a bad fit and taking an extra year to graduate.

3

HOW CAN DOING A SELF-INVENTORY HELP ME ASSESS WHICH CAREERS I WILL FIND FULFILLING?

Career inventory tests are great, but some true introspection will help you tap into the knowledge of exactly what you love and will find fulfilling as a career. The old axiom still rings true: Find a job you love, and you will never work a day in your life. In my own life, I'm so passionate about finding the right school match for every student that I often take phone calls from families while on vacation. I'm often criticized for this, but taking these calls doesn't feel like work to me, because I find it fulfilling.

Think about the books you like to read for recreation. When you read, you are thirsting for knowledge. These choices are a window to your soul. Also think about the television shows you watch. Do you like

CSI? Maybe a career in forensics is right for you. If you're watching *CSPAN*, politics could be your future. Animal Planet's *The Vet Life*? Veterinary medicine could be your true passion.

One last thing to think about is where you choose to spend your money. The Bible is right in Matthew 6:21, which says, "where your treasure is, there your heart will be also."

I also encourage you to pay attention to what comes easy to you. Listen carefully to where others affirm that you are gifted. It may come from friends, relatives, or teachers. Here is what Proverbs 18:16 says: "A man's gift makes room for him, and brings him before great men."

Jennifer, a student I once worked with, claimed she hated to read. It really bothered her dad, because he was such an avid reader. I witnessed a heated argument over this, during which Jennifer's dad said that everyone likes to read once they learn what they love. One day, Jennifer told me she'd found an amazing book called *The Skin I'm In* by Sharon G. Flake. The book tells the story of a seventh grader who has low self-esteem because of her dark skin color. I wasn't surprised when Jennifer told me she'd realized that what she truly wanted to do was to provide counseling guidance to middle school girls.

4

WHAT FREE RESOURCES CAN I USE TO IDENTIFY WHAT THE BEST JOBS WILL BE IN THE FUTURE?

One of the most common mistakes students make is assuming that just because they graduated and have a degree, opportunities will open up to them like Moses parting the Red Sea. The truth is that jobs in the medical field, computer science, finance, and engineering are growing much faster than jobs in anthropology and graphic design.

Before choosing a major, take the results from your online major and career tests and study what those jobs will look like in the future. The best source for this is the Bureau of Labor Statistics Occupational Outlook Handbook. The OOH runs articles on the 20 fastest-growing jobs.

If you find you're not interested in those, you can check the projected growth rate for *all* jobs. Find the OOH at https://www.bls.gov

Just because your intended career path has only a modest growth forecast doesn't mean you should automatically reject it. It will, however, mean that you'll need to work harder, network better, and really research to understand what steps you'll have to take to land a quality job in your desired profession.

Tammy says that if she had to do it all over again, she wouldn't have been a dance major. She had no idea how hard it would be to find a job that used her major and feels like she'd have been much further ahead after graduating if she'd majored in something else. You can avoid this problem by researching the job market for your intended major.

5

HOW CAN THE INTERNET HELP ME LEARN WHAT A TYPICAL DAY LOOKS LIKE IN THE CAREER I'M CONSIDERING?

Once again, the Bureau of Labor Statistics Occupational Outlook Handbook is your best source for this information. Use the Occupational Finder feature at https://bls.gov/ooh/occupation-finder.htm. Type your desired career into the search bar.

For a work description, click on the "What They Do" tab. Also check out the "Work Environment tab" and other areas of interest to learn more about the career.

http://careers.org is another valuable resource.

When I met Jackie, she was a newlywed living in Philadelphia and we were attending the same church. Jackie looked sad one day, and I asked her what was wrong. She said, "Since I was five years old, I've wanted to be a doctor. Now, I am in a joint PhD and MD program at the University of Pennsylvania, and I start my days at 5:00 a.m. and end them very late in the evening. I don't see how I can have children. I've realized I wanted to be a doctor because my dad kept telling me I should be a doctor. I just wish I'd known what I was getting into before I went down this path." Always learn what the day-to-day life of someone in your career could look like.

6

HOW CAN THE INTERNET HELP ME LEARN WHAT SALARY I CAN EXPECT IN VARIOUS PROFESSIONS?

Find salary information at http://careers.org/salaries/step1 using the salary tool. The Occupational Outlook Handbook at the Bureau of Labor Statistics also has a "Pay" tab.

My favorite resource for this information is https://payscale.com. This website updates salary information on a daily basis using compensation data from over 40 million employees, and provides accurate pay projections based on where you live. Payscale has information on over 14,000 unique job titles and covers more than ten countries. Their sophisticated model uses over 250 factors that impact the accuracy of their projections. I encourage every person to consult this tool when they are considering a particular major and the career that follows it.

You can make a great case that the best comprehensive website for this important information is the government's College Scorecard: https://collegescorecard.ed.gov/. Here is how Wikipedia describes the value of the College Scorecard:

"The College Scorecard is an online tool, created by the United States government, for consumers to compare the cost and value of higher education institutions in the United States. It displays data in five areas: cost, graduation rate, employment rate, average amount borrowed, and loan default rate."

Simone was passionate about environmental activism, so she went to school to major in Environmental Studies. She secured a job and loved what she did, but one day she said to me, "I just can't take it anymore. I can barely pay my rent, my car expenses, and my grocery bill, and I don't even have any kids." She loved the job, but left it because the compensation forced sacrifices that became too much for her to bear. Had she consulted Payscale or other resources, she might not have been in for such a rude awakening.

7

HOW CAN THE INTERNET HELP ME UNDERSTAND WHAT STEPS I NEED TO TAKE TO REACH MY CAREER OBJECTIVES?

You have identified college majors that match your interests through surveys and self-assessment, and you've looked at what the career is actually like. You have checked out the job prospects for the future, and you feel like you can live with the compensation. Now it is time to find out how to actually *become* the professional you aspire to be.

Return to the OOH's Occupational Finder at http://bls.gov/ooh/occupational-finder.htm. Let's enter "school counselor" as an example, but this time we'll click on "How to Become One."

Also try a Google search for "College Navigator" and search for colleges that offer your major of interest. Give a call to the Department of

Interest for each school to ask what they recommend you do to become what you want to be.

If you're the parent, you can help your child by tapping into your network to talk to any school counselors you know. You can also tap into your friend network or social media network to reach further to find real-life models your child can talk to about their path into their career.

Angela was a high school senior who wanted to become a school counselor. She knew she needed a master's in school counseling, but she wanted to know what she could do earlier to reach her goal. In guiding her, I learned that the University of Georgia has one of the top programs in the nation in school counseling. I called and spoke to a student affairs professional who assists applicants as they apply. One of the key hints she gave me was to volunteer as much as you possibly can with youth in a wide range of different contexts. Angela was able to make a plan based on this recommendation.

8

HOW CAN I USE SHADOW DAYS AND INTERNSHIPS TO CONFIRM MY AREAS OF CAREER INTEREST?

Shadow days mean you can spend the day following someone who currently does what you aspire to do. By sticking to them like you are their shadow, you can learn things you won't find in a book or on the Internet.

Internships are like protracted shadow days, as they last longer. Internships usually last anywhere between two weeks and a year. They may be paid or unpaid, and you can sometimes earn credits for school through internships.

Let's say, for example, that you're thinking about becoming a physical therapist, and you don't know any physical therapists. You should ask all the adults you know if they know any physical therapists. If you ask enough people, you'll eventually find someone who does. You should then ask them if they'll help set up a meeting between you and this physical therapist. At the meeting, ask for a shadow day or for the opportunity to do an internship with them, and let them know that you'll perform whatever tasks they need in exchange for an up-close look at what the job is really like.

I do not mean to imply that if you follow the course I have laid out that you will not change your major or your career plans once you get to college. Major changes in college are inevitable, but utilizing the plan I have shared here will, at a minimum, help you identify your general areas of interest.

I met Dianne when she was a tenth grader working at the register of a Giant grocery store in Exton, Pennsylvania. She told me she'd wanted to be a dentist since she was six years old. Dianne was a student at the Westtown School, where my oldest daughter would be attending school in the fall. Dianne and I kept in touch, and during her senior year, I learned that for her senior project, she had set up a three-week unpaid internship in a dental office. Through that internship, Dianne learned something surprising: she hated dentistry. That internship was one of the best educational decisions she ever made, as it gave her a close-up look at the job she thought she wanted. Today, Dianne is a psychologist, and she couldn't be happier.

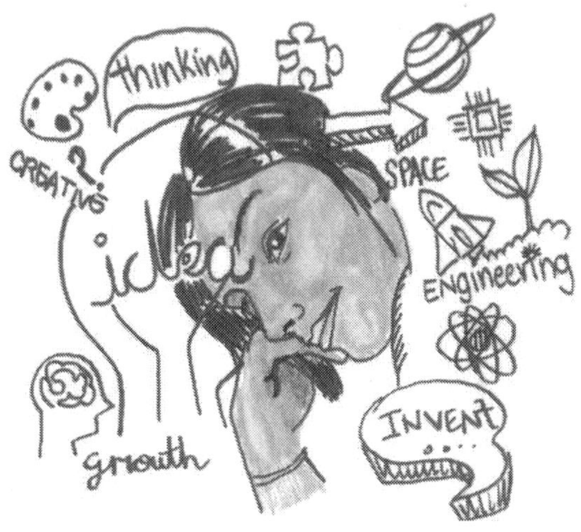

9

How can I prepare for the jobs that will be here in the future?

Many employment experts project that for students entering pre-kindergarten now, two-thirds of the jobs that will exist when they enter the workforce are not even on the radar today.

Ten years ago, who would have imagined that jobs like social media manager, Uber driver, and mobile app developer would be so popular? Who knew that cyber security engineers would even exist, let alone make over $100,000 in most locations? I had never heard of a life coach while I was growing up, and now I've met four just in the past six months. So how do you prepare for the job market when you don't know yet where the demand will be?

According to an article published on January 19, 2016, by the World Economic Forum, the ten most valuable skills in 2020 and beyond will be complex problem solving, critical thinking, creativity, people management, coordinating with others, emotional intelligence, judgment and decision-making, service orientation, negotiation, and cognitive flexibility. A lot of preparation for jobs involving these skills comes from the social sciences and humanities, so don't understate the value of a strong liberal arts foundation when choosing a college.

I seriously considered adding a chapter on the value of liberal arts colleges in this book. Their interdisciplinary approach to education, coupled with the way they develop critical thinkers, writers, speakers, and collaborators, is an ideal preparation for the jobs in the future. There are a lot of pejorative comments about the value of liberal arts colleges in the media, but I have been very impressed by the skillset and career trajectory I have seen from students I have coached that have gone to liberal arts colleges.

I had dinner with Anika three years after she had graduated from high school. I had helped her through the college selection process, and she was now a political science major with a minor in sociology. I remember being awestruck by her ability to synthesize information and to think critically outside the box. I complimented her on her stunning thinking skills and asked her where they'd come from. She credited her interdisciplinary studies and liberal arts foundation. Today, Anika is a highly-respected attorney.

10

A CHALLENGE FOR PARENTS ABOUT YOUR CHILD'S CAREER SELECTION ...

I might offend some parents here, but I'm a straight shooter. Your child's choice of profession is not your chance at a do-over. It is not your chance to correct mistakes you feel you have made. This also applies to the college your child selects.

You have lived your life and made a number of choices along the way about what you wanted to do with it. How would you feel if you hadn't been allowed to make those decisions for yourself? I know you mean well. You love your child with all your heart. Are you trying to get them to become a doctor, lawyer, or engineer because you believe it will lead to better life opportunities? Guess what: you may be right. But it is your child's life, and they may not be satisfied doing what you want them to do. Even if they end up satisfied with a career you encourage them to pursue, part of growing up is hitting your head against the wall and learning from your own mistakes.

Don't read this and think, "You are absolutely right. It's really sad when parents act like this." The truth is, we all live vicariously through our children sometimes, and it's natural to want them to do well. But we can't live in denial about the moments we try to make their decisions for them based on our own regrets or accomplishments.

I once told my daughter, Joy, that if she took some marketing courses in college and became an active tour guide, she could transition to a college admissions job, and then after five years, she could come work with me. She could have her own clients and eventually take over my private college counseling practice. Joy said to me, "Dad, that's your thing. That isn't my thing." It was hard to hear, but she was right.

Marilyn was a mother who met with me to discuss the future of her seventh-grade daughter, Nancy. Marilyn told me, "Nancy is going to be a veterinarian, but she's also getting an MBA so she can have her own performing arts studio as well."

I said, "It seems like you have all of this planned out. What if Nancy changes her mind?"

Marilyn replied, "I know what I want for her; I have known this since she was in the second grade."

It's difficult to avoid making plans for our children, but it's important they make their own plans and decisions. Nancy needed to be able to learn for herself what she wanted to do.

Section 2

Building the Right College List

11

WHAT IS THE DIFFERENCE BETWEEN "HOLISTIC ADMISSIONS" AND "ADMISSION BY THE NUMBERS"?

Admission by the numbers means that only test scores and GPA (Grade Point Average) determine acceptance. Many colleges treat these as the two "vital signs," kind of like doctors with blood pressure and pulse. In fairness to these schools, many concede that they wish they could take other factors into consideration, but a lack of staffing in their admissions offices forces them to automate the process with computers. A lot of colleges will also factor the rigor of the course into their admissions-by-the-numbers formula. It is also very common for colleges to differentiate between the five core courses of math, science, history, English, and foreign language versus the electives. This is often referred to as Academic GPA or Core GPA.

There are two variations to admission by the numbers. The first one I call the "mandatory minimum method," in which you must have at least a certain GPA or test score to be admitted, no matter how impressive your numbers. At these schools, you could theoretically graduate at the top of your high school class and still not meet the mandatory minimum for admission to a particular school.

The other variation is often called a "freshman index formula" or an "eligibility index." In this approach, it's still all about the numbers, but a higher GPA can make up for lower test scores. At schools that use this approach, like the California state schools, for example, bonus points are often given to students who take advanced courses. Some state schools will also prioritize state residency, and some majors may require higher numbers, but it's still all about the numbers.

Colleges that use these eligibility indexes are very transparent about their admissions criteria. They will usually have a calculator on their websites. Many of them will have tables that show the various test scores you will need depending on your GPA.

Here is an actual example from the University of West Georgia for 2018 using the Redesigned SAT. This comes directly from the undergraduate admission section of their website.

Putting it All Together

Students must have a minimum Freshman Index of 2120.

Freshman Index Formula:

- SAT*: Freshman Index = (500 x Academic High School GPA) + (Critical Reading SAT* + Math SAT*)
- ACT: Freshman Index = (500 x Academic High School GPA) + (ACT Composite x 42) + 88.

Holistic admissions is by far the most accurate way to assess a student. This approach looks at the whole student, using factors like essays, recommendations, interviews, extracurricular activities, demonstrated interest, institutional priorities, and more.

"Holistic admissions" has become a buzzword phrase. Most prestigious schools use it, and others want to claim it. Two women could say they are joggers, but one jogs one mile once a week and the other jogs five miles a day five times a week. This is sort of how holistic admissions is. UCLA and Scripps are two schools in the Greater LA area that claim they do holistic admissions, but Scripps is looking at more variables in their version of holistic assessment.

Knowing how you'll be evaluated helps you develop an effective admissions strategy. There are many places you can look to find this information, but my favorite is http://bigfuture.collegeboard.org. This site is highly accurate, easy to use, and for what it's worth, it's also aesthetically pleasing. Use the search bar to find the college you're interested in, then click the "Applying" tab, "the "What's Important" tab, and the "Application Requirements" tab.

I also love using http://www.collegedata.com for getting an accurate understanding of the admission selection criteria. Enter any college into the search bar and click the admissions tab. Then scroll down to the "Selection of Students" section and you will see the admission criteria. Try both websites and see which one you like the most. Recently, more of the students I coach have been preferring CollegeData over BigFuture when I have shared this information with them.

When Mr. Watson called me, he was livid. I had to hold the phone six inches from my ears, he was yelling so loudly. His daughter had earned a 1550 on the SAT and had a very high GPA, but she had been wait-listed at Princeton while another strong student with lower scores and GPA had been admitted. He couldn't understand what had gone wrong. Mr. Watson thought Princeton handled its admissions by the numbers, but they actually use holistic admissions.

12

HOW MANY COLLEGES SHOULD I APPLY TO?

Anyone who gives you a magic number doesn't know what they're talking about. Individual situations vary.

With the growth of the Common Application, applying to multiple schools has become much easier. According to the National Association for College Admission Counseling (NACAC), the number of students applying to seven or more schools reached 36 percent in 2015, up from 17 percent in 2005, and only 9 percent in 1990. This is compounded because college admissions deans are usually evaluated partly on whether they generate more applications than the year before. This leads to more creative ways of generating applications, like VIP Applications, and the waiving of application fees.

My recommendations are usually to apply to two to four Reach schools, two to four Mid-range schools, two to four Likely schools, and one Safety school. Every school on your list should be a financial match.

Students who need financial aid and are undocumented or are applying to highly selective schools should plan to apply on the higher number range of my recommendations.

Applying to too many schools wastes your money and causes you to produce lower-quality applications if you spread yourself thin. It takes a lot of time to generate a quality application. It involves research, relationship building, and plenty of time editing. Most counselors and admissions officers are concerned about how many colleges some students are applying to.

In the past, students used to spend more time researching schools, and the fact that a school was being applied to meant something. Now, many students are applying to twenty or more schools, and they figure they will see where they get in and then start doing their research. This is forcing colleges to prioritize early decision applicants and to use more sophisticated methods of assessing who is really interested and who is not. According to the 2015 NACAC State of College Admissions report, "Between Fall 2014 and Fall 2015, colleges reported average increases of 10 percent in the number of early decision applicants." The ease of applying through the Common Application is one reason MIT and Georgetown do not accept the Common App.

I recently had a firm disagreement with the founder of a large independent consulting company. He was advocating that his clients apply to between 15-25 colleges. It really struck a nerve with me because of my nine years traveling all over the country recruiting students. I told him that if I was in college admissions and I knew someone came from his firm and was giving this advice, it wouldn't work in his favor. He is telling colleges that they have between a 4 percent (1 in 25) to a 6.67 percent (1 in 15) chance of enrolling one of his students.

You have to think of yourself, but you also have to think of what's fair to the colleges. Do your homework and you can get your list down to a number of colleges that is fair to you and fair to the colleges you are applying to.

On November 14, the *New York Times* published an article titled "Applications by the Dozen, as Anxious Seniors Hedge College Bets." In the article, Brandon Kosatka, Director of Student Services at the Thomas Jefferson High School for Science and Technology in Alexandria, VA, said he had recently worked with a student who had applied to 56 colleges. Students are applying to more colleges than ever before!

13

WHAT ARE "LOTTERY SCHOOLS," "REACH SCHOOLS," "MID-RANGE SCHOOLS," "LIKELY SCHOOLS," AND "SAFETY SCHOOLS"?

Lottery school: a college for which your qualifications are so far away from making you a competitive applicant that applying would be a waste of time and money. Getting in would be as difficult as winning the lottery.

Reach school: you have a possible, but not probable, chance of admission. Your qualifications may be slightly lower than the profile of a student they typically admit. Some colleges are so selective that they are Reach schools for practically everyone who applies there.

Mid-range school: this is a school to which you wouldn't be surprised either way about being admitted or denied, because your qualifications put you in a range where admission would be hard to predict. These schools are sometimes referred to as "target schools," "match schools," coin tosses," or "50/50 schools."

Likely school or Probable school: your qualifications are clearly stronger than the average admitted student, but there is at least some possibility you could be denied or waitlisted.

Safety school: you are nearly 100 percent sure you will be admitted. The only schools you can use as Safety schools are those that admit by the numbers, and you know you clearly meet their requirements. What many people call Safety schools are actually Likely schools, so be honest with yourself when you make your list. There are a number of credible places for reliable data to help you discern how your qualifications compare with students they typically accept, but I recommend: http://bigfuture.collegeboard.org or http://www.collegedata.com.

You can also try an Internet search with the name of the college you're interested in and the words "Common Data Set," although not every school provides the information. The Common Data Set is the most comprehensive source of information on how admissions decisions are made. It is a collaborative effort to amass knowledge from the College Board, *Peterson's, U.S. News,* and Wintergreen/Orchard House. Common Data Set, aka CDS, is divided into 10 categories:

A. General Information
B. Enrollment and Persistence
C. First-Time, First-Year (Freshmen) Admission
D. Transfer Admission
E. Academic Offerings and Policies
F. Student Life
G. Annual Expenses
H. Financial Aid
I. Instructional Faculty and Class Size
J. Degrees Conferred

I had to console Beth when news of college admissions decisions began to come in. She was running through the school halls nearly hysterical; tears poured down her cheeks and her self-esteem was at an all-time low. Beth had learned that American University had accepted 15 students from her private high school the year before, and she didn't know anyone who had applied and hadn't been accepted other than herself.

Beth had made three mistakes: first, she'd considered American a Safety school when it was really a Likely school. Second, she hadn't considered that sometimes you don't get into your Likely schools. Third, she didn't realize that when a school uses holistic admissions, there are no guarantees of getting accepted.

14

WHY IS IT IMPORTANT TO HAVE FINANCIAL MATCH SCHOOLS AT VARIOUS LEVELS OF SELECTIVITY?

Applying to schools at a variety of selectivity levels is important, but you need to make sure every school you apply to is affordable to you. Not making sure of this before applying is one of the biggest mistakes students and parents make.

I recommend students apply to a few Reach schools because sometimes, a rising tide lifts all boats. In other words, for ambitious students, Reach schools will be comprised of other high-achieving students who will challenge and bring out the best in each other. Surrounding yourself with other high achieving students also helps you prepare a solid network you can use later in life. Reach schools also often have a lot of money, and their aid packages can be some of the most generous. This is particularly true for schools that have a strong need-based aid program, when the applying student qualifies for a lot of financial aid. These schools often have excellent reputations.

That said, do not always feel compelled to choose the most selective school to which you are admitted. You will face a lot of pressure to do this if you attend certain schools in this country. This is another common mistake.

I was really proud of Joy's friend, Kyelin. Kyelin was a straight-A student for all four years with plenty of academic rigor, high testing, and great teacher recommendations. She could have gone to virtually any college in the country, but she knew that Xavier University of Louisiana produces the most black doctors in the nation, year after year. She rejected the mentality that said she should select a Reach school over Xavier just because it is harder to get in.

Mid-range schools are important because applying only to Reach schools can be emotionally deflating, and lots of rejection isn't great for anyone's self-esteem. These schools present a balance between the advantages of a Reach school and the higher acceptance probability of a Likely school.

Likely schools and Safety schools are extremely important. The goal is to attend college, so apply to schools you are very likely to be admitted to. At the same time, be sure to apply to Likely schools that you actually would be happy to attend. Try not to fixate on one or two schools, and approach application season with the mindset that all of your schools are great and you would be happy to attend any of them.

Peter was an outstanding student who applied to a range of schools, all of which I made sure would meet his financial needs. The first decision Peter received was a denial. I knew how ambitious Peter was, and I prepared myself to take on a different counselor role: that of encourager and consoler instead of information-sharer. I said to him, "I'm so sorry, Peter. Stay positive, because good news will come your way."

Peter replied, "Teacher Mark, I love all of the schools I applied to and any of them will provide plenty of opportunities for me. I'm not worried about getting into one school."

I wish I could get everyone to think like Peter!

15

WHAT IS A COLLEGE ADMISSION CALCULATOR, AND HOW CAN IT HELP ME BUILD MY COLLEGE LIST?

A college admission calculator uses horizontal and vertical axes to plot ACT or SAT scores and GPAs. These calculators use different colors to differentiate between students who were accepted, denied, and waitlisted. Another name for a college admission calculator is a "scattergram." Obviously, if you want credible results, you must enter accurate information.

My personal favorite scattergram that is available to everyone is from Cappex. Look up a college, go to the "Admissions" tab, and click the "What are my chances?" link. Find it at https://cappex.com/hq/scattergram.

In addition to using different colors for accepted, denied, and wait-listed students, Cappex has a color for students who were accepted but won't attend, and for the point where your test scores and GPA intersect, so you can see how students with profiles similar to yours fared. What I love most about this calculator is that it's based off self-reported actual admissions decisions, with millions in their database.

If you work for a CBO that helps underrepresented students, Cappex has spun off a similar website called www.collegegreenlight.com that works the exact same way as Cappex, but it is targeted to under-resourced and under-represented students. It offers the same scattergrams and the "What are my chances?" feature, but it also allows a counselor to see all of their students' profiles. I use http://www.collegegreenlight.com.com for keeping track of my KIPP students, and I find it to be an invaluable resource. This is a free service, and I cannot recommend it highly enough.

Cappex and College Greenlight use the Integrated Postsecondary Education Data System (IPEDS) for their source of data. IPEDS is the government's primary source of data for colleges, universities, and technical and vocational schools.

Also check out the calculators from Niche (https://niche.com/colleges/admissions-calculator) and Parchment (https://parchment.com/c/college/search/browse).

If your school subscribes to Hobsons' Naviance, you will absolutely want to check out their scattergrams, because they'll reveal admissions information about students from your actual high school. Naviance is now used by 40 percent of schools across the country. If your school uses Naviance, you are blessed. It is expensive, and your school has made a big investment in your college counseling.

This is a tremendous organization and communication tool between you and your counselor and teachers. You'll get notifications of college visits to your school, important deadlines, etc. Your counselor will probably also use the message feature to send you important messages about the college process. You can submit transcripts and teacher recommendations through Naviance. I strongly recommend you go through a Naviance tutorial and master all of the features available to you with their scattergrams and their other information on their college tab.

It's extremely important to note that you can't use these calculators to conclude whether you'll absolutely be accepted or denied to any given school. There are too many variables to consider. Sometimes when students learn about scattergrams they put too much or too little confidence in their likelihood of admission. There is a reason there are a lot of outlier decisions. Colleges have their institutional priorities that lead them to take students with lower scores and grades. However, they are incredibly useful tools for developing a realistic perspective on your admission chances.

Tamar was like a lot of students I work with; she was a very competitive applicant, but she lacked confidence because her test scores were not as high as the average scores at the colleges she was interested in, and it was causing her to doubt herself. I had her complete a detailed Cappex account and enter the schools she was interested in. When she clicked the "Colleges" tab and looked at the "Chances" bar, it really gave her confidence and it let her double check and confirm what her Reach, Mid-range, and Likely schools were.

16

Important Criteria to Determine Whether a College Is a Match for Me

This list of criteria is for both parents and students to think about. Many of these factors may already be on your radar, but if not, they'll help you consider things you may not have thought of when starting to build your college list.

1. Academic Difficulty Level

- Valued by bright and ambitious students who want to be challenged and want to see how they measure up
- Important to very social students who are concerned about work/life balance
- Important to students questioning their academic self-confidence

א When I am helping them build their college lists, I ask the students I coach, "How rigorous do you want your college classes to be in comparison to your current high school curriculum?"

James attended a very rigorous high school. When I met with him, he was stressed out and consistently going to bed at 1:00 a.m. In our consultation, James told me, "I don't want a college as hard as my high school."

2. Campus Beauty

- א Some students know what they're looking for in the aesthetics of a campus and articulate it upfront, while others are moved by the beauty of the campus after their visit.
- א Beauty is in the eye of the beholder and is highly subjective.
- א Most students care at least a little about what their campus looks like, but for some it's a major factor.
- א The best way to know this is by visiting a wide range of different colleges and seeing what campus 'feel' you are looking for. Beauty is only one component of campus feel, but for a lot of students it is an important one.

Wang was obsessed with choosing a college that was scintillating in its beauty. She once told me, "If I'm going to live there for four years, why would I not want it to be beautiful?" Wang wanted her campus to look like a resort. She flipped through the promotional materials each school sent her, and unless it was striking, she had no interest in visiting the school.

3. CAMPUS RULES

- I don't usually have students who use rules to select their college, but many will use this factor to cross a college off their list.
- Parents may also feel strongly about certain policies.
- Schools may have rules surrounding students having a car on campus, policies on drinking, curfews and coed visitation policies, requirements about living on campus, and rules about meal plans.

Robert was a student who had originally looked at traditional engineering schools, but chose instead to go into the Coast Guard. Later, I was talking to Rob and asked his opinion on who is not a good fit for the Coast Guard.

Rob immediately said, "Students who don't like a lot of rules and a lot of structure."

4. CAREER PLACEMENT

- ℵ This factor is rising in importance as the changing economy causes more students to graduate college without jobs waiting for them.
- ℵ The Career Placement office is one of the most valuable and most under-utilized resources on college campuses.
- ℵ The Career Placement office can help students with interview preparation, internships, résumés, and career guidance, and they often bring job fairs and actual job offers to campus.

Jeff, who had been a dean of admissions for over a decade and had 20 years of experience in college admissions, was speaking on a panel in the Philadelphia area. Of recent changes in students' interest in career placement, Jeff said, "Never before in my 20 years have I had so many parents ask about the ROI on their investment in my school, saying that it is no longer assumed that their child will graduate from my school with a great opportunity awaiting them. We have to beef up our Career Center to prove our value like never before."

5. CLASS SIZE

Those who care about this one *really* care. Small classes are the equivalent of individualized and personalized education, and this is what parents want. I once did a survey of twenty-five desirable characteristics and how important parents at a private high school thought these traits were. A personalized education with individual attention scored off the charts. Often, students don't care about this, and some students I have worked with actually prefer large classes.

It has been 35 years since I enrolled in college at Michigan State University. My memory has faded, but I do remember six particular classes. I remember a sociology course with an internationally-renown Russian professor. I remember my political science course on the "Ugly American." I remember my Marriage and the Family class in which the twelve of us students critiqued each other's papers. I remember a computer science class, and an urban sociology class called "The Ghetto." Most of my classes at MSU were large, but those are not the ones I remember. That is the impact of small classes.

6. CLUBS AND ORGANIZATIONS

- ℵ Sororities and fraternities
- ℵ Spiritual growth organizations
- ℵ Race-based affinity groups
- ℵ Women in STEM organizations
- ℵ Community service organizations
- ℵ Entrepreneurial organizations
- ℵ Ultimate Frisbee and other recreational clubs
- ℵ Robotics
- ℵ Debate, etc.

Before Mo went to boarding school at Choate, he had not heard of Ultimate Frisbee. He gave it a try, and sure enough, he loved it. Mo went on to attend Ultimate Frisbee summer camps, and he played all four years in high school. When I asked him what was important to him in a college, one thing he said was, "I'd like an Ultimate Frisbee club. I know this sounds strange, but it's the way I relieve stress." Not strange at all! You might find that clubs and organizations are an important outlet for you, too.

7. COLLEGE SIZE

- Intimate: under 5000 students
- Small school: 5000-15,000 students
- Midsize school: 15,000-25,000 students
- Mega school: 25,000+

Different people can feel very strongly about different school sizes. Ronnie, a parent I worked with, was looking for a school for her daughter with 4000-6000 students. She loved Wake Forest, Richmond, and Valparaiso, but size was a factor she wasn't willing to compromise on.

There are other significant factors when you consider size, such as:

- ℵ percentage of undergraduate vs. graduate students
- ℵ how many students live on or off campus
- ℵ how many students are adults or non-traditional students

8. CONSERVATIVE VS. LIBERAL CULTURE

- ℵ Dress
- ℵ Social rules
- ℵ Politics and hot social topics on campus
- ℵ Religion
- ℵ Professors' perspectives

Liz was sick of the rules at her boarding school concerning tattoos and piercings. She was darn sure she was not going to be so restricted in college. As a result, Liz gravitated towards schools like Hampshire, Sarah Lawrence, Reed, Bard, Guilford, and Warren Wilson, where she felt she'd be able to express her individuality.

9. COST

This seems to be a factor at least 90 percent of the time, and is usually a big one even for wealthy families. I've had many wealthy parents tell me, "I still need to think of our other children, graduate school, and our retirement."

Cost can determine whether someone stays in state or goes out, whether they go private or public, and whether they live on campus or stay home and commute.

"Sticker shock" stresses out parents and students alike.

Parental expectations surrounding cost can often be unrealistic, especially with certain institutions, leading to tough conversations.

It's important for parents to establish and communicate to their child early about how much they can and will pay; I see the most family turmoil over money when parents change their tune, pulling a bait-and-switch on their student.

Parents are typically responsible for providing the college with the money to cover their Expected Family Contribution (EFC) to the student's educational costs.

Consider whether you'll need to have the "loan conversation" when you discuss paying for college (see the section "Paying for College" for more information).

When I asked Fred and his parents how much, if any, money they expected Fred to contribute to his education, his parents looked at each other and said, "About $5000 a year." Fred's eyes almost popped out of his head. He said, "You never told me that I had to pay. I thought you were paying!" These are the conversations that should happen early on in the process to avoid surprises and unrealistic expectations.

10. COURSE OFFERINGS

Online and/or hybrid course opportunities are changing college education. Consider the breadth of courses from which you can select. Students who want a wide range of courses usually are also interested in larger schools. Study abroad opportunities fall under this category.

Course offerings available through consortium affiliations fits here.

11. CURRICULAR APPROACH

Some schools have an intense core curriculum, like Columbia University and its fairly rigid requirements.

Other schools have a wide-open curriculum, like Brown, Amherst, or Grinnell.

Jennifer didn't just dislike math. She loathed and despised it. When we discussed what mattered to her in a college list, she said, "I don't ever want to take a math class again." I knew we needed to look at colleges that had a very open curriculum. Jennifer fell in love with Brown University, got accepted, and had a great four-year experience.

12. DISTANCE FROM HOME

This can be an important factor for many students and usually for parents, too; it adds cost, and parents often don't want to be very far from their children.

The additional cost of faraway schools not only includes airline tickets, but also out-of-state tuition if a school is outside the student's home state.

Apart from cost, students and parents may sometimes feel a school is just too far away from their support base, making them feel disconnected.

For many students, there is also such a thing as being *too* close to home. A lot of times they will articulate this to me by saying, "I want to leave the state," but they are really saying, "I want a different geographical experience."

My daughter Joy wanted to play college basketball, and Oglethorpe was recruiting her hard. We had been to multiple games and had visited the school twice. She liked the academic quality, the campus, the people, and the neighborhood, but she was still hung up. One day, Joy confessed to me, "It's just too close. It's 45 minutes away from my home. I need to go at least two hours away."

13. DIVERSITY

Really think hard about this one: do you want a college where you'll meet many people like yourself? Or would you rather go somewhere you'll meet a wide range of different people?

Think about:

- ℵ Race and ethnicity
- ℵ International students
- ℵ Cultural perspective
- ℵ Socio-economic diversity
- ℵ Sexual orientation
- ℵ Mindset and worldview
- ℵ Political perspective
- ℵ Private vs. public student body
- ℵ Religion

Roger was excited to leave Texas for a selective liberal arts school on the West Coast. I was surprised when, after a year there, he wanted to transfer. When I asked Roger why he had decided to leave that school, he said, "There are too many blond-haired, blue-eyed kids like me at my school. The place was just too cookie-cutter for what I was looking for."

14. FACILITIES

This can be a big factor, particularly when it comes to residence halls. Many colleges are abandoning traditional-style housing and investing in suite-style housing. Dorms matter a lot to students.

Also consider how important the following facilities are to you: libraries, athletic facilities, dining options, wellness centers, student centers, theaters, parking, etc.

My youngest daughter Joy and I were touring a school together in North Carolina, and when we got to the residence halls, she gave me that look. I knew what that meant: "Strike 1. I just can't see myself living here." When we got to the Student Center, she said, "It looks like a middle school student center at an underfunded school." You may get three strikes in baseball, but two strikes were enough to take this school off Joy's list.

15. FOOD

This is a huge factor for most students. I knew food was important, but it wasn't until I heard how much it mattered to students in the college admission process that it really resonated with me.

Most students complain about their food on campus. It is almost a teenage rite of passage, but try it yourself. If you have special dietary needs, you should talk to the kitchen staff about how they will handle your special diet or your food allergies.

> Malcolm was a top student at his highly selective private school and graduated as valedictorian. Despite his strong focus on academics, food was a surprisingly important factor for Malcolm. He was obsessed with Thai food and knew he wasn't going to attend a school without a selection of Thai restaurants around. When he realized his top-choice school had 13 Thai restaurants in a 15-mile radius, he was sold.

16. FRIENDLINESS

This impacts campus feel, so I hear it more on the backend when students are discussing what they look for in a college. I hear it both ways: "That place was cold," or "I just felt so comfortable there." Not every student needs this. Some students prefer more anonymity, but no one wants a place that feels cold and uncaring.

Before her senior year of high school, my oldest daughter Karis attended a summer program called the July Experience at Davidson College. She took classes with Davidson professors for three weeks, and after those three weeks were over, she was sold on attending Davidson for college. She had bonded especially well with a Latin American Studies professor, Dr. Magdalena Maiz-Peña. They exchanged numbers and sent text messages throughout the school year.

When Karis moved into her residence hall as a freshman, she sent Dr. Maiz-Peña a text to say we were an hour away from arrival. Dr. Maiz-Peña asked us to meet her in the Student Center, and when we arrived, she ran to give Karis the kind of bearhug and long embrace I thought was only for grandmothers to give. I knew at that moment that Karis had found a friendly place that could be her home away from home for the next four years.

17. GRADUATION RATE

This factor is rising in importance with more emphasis from the government and college rankings. Students and parents are more interested, especially in the four-year graduation rate. College Navigator and Big Future are good sources for this data but http://www.collegeresults.org/ and http://collegecompletion.chronicle.com/ are outstanding websites to research graduation rates. I strongly recommend that you explore these websites.

18. HBCU OR PWI

Historically Black Colleges and Universities (HBCUs) were founded after the Civil War, when legal segregation was still the law of the land. There are 107 private and public HBCUs, and most of them are in the former Confederate states of the South. Students of all races and from all countries are welcome to attend an HBCU, and students may select them for similar reasons to why some women select women's colleges, including:

- ℵ The desire to be at a school designed with them in mind
- ℵ The desire to meet caring and supportive adults and students
- ℵ The feeling that seeing many brilliant professors who look like them will be inspiring and empowering

- ℵ The nurturing quality of these schools

PWI, or Predominantly White Institution, refers to any institution that wasn't labeled an HBCU prior to 1964. The raging debate in many black families is whether a PWI or an HBCU is the better option, but I think both options deserve respect. It is all about the right school match for you. Some students may find an almost all-black environment to be lacking in racial diversity for them, and this can be important even though it's only a short period of their lives. Others say that attending an HBCU was the best decision they could have made.

> I was one of the few black kids in my high school, and I got tired of all of the other students expecting me to be the voice for the black race. I can still remember in United States history class when slavery was discussed and heads would turn to look at me and see what I was thinking. I almost attended Howard University, because for those four years of my life, I wanted not to be a minority. In the end, though, I chose to attend Michigan State. The world is not black, and I wanted exposure to many different cultures. Still, MSU had 3600 black students, and it was important to me to know that I'd find others like me and I would not be alone.
>
> Nicole was skeptical of attending a Historically Black College because, as she reasoned, "Most of the country is not black, so why should I be in a mostly-black environment for four years?" Despite her reservations, she decided to visit North Carolina A&T, and she felt at home on her very first visit. She applied, was accepted, enrolled, and graduated.
>
> Nicole told me a decade later that attending an HBCU was one of the best decisions she'd ever made. She said, "I was someone who I thought was self-confident, but having all of those brilliant professors who looked like me and cared about me took my confidence to a whole new level, and that has remained with me until this day."

19. INFLUENCERS

This refers to the people in the student's life who may have some influence, or *want* to have some influence, over college choices.

The noncustodial parent is a big factor for some families. A fairly common situation goes something like this: A student lives with Mom as the custodial parent, but Dad's income is going to be an important part of paying for college, and Dad has strong views about where the student should go to school. Families would be wise to anticipate and work through these conversations early, as all too often I see them hold up the process and put serious stress on families.

Grandparents often also have a significance influence on college choices, and sometimes other relatives do, too. For example, say Uncle Bob has a strong opinion on where you should go to college. You're very close to Uncle Bob, and he's pretty financially stable. He is offering to provide a significant portion of the money needed for college expenses, but he wants his voice heard about where you decide to go. I've also seen some family drama with these situations, because sometimes money comes with strings attached.

In my early counseling days, I faced situations where divorced parents didn't seem to be on the same page. A single mom might say she made all of the educational decisions and Dad deferred to her, but Dad showed up with strong opinions later, and it turned out that Mom's earlier statement had been more wishful thinking than reality.

On one occasion, I was hearing completely different details from each parent, and I told the father I'd like to hold a joint conference with both parents to make sure everyone was on the same page. That father told me, "I will not be in the same room with that woman."

If you have influences in your orbit that may chime in on your decision, or other family situations that could affect your college search process, you'll need to work through these in advance to help things move smoothly when time really counts.

20. INSTRUCTOR QUALITY/ACCESS/STYLE

There is a growing trend for students to read reviews on RateMyProfessor.com as part of their college research.

I have tended to see a high premium on instructor access with students who were very successful in high school.

- ℵ Families who value small classes also value instructor access.
- ℵ How important is it for your teachers to know who you are?
- ℵ Some students consider discussion-based vs. lecture-based course models

Recently, I visited Claremont, California to meet with a former student who was a freshman at Pomona College. While I waited for our meeting time, I sat on a bench in a busy spot on campus and told students who walked by that I was a college counselor and would like to ask them a few questions if they didn't mind. I asked them what they liked most about Pomona, and what was the one thing they'd change. The most frequent positive answer I got was, "The amount of access I have to my instructors."

21. LOCATION AND SURROUNDING COMMUNITY

I highly recommend that families use http://city-data.com to search the zip code for schools they're interested in and carefully read the detailed profile and the message board posts. This will help you learn inside information about the college's location.

Also consider the geography. Is skiing important to you? Do you need to be near the beach? Will you need easy access to a reliable airport? Are any relatives or members of your support system close by? Students may also consider proximity to various stores or to a church, synagogue, or mosque. Ladies often really value having quality beauty parlors close to the college. I've noticed that the environment where a student grew up usually influences their expectations for a college, so these are all things to think about.

I was talking to my friend Jamal, who is also an Atlanta-based college counselor, and he commented that it seems to be so hard for students from Atlanta to be happy with the location of a college. Jamal said, "Students have to realize they aren't going to get Atlanta. They're used to going to Buckhead; Midtown; Falcons, Hawks, and Braves Games; and Perimeter, Lennox, and Cumberland malls; and you are rarely going to find that much to do in most college towns."

If you set your expectations based on the place you grew up, you may be either disappointed or impressed, depending on where you're from and what you like or dislike about it.

22. NAME RECOGNITION AND PRESTIGE

This is another big factor—often the biggest factor for students and parents, even though many times they are not honest with me, or with themselves, about how much prestige is going to trump whether a school is a match in their decision-making process. As college degrees become more common, the mindset among the middle class has transitioned from "Did you go to college?" to "Did you go to a good college?"

Of all the factors I help families consider, this is the one about which they are most often not honest with me at the beginning of the process: parents often say they want the best school match for their student, but what it comes down to is that they really want the school with the biggest name. This is especially true for students who attend very prestigious, selective, private high schools. The social pressure to attend certain schools is off the charts, and personal validation and self-worth are on the line.

As a counselor, I appreciate the honesty upfront. If this is going to be a top factor, I'll help families build their list with that in mind. That said, I do sometimes feel concerned when I see too much focus on school name. That focus often comes with a belief that the degree will magically open doors that really are only opened by your excellence at what you do and your ability to network with the right people.

It's also worth saying that parents have to be honest with themselves about whether they are seeing their child's college choice as a validation of their own self-worth and intelligence.

When I was doing boarding school admissions, I had a meeting with a New York City placement director and he was expressing his frustration to me about how he will often recommend schools that will be great for the students and parents will reject them because they don't have a big enough name. I will never forget what he then said. He shared a specific time when he'd recommended a boarding school for a wealthy New York dad and the dad said, "You don't understand; I need a name that will play well at the club."

The same mindset is prevalent in college admissions. This obsession with having a name is causing some families to abandon their retirement savings and accumulate unsustainable amounts of debt. I see this far too often.

Donald and I were roommates at an admission conference in San Antonio where we were seeking more professional training. Donald was venting, and I was listening. He said, "I went to Bates College in Maine, and I busted my butt. It was rigorous. I would talk to some of my friends who had gone to big state schools, and they didn't have nearly the homework load that I had. But now that I've graduated, I tell people I went to Bates and it's not uncommon for them to say they've never heard of it and ask me if it's a community college."

Donald was clearly upset that he wasn't being recognized for his four years of hard work at a tough college with a small name. Bates is an exceptional school, one of my favorites, but some can handle this well, and others can't. This is where self-awareness is so important when building your college list.

23. ON-CAMPUS VS. OFF-CAMPUS LIVING

Is the school more resident-based, or more commuter-based? For students who are new to the college admissions process, this is not usually a primary reason a school is selected, but it can be a reason one gets crossed off a list.

As students learn more about how a residential experience differs from a commuter campus, they tend to value this more when it comes to which schools they select.

Non-traditional students, such as adults who are taking evening classes, may actually like the more commuter-based vibe because they will find more students like themselves there.

This question will impact the general feel of the campus on a visit.

24. RELIGIOUS AFFILIATION

This includes Catholic, Jesuit, Seventh-day Adventist, Christian, or even specific denominational schools.

Some students want this, and others don't.

This is a non-factor for many students, but for those to whom this matters, it's important; if you want to be surrounded by students and faculty who share your worldview from a religious perspective, you'll want to prioritize schools in that circle.

25. RESEARCH OPPORTUNITIES

Only my top students ask about this, usually, students who know they eventually want a PhD. Parents with advanced degrees typically also prioritize this in the college search process.

I have noticed that more students value research opportunities now than when I first started doing college coaching.

26. SAFETY AND SECURITY

This is a big factor for students, but also parents: they're letting "their babies" go out into the world for the first time. When I do a coaching session and I take families through these thirty-two areas of college compatibility, most of the time the parent defers to the student. But when it comes to safety and security, cost, and, sometimes, distance from home, this is when parents speak up.

Think about consulting crime statistics on http://city-data.com and College Navigator.

Consider the overall safety feeling you get from the campus and community while on a visit.

When I attended the Valdosta State orientation for new freshmen and their parents, the end of the day brought a one-hour parent question-and-answer session with ten school administrators. Eight of the first ten questions were about campus safety, and for good reason. 29 days earlier, Governor Nathan Deal had signed legislation allowing people with permits to carry concealed handguns on Georgia's public college campuses. Faculty and administrators had done everything they could to oppose the legislation, including picketing a week before graduation, but parents still peppered them with difficult questions.

When my parents dropped me off for my first day of college in 1982 at Michigan State, we embraced and said goodbye. I was excited, rather than nervous. 45 minutes later, I heard a knock on my residence hall door. It was my dad. "Son, I just thought you might need some light bulbs so I went around the corner and got you some," he said.

To this day, I've never told him, but I saw the tear that was rolling down his cheek when I answered that knock. He'd had a nephew leave home one day and never return, and he was scared for me. Campus safety matters, and it's a factor that often grows for families as they move through the college selection process.

27. SCHOOL SPIRIT

This can be a big factor for sports fans whose idea of a great time is going to the big game with friends and feeling the electricity in the air.

Interestingly, I also meet many students who are not into sports, but who still care a great deal about school spirit. They may not watch the game at home by themselves, but the social side of these gatherings is their vision of what makes college fun.

Other students I coach don't really care about athletic school spirit, but they want to be surrounded by students who feel proud to attend the college. This is another form of school spirit that is important to reflect on.

Lisa Shannon was a brilliant student and a competitive applicant at some of the most selective colleges in the country. Why did she select USC over Ivy League choices? She told me, "I would die if I didn't have my tailgating and big-time football fix on Saturday afternoons."

28. SINGLE GENDER VS. COED

Almost everyone has a strong opinion one way or another. I like to see women visit a women's college with an open mind, because they will often see value there that wouldn't be seen without a visit.

I like to mention that the Webb Schools in Claremont California use a very unique model of education. Students are separated by gender in ninth and tenth grade, and they come together for a coed experience for eleventh and twelfth grade. When it comes to selecting a college, 20-25 percent of graduating women choose a women's college. Women's colleges often develop confidence and inspire women to try careers they otherwise wouldn't attempt. They develop leadership and produce a friendship bond that is inexplicable. Still, single gender schools are not for everyone, and when students are adamant that they won't consider it, I get that, and I move on. I wish I had a dollar for every student who has said to me, "Girls are too catty. I don't want to be around them 24/7."

All single gender schools have coed schools they partner with for social events. Before young women rule out single gender schools, they should explore the coed opportunities because oftentimes they extend to the classroom.

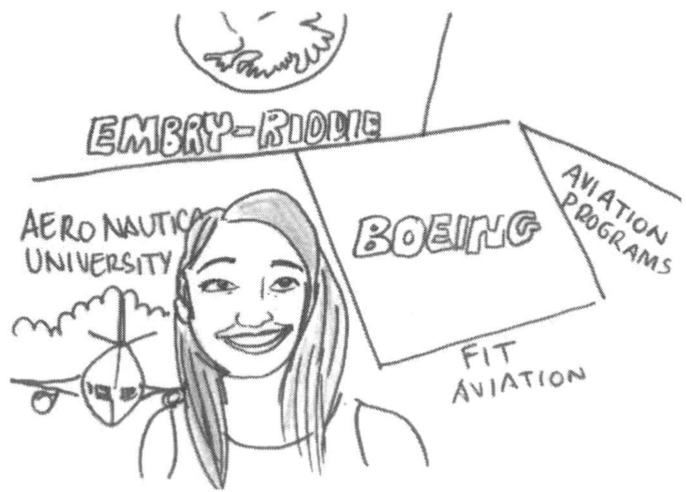

29. STRENGTH IN YOUR MAJOR

This is particularly important for unique and intense majors, such as aerospace engineering, which may not be offered at all colleges.

This is a major factor for students who already know what they wish to study. Even if you know you may switch majors (surveys suggest that 80 percent of students do at some point), you'll still want to go in with a plan, and choosing a school that's weak in your area of interest is not a good plan.

Candace had been in a flight program since she was 11 years old. She had known from a young age that she wanted to be a pilot. When it came time to select colleges, we knew we needed to look at schools such as Embry Riddle, Florida Institute of Technology, and others with a strong aeronautics program.

30. SPORTS AND PERFORMING ARTS

This is important for students who want to play sports at the highest level: consider your potential for playing time, the coaching staff, division, etc.

It also applies to students who want to participate in activities like orchestra, marching band, cheerleading, and choral groups.

There may be scholarships associated with these opportunities.

These are a non-factor for those who are not interested.

Nakevia was not only a sprinter: she was a very good sprinter. Her fastest time in her 4x400 split was 55.1 during her junior year of high school. She loved to run, and had aspirations of becoming an Olympian. A runner since the age of six, it was her stress outlet as well. You would think the grueling spring season would burn her out, but not Nakevia; she also ran cross-country in the fall. When it came to building her college list, we knew we needed to make sure any school on her list had a stellar track coach.

31. STUDENT SUPPORT

- Another factor emphasized more by parents than by students
- Big factor for students with learning differences
- Availability of tutoring
- Counseling services
- Educational seminars and workshops
- Writing support
- Living/learning communities
- Affinity groups and supports for students of color
- Women's groups at engineering schools
- Support for international students
- Disability services
- Emphasized more frequently by colleges now, with more focus on retention rates, graduation rates, mental health, and suicide prevention
- Support for first-generation students. First-generation students are the first students in their family (generation) to graduate from a college with a bachelor's degree.

32. WEATHER

If you know you hate the cold, why go to a school in a frigid locale where you'll freeze for half the year when there are other options? On the flipside, some students know they have very little tolerance for heat or humidity and want to take that into consideration as well. This is a place you'll be spending at least nine months a year for the next four years, so make sure it's a place you can enjoy living.

I had worked with Tonya years before when I helped place her at her outstanding Massachusetts boarding school, and now she was back for college counseling. As much as Tonya had loved her school, she'd previously lived all of her life in Florida and Georgia, and the hard Massachusetts winters were taking a toll on her. She told me once, "It gets cold here in September, and it's still cold in April." When it came to her college list, we focused on quality schools in warmer climates.

17

HOW CAN I USE THE SCHOOL'S WEBSITE TO TELL WHETHER THAT SCHOOL SHOULD BE ON MY LIST?

Less than 1 percent of the families I work with use school websites as much or as effectively as they should. There's a gold mine of information there!

Start at the homepage and read everything in the "About" section, or whatever it's named for that school. This is where schools talk about what makes them distinctive and what they most pride themselves for.

- ℵ Be sure to read the mission statement. If you can't find it, try a Google search for "mission statement" with the names of colleges you're interested in. Ask yourself if you fit into their vision.

- ℵ Read about any strategic plans they have. This will let you know what that school's project priorities are for the next 5-10 years.
- ℵ Click every tab under their Admissions section. You will want to read about deadlines, requirements, freshman profiles, etc. You will also want to watch any admission videos they might have.
- ℵ Make sure you check out the frequently asked question section. Most schools have stupendous FAQ sections that will answer many of your questions.
- ℵ Don't forget to sign up for their mailing list!
- ℵ Look for admissions events to see when open houses are being hosted. See if the college lists when they may have representatives traveling to your area.
- ℵ If there's a Meet the Staff section, read the backgrounds of the admissions officers.
- ℵ Explore the school's social media sites and look for interactive opportunities, like chats with current students. Many schools, like MIT and Dartmouth, have outstanding blogs that you are going to want to read.
- ℵ A lot of schools run great articles with tips on how to complete various portions of the admission application with excellence.
- ℵ You are going to want to know the policies on things like interviews, submitting additional information beyond what is required, etc.
- ℵ Thoroughly explore any and all scholarship and aid information, with particular attention to the process, qualifications, and deadlines.
- ℵ There is a lot of information on cost, and most students will need to look through this carefully.
- ℵ Explore the Academics section, looking at the courses and descriptions in the course catalog. Look for core requirements, requirements in your major(s) of interest, special features like research opportunities, study abroad, and anything else of interest to you.
- ℵ Visit the Campus Life section for information on housing, food, clubs, and activities.

- ℵ See if you can find back issues of the school newspaper online to read. This is an invaluable source of unfiltered information. I strongly recommend that you read back issues.
- ℵ Read up on athletics if that's important to you.
- ℵ Many schools have a "quick links" section that can easily direct you to other important information.
- ℵ When in doubt, click on every tab on the home page under the major headers, read, and take notes.

I was talking with Danielle about her great undergraduate experience at Spelman College. She said, "A lot of people talk about how much Spelman costs, but I went to their website and I found they had scholarships for current students that most of my classmates didn't even know about. You needed to do well in school and complete a special scholarship application in the spring, but I did it, and I was successful at getting enough scholarship money to make Spelman affordable."

18

A NEW AND CREATIVE APPROACH TO LEARNING WHICH COLLEGES ARE INTERESTED IN ME

The traditional way to find a college is totally reliant on discovering the college yourself. You may hear about it through word of mouth, or you may go to a school fair or an information session, but it's up to you to initiate the exploration of that school.

In 2006, Cappex came up with a new model that has been wildly successful. You can visit Cappex.com and fill out a detailed profile that includes all of your contact information. You'll also fill out your grades by subject for every course, your test scores, interests, and more. Colleges who have a partnership with Cappex can then share your information, and if they are interested, Cappex will notify you and allow you to express interest and look for information, or simply decline. More than eight million students and around 20,000 school counselors have signed up and created profiles. This is invaluable to colleges, because they learn about students who may have flown under the radar in their traditional recruiting.

Cappex also works with colleges to create customized messages which appear in students' inboxes. Students are encouraged to rank schools according to their interest levels, and colleges are able to not only find potential students, but also gauge their interest in the school. It's a win-win situation. Cappex also produces outstanding reports for colleges in their dashboards to further help them track potential students. In addition to other features, Cappex has an outstanding scholarship identification process and has its own application that is free for students. More and more colleges are accepting this application format.

19

How can I use college reviews to learn more about schools I'm considering?

You'll save a lot of money on college visits—hundreds or even thousands—using the series of steps we've discussed through Section 2. That said, there is always another way to learn about a given school.

My favorite site for college reviews is https://www.niche.com This site is also a great tool for looking into the college's town.

It can be interesting to look up Niche's reviews on K-12 schools as well, to see how accurate you feel they are about your own high school.

Each college earns a letter grade based on reviews in thirteen categories:

- Overall grade
- Academics

- ℵ Diversity
- ℵ Athletics
- ℵ Professors
- ℵ Dorms
- ℵ Student life
- ℵ Value
- ℵ Campus
- ℵ Party scene
- ℵ Location
- ℵ Campus food
- ℵ Safety

You can read reviews in each category, look at scattergrams, and more. Think of yourself as an investigator of the school as you whittle your list down and come up with a list of questions you can ask an admissions counselor or a current student while on a visit. Remember what you're looking for in a school.

Another favorite review site is https://www.unigo.com I also think discussion forums can be a valuable resource. The largest one I know of is College Confidential. I'm sure many college admissions representatives are recoiling at the very mention of this site, because it certainly has its flaws. It is a message board, after all! Still, it's worth mentioning, as you can find a wealth of information from these unfiltered posts. I trust that you can discern between the jewels and the junk. Don't waste your time reading their wildly inaccurate "Chance me" threads and don't get caught up in their obsession with prestige and rankings. Find the confidential message boards at http://talk.collegeconfidential.com. There are some great links to articles in school newspapers on College Confidential. It is not surprising to see an actual admissions rep come on the College Confidential school message boards to interact with potential students and to dispel false rumors.

There are some college guidebooks that are invaluable. The *Fiske Guide to the Colleges* and the *Hidden Ivies* (2016 version) are must-haves. I tell all my clients to get these two books and the *Best 382 Colleges* by the Princeton Review. While there is clearly a subjective quality to these descriptions, they are usually quite accurate and if you can afford it, spend the $50 and get all three books. If your funds are tight right now, get to your library or Barnes and Noble and start reading these three books.

You should also know that reviews of HBCUs from people who did not attend an HBCU are often faulty. The same is true for reviews of women's colleges by a man, or even by a woman who never attended a women's college. They are suspect because there are intangible benefits for the right person who has these experiences.

Finally, a word about reviews: their strength is in their numbers. There will always be disgruntled students with an axe to grind, and there will always be someone with a sanguine perspective that strains credulity. Overall, however, this is a great resource. I have been impressed with how well the reviews depict a school when you get the chance to read over a hundred of them. I looked up my daughters' colleges, and last time I checked niche.com, Valdosta State had 2000 reviews and Davidson College had nearly 300.

One group of students and parents I work with who understand the subjectivity and limitations of reviews are the parents who have attended HBCUs and had a great experience. Some of the websites and books that do reviews don't understand the value of women's colleges or HBCUs for many students. An example is my friend Leonard McReynolds who wouldn't trade his Morehouse College experience for any college in America. His wife Jennifer would say the same thing about her Spelman College experience. I definitely recommend reading quality reviews. They have their place, but consider the source–and there is no substitute for a college visit.

20

WHAT OPTIONS ARE THERE FOR FAMILIES WHO CAN'T AFFORD TO VISIT COLLEGES, OR DON'T HAVE THE TIME?

Even if time and money aren't an issue for your family, I encourage you to take these steps. Everyone's time is valuable.

You want to find out when the colleges you are interested in are coming to your area for fairs or information sessions. You want to meet the admission counselors, get your questions answered, and hear their presentations.

Visit YouTube and type your college name into the search bar. If you find a college tour, watch the video. Also check for interviews and a wide range of other materials the school may have made available. Most colleges have a YouTube channel with official materials, but you'll likely find random videos uploaded by students to be the most helpful, as they are not an extension of the school's marketing efforts.

For additional video tours, also visit Nacho, formerly called YOUniversity, at http://youniversitytv.com/category/college. You'll find hundreds of video tours. Notice the date of the tours you watch. Some are significantly more recent than others.

You may also find a video tour or a virtual tour on the college website. You will certainly find helpful interactive chat sessions, blogs, social media outlets, and webinars.

Lastly, I recommend https://www.youvisit.com/education/. YouVisit's cutting edge virtual campus tours allow you to use the Internet to explore over 400 educational institutions across North America.

It is really important that you utilize these sources because time and money are at a premium and you can squander a lot of time and money visiting colleges that you have no interest in. Had you just done a little more research, you would have known that.

When I recommended the University of Richmond to Bert, he was originally skeptical, and so were his parents. Bert thought what most students and parents think: he hadn't heard of the University of Richmond, so it must not be any good. I told him I'd worked with six students who had attended Richmond, and while it hadn't always been easy, all six said they'd do it all over again if they had to. I sensed that this piqued Bert's interest, but I felt like they were only agreeing to a visit to appease me.

I decided to send them a number of YouTube videos, and one video in particular inspired them. The video was taken at graduation, and senior after senior gave a brief interview. Bert and his family were really impressed with these students, and the rest is history. Bert graduated from Richmond recently, and then was hired to do research and teach classes there. Imagine if he hadn't watched those YouTube videos.

21

How can I do a self-assessment of what my family can really afford to pay for college?

This is a question and answer mainly for parents, but students need to also be part of this process. Start by making a list of all your current monthly expenses. I strongly recommend you use financial software; I have used Mint.com for years, and it is invaluable. Include absolutely everything that you spend. Let's say you do this and find that your expenses are $6000 a month.

Next, make a list of all of your current monthly income streams. This list should include all full-time and part-time jobs for parents and the college-bound student, and any child support, alimony, rental properties, etc. Let's say this comes to $7000. It looks like you have $1000 a month for college, but wait—your emergency account is not built up to six months' worth of living expenses, so you allocate $250 a month to that.

Add any other resources you expect to be able to use. Let's say you have ...

- ℵ $3000 a year in overage
- ℵ $3000/per year ($12,000 saved) in a 529 Plan
- ℵ $1000 that Grandma says she will give
- ℵ $500/per year ($2000 total) in an educational IRA
- ℵ $3000 from Catholic school tuition savings for twelfth grade
- ℵ $1100 when ACT test prep is over
- ℵ $1500 from the student's projected summer-job-for-college earnings
- ℵ $2000 projected savings on food, gas, and utilities that won't be spent on the college-bound child once he/she has moved out
- ℵ $2500 from the American Opportunity Tax Credit (see chapter 157 in Section 4)
- ℵ $5000 in the form of a Stafford student loan
- ℵ $500 from an outside scholarship you won

The total now comes to $23,100. Now, look at adjustments you can make to your lifestyle. You agree to spend $1500 on your annual family vacation instead of $2500, and Mom feels she can work ten more hours a week at $12 an hour now that she isn't running the student around so much. You add $4000 from these resources.

Now you have $28,100 a year for college. This is your bottom line, and you can't go over it. You absolutely have to know this number before you start your college search. Would you shop for a car without knowing how much you can spend? Of course not, and yet this is exactly what many families do when shopping for college.

Now it is time to have what I call, "The Big Conversation." This is where the parents tell the child that this is the maximum amount you are spending on college. You discuss how paying for college is a shared responsibility and you make it clear what the expectations are for what you each will contribute.

In 2009, we moved from West Chester, PA, to Metro Atlanta, and we were house shopping. My mom gave me great advice. Mom said two things: 1) There is always something bigger and better out there, so don't get greedy, and 2) Set a maximum on what you can pay, and don't go over it.

I carried this information over to the college search process. If you don't do the same, you'll be swept away by your child's dream school, your desire to make your child happy, and the college marketing blitz.

22

HOW CAN I FIND OUT IF A SCHOOL IS AFFORDABLE BEFORE VISITING?

Most college counselors help students create a balance between Reach, Mid-range, Likely, and Safety schools, but I've found that affordability isn't put to the test as often as it needs to be. If you get into a school that you can't afford to attend, it's not another notch in your belt or a trophy. It's a waste of time and money.

Most students and parents don't realize they can get a fairly reliable projection of what they'll be asked to pay before they even visit or apply. If you want a quick read with a range of what you might likely be asked to pay, go to College Reality Check at https://collegerealitycheck.com/en/ and use their Compare Colleges feature. You can compare up to five colleges at one time. Compare the colleges by net price, which is the amount you'll have to pay after grants and scholarships, as opposed to sticker price, which is what's listed on the school's website as its full cost.

College Reality Check has reliable information on over 3800 colleges. Make sure that you select Family Income Range and select the range that best fits your family.

For even more precise information on a specific school, I recommend the Department of Education's Cost Calculator, which you can find at https://collegecost.ed.gov/netpricecenter.aspx You'll have to go through the process one school at a time.

College Board also has a great net price calculator at https://bigfuture.collegeboard.org/pay-for-college/tools-calculators

Remember that the figures from College Reality Check won't take into account specific scholarships that you may be awarded. Their figures will be based on the average amount that a typical student at your income level would be asked to pay. A school that doesn't look affordable using this tool can become eminently affordable with a $20,000 scholarship, if you earn it.

When Robert came to me, he and his parents had already committed to spending nearly $1500 to go on a tour of some California colleges, and just about every college on the tour had a net price well above their price range. I wished I'd met them before they had made that commitment, because I could have walked them through using a good net price calculator to help them target schools that were more affordable for their family.

23

HOW DO I KNOW IF A COLLEGE IS STRONG IN MY MAJOR BEFORE I VISIT?

- ℵ Visit https://collegeexpress.com and look at their list of majors. You can compare schools based on survey research of the best schools for each major.
- ℵ Get a totally different perspective using the *US News* list of top colleges by major. You can find this list using a Google search. I despise *US News* cumulative rankings, but their top colleges by major are much better.
- ℵ I also like to use College Navigator to search by college. You can use this tool to learn how many students earned degrees in your major of interest. Take a look at whether advanced degrees are offered in that subject area.
- ℵ Go to https://bigfuture.collegeboard.org and after you have looked up the colleges you are interested in, click their

"Majors and Learning Environment" tab to see if the major you are considering is a prominent major at the college you are researching.

- ℵ Visit the college's website and look up their curriculum offerings in your area of interest. Look into the faculty and read about their experience and qualifications.
- ℵ If you can, start a conversation with a faculty member in your area of interest, and try asking them for the names of a few other schools with outstanding programs in their area of expertise.

RateMyProfessors.com is the largest online destination for professor ratings. The site has 8,000+ schools, 1.4 million professors, and almost 20 million ratings. One of the great features of this website is your ability to search for professor ratings by department. Professors despise this site, and, of course, sometimes professors get bad reviews when they shouldn't, but I have been impressed with how well the ratings have correlated with what my own kids and the students I coach feel about a professor.

Another great source for department reviews is the Princeton Review's *Best 382 Colleges*. They use their own methodology to come up with their list of the top schools in the following 15 popular college majors: accounting, biology, business/finance, communications, computer science/computer engineering, criminology, education, engineering, English lit and language majors, history, journalism, marketing and sales, mechanical engineering, political science/government, and psychology.

In Chapter 28, you will see my perspective on rankings. Don't take any of these as gospel, but if you consult all of these sources and you see the same schools popping up over and over, with different sources that use different methodologies, you can be confident the department is strong. You can't say it is number three in the country with any semblance of objectivity, but you can be confident you can get an excellent education there in your area of interest.

My daughter Joy was very interested in Armstrong State University. They were recruiting her for basketball, and she liked the basketball coach, the school size, and the location. However, Joy wants to be a school counselor, so I took her through College Navigator and we looked through the programs and majors. In the most recent year, 181 students had graduated as registered nurses, 92 in health professions and related clinical sciences, and 66 had graduated in medical radiologic technology/science and radiation therapy. Almost half the graduates were in the health sciences, and the school did not offer a master's in school counseling. Joy realized that while Armstrong State University was a good school for her in some ways, it was a better plan for her to focus on schools that were stronger in her area of interest.

24

HOW CAN I MAKE THE MOST OF COLLEGE VISITS?

- ℵ Plan visits well in advance; visits can be expensive and you want to maximize their value.
- ℵ Sign up online for your desired tour time, and sign up for an information session.
- ℵ Arrive 30 minutes early to your tour or information session. A lot of colleges have very poor signage and finding a parking spot will often take you 15-20 minutes, so factor that into your timeframe.
- ℵ Never try to visit more than two colleges in one day. If you are visiting two in one day, try to select the first available tour time and information session for one school, and a time after lunch for the second school. Each school on your

list deserves time, and you want to leave plenty of time to get to the second school. As Chris Gruber, Dean of Admission at Davidson College, likes to say, you shouldn't spend more time at the car lot buying a car than you spend on the campus of the school you will attend for the next four-plus years.

- Dean Gruber has wise advice when he says take the tour and attend the information session, but then double your time on campus to get the feel and understand the culture.
- Your visit is your chance to explore whatever is important to you. Think about setting up a meeting with a professor in your department of interest. You can request to meet with a coach, someone in the theater department, the faculty liaison to a club, or any other area that is of interest to you. If you work on this well in advance, you'll likely be successful.
- Ask about sitting in on a class in your area of interest.
- Some schools allow you to meet with an admissions counselor after the tour. Don't skip this opportunity if it's offered.
- Set up a meeting with someone in the financial aid office if you have questions about financial aid.
- Build an extra hour into your time on campus. Use this time to find a busy spot on campus and ask students who walk by if you can ask them a few questions. I do this as a counselor and 90 percent of the time, students are willing to talk with me. Even those who aren't are polite. Ask the students what they like most about their college, and one thing they would change if they could.
- If sports are important to you, attend a game. Karis and I attended basketball games at both Davidson and Richmond when she was visiting those schools. If theater is important to you, attend a play. These visits take time and that is why you should use the books I recommended and online research to narrow the list down.
- Let's say you have ten colleges on your college list. I'd rather you go deep on visits to five than skim the surface and

visit all ten. You should select the five you are most interested in. Remember, you can visit the others (if you are admitted) in the spring.

- You should prioritize your favorite schools, your Reach schools, and your Mid-range schools. You should also prioritize any school that factors demonstrated interest into its decision-making process.
- Take pictures of campus because the schools will start to run together in your mind if you don't do this.
- Try to eat a meal in the dining hall—you may need to purchase a meal ticket. Watch and observe how the students act.
- After you leave it, record your impressions of a college in a journal or in a Notes app on your phone. Learn to trust your gut. This is very important.

When my oldest daughter Karis was visiting colleges, we visited the University of Richmond, and Karis set up a lunch meeting with the admissions representative who was assigned to handle the area we lived in. We then talked with 17 students about what they liked and didn't like. One happened to be from West Chester, PA, where Karis had lived for twelve years. The student loved Richmond and went on and on, giving us her thoughts. You may only ask one or two questions, but sometimes students will share so much more.

25

WHY AM I RECEIVING ALL OF THESE COLLEGE MAILERS AT MY HOME, AND DOES THAT MEAN I'LL BE ADMITTED?

Over 1100 colleges purchase student lists from College Board and the ACT. They use PSAT, SAT, SAT Subject Test, ACT, and AP scores to target students who may be admissible applicants. The largest purveyor of names to colleges is College Board's Student Search Service (SSS), which gives colleges access to the information of almost seven million test takers. The SSS can also provide colleges with precisely-located students who meet specific criteria, and information about where students went to high school.

The ACT offers a similar service, in which students are asked at the beginning of the test if colleges can contact them. Most students opt in, and the mailings begin. Colleges target students based on test scores, self-reported GPA, geography, gender, ethnicity, intended major, religious preference, activities, and other factors.

Most colleges find this to be an effective way to discover and enroll appropriate students. Other colleges want you to apply even if they know you aren't a viable applicant, because more applications mean the acceptance rate is lower, which makes the college look stronger. This, in turn, leads to applications from stronger students, increased donations, and increased prestige. College admission counselors know that scarcity drives up the value of their brand.

Students need to know that being blitzed by mailers means a college wants you to apply, but it doesn't mean you'll be guaranteed admission.

My daughter Karis received 29 mailings from Vanderbilt, and that didn't even count emails. NYU sent her an envelope with large bold print that said "NYU is impressed with you." Southern Illinois said in all caps, "WE'VE DETERMINED THAT YOUR QUALIFICATIONS MAKE YOU A GREAT CANDIDATE FOR A GENEROUS ACADEMIC SCHOLARSHIP." These colleges didn't have her transcript, essays, recommendations, or application. They advertised based on test scores, and this is something to keep in mind when you receive mailers.

26

WHAT IF MAY 1 ARRIVES AND I STILL HAVEN'T BEEN ACCEPTED ANYWHERE?

There is a name for May 1 amongst college admissions professionals. It is known as the "National Candidate Reply Date." This is the day that most schools require you to have submitted a signed contract and deposit.

So what happens if you didn't get accepted anywhere, and therefore cannot submit a contract and a deposit? Don't be discouraged. There are still plenty of schools that have rolling admissions right up through the beginning of the school year.

You can visit https://nacacnet.org around May 4 to view Space Availability reports that show which schools still have openings after that date. Try using the search filters to change your criteria, such as majors, school size, and location. Pick up the phone and call the schools that your search reveals to find out who is still accepting applications.

You can also use a tool like College Navigator to search for colleges that accept over 80 percent of their students. Usually these colleges will still be admitting students in May.

When Janean came to me, she had just barely made it across the finish line to graduation. She'd graduated in the bottom 15 percent over her class with a 2.1 GPA and had earned a 12 on the English section of the ACT. Furthermore, it was mid-June, and she hadn't been accepted anywhere. I assured her there would be plenty of schools interested in her, and four days later, I called her with the names of five schools that were going to admit her and offered some of the things that were important to her in a college. Janean is a freshman in college right now; she is living in the dorm and she is enjoying college life.

27

WHAT IS THE PARENTS' ROLE IN DECIDING WHICH COLLEGES TO APPLY TO, AND WHICH ONE TO SELECT?

Parents have a major role in this process. They should set financial parameters, and the EFC (Expected Family Contribution) is almost always based on parents' income and assets. In my opinion, parents have an obligation to pay the EFC portion of the cost of college.

One of the biggest mistakes I see parents make is believing that it is their parental obligation to help their child attend their dream school regardless of the cost. This is a colossal mistake that can be financial suicide. Set limits on what you can pay and let your student know well in advance, but don't be afraid to sacrifice. Ask your child to sacrifice because your child is getting something that will be invaluable for the rest of their life. Students who cannot handle this reality need not get their way, as they have much growing to do in the entitlement department.

Parents can help students work through applications and review them afterwards, but they absolutely should not complete the applications or write the essays. Parents can also arrange the logistics for college visits, help do scholarship research, and fill out financial aid paperwork. Even though FAFSA and CSS profiles are in the student's name, in my experience, parents do need to take the lead on these. The complicated paperwork largely revolves around parents' tax returns. Parents can also be the point people if a FAFSA verification request occurs.

Not everyone will agree with me on this one, but I do believe parents have the veto power over a school that they don't believe will provide a quality education for their child. I believe parents should allow their kids to take the lead in the process, and students should come up with a list of affordable schools. Parents can then mark which schools they approve of, and should let their students select from the mutually agreed-upon schools.

A lot of parents from different cultures believe they should be the ones driving the process and not their child. I understand this and I respect this, but just know that your child is coming to America, and colleges don't want to hear you say, "I make the calls in my country."

Parents can help keep students on track with deadlines if it's helpful and necessary, and should be a constant source of encouragement. Finally, parents should accept the college a student selects. If parents have a scintilla of doubt about the school a student is selecting, the student will detect it. Parents may need to slightly adjust what responsibilities they take on, depending on the independence and maturity of their child.

Iris and her mom worked exceptionally well together. Iris's mom handled the logistics of arranging their college visits and checked up periodically–without nagging–to make sure Iris was on top of the deadlines. Iris's parents took a lead role on financial matters, but neither parent tried to write her essay, and they empowered Iris to select the college she wanted to attend, even if it wasn't the school they would have selected for her.

28

HOW MUCH WEIGHT SHOULD I PUT ON COLLEGE RANKINGS?

If I started out by telling you to ignore the rankings, you wouldn't listen to me: the rankings are too intriguing and enticing not to at least take a sneak peek. I know my families are looking at them, so what I want to do is discuss the value of the rankings, the flaws of the rankings, and the danger of the rankings. I want to encourage responsible use of the rankings.

What would you think if you were a boy in high school and you were dating a girl at your high school, and I came up to you and said, "I have ranked all of the girls in our school from number 1 to number 1000 and I just want to ask, why are you dating number 87 when number 16 on my rankings has a crush on you?"

First of all, you would look at me like I was insane, but here is what you would probably be thinking: "How do you know what personality meshes with my personality? How do you know whether the girls you ranked ahead of my girlfriend have the same interests I have? How do you know who I find to be physically attractive?"

I have so much respect for the approach that the Princeton Review takes in their excellent book, *The Best 382 Colleges*. They do rank colleges, and even though that is not precise, they refuse to do an aggregate or cumulative ranking. They refuse to say, "School X is better than School Y." Here is what they say instead: "The Princeton Review does not rank the schools in the book overall, 1 to 382, hierarchically or in a single list category. The Princeton Review reports the top 20 schools (of the 382 in the book) for each of its 62 different ranking list categories–but does not report ranks beyond the top 20 in any category (i.e. schools ranked 21 to 382)" (*The Best 382 Colleges*, 2018 edition).

There are so many college rankings, and they are all over the place when it comes to where a college is ranked. This is because they all have different formulas. You will often hear *US News* rankings quoted. They were the first source to really promote an aggregate ranking. They did this over 35 years ago, and they were so popular that now their college rankings are what they are primarily known for, and they have become a complete non-factor as a news agency.

After years of railing against the USNWR rankings and how biased and inaccurate they are, a slew of others have jumped into the rankings game, coming up with their own formulas, often much better than *US News* formula, but still inadequate to properly reflect your values and what you want in a college experience.

Here are a fourteen of the other rankings that have sprung up in the few decades:

- ℵ *Washington Monthly*
- ℵ *Forbes*

- *Kiplinger*
- *Niche*
- *Princeton Review*
- *Business Week*
- *Newsweek*
- *Times Higher Education World University Rankings*
- *Center for World University Rankings*
- *Parchment Student Choice College Rankings*
- *Collegiate Choice*
- *Money Magazine*
- *College Factual Rankings*
- *College Score Card*

At first I was disheartened when all of these rankings started springing up, because in my experience as a college coach, parents and students put entirely too much weight on the rankings. But over time, I began to like the spate of new rankings, because they enabled me to make a point I have been making since the early 90s when I worked in college admissions: You have to use your own value system to come up with a personal ranking that reflects what you value, and in the right apportionment that you value the school characteristics.

Let's look at a few examples of how this collection of rankings undermines the perceived precision of accuracy that the public affords them.

CUNY (College of New York) Baruch College is number two in the *Money Magazine* college rankings, but in *USNWR* they do not even make the national rankings and only come in 20th in their region.

The *Times Higher Education* World University Rankings has Dartmouth at 104, but they are 11th in *USNWR.*

Wesleyan University is 374th in the Center for World University Rankings, but tenth with *Kiplinger.*

Berea College is number one with *Washington Monthly,* but number 367 with *Forbes.*

The best article I have ever read on the college rankings was published on August 9, 2016, by Jeremy Ratcliff, and it is titled, "Deciphering the Different College Rankings." I strongly encourage you to Google this article. Ratcliff talks about how in high school, he was rankings-obsessed, but then he decided to do a study of the rankings. In this article, he goes over the different formulas for a bunch of the rankings and then he draws attention to their biases. For example, Ratcliff says *USNWR* is biased against regional universities and up-and-coming universities. I would also add that it is biased against public colleges; it doesn't do enough surveying of students about their experiences, and it definitely doesn't factor in the value of racial and socio-economic diversity into its rankings.

If you want to read the best article I have ever read about the deleterious impact *USNWR* college rankings have had on American higher education, I strongly encourage you to Google the following article: "How *U.S. News* College Rankings Promote Economic Inequality on Campus," September 10, 2017, by Benjamin Wermund of Politico.

The *Washington Monthly* rankings do a great job of looking at whether a college improves society by educating the less fortunate, but they do not even look at political diversity and cultural intolerance. They rank Washington & Lee, where General Lee was serving as president when he died and became the school's namesake, as the seventh ranked school in the country. W & L has its strengths, but the student body overwhelmingly voted for Donald Trump, so for a lot of the students I work with, when they go through the process of assessing the political and cultural environment they want, there is no way Washington and Lee is going to be the seventh ranked school based on what they are looking for. According to collegedata.com, fewer than 1 in 40 W & L students are black. That is not going to be enough racial diversity for most of the students I work with, so the number seven ranking is irrelevant.

You'll also want to be wary of any rankings a school shares with you on your campus visit. It isn't that they're lying, it's just that with so many rankings available, it's easy for a school to find a set of rankings that makes them look good. Colleges use these because it comes across as objective and outside substantiation.

I know it may seem like I am anti-rankings, but I have a lot more respect for rankings that are based on surveys and for rankings that are in an individual category. For example, the *USNWR* has a pretty good formula for ranking which colleges are the most selective, but where they go off the tracks is by telling you college X is the best overall college. Our brains like to put things in order, so these ordinal rankings can be seductive. Have you ever noticed how the rankings change every year? They need to sell magazines, so they keep changing their formula, revealing just how imprecise the rankings are.

The Princeton Review takes 62 different categories, and they survey around 140,000 students, about 375 per campus, and they come up with the top 20 list using scientific survey methods. I respect the formula, but it still has to be processed through your value system and what you want. When they say, "the following top 20 schools have the best campus food," I know it is based on a large enough sample size. Ditto for their question about the top 20 colleges where professors get high marks. But it isn't perfect, because all you have to do is look back the year before and you will see that by surveying different people you get different results.

Let me share an example of how to combine responsible use of the rankings with customizing the rankings to reflect your values.

I think *Bloomberg*'s *Business Week* does as good a job as any rankings at having a respectable formula. For their 2016 top undergraduate business schools, they surveyed over 30,000 students and 600 companies, and here is how they weight everything in their formula:

Employer Survey (40 percent of total score): Feedback from recruiters who hire recent business graduates on how well schools prepared students for jobs at their companies.

Student Survey (35 percent): Students' own ratings of the campus, career services department, and faculty and administrators.

Starting Salary (15 percent): The base compensation of students who had jobs lined up, adjusted for salary variation across industries and regions.

Internship (10 percent): The percentage of a school's graduates who had at least one internship at any time during college.

While this is nice, what if a school is in the boonies and you would die if you were not in the city? What if a school is in freezing cold weather and you get depressed without your large dose of sunshine? What if you value a racially and socio-economically diverse student body? What if cost is a concern? None of those things are factored into *Bloomberg*'s rankings. In Chapter 16, I discuss the 32 factors that will help you determine the right college for you.

Ratcliff's summary of his article was so on point; I agree with every single word:

> I hope you can take one thing away from it: college rankings should only be taken with a grain of salt. No college ranking can accurately say where you will be the most successful, feel the most comfortable, make your closest friends, or meet professors who will impact your life the in ways you simply cannot predict as a high school senior. College rankings are made by people who try to arbitrarily weigh your college experience for you without knowing what you value.

Joy and I visited a college that had twice been recognized by a highly-respected publication as the most beautiful college in the country. The school was proud of this, and the tour guide repeated their ranking twice. Joy thought that the campus was a complete eyesore, and I tended to agree with her. She still talks about how ugly that place was! Be careful how much stock you put into college rankings, because subjectivity always comes into play in their creation.

SECTION 3

GETTING ACCEPTED WHERE YOU APPLY

29

WHAT ARE ADMISSIONS COUNSELORS REALLY LOOKING FOR?

I like to break this down into seven key things admissions counselors are seeking. Remember our conversation in Section 2 about admission by the numbers versus holistic admissions? If a school admits by numbers, they won't use everything I list here to evaluate your application, but they'll still want an applicant they admit to have these traits. For holistic admissions schools, they are even more important.

1. They want to see your authentic self. There is so much pretense, packaging, and posturing in the application process, and admissions counselors are very good at picking out the "real thing." They'll assess your authenticity with your application,

your essays, recommendations, interviews, if they do any, and any impressions you've created in your interactions.

2. They are looking for admirable character traits that they need more of on their campus, such as the ability to build amiable relationships with a diverse population of students, a positive attitude, personal integrity, willingness to try new things, creativity, strong work ethic, emotional stability, grit and resilience, likeability, a caring attitude, and leadership.
3. They want students who have an insatiable love of learning, and they want students who can excel in their academic program. They want students that will elevate the classroom experience and learning environment for the other students and the professors. This is evaluated based on teacher recommendations, test scores, grades, demonstrated academic rigor, writing ability, intellectual curiosity, and grade trajectory.
4. They want to get a clear sense of where and how you'll contribute to the community outside the classroom. Admissions counselors will look at how you contributed to your community in high school and your local community. They will look at what you articulate as your interests, and they'll project what you might accomplish on their campus.
5. They're looking at their institutional priorities and whether they need more applicants like you. See Chapter 74 on "hooks."
6. They want to know how likely you are to choose their school. See Chapter 58 on demonstrated interest.
7. They'll evaluate whether you're a match for their campus culture and course and major offerings.

If I had to pick two words to summarize what they are looking for, I would select the following two words: Positive Impact.

When I am asked to share what is the single best predictor a school will get "positive impact" in and outside of the classroom, I don't say grades, test scores, rigor, writing, interview skills, or extracurricular talent. The best predictor I have seen, which is usually "spot on," is this: someone that teachers absolutely love to teach. This is particularly true if the teachers are teaching a very rigorous class at a rigorous school and if they know the student very well. In order for this test to be valid, a teacher has got to be gut-wrenchingly honest in their recommendations. I call this "painting the picture with the warts." If an AO (admission officer) could have teachers who wrote recommendations like this, in addition to having the transcript and a quality School Profile, they would make decisions they would not regret 95 percent of the time, in my opinion. This test encompasses the academic and the character factors, but each piece of the application reveals something of value.

> When I first met with Lorraine and her mom, one of the first things Ms. Robinson asked me was, "What do colleges want Lorraine to be involved in now?" She wanted to know what extracurricular activities her daughter should be involved in to be accepted to a selective school. The truth is, though, colleges find this question frustrating. They want to know what you're passionate about to get you involved in what inspires *you*, not what you think inspires *them*.

30

What are the four types of Grade Point Averages (GPA)?

GPA is a way of taking your grades for all the years of high school and translating them into a number. There are lots of different scales, but the most common is A=4, B=3, C=2, D=1, and F=0. The numbers are then averaged together. For example, if you had three As and three Bs, your GPA would be a 3.5.

The four types of GPAs your school could use are core weighted, cumulative weighted, core unweighted, and cumulative unweighted. As if that isn't confusing enough, colleges and scholarship organizations often create their own GPA and will recalculate yours in order to compare it to others using their rules. This creates a level playing field. Read the fine print carefully when you read a school's information on GPA.

- Weighted vs. unweighted: Weighted GPA gives extra points (or weight) for taking honors, AP, or IB courses. This is like putting a 10-pound bag of potatoes on the scale before you even add your grades in. The side with the extra potatoes (the advanced courses) won't ever be lower than the unweighted GPA. Schools that use an unweighted GPA do not give "bonus points" for taking more difficult versions of classes.
- Core vs. cumulative: Your core GPA only counts the following five subjects: math, science, history, English, and foreign language. Cumulative GPA includes elective classes such as health courses, art, and others.

I have the privilege of serving with and learning from Peter Johnson, Senior Associate Director of Admissions at Columbia University, as fellow board members for http://gotocollegenyc.org. Peter is one of the wisest and most experienced admission professionals in the nation. One axiom I have heard Peter use on more than one occasion is, "We do not admit statistics to an institution; we admit students to an educational community." Grades are very important, but this quote puts them in perspective.

When Janice called me, she was sad. She had thought her daughter, a student at a very good private school, would be receiving a Zell Miller scholarship to cover all of her tuition at any of Georgia's public colleges. The requirements for the scholarship were a 3.7 GPA and a 26 on the ACT or 1200 on the SAT. Janice never questioned her daughter's eligibility, but what she hadn't thought about was that her daughter's school used a weighted GPA that gave extra points for advanced courses. The Zell Miller scholarship only allows extra points for AP or IB courses, and never more than a 4.0 for an A.

When Janice's daughter's GPA was recalculated for the scholarship's rules, she fell just short of qualifying, with a GPA of 3.698, which the scholarship committee would not round up. You can prevent a lot of heartache by making sure you know how your high school and any colleges or scholarships you're interested in will calculate your GPA.

31

Is it better to earn a B in an advanced course or an A in a standard-level course?

From an admissions standpoint, it depends. Some colleges will only look at an unweighted GPA, even if your transcript displays a weighted GPA.

For most highly selective schools that use holistic admissions, excelling academically with rigorous courses is the biggest factor determining your admissions chances. Usually, for highly selective schools, this means a B in a more rigorous class will be more valued than an A in an easier class. However, which option helps you get admitted is a more complicated question that can only be handled on a case-by-case basis.

Other things to consider when you're thinking about this question:

- ℵ What are your other grades?
- ℵ Is this likely to be your only B in a sea of As, or are you more of an A/B student in general?
- ℵ What is your work/life balance?
- ℵ Can you handle extra rigor without undue stress?
- ℵ Can you be happy and enjoy high school and handle the rigor? If not, don't do it. You don't have to go to Brand Name University. This is really my bottom-line test. There are a lot of high school students taking advanced classes because they have heard the colleges value them, but they have no business taking the courses they are in. Here are a few other questions I ask:
- ℵ What subject is the course in? Is it related to your major?
- ℵ Which colleges are you most interested in?
- ℵ Are you likely to earn a high B, low B, or mid-B? (If it's going to be a mid- or high B and you're generally a straight-A student, I'll usually recommend taking the more rigorous course if you can maintain a good work/life balance.)

Let me go back to my statement about which colleges you're most interested in. There are 40,000 high schools in this country. This means that there are 80,000 valedictorians and salutatorians in the United States, and then there are all of these international students. A lot of these students apply to Stanford, MIT, Yale, Harvard, Princeton, Columbia, and a few other ridiculously selective schools. These schools accept between 1500-2000 students a year. You do the math: 80,000 valedictorians and salutatorians and thousands more brilliant international students for 1500-2000 acceptance letters.

I have heard several admissions officers from these schools ask this question, and on more than one occasion I have heard them honestly say, "Take the advanced class and get an A." Am I saying you can't get in these schools with a B on your transcript? Of course not. I've seen every one of these schools take a student with a B. But I do want to be clear about how selective some of these schools are. According to a former Stanford admissions counselor, they denied over 70 percent of students with perfect test scores and a 4.0 GPA in a recent year.

Colleges tend to hate this question. They want the students to take the hardest courses they can handle because they want them to be intellectually stimulated because of their thirst to learn, but they also want you to be happy in high school and not unduly stressed out. Some admission counselors refer to students who take courses to get A's as Grade Grubbers. I am sympathetic to the college perspective and the student perspective. I do want students to know that if you don't make it into Brand Name U, it will not have any correlation with your success in life or your happiness in life. That will be based not on where you go, but on what you do when you get to college and what you do when you get out of college.

Anthony was an exceptional student. He had virtually straight A's, and nearly perfect test scores. Anthony decided to apply to a school through early decision, a method that would significantly increase his chances of admission, but that committed him to that school if accepted. Anthony was an underrepresented student of color, and he applied to a school where he had alumni status. His parents were surprised when he was not admitted, and made a call to their college counselor. When his counselor followed up with the college, it turned out that despite his high grades and test scores and his other positive factors, the rigor of Anthony's courses was not at the same high level of the students against whom he was competing.

32

HOW DO COLLEGES EVALUATE MY GRADE TRENDS?

Grade trends are extremely important for schools that use holistic admissions. Colleges know that a student's twelfth-grade performance is a better indicator of college readiness than their ninth-grade performance.

There are six different grade trends a student could have; four are negative, while two are positive.

The negative grade trends are:

- ℵ Consistently low
- ℵ Downward trend: your grades begin high in ninth grade and go down each year
- ℵ Consistently average

- "Rollercoaster" grade pattern: your grades bounce around unpredictably between high and low
- Here is how Jim Miller, the former Dean of Admissions at Brown, puts it: "The kiss of death in any college admission process is a declining record."

The positive grade trends are:

- Consistently high from ninth to twelfth grade
- Upward trend from ninth through twelfth grade

Joyce was a student I worked with who transferred in tenth grade from an average high school to an incredibly rigorous one. The transition was difficult and impacted Joyce's grades in Latin and math. She received two C's in tenth grade in those courses, but had an outstanding eleventh grade and an even better start to her twelfth-grade year. Joyce was rewarded for her upward grade trend and was admitted to a handful of highly competitive colleges. Joyce wisely used the addendum at the end of the Common App to explain that the difference in rigor from her previous school to her new school took some time to adjust to. She talked about how her grades suffered at first, but she met with teachers and worked hard and caught up to her peers.

33

HOW DO COLLEGES EVALUATE MY CLASS RANKING?

Class ranking is a number that tells you where your GPA falls in a ranking of everyone in your high school class. For example, if your ranking is 282 out of a class of 328, that means 281 students have a higher GPA than you do.

You could make the case that class ranking is even more important than your grades themselves because it puts your grades into context and minimizes the effect of grade inflation. When I pick up a new client and they have a 3.92 GPA, it really doesn't tell me very much until I can see their School Profile and their class rank. There are times I can't get this, and I know it may seem awkward but I ask them and their parents how many students they feel are ranked ahead of them in their class.

Having said that, colleges have trended towards putting less emphasis on class ranking, as fewer high schools are including this information on transcripts. This is particularly true of private high schools and public schools in upper-middle class areas. Unfortunately, the decreased visibility of class rankings places more emphasis on test scores.

Why is class ranking being reported less often? Several reasons. First, some believe it introduces a divisive and competitive culture that pits students against one another. Second, it is thought to lead students to focus too heavily on grades and loading up on "easy A" courses. Third, administrators can't agree on how much weight to give to advanced or honors classes in class ranking. Lastly, class ranking makes it more difficult for students to be admitted to competitive schools because very strong high schools may have many excellent students, and an outstanding student who ranks 30th in their class could be valedictorian at a less rigorous high school. The concern is that colleges will not make this adjustment as appropriate, leading to stiffer competition in their evaluation.

> Kathy Boccella of the *Philadelphia Inquirer* wrote an article on October 30, 2016, entitled, "More Top High Schools Drop out of Class-Rank System." Boccella shared evidence that rank can hurt students. "For the West Chester Area School District, the last straw for class rank came when a University of Pennsylvania admissions officer told school officials that a highly qualified graduate had been rejected because she was ranked 15th out of 320 students. They said, 'If you didn't rank her, she would have gotten in,'" Superintendent James Scanlon said of the student, who had earned a 3.9 grade point average in the high-achieving Chester County district. Now West Chester may be joining a growing number of districts around the country in eliminating class rank in its high schools.

High schools are also becoming more creative at hiding their class rankings. According to a May 2015 article published in the *Washington Post*, at Washington-Lee High school in Arlington, VA, 117 students all shared the title of valedictorian because this school awarded the title to any student with a GPA above 4.0. This same article quoted a Tufts University admissions dean who said that only one out of every five applicants displayed a class ranking on their transcripts last year at Tufts.

When Jim and his mom came to me, they were very focused on test scores, but Jim had already received an ACT score in the low 30s. I noticed that his school transcripts provided a class ranking, and that Jim was just outside the top 10% of his class. I told Jim and his mom that his ACT score was fine, and we should instead focus on improving his grades to raise his ranking to the top 10% of his graduating class. "Your school provides a ranking," I said, "so this will be closely looked at, and there are schools that want their applicants in the top 10% of their classes so they can report this to *US News and World Report*." In Jim's case, class ranking was particularly important.

34

WHAT HOPE IS THERE FOR ME IF I AM ONLY A C STUDENT?

There is a lot of hope for C students. Hundreds of colleges practice what is known as Open Enrollment, meaning they accept any student who applies as long as they have either a diploma or a GED.

There are far more colleges than people realize that are accepting a very high percentage of their applicants. Visit College Navigator and click the "More Search Options" button to search for colleges that accept more than 80 percent of their applicants.

I have had the privilege of working with two sisters who started a foundation to help under-resourced students so they can have access to quality education. I would mention their names, but they like to be anonymous. Their dad made a lot of money, and he passed it on to them. He also gave a very large gift to his alma mater, Presbyterian College, to establish a scholarship. The scholarship at Presbyterian is for a hard-working C student. He wanted it to be for the C student because *he* had been a hard-working C student at Presbyterian because of his learning difference. Don't ever mentally put limits on what you believe you can accomplish because you are a C student.

You should also not dismiss technical colleges and community colleges. These two-year programs can be very attractive, and technical colleges can lead to many outstanding jobs. Those colleges are also sometimes called trade schools, vocational colleges, or career colleges, because they focus on specific, career-based training. Examples include cosmetology, medical imaging, welding, and automotive tech. They have excellent hands-on training, and if you follow the blueprint we laid out in Section 1, you can choose a field where there are ample jobs awaiting you when you finish your two-year program.

Jackson was enrolled in a four-year college, but one day he said to himself, "Why am I doing this? I have loved cars since I was a little kid, and all I really want to do is work on cars." Jackson transferred to a two-year technical school where he received his automotive training, and he has never regretted his decision. Today he is doing what he loves, working on cars. As long as he is really helping people, Jackson is highly successful according to the definition of success we set in Chapter 1.

Community colleges, also known as junior colleges, offer associate degrees. They can also lead to many career opportunities, but they generally require more core classroom instruction in subjects like math, English, and science. The better academic community colleges establish Articulation Agreements with other four-year colleges to approve, in advance, the acceptance of credit hours earned at the institution to facilitate the transfer of students into four-year colleges after earning their two-year community college degree.

35

WHICH OF MY GRADES DO COLLEGES SEE IN MY SENIOR YEAR BEFORE THEY MAKE THEIR ADMISSIONS DECISIONS?

At the time schools make their admissions decisions, they will usually have seen your grades from your most recently-completed and reported quarter, trimester, or semester. Policies are all over the place when it comes to what senior grades they require in order to make a decision. UCLA receives about 120,000 applications a year, the most in the nation, and they recalculate a GPA based only on tenth and eleventh grade grades. Many public schools will even accept students at the end of their junior year—usually schools that practice rolling admissions (this means they evaluate and accept/deny students as they apply and stop when they are full, instead of waiting until a specific deadline to evaluate all applicants).

Most selective private colleges will require your first semester senior year grades in addition to a counselor report from your counselor. One of the biggest myths out there is that the senior year does not count toward college decisions. It does!

If you read this section's earlier question about grade trends, then you know that how you finish your senior year is extremely important. Don't let your grades taper off with a case of "senioritis" or the "senior slump." Another major mistake seniors make is taking a lighter load. If you are looking at a highly selective school and you only take four core classes as a senior, you may as well not even bother to apply. There are always exceptions to this (like for recruited athletes in revenue-producing sports), but there are not very many.

High schools on a trimester system sometimes submit their second trimester grades in time for college decisions made from mid-March to April 1, but it's far more common for first trimester grades to be the last grades a college sees before making its decision.

Most importantly, however, students should NOT think they can allow their grades to slide after January. Admissions representatives sometimes call counselors in mid-February and ask for an updated progress report.

You may be thinking, what about schools where students have an early decision deadline of November 1? Some schools will use the end-of-year junior grades, but most will try hard to get a fall grade update. Lee Coffin, Dartmouth's Dean of Admission, makes it very clear that when an early decision applicant is admitted in December, they will require the school counselor to submit the January grades. This isn't just Dartmouth. This is standard practice at selective schools that practice holistic admissions.

Janean was very fortunate. After three years of solid grades, she was tanking in her senior year and despite phenomenal test scores, I suspected she was unlikely to be admitted to her Reach or Mid-Range schools. However, she had a great high school counselor who was working with her in addition to my guidance, and Janean's school was on a trimester system. Janean hunkered down and brought her grades up nicely in the second trimester of her senior year and was offered a generous financial aid package by Johns Hopkins. There was no way she would have received that acceptance without a strong senior year.

36

HOW WILL A SELECTIVE COLLEGE EVALUATE COURSES I'VE DECIDED TO TAKE?

The more selective the college, the more scrutiny applied to your curriculum, and the more rigor that will be expected. You will be expected to have increased your level of academic rigor each year. I heard Jenny Rickard, the former Dean of Admission at Bryn Mawr College, speak and here is what Jenny said: "The thing that we are most obsessed about is the transcript."

Colleges will also look at the major you are interested in and that will impact where they will expect to see rigor and success. This is especially true if you are applying to a university where you have to select a school within the university at the time you apply. For example, if you apply to UPenn as an engineering major, they will expect you to have taken and excelled in high level math and physics. If you apply to the Wharton School of Business, they will expect you to have had success at high level calculus because their economics and finance curriculum is very calculus-based.

In general, if you indicate that you want to be a Spanish major and you only took the bare minimum of two foreign language classes, it will not serve you well in your evaluation by a selective school. Your curriculum will be seen through the prism of what you want to study. If you indicate you want to be a doctor, you can expect more scrutiny in your advanced science and advanced math courses.

Every year, the NACAC issues the State of College Admissions report. This is a professionally-done research project that involves surveying over a thousand colleges by asking them what matters most to them in terms of college applications, recruitment and yield strategies, and factors in admissions decisions. Year after year, the number one factor determining admission is the grades students receive in rigorous classes. Every year of the report, grades in college prep classes are ranked to be of considerable importance by between 79-87 percent of admissions offices and it is usually considered to be of moderate important by more than 10 percent. It has been the number one factor in determining who gets in for fifteen consecutive years.

Many students aren't aware of this, but from the standpoint of a selective college using holistic admissions, two students could have taken five AP courses, and one student's rigor could be very impressive while the other's is considered woefully inadequate. How? It's all in *which* courses were of an advanced level.

Very selective colleges want to see you take the most rigorous courses that your school offers in either four or five of the core areas: math, science, English, history, and foreign language. This is sometimes called "maxing out the curriculum." In certain instances, you can get away with just doing this in three out of five subject areas, but then you'll need some additional hooks. Selective schools using holistic admissions won't hold it against you if your school doesn't offer AP or IB courses. They'll only judge you in light of the opportunities at your school.

Very selective schools, with few exceptions, will usually want to see calculus on your transcript. For those that make exceptions, not making it to pre-calculus is usually the kiss of death. In other subject areas, it's usually in a student's best interest to take physics, chemistry, and biology. Some states, like Georgia, require four years of science in order to attend any of their public schools.

Colleges will look at your number of AP and IB courses if your school offers these courses. If you took these courses in the junior year, they will look to see what scores you got on the AP and IB exams. Scores for the senior year are not available until after admission decisions are made. If you got a 5 on an AP exam but you only got a B, they will likely conclude that the class was very rigorous and perhaps the grading was tough. However, if you got an A but you got a 1 or a 2 on an AP exam, they will likely assume that the class lacked rigor and there was grade inflation.

The most selective schools differentiate between students who get their high grades because they want to get in a selective college, or because they like the recognition of being valedictorian, or because they want the accomplishment of achieving a goal. They want the student who has an omnivorous thirst to learn. They want the student who stimulates and elevates class discussion. They want the student who thinks well on his or her feet. They want the student who challenges the thinking and perspectives of their fellow classmates and their teachers, as long as it is done in a respectful way. This isn't always easy to detect, and choosing to take an academically rigorous schedule is consistent with having a deep love of learning.

My daughter Karis took five AP courses in high school, but two were AP Language and AP Literature, both considered part of English, so this is seen as doubling up. She also took AP US History and AP Government, and this was doubling up again. She took AP Spanish, but she did not take an AP course in math or science, so this was a big weakness in her curriculum for her consideration at Davidson, since her school did offer APs in both. Her A in non-AP calculus helped, but the admissions office at Davidson urged me to counsel her to take an AP science course.

Science was Karis's weakness. If she got a C or even a C+ in an AP science course, this would have been worse than not taking AP at all. Fortunately for her, she did exceptionally well at Davidson's three-week July Experience the summer before her senior year. Without this success over the summer and the recommendation that came from one of Davidson's own professors, I think there's a good chance she would have been waitlisted due to not maxing out her curriculum.

13 years ago, I attended an information session at the College of William and Mary. I was very impressed with the senior leader who led the presentation, and I spent some one-on-one time with her after the tour to share what each of us did. When I told her I did college counseling, she told me she had been thinking about leaving admissions to do work similar to mine. I was surprised, because she'd seemed to content in her role. When I asked her why, she said, "By the time I see them, it is often too late. I meet so many great kids who I know could be successful here, but because they didn't take the right classes, we can't admit them." Less than a month later, she sent me an email to say she'd moved on from her job to transition into a counseling role where she could better guide students to admission at colleges of their choice.

37

WHAT IS THE PSAT, AND WHY IS IT IMPORTANT?

The PSAT is the Preliminary SAT, designed by the College Board and implemented in 1971. It was intended to be a diagnostic tool to assess your strengths and weaknesses in advance of the SAT, and it's your first opportunity to take a college entrance-level exam. PSAT scores are not used for college admission applications, but are considered for entry into the National Merit Scholarship Program. The test is usually taken in October of eleventh grade. There are also PSAT 8/9 and PSAT 10 tests designed for students in grades eight through ten, but these are just for practice and general assessment of your skills. While SATs are administered at nationally-assigned test centers, the PSAT is given at your individual high school.

The test takes two hours and 45 minutes to complete, and scores range from 320 to 1520. Each question is multiple-choice and has four choices. The time and question breakdown is as follows:

Section	Time	Number of Questions
Reading	60 minutes	48 questions
Writing and Language	35 minutes	44 questions
Math	70 minutes	47 questions
Total	165 minutes	139 questions

These scores are important if you plan to compete for national merit scholarships. This is particularly true of national merit scholarships offered by the universities themselves. These are usually very generous, but are highly competitive as only 1 in 200 high school students qualify as a National Merit Scholar.

Some people wonder why the PSAT is out of 1520 and the SAT is out of 1600. The PSAT leaves off the most advanced type questions that the SAT asks, and that accounts for these 80 points. These are usually in trigonometry and advance science questions, and many students may not have had the course work for these questions yet. Nevertheless, your PSAT score is a pretty good barometer of what SAT score your skillset has you currently tracking toward. The one exception is for the extremely high PSAT (high 1400s) tester. They are likely on pace for the mid to high 1500s on the SAT.

A homeschooled student can take the PSAT, but they must contact a local school principal well in advance to make these arrangements.

Janet called me, stressed out. She had just received her PSAT scores, and while she was a straight-A student at one of the most respected high schools in the country, she was not a great test taker. "Mr. Stucker," she said, "I only got a 1140 on my PSAT." I told her, "This is a great opportunity for us to dive deeper into your scores to see where you did well and where you need to bolster your skills." I assured her that her PSATs would not be part of her college application, and she brightened up at the thought of the PSAT as a no-stress test that could help her prepare for the SAT.

38

What is the National Merit Scholarship Program?

About 1 out of every 200 students who takes the PSAT (usually as eleventh graders) will eventually become a National Merit Scholar. This program was launched in 1955 by the not-for-profit National Merit Scholarship Corp.

The National Merit Scholar program has five levels of recognition.

Level 1: Program Recognition

This level applies to the top 50,000 (about 3 percent) of the 1.6 million students who take the PSAT in whichever year their local high school determines is their "official" year (nearly always eleventh grade, but sometimes tenth grade). Each state gets a portion of the 50,000, determined by the state's population. Reading, writing, language, and math scores are doubled to create the Selection Index.

Level 2: Commended Scholar

The 34,000 students with the highest scores are recognized the following September.

Level 3: Semi-Finalist

The 16,000 students with the highest scores are also recognized the following September. Semi-finalists must complete a detailed application, and their academic record and character are closely evaluated.

Level 4: Finalist

15,000 of the 16,000 semi-finalists will become finalists, notified in February of their senior year.

Level 5: National Merit Scholar

8000 students, or about half of the finalists, become actual National Merit Scholars. This decision is based on a holistic review that includes essays, recommendations, grades, curriculum, leadership, volunteerism, SAT scores, and other factors.

The NMSC awards these students with $2500. There are some corporate sponsorships that can exceed the $2500, but they are mostly for employees' children who work for one of these corporate sponsors. The bigger prize, however, comes from over 50 universities that offer full scholarships to national merit award winners. The list of colleges offering these generous awards includes a few flagship schools in the south, such as Mississippi, Kentucky, and Alabama, but the majority of the colleges that offer these full scholarships are rarely first-choice schools for most students.

I've had the same disagreement over the PSAT with two different companies who have done test preparation for students I work with. They've said, "Mark, you need to send students to us sooner so we can prepare them for the PSAT in order to become National Merit Scholars." My response is that only 1 in 200 students is a National Merit Scholar, so unless a student is already a good test taker, a prep course is unlikely to turn them into a National Merit Scholar. Even then, being a top tester isn't enough to get them the award, and if they do receive it, they may not even want to attend one of the colleges that offers a generous scholarship to winners. Students should value their PSAT scores, but not view PSATs and the National Merit Scholar program as the end-all, be-all of prestige and scholarship.

39

What is the ACT?

The ACT is currently the most taken college entrance exam, with almost 2.1 million annual test takers. It surpassed the SAT for the first time in 2012.

Founded in 1959 in Iowa, the test is designed to be a curriculum-based achievement test that measures what a student learned in high school. It was intended to be a clear alternative to the aptitude-oriented SAT test. Test scores ranges from 1 to 36, with the current average score being 20.8. Test sections include English, math, reading, science, and an optional essay.

On http://act.org, the test length is described as "215 multiple-choice questions [taking] approximately 3 hours and 30 minutes to complete, including a short break (or just over four hours if you are taking the ACT with writing). Actual testing time is 2 hours and 55 minutes (plus 40 minutes if you are taking the ACT with writing)."

The breakdown of each section is as follows:

Section	# of Questions & Time Limit	Content/Skills Covered	Question Types
English	75 questions in 45 min.	grammar & usage, punctuation, sentence structure, strategy, organization, and style	four-choice, multiple-choice usage/mechanics and rhetorical skills questions
Math	60 questions in 60 min.	pre-algebra, elementary algebra, intermediate algebra, coordinate geometry, plane geometry, and trigonometry	five-choice, multiple-choice questions
Reading	40 questions in 35 min.	reading comprehension of what is directly stated or implied	four-choice, multiple-choice referring and reasoning questions
Science	40 questions in 35 min.	interpretation, analysis, evaluation, reasoning, and problem solving	four-choice, multiple-choice data representation, research summaries, and conflicting viewpoints questions
Writing (optional)	1 essay in 40 min.	writing skills	essay prompt

A number of states require the ACT as their official test for public high school students to measure whether their students are meeting state and federal educational goals. Students can sign up at http://act.org, and they are advised to do so at least six weeks before a test in order to avoid late fees and to ensure their testing location of choice has not filled up.

Currently, the ACT is offered seven times a year in the United States, in February, April, June, July, September, October, and December. It is offered internationally five times a year. See http://act.org for those dates. The addition of the July date is new, and it is exciting because students have the most time to prepare for these tests in the summer, and now they can prepare and take the test over the summer.

Bridgit wasn't sure whether she should take the ACT, or the SAT. She had scored a 1080 on a practice SAT and 21 on a practice ACT. When we discussed where she should place her focus, I explained that her scores were equivalent, so like most students, she would likely score the same on both tests. I asked her which test she had liked the most, and before I could even finish asking, she said with certainty that she preferred the ACT. I told her, "You have your answer. You are going to have to be immersed in this material pretty diligently, and if you like the ACT more, it will be easier to stay motivated and disciplined." You can use the same method to help you choose between tests.

When you sign up for the ACT, you can select four colleges where your score reports will be sent for free. I recommend that you do not use these free score reports for your more selective schools. You can always add colleges later, but these reports require a fee. (For 2018 the cost is $12 per college, but it usually goes up a little every few years). Score reports are ordered on the ACT website, and expedited shipping is available for a premium fee.

40

WHAT IS THE SAT?

Founded in 1926 as the Scholastic Aptitude Test, the SAT has undergone several iterations, with two of the most major overhauls happening in 2005 and 2016. Along with the ACT, it is one of the two most commonly-accepted tests for undergraduate admission to United States colleges.

Test scores range from 400 to 1600, and sections include English, math (calculator, non-calculator, and free response), and reading. The national average score for the population at large is 1020, and for college-bound students the average is 1083. Of course, there is variation in average scores each year.

The SAT is offered in March, May, June, August, October, November, and December. The August SAT is new, and this can help take some of the pressure off of students during the school year. Just as with the ACT, students should plan to sign up at least six weeks in advance to avoid late fees and to secure their preferred test location. You can sign up for the SAT at http://collegeboard.org/register.

When you sign up for the SAT, you can select four colleges to send your score reports to for free. I recommend using your free score reports for your Likely and Safety schools. You can always add colleges later, and the fee for this in 2018 is currently $11.50 per college, but it usually goes up a little every few years. You can do this on the College Board website.

The score ranges for the most recent version of the SAT (reported from College Board) are:

SAT Score Reported	Details	Score Range
Total score	Sum of the two section scores.	400–1600
Section scores (2)	Evidence-Based Reading and Writing, and Math.	200–800
Test scores (3)	Reading, Writing and Language, and Math.	10–40
SAT Essay scores (3) *The SAT Essay is optional.*	Reading, Analysis, and Writing.	2–8
Cross-test scores (2)	Analysis in History/Social Studies and Analysis in Science. Based on selected questions in the Reading, Writing and Language, and Math Tests. These scores show how well you use your skills to analyze texts and solve problems in these subject areas.	10–40

SAT Score Reported	Details	Score Range
Subscores (7)	Reading and Writing and Language: Command of Evidence and Words in Context. Writing and Language: Expression of Ideas and Standard English Conventions. Math: Heart of Algebra, Problem Solving and Data Analysis, and Passport to Advanced Math.	1–15

Rachel was a reader; she always had a book in her hands. She would devour both fiction and nonfiction, popular young adult books like *Harry Potter* and the *Hunger Games*, and more sophisticated reads like the *New York Times* and the *Wall Street Journal*. Rachel wanted to take both the SAT and the ACT, and she scored much higher on the SAT. I've seen some voracious readers do better on the ACT, but most of the time, my students who read as much as Rachel score higher on the SAT. This makes sense, because the SAT's reading comprehension passages are more complex than the ACT's, giving students with very strong reading skills an extra chance to shine.

41

How is the "new" SAT different from the "old" SAT?

Students who took the SAT before 2005 took it with a 1600-point score system. From 2005 to 2016, a 2400-point scale was used, but in March 2016 the SAT returned to a 1600-point scale.

The "old" 2400-point test had maximum math, critical reading, and writing scores of 800 each. The new test, which has a maximum score of 1600, which is a similar scale to the one your parents took, has just two required sections: math and "evidence-based reading and writing." Each is still worth up to 800 points. The writing test is now optional, and is scored differently. The old test offered five multiple choice options per question, but now there are only four.

One of the biggest changes to the newest SAT was in scoring, with the elimination of a "guessing penalty." For decades, the SAT had a quarter-point deduction if you got an answer incorrect, while no points were deducted (or awarded) for an answer left blank. The ACT never had this penalty, which is one reason more students began to gravitate toward the ACT. Now, the newest SAT does not have this penalty.

Another change to scoring is that new SAT scores are inflated compared to the previous test. The average-scoring student will score 60-80 points higher on the new SAT, but this inflation diminishes as the score rises. For details on the conversion scale, check College Board's website. The new SAT also has "sub-scores" out of 40 in reading, writing and language, and math. Colleges are emphasizing these sub-scores more heavily. For example, Georgia Southern requires a 1090 on the redesigned SAT for admission for 2018-19, but they also require a 24 on the reading sub-score and a 22 on the math sub-score. Sub-scores and the composite scores matter for colleges with the redesigned SAT. Don't confuse a 32 in math on the SAT with a 32 on the ACT, as they are not the same.

The new test is significantly shorter than the previous version. The length of the test in the 2005-2015 version is one of the major reasons the ACT surpassed the SAT in the number of test takers. By dropping the SAT's essay requirement, the test became nearly an hour shorter for students who don't take this optional section. However, if you have a very high GPA, I do recommend taking the writing portion. Several competitive colleges either require or recommend this section. Even if you don't think you will apply to one of these schools, it's still best to take that portion—if you don't take it and you add a school to your list later that requires the writing portion, you'll have to re-take the SAT. Not fun! You can find out which schools currently recommend the writing portion at http://compassprep.com/act-writing-and-sat-essay-requirements.

The SAT has historically been more of a reasoning test, while the ACT measured content mastery. However, the new SAT moves more in the direction of the ACT, blurring these lines. Other differences in the new SAT include:

- ℵ Two math sections, one allowing a calculator
- ℵ No "complete-the-sentence" vocabulary section
- ℵ More algebra and more higher-level math, but less geometry

- ℵ The new essay score contains three scores ranging from 2-8, one each for reading, analysis, and writing (the essay score is no longer out of 800)
- ℵ The new SAT is more formally referred to as "the redesigned SAT"

Evelyn was so happy when she got her new SAT scores. She was a student in the class of 2017, and was given the option of taking either the new test or the old test. The highest score Evelyn had received on the old test's practice test was 1020, and she decided to take the new test, finishing with a score of 1070. She was excited about her score, and I hated to break the news that this score was equivalent to a 990 on the old test. Evelyn hadn't realized the new test scores were inflated. Understanding the scoring system can save you a lot of heartbreak.

42

WHAT ARE THE DIFFERENCES BETWEEN THE ACT AND THE SAT?

These two tests are more similar than ever in 2017, after the SAT's most recent changes in 2016.

The best explanation of the differences I've ever seen comes from arguably the best comprehensive college admission book on the market today, *Admission Matters* by Sally P. Springer. Here's what these pros have to say on the subject.

For the reading section, "the SAT has about twice as many vocabulary questions as the ACT ... The SAT reading section has five reading passages, two of which include graphs or charts. The ACT reading section has four reading passages, with no graphs or charts." The average reading level of the SAT passages is "two grades higher than the average grade level of corresponding ACT passages."

According to Springer, in the math section:

> The ACT places greater emphasis on geometry than the SAT—about 25 percent of its math questions are geometry-based, compared with only about 5 percent of math questions on the SAT ... The SAT places greater emphasis on algebra, word problems, and data analysis questions using tables and charts ... The ACT Math test includes a small number of questions that require knowledge of some advanced topics in mathematics ... Roughly 75 percent of SAT Math questions are multiple choice, and 24 percent are 'fill-in.' All ACT Math questions are multiple choice ... You can use a calculator on all ACT Math questions. The SAT has a calculator-allowed section and a no-calculator section.

Most questions are multiple choice, with four options for both tests, but the ACT has some math questions with five choices.

Jed Applerouth has a PhD in Educational Psychology and he and Saul Khan are more knowledgeable about the technical differences between the tests than anyone else I have heard address this subject. Jed is an educational innovator who started the outstanding Applerouth test prep company. I recently heard Jed speak and he repeatedly pointed out how much more focused the Redesigned SAT is on advanced reading and critical thinking. There are 30 more minutes on reading on the redesigned SAT than there are on the ACT. He also said that the non-calculator math section is challenging students because they have to do long math division and multiplying by decimals and kids aren't used to doing that anymore without a calculator.

Like most experts, Jed points out how timing issues present a bigger challenge on the ACT than the SAT, but he says the non-calculator section and even the calculator section on the SAT are the two sections that students are struggling to complete in time. Dr. Applerouth points out that the SAT gives students 43 percent more time on reading questions, 40 percent more time on math questions, and 33 percent more time on writing questions. Jed is working on a new ACT book that I can't wait to buy.

The ACT is rigorous when it comes to high-level math. It has a lot more trigonometry and according to Jed, the advanced topics cover so much material that he is trying to figure out how to cover all of them in his new book without making a 1400-page book.

The science section is only found on the ACT. Here is how Springer puts it: "The ACT Science section tests your ability to analyze charts and graphs and draw conclusions about scientific information ... This section is not a test of scientific knowledge as such, but instead focuses on logic and scientific thinking." A lot of people think the science section on the ACT consists of an entire new realm of knowledge that you'll need, and this is just not the case. It will not require much knowledge of chemistry, physics, geology, or biology. This is another one of those widespread myths I hear regularly. The science section is reading and interpreting tables and graphs. However, there is some advanced scientific knowledge required for a small number of questions.

In the optional essay section, "the SAT essay asks you to analyze a passage by discussing how the author uses evidence and develops the argument ... [while] the ACT essay asks you to write a persuasive argument in response to a passage dealing with a specific, contemporary issue."

I recently gave an in-home presentation to six families in West Chester, PA, joined by another counselor. The other counselor mentioned that you needed to be skilled in science to do well on the ACT, but I disagree, as this section is more about logic than specific knowledge. However, this myth that you must be good at science to excel on the ACT exists not only with students and parents, but with some counselors as well.

The SAT has fewer questions in each section than the ACT, but it takes longer to complete these questions. The ACT expects the test taker to move through the questions at a fairly rapid pace. This is arguably the biggest difference between the two tests, and if you are not a fast test taker, the ACT may not be the best choice for you. Time-wise, the ACT is 15 minutes shorter with the writing tests included; without the writing test it is only five minutes shorter, which is negligible.

Both tests have no guessing penalty, an optional writing section, and will test your knowledge of grammar, your ability to read a passage and understand it, and your skills in algebra, geometry, and trigonometry.

"I am now convinced that it doesn't matter to colleges if my son takes the ACT or the SAT"

43

DOES IT MATTER WHETHER I TAKE THE ACT OR THE SAT?

In a way, no. Both tests are accepted universally. Because each test has close to half the country taking it, it would be terrible business for any college to insist that students take a specific test.

The SAT continues to be the most frequently-administered test on both coasts, while the ACT has been more popular between the coasts. Recently, the ACT has been increasing in popularity along the coasts, and many believe this is a major reason for the SAT's 2016 overhaul, which made it more similar to the ACT.

The early evidence suggests that the redesigned SAT is effectively leading some states to abandon the ACT and use the SAT for their state contracts. I was shocked when I learned some time ago that the states of Illinois and Michigan (the heart of ACT country) were switching from the ACT to the SAT. On September 13, 2017, Jed Applerouth wrote an excellent article entitled, "ACT Loses Ground to Redesigned SAT" that explains how the SAT is surging. Here is what Dr. Applerouth wrote:

> The ACT's annual report, released late last week, revealed that the retooled and redesigned SAT is on a comeback, at the expense of the ACT.
>
> The SAT had been fairly stagnant for years, administered to 1.65 million students in 2011 and then to 1.64 million students in 2016. During that time, David Coleman led the College Board through a major transition, overhauling the flagship SAT, aligning it with the Common Core State Standards in hopes of gaining more state-contracts. It was a gamble, but one that eventually began to pay off when states including Michigan, Illinois, and Colorado, swapped their ACT contracts for SAT contracts. Although the official report for the class of 2017 has yet to be released, College Board officials have announced that over 1.8 million students in that class have taken the SAT, marking the most significant growth in decades. The SAT's gains are coming partially at the expense of the ACT which shed 60,000 students, dipping from 2.09 million students to 2.03 million.

Ultimately, you should consult this book and others for the differences between the two tests and take the one that is better suited for you. If you want a more in-depth analysis of the differences between the tests, I recommend signing up for one of Jed Applerouth's webinars at https://www.applerouth.com/#. He doesn't charge for these webinars, and you will get a chance to ask him questions.

It's worth mentioning that there's a myth that black students tend to do better on the ACT. However, this is urban folklore. It's a case-by-case assessment. One black student I worked with this year got a 16 on her ACT (24th percentile) and a 1370 (95th percentile) on her SAT. Regardless of race, I used to find that 80 percent of everyone did as well on the SAT as the ACT, but with the new SAT being more similar to the ACT, I'm expecting those numbers to be closer to 90 percent.

Cost-wise, both tests are around $50 if you sign up on time. You will pay around $15 more if you sign up for the longer test that includes the writing section. Students who qualify for the free or reduced lunch program are also eligible to receive two fee waivers for both tests and can sign up for free.

Roger was a dad who was convinced that colleges value the SAT over the ACT. Usually, when I get parents like this, I find that they grew up in the northeast, where more students take the SAT. I showed him multiple schools' websites stating that they don't treat ACT test takers any differently from SAT test takers. When Roger found out that more students in general take the ACT, I was able to convince him that colleges are unlikely to punish students for taking the test that most students take.

44

How do I know whether the ACT or the SAT test is better for me?

There are many excellent online tests that can help you determine this, and a good tutor or test prep center can easily determine the test that you're better suited for. You'll want to settle on which test you're better at earlier on in your process, so you can focus on one and ignore the other.

In general, the SAT is very verbal-dominant, while the ACT is more analytical and comprehensive. If you're not a fast test taker, the ACT could present an extra challenge for you. If you are a math whiz like Kyrah, one of the students I am working with, the ACT is probably for you.

If you do decide that the ACT is for you, then I strongly recommend that you work on your pacing. The students I have seen have sizable score gains on their ACT almost always learn how to not question themselves and answer the questions in less time.

One of the test prep pros I work with, Daisy Abdur-Rahman, can usually figure out what is best for a student based on how well they do on the science section of the practice ACT. She also looks at whether a student is verbal dominant or math dominant in her assessment of what test is best for each student.

I do strongly advocate that every student take one practice SAT and one practice ACT in real, test-like conditions in order to determine which test is best for them. Too many students don't go through this process with an open mind.

Many students do equally well on both practice tests, so I ask which they liked better. They almost always have a preferred test. I advise them to take that test. Because you'll be spending a lot of time with this material, it's best if you choose the material you dislike the least. I was going to say "choose the material you like the best," but let's be honest. Who likes test prep?

Monica started out doing the right thing. She took both practice tests, and since she'd done better on the SAT practice test, she started preparing to take the real SAT. Ultimately, though, Monica couldn't commit. After getting another SAT practice score, she'd flip over and start preparing for the ACT instead. Even though she started her test prep in 10th grade, she was still flip-flopping by 12th grade. Don't waste your time and money flip-flopping. Do an assessment, trust the results, and stick with one test.

45

HOW MANY TIMES SHOULD I TAKE THE ACT OR THE SAT?

Ideally, you'll take a number of practice tests, but not more than three "real" tests. I like to see students take the real test twice. Some students nail their score the first time and there's no "need" to take it again, but I generally advise taking it a second time anyway.

If you're taking quality practice tests and seeing score gains, you're ready to take the official test.

Here is my ideal timeline: Begin prepping in the summer between tenth and eleventh grade, and take your first test in August (SAT) or July/September (ACT). You could also take one of the fall administrations, but you'll definitely want to take your first test no later than December of your junior year, and within two weeks of when your test prep course ends so you're still on the ball. If you know you aren't a great test taker, you may want to begin during the summer between ninth and tenth grade. If you read widely and take your math class seriously, you will be preparing in elementary and middle school without even thinking about an ACT or an SAT.

Don't be discouraged if you're reading this after those dates have already passed for you. There's still time!

Be aware that if you're planning to take SAT Subject Tests, you can't take them during the same month as the main SAT, because the test administrations occur simultaneously. You'll need to plan accordingly. Usually, you will be taking the Subject Test after the course in school that aligns with that material has just ended.

One of the mistakes I made with my daughter Karis that I haven't made since was to have her take an official SAT at the end of 10th grade, just to get used to the testing atmosphere. She scored exactly the same as she had on her practice tests, but after more prep, she ended up taking the official SAT four times! This is once more than the maximum number of times I like to see a student test. Remember, there are some schools that monitor the number of times a student takes a test, and they will treat your scores differently if they see you've taken it many times. I see tremendous value to taking the test more than three times, but this is what practice tests are for. You can take practice tests in a group setting under real test-like conditions if you'd like to get a feel for the test atmosphere. There's no need to take an official test before you're ready.

There is no need to take the official test for both tests. The practice tests are very good at helping you determine which test will likely result in a stronger score for you, and with the help of a tutor, you should be able to choose the best test and save money, time, and stress.

46

WHAT TIPS CAN I USE TO IMPROVE MY ACT OR SAT SCORES?

Read daily! Great reading ideas include the *Washington Post*, the *New York Times*, and well-written magazines like *TIME* and *Newsweek.* Find material that interests you so this will come naturally. Reading frequently will help improve your comprehension.

- ℵ Sign up for *Word of the Day* at Dictionary.com. Look at how the word is used in context, and try using it on your parents. You can also find another friend who signs up for *Word of the Day* and use the word in context with each other.
- ℵ Work on test-taking strategies with your tutor or through your free online test prep.

- ℵ Take practice tests often, and identify your strengths and weaknesses. Work on both, improving on your weaknesses and making your strengths even stronger.
- ℵ Know the structure of each test before you take it.
- ℵ If you really struggle with time on tests, learn how to become effective at skimming by reading the first and last paragraphs in full, and the first and last sentence of the other paragraphs.
- ℵ Don't dwell on one question too long. Be attentive to your pacing.
- ℵ Go with your gut: when guessing, choose the first answer that comes to your mind.
- ℵ Get plenty of rest the night before, and fuel your body with nutrients by eating a solid, healthy breakfast the morning of the test.
- ℵ Find a great tutor who is a good match for your personality, learning style, and budget.
- ℵ If you are doing free online or low-cost online prep, find an accountability partner who will make sure you study when you say you're going to.

Chris saw a quantum leap in his SAT score: 400 points! He attributed his score gains to his test prep instructor and plan. Chris had a committed and talented test prep pro that he worked with one on one, but he also attributed his score improvement to his practice tests. He disciplined himself to take a practice SAT every week for eight straight weeks leading up to the test. On the week before the real test, he took his practice test at the same time of day as the real test would be taken, and he did everything he could to create the same testing conditions. He then went back and analyzed why he made his mistakes and how to minimize them on test day.

47

WHAT IS A COMPETITIVE SAT OR ACT SCORE?

For the SAT, this information comes from College Board's publication, "SAT: Understanding Scores 2016." You can find it at https://collegereadiness.collegeboard.org/sat/scores/understanding-scores

You can find ACT scores by percentile at: http://www.act.org/content/dam/act/unsecured/documents/Multiple_Choice_STEM_Ranks2016.pdf

If you're in the 50th percentile, you scored better than half of other test takers. If you're in the 75th percentile, you scored better than 75 percent of test takers. The key with percentile is to be aware of the cohort group you're being compared to.

The National Sample is based on all students in the nation, college-bound or not. The User percentiles require higher scores to reach the same percentiles, because they are based on United States students who take the SAT and are college-bound.

In order to know if your score is competitive, you need to know how your scores compare to others like you who are applying to a particular college. See Chapter 11 in Section 2.

Olufemi Ogundele is the Assistant Dean of Admission for Diversity Outreach at Stanford. He is someone I regard as a rising star on the national scene of college admission. His ability to articulate various nuances of holistic admissions is as insightful as anyone I have heard speak on this subject. One thing Olufemi says about the role of test scores that is so true is the following: "Testing matters more than you like, but less than you think."

I was talking to Jasmine's mom, Kennedy, about Jasmine's test scores. She started by saying, "Jasmine sucks at the ACT. Her score is only a 26." I have noticed that students at highly competitive schools have a really skewed view of what a competitive test score is. The fact is, the national average for the ACT is 20.8, and a 26 won't get Jasmine into Cal Tech, even though it put her in the top 17 percent of ACT test takers that year. For your score to be competitive, it needs to be competitive with the students who are applying to the same schools you're applying to, not just with the national average.

48

WHAT IS THE RECOMMENDED TIMELINE FOR TAKING THE ACT OR SAT?

Unless you're in a competitive program like the Duke Tip program, there's no need to take the ACT or SAT in seventh grade.

You can take the PSAT 8/9 in eighth or ninth grade if your school administers it. You can then use KhanAcademy.org's free service to sync your test scores with their advanced computer software, which will generate questions to target your areas of need. At such an early point in the game, you shouldn't obsess over test prep, but you should be following our guidelines for how to improve your test scores.

If your school doesn't offer the PSAT 8/9 or the PSAT 10, you can access practice tests and take that test. I'm not advocating taking the test more than once a year at an early age.

If you're an ACT person, the ACT now offers PreACT, which helps students prepare for the ACT.

Here is what the ACT website says about their low-cost test prep plan designed to compete with Khan Academy: "Through ACT® Kaplan® Online Prep Live, get live instruction and practice on ACT test subjects through a virtual classroom experience that delivers all the benefits of expert instruction at an accessible price."

You can devotedly prep for the ACT/SAT in the summer after tenth and the fall of eleventh grade, because you want to be done with your test scores before you begin twelfth grade. It pains me to tell you to devote so much time and resources to test prep, but until more colleges go "test optional" for scholarships and not just admission, it's in your best interest to prepare this way.

If you find that you have significant gaps in your test scores and it is determined that it isn't a timing issue, I strongly encourage you to find a teacher who is adroit in your area of weakness for subject tutoring to fill in your academic gaps. Subject tutoring is often done by the same person who does test prep tutoring.

When I met Janet, I was helping her with college counseling for her second child, but she proudly told me of an approach she had used with her oldest. She shared how she'd administered the SAT to her oldest daughter at least twice a year beginning in sixth grade, and that her daughter took the test a total of 17 different times. She thought she was impressing me, but all I could think was, "Poor kid! Her memory of her childhood is going to be that she missed out on fun because she was forced to take the SAT 17 different times."

I'm all about preparation, but there is such a thing as going over the top.

49

How can I use the SAT Subject Tests to stand out?

Parents who are over 40 may remember the term "SAT 2," the old name for SAT Subject Tests. These tests are one-hour, multiple-choice tests that are designed to test a student's subject mastery of that specific academic content. There are 20 different SAT Subject Tests and they're administered concurrently with the main SAT, so a student cannot take a Subject Test during the same month as the traditional SAT.

SAT Subject Tests are becoming less common and receiving less emphasis these days. It isn't that schools don't value them—it's more that unless someone is receiving quality advising, a student may not even know these tests exist, let alone prepare and sign up in time. As a result, colleges lose out on great applicants they would love to have in their candidate pool. Many schools also feel that they can get a good read on content mastery based on how well students are doing on the ACT. In fact, the ACT is seen as such a good barometer of your content mastery that there are very few schools that still require students to take two SAT Subject Tests if they have taken the ACT. Usually these are engineering schools that are highly selective, and they will often dictate what tests they want you to take.

The ACT doesn't have an equivalent to SAT Subject Tests, because it was designed as a curriculum-based test in protest to the SAT, which was designed as an aptitude test.

As a consultant, I love SAT Subject Tests because I can have my students use Subject Test practice test materials to see in which areas they test best. Then, I have them take the tests they're best at, and only send in the scores to colleges if they do well. The best time to take these tests is after you have just completed the subject matter in school that corresponds to the tests. The June SAT administration is a great time to take Subject Tests. It is also great to take these after you have taken a junior year AP exam that corresponds to the subject matter.

Even though there are twenty Subject Tests, there are only ten tests that have more than 15,000 students in the country who are taking them. Here are the ten tests arranged according to how many students are taking them:

1. Math 2
2. Chemistry
3. US History
4. Math 1
5. Physics
6. Literature
7. Biology-Molecular
8. Biology-Ecological
9. Spanish
10. World History

My advice is to only take Subject Tests from this list of ten. When a college has received so few tests, they really don't know how much weight to put on the test because they don't have reliable benchmarks. In other words, the less students that take a Subject Test, the more likely a college is to put little weight on the test results. If you are looking at applying to an engineering school, Math 2 and physics are the ones that are ideal to take. When an engineering school does not require Subject Tests, but you take Math 2 and physics and do well on them, you are going to raise some eyebrows with the admissions committee in a positive way. In general, test scores in math and science are a more substantial part of how engineering applicants are evaluated than most of the applicants who are selecting other college majors. Studying effectively for Subject Tests really will result in sizable score gains.

The only tests that have really been growing are Math 2, chemistry, biology, world history, and physics. The test is almost being relegated to engineering and advanced science tests. There are about twice as many students taking the Math 2 exam as there are any other Subject Tests. One seasoned admission dean I know told me he expects the test to be obsolete in the next five years, but for now, it is a great chance to stand out from others. He personally found the test to be very helpful but he knows that so many students will not complete their applications if you require the test unless they are getting quality counseling.

Many schools' own internal research indicates that excelling on SAT Subject Tests correlates well with success in the classroom. Jenny Rickard, the Chief Enrollment and Communications Officer Bryn Mawr College, was so impressed with the correlation their own research revealed between academic success and high SAT Subject scores that Jenny says it played a major role in their decision to go Test Flexible in 2009. However, with a national average of around 350 to 1 school counselors to students in public high schools, most public school students have never even heard of a Subject Test. After Rikard left, Bryn Mawr went from Test Flexible to Test Optional in the summer of 2014.

I was talking to Jess Lord, the outstanding Dean of Admission at Haverford College, about their decision to not require Subject Tests anymore. I said, "Jess, I am really glad you no longer require Subject Tests because in my opinion, you were missing out on so many public school applicants who don't even know they exist."

Jess said, "It was a tough decision for us because how students did on some of those Subject Tests really was a good indication of whether they could handle our academic rigor."

I then said, "So do you regret not requiring them?

Jess said, "No, I have no regrets."

He went on to say, "A higher percentage of the students that started our application this year completed it and it is hard to not see that as having some correlation to our decision to not require Subject Tests."

What I want you to take away from this is that the highly selective prestigious private schools like Bryn Mawr and Haverford that do comprehensive holistic admissions may not require the Subject Tests, but they respect them, and this represents an opportunity for you.

Liz was interested in applying to competitive schools, but she was also relieved to find out that the schools on her list did not require Subject Tests. I told her that Subject Tests represented a great opportunity for her, because she could take a few tests, see how well she did on them, and send in the scores only if she scored in the high 600s or better. She took three tests and her scores were in the high 700s, low 700s, and low 600s, but her schools only saw the two 700-range test scores. For the schools you apply to, scores in the high 600s are usually worth submitting, but I wouldn't submit scores under 650 because most of the tests have median scores around 650. Remember, only the most able students are taking these tests.

50

WHAT ARE "SUPERSCORING" AND "SCORE CHOICE"?

"Superscoring" is the widespread practice of allowing a student to count different section scores from different administrations of a test toward the aggregate total score. For example, let's say you take the SAT test in August and you score a 600 on the evidence-based reading and writing section and a 500 on the math section. Your cumulative score would be 1100. However, let's say you take the test again in December and you score a 500 on the reading section and 600 in the math. Instead of having another 1100, you would be able to have a cumulative score of 1200 by only counting the two 600s. Once you post a score, it cannot be taken away from you even if you score lower in the section on a future test. Most colleges superscore for the SAT and ACT, but you'll want to read the college's policy on this, because there *are* schools that do not accept superscores for one or both tests.

There are also colleges that have different policies for test score requirements for international students.

"Score choice" allows you to decide which test scores you will submit to each college, so you can choose to send only your best scores. Most colleges permit score choice for the SAT and SAT Subject Tests as well as the ACT, but there are exceptions, so read the fine print. Schools who don't allow this see it this way: if one student takes the ACT or SAT seven times, but other students only have the opportunity to take it once, this is important information they should have access to when they evaluate scores. As of the fall of 2017, schools that reject score choice include, but are not limited to, Rice, Cornell, UPenn, Stetson, Pomona, Yale, Howard, Georgetown, Maryland, the UC System, Stanford, University of Kentucky, and Florida A&M. There are around 100 colleges that require all scores to be submitted, and they range in selectivity. This is an integrity issue, because while you may be able to get away with not sending all your scores, you have to live with your conscience.

When I was explaining to Bart how superscoring worked, he was giddy with excitement. He could not believe that if he bombed one section of the SAT and improved the next time, his previous score would not be counted against him. He said to me, "These colleges are really generous to their students." I told him that may be true, but to also remember that colleges want to have the highest test scores possible to list on their websites and publications, because it makes them look good.

51

HOW DO I SELECT A TEST PREP OR TUTORING COMPANY?

There are many factors to consider when choosing a tutor or test prep company. Consider the following.

- ℵ Referral is usually the best approach, but do your homework.
- ℵ Ask for referrals and follow up to ask them the tough questions.
- ℵ Avoid falling for the hard sell or paying a fortune upfront.
- ℵ Trust your instincts.
- ℵ Is the process described specific to your needs and learning style, or is it a one-size-fits-all approach?
- ℵ Will the location work well for your family?
- ℵ Do the time slots work well for your schedule?

- ℵ Can you sit in on a class or observe a session?
- ℵ What is the philosophy of the test prep and does it match your belief system?
- ℵ Do they seem to care more about helping students or making money?
- ℵ Do you like the instructor and find them motivating?
- ℵ Is it a positive environment with positive and likeable teachers?
- ℵ When you are quoted stats and results, are those the results from people you'll be working with, or are they the results of a rock star tutor you'll never be meeting?
- ℵ How many hours of test prep can you get within your budget?
- ℵ Will the requirements and expectations of the course fit in with your other responsibilities so you can still maintain balanced excellence in your life?

One mistake I find families make is putting too much emphasis on the test prep company and not enough on the individual teacher teaching the class. In Atlanta, my students have worked with many outstanding test prep instructors at SuccessPrep, MathSP, Kaplan, Varsity Tutors, Applerouth, and Princeton Review, but not all instructors are equal. Think of your child's school. Are all the teachers equal there? Test prep is no different. Focus more on who is going to be teaching your child than the brand name of the tutoring company.

Daniel DiPiazza was a test prep pro I worked with very closely before he moved away. He used to sit down with students on the first session and say, "I get it. You'd rather be with your girlfriend right now. You'd rather be playing video games or watching Netflix. I know, test prep is boring, and I'm only 24, so that's exactly what I was thinking seven years ago when my mom made me take a dumb test prep class." Immediately, the students would loosen up, relax, and think (and often say), "I'm going to like working with you; this may not be that bad." Daniel had the gift of likeability with his students, and it's not everything, but it's important.

52

IS IT BETTER TO DO ONLINE TEST PREP, ONE-ON-ONE TEST PREP, OR GROUP TEST PREP?

Very few students would have the same options for college with and without test prep. Parents who invest properly in test prep often help provide their child with better and more affordable choices for college. It really is an investment, and some prep is better than no prep.

Group sessions are an option for a good score, but rarely the best option for a great score. Regardless, students who work hard and have a great teacher will still make sizeable scoring gains with group sessions. One-on-one sessions usually result in the largest score gains, but are generally the most expensive option. The bottom line is that different students have different styles, and some will even do better in small groups than they do individually.

Another effective option to consider is combining methods if possible. A combination of small group prep and individual prep is a great bang for your buck. Smaller group sizes are better, and it's important that the teacher is highly skilled. The best option is a star teacher in a small class, but there is a lot of research supporting the idea that a superstar instructor is really what matters most—even more than class size. This is true with subject matter instruction in schools, as well. For test prep, it's less about the company and more about the instructor you'll be working with.

Students shouldn't have to pay exorbitant prices for test prep, even one-on-one test prep. There are great, talented, and caring test prep pros who will do test prep via SKYPE at reasonable rates if you live in an area where in-person test prep is especially expensive. Admission officers will tell you not to make test prep an extracurricular activity.

Some students are so highly motivated and so disciplined that they can excel with online prep, which is better than it's ever been. For some students, this is all their families can afford, or all that fits their hectic schedule. However, students who can truly excel in online prep are rare, and most students do better with face-to-face accountability. For those who use online test prep, I strongly recommend an accountability partner. A parent can be a great option if the student won't rebel against that idea.

For students taking the SAT, I cannot speak highly enough about the quality of the free online tutoring that Khan Academy is producing. Saul Khan is devoted to eliminating the gap that wealthy and under-resourced students have when it comes to test prep. I met Saul in Arizona a few years ago and he said, "My goal is not to have the best free prep but the best test prep, period."

A few years ago, I had a test prep company named Applerouth give a few test prep classes for my students. As we were sitting down and doing some pre-class planning, they recommended their six-pack class. First of all, the name was clever, but what really excited me about this plan was the structure. The students had 15 hours of classroom time in small groups, but then they had six hours of one-on-one instruction after the classroom portion was completed. The six hours were customized to the area of greatest need that the students demonstrated in the small group class.

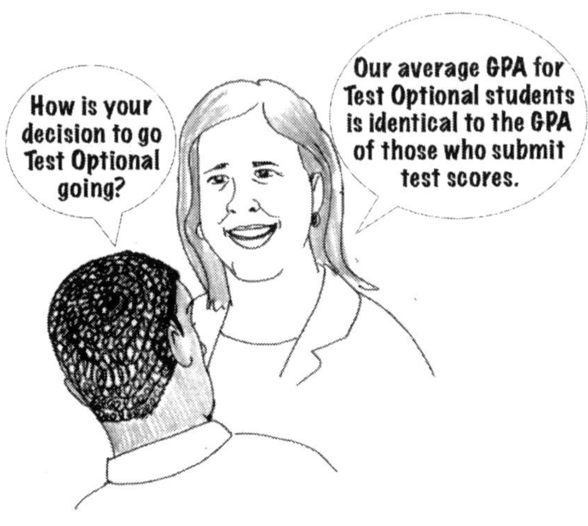

53

WHY ARE AN INCREASING NUMBER OF SCHOOLS NOT REQUIRING STANDARDIZED TEST SCORES THESE DAYS?

Schools have always known that a student is more than a number. They know that what you do over four years matters more in revealing who you really are than what you do during a four-hour test.

They also know that if your testing is below certain thresholds, this is a significant academic risk factor. This is particularly true for majors like engineering and pre-med. Courses like organic chemistry, biochemistry, and linear algebra are usually a major problem if you go to a school where your test scores are significantly lower than those of your peers. In most instances, students with extremely low scores will predictably struggle in certain majors. Personally, I've noticed that testing doesn't correlate as closely with grades as you would expect, but it does correlate with how hard a student has to work for their grades.

Lloyd Thacker is the Founder and Executive Director of the Education Conservancy, a nonprofit organization dedicated to reforming college admission practices. He has spoken out about the problems with test-prep-dominated culture for decades.

Bob Schaeffer, Director of FairTest, has played an even bigger role at aggressively combating the abuse and misuse of testing with alacrity and zeal since FairTest was founded in 2007. Schaeffer notes that since the redesigned SAT was announced, schools have been dropping their test mandates at a rapid pace. Schools like Bowdoin and Bates, which have been test optional for decades, have done studies on students they admitted without test scores and their research shows excellent outcomes in the GPAs and graduation rates of these students.

Colleges that are passionate about diversity can also admit a more diverse applicant pool without test scores being an impediment to admissions. Other colleges don't like how the multi-billion-dollar test prep business adds stress to the lives of students and greatly advantages affluent families who can pay thousands of dollars for quality test prep.

Here is how selective schools that use holistic admissions view test scores. They know that they are highly correlated to family income, and they do not believe poorer kids are inherently less smart. They will read your test scores through the prism of your family income. In other words, don't expect much grace if your test scores are outside a school's 25th-75th percentiles if you are affluent, unless you have some powerful hooks. The combination of the bias toward affluent families coupled with the test prep wealthy families can afford makes schools cynical of the objectivity and value of the ACT and the SAT.

I got a call from a test prep company last week. They were hoping I would start referring to them. I asked what they charged and they said, "If you pay a membership fee of over $500 a year you can get it for $99 an hour for a newer tutor, but if you want the best tutors we have, it will be $699 an hour." I said, "$699?" I was told, "You should see how amazing our $699 an hour tutors are." Colleges know this, and it really bothers them to feel they are implementing policies that are biased toward the wealthy, leading more and more to go test optional. The liberal arts colleges have been the leaders in the test optional movement.

The test optional movement is growing and it has real momentum. I predict one, if not several, of the Ivy League schools will go test optional in the next five years and that will lead a lot of their competitors to follow suit. Last week I had a great meeting with Cortney Lima, the effervescent Assistant Director of Admissions at Worcester Polytechnic Institute. I was thrilled to learn that even a high-powered prestigious engineering school like WPI has now gone test optional. The engineering schools love their numbers, so when a high-powered math-oriented school like WPI says they can make admissions decisions they are confident in without test scores, the dominos are starting to fall on the billion-dollar test prep business.

There is value to testing for a college in the assessment process, but at what price? I agree with something Jim Miller, the former Dean of Admissions at Brown, said, "Testing helps us at the top and the bottom end. In the middle they don't predict much, but they help us at the top and at the bottom." The question almost every selective college is asking is, is it worth the stress it creates with teenagers? Is it fair to put so much weight on a test that wealthy families can pay $699 an hour to raise their scores with some superstar test prep guru and then get merit aid because they had the resources to buy themselves a scholarship? WPI, Wake Forest, and so many other schools are coming to the conclusion that no, it is not fair.

Miller talks about how in his last year at Brown one student submitted twelve different SAT scores. Some colleges are saying to themselves, have we created a monster? Could we still make admissions decisions that serve our institution well without all the stress, misplaced priorities, and bias to the wealthy that comes with the test prep industry which has become a multi-billion-dollar industry?

Some colleges go test optional in order to become more selective. The thinking is that they'll get more publicity and applicants if they go test optional, and then they'll only have to list the test scores of high-scoring students who submitted their scores. The colleges can also increase their average test scores, which will be listed in the books and on websites, because with test optional schools, the higher-testing students still submit their test scores. This way, their applications will go up, their admission rate will go down, and their average test scores will increase. Most of the time, humans have mixed motives in what we do and I believe that applies here. You can want to help provide access to your school by removing a barrier to entry while simultaneously knowing that you will likely decrease your admit rate, raise your average scores, and improve your position in the brand-conscious college admissions marketplace.

A few years ago, I met with the dean of admissions at Wake Forest University at a college fair. They had gone test optional two years before, and I wanted to know how it was going. She told me, "Well, it's a lot of work, because we have to do so much research on each feeder school, and our interviews take a lot of time. But it's one of the best decisions we've made. It allows us to increase our diversity, and the average GPA for our test optional students is identical to the GPA of those who submit test scores."

54

WHAT ARE THE DIFFERENT VARIATIONS OF "TEST OPTIONAL" AND "TEST FLEXIBLE" COLLEGES?

Consider FairTest your Bible when it comes to test optional and test flexible colleges. Find that information at http://fairtest.org/university/optional

When you visit this invaluable site, you'll see the 950+ schools that are test optional or test flexible. Each will have a number listed after it to reflect the various ways in which a school might be test optional or test flexible. The descriptions of possibilities below come directly from the FairTest website.

- א SAT/ACT used only for placement and/or academic advising

- א SAT/ACT required only from out-of-state applicants
- א SAT/ACT may be required but considered only when minimum GPA and class rank is not met
- א SAT/ACT required for some programs
- א Test flexible: SAT/ACT not required if other college level exams specified by school, such as SAT Subject Tests, Advanced Placement tests, or International Baccalaureate are submitted—contact school for details
- א Placement test or school-specific admissions exam score not required if submitting ACT/SAT scores

Here is a look at Colby College's discussion of their requirements for test scores going into the 2017-2018 admission year. Colby is an example of a test flexible, not a test optional, school. Notice how user-friendly their appeal is to allow a student to showcase their strengths:

> You'll need to provide us with standardized test results for either the SAT, ACT, or two SAT Subject Tests. We use these scores as part of our holistic application review. You may self-report your scores when applying to Colby, either by reporting them on your application to Colby or sending a pdf copy of your score report via email (*admissions@colby.edu*) or fax (207-859-4828). Official scores will be required only for students choosing to enroll at Colby. We believe in transparency in the admissions process and encourage you to send us all of your standardized test scores. We will only consider the scores that put you in the most competitive position in our applicant pool.

55

WHAT ARE THE 15 DIFFERENT WAYS I CAN APPLY TO COLLEGE?

1. **Regular Admissions:** All applications are due on a specific date (often between January 1 and February 15), but applications pile up, and once they are reviewed, all students are notified on the same date. A student who applies in September is not notified any earlier than a student who applied on the last day before the deadline. This is the most common way students apply to four-year colleges.
2. **Rolling Admissions:** Admission decisions are made on a first-come, first-served basis. It pays to apply early, because there are more openings and less competition for those open slots. Decisions are usually made two to four weeks after an application arrives. This is a common method with large public schools.

Some schools start making decisions as early as July after junior year. The window is usually open for at least six months, and some schools have no official final deadline.

3. **Modified Rolling Admissions:** Instead of rolling out decisions two to four weeks after applications are completed, every so often decisions are released. The University of Michigan uses modified rolling admissions and they release decisions four times a year, but they don't post the dates of these rolled-out decisions.
4. **Early Action, aka EA:** You submit your application early and you are informed of the admission decision early, but you are not bound to attend if admitted. You can enroll early, wait until May 1, or choose not to enroll at all.
5. **Restricted Early Action:** This method is similar to EA, but you cannot apply to more than one school through its early program (if they have one). Many people call this method "Single Choice EA." You can count the schools that offer this on two hands, and they are the most selective schools in the nation. In fact, their brand is so strong that they don't feel the need to lock students in to avoid competition the way their competitor early decision schools do.
6. **Early Decision, aka ED I:** You apply early (usually between October 15and November 15), but if you are admitted, you are bound to attend that school and you must withdraw any pending applications you have submitted to other schools. Oftentimes, a parent signature and a school counselor signature are required for letting the student know you are making a binding commitment. You cannot apply ED to more than one ED school at the same time. Approximately 10 percent of accredited colleges offer ED, and they are usually selective private schools.
7. **Early Decision II, aka ED II:** This is a second round of ED, with later dates. The deadlines are usually between January 1 and February 1, and the notification date is usually between February 1 and March 1.
8. **Early Action II, aka EA II:** This is similar to ED II, but not binding.
9. **Open Admissions:** As long as the school is not full, any student who graduates from high school or has a GED will be admitted.

Online schools and community colleges use an open admissions policy almost all of the time.

10. **Early Evaluation:** Students who apply through regular admissions receive general feedback before other students in the same applicant pool if they request an early evaluation. Very few schools offer early evaluation, but this option allows students to be notified in late February of whether they are a "likely" admission, a "possible" admission, or "unlikely" to be admitted. A final official decision still comes out about a month later. Wellesley College is an example of a school that offers early evaluation, and in their case, they offer official early evaluation. Some schools do an unofficial early evaluation for their most desirable applicants. These are often referred to as Likely Letters or Wink Letters, as they give a hint that something positive is to come.
11. **Deferred Admissions:** There are really two types of deferred admissions. In the first, a student applying early can be deferred to the regular round so he/she can be compared to the other applicants. If an ED applicant is deferred to the regular round, they are no longer bound to attend if they are admitted. Highly selective schools rarely admit a deferred applicant in the regular round. A second type of deferred admissions occurs when a student is accepted, but then requests to take a gap year. A gap year defers the student's matriculation until the following year.
12. **Late Admissions:** This method applies to schools that are still taking applications after May 1. Some may take applications well into late summer.
13. **Transfer Admissions:** Students who are transferring from one college to another will be sent to a different applicant pool and evaluated differently.
14. **VIP Admissions:** The VIP applications offer a quick, simplified application process and often stress the admission offer being only good for a "limited time." Usually, the applicant is told how special they are and how they may be eligible for merit money. Usually the application fees are waived, and usually much of the application is already completed, so the student has very little work to do to complete it. A lot of the students I worked with this year received these VIP applications from Tulane this year. This is sometimes referred to as Priority Admissions.

15. **Transfer Instant Decision:** Colleges like Rowan, Drexel, and so many others utilize this method. Here is what Drexel's website says about Transfer Instant Decision Days, "Submitting a college application doesn't have to mean weeks of waiting for a decision. Prospective transfer students can make an appointment to meet with an admissions counselor and receive an admission decision that day."

Your head may already be spinning from all of these methods, but there are variations of policies even within the admissions processes I listed above. Stanford is one of the few schools that offers restrictive admissions, but according to their website, here are the exceptions they make:

- א The student may apply to any college/university with early deadlines for scholarships or special academic programs as long as the decision is non-binding.
- א The student may apply to any *public* college/university with a non-binding early application option.
- א The student may apply to any college/university with a non-binding rolling admission process.
- א The student may apply to any foreign college/university on any application schedule.

Jim was a strong student who had applied to a very competitive list of schools, but we all knew at least one school where he'd be admitted. Dartmouth College had sent him a Wink Letter more than a month before they sent out their regular admissions notices. The Wink Letter made Jim sound like they were salivating to have him on campus, so we knew he was in at Dartmouth.

56

WHAT ARE THE PROS AND CONS OF APPLYING TO A SCHOOL THROUGH EARLY DECISION?

Advantages:

Acceptance rates are higher for early decision applicants; in many cases, they are significantly higher. The ability for a college to lock a student in helps them immensely with their planning, and oftentimes they will reward this by admitting a student who would otherwise have been waitlisted or denied in the regular admission round. The students who apply early are excited to attend their first-choice school, and schools see value to having their enthusiasm on campus, and they admit kids they would waitlist in the regular round. I was talking to a highly selective college about an applicant a few years ago and the admission officer said to me, "He doesn't need to apply ED." I knew exactly what she meant.

Some applicants who are on the cusp need the extra thumb on the scale that ED applicants receive, but others are strong enough to be accepted in the regular round. Some studies have shown that applying ED is worth as much as 150 points on your SAT scores, but I caution people from taking those reports as gospel. The truth is, the advantage will vary tremendously from one school to another. The basic rule I want you to know is that there is a high correlation between the yield that a college has and how much weight they put on ED. The lower the yield, the more ED will benefit you. The same is true for demonstrated interest.

A student who is admitted finds out as much as four and a half months earlier than they'd find out in the regular round. This can make their senior year much more relaxing and enjoyable.

ED can save on application fees, and a student will save time and money by not completing those other applications or visiting other schools in the spring.

Once you know where you are going, you can start to visit the college and begin the acclimation process as early as January, instead of having to wait until April or May.

Disadvantages:

Students are entering into a binding commitment to pay what that schools asks them to pay, even before they have a chance to see what the *other* schools they're interested in would ask them to pay. They even have to withdraw their applications from the other schools if they're admitted. This is a major disadvantage for students for whom paying what the ED school asks for would be a hardship to their family. Many schools use financial aid as an enrollment management tool. This allows them to spread their aid further if a group of applicants are so zealous to apply early that they are not comparing aid awards. Many less-wealthy schools do not give their best offers to those who apply early, but many other schools offer the exact same packages in the early round.

Notice that I did not say, "ED is always a disadvantage for students who need a lot of money." This is a myth that I hear too often. Some of the schools that offer ED are some of the wealthiest and most generous colleges in the country, but if the basic EFC formula the school uses is inadequate for your needs and you are relying on merit aid to make college affordable, then applying ED is probably not for you.

I find myself talking a lot of families out of applying ED for this reason. It is admissions malpractice to apply ED to a school without completing their net price calculator and agreeing that, yes, you can afford what they project you will have to pay.

ED is also a disadvantage if a student has not thoroughly done their homework on the school, and part of this homework must involve an onsite visit. Remember, you are making a binding commitment. I don't like to see a student apply ED when they have never visited. This would be like making a four-year commitment to dating the same girl before you have had a first date.

Students who apply ED and are denied have to deal with rejection while continuing to do an excellent job completing their other applications and finishing strong in their senior year. The long wait until the regular admission round of decisions is released can be tough on emotions.

When Frank identified Vassar as his top choice, he decided to apply early decision. Later, his rejection knocked the wind out of him like a sucker punch to the gut. Still, he showed the grit of truly successful people by bouncing back and applying ED again to Brandeis in the second round of early decision, which is offered by fewer than 100 colleges. He was admitted in this round, and Frank may as well have been doing cartwheels, he was so ecstatic.

Frank said, "Things happen for a reason. Brandeis is actually the better fit."

My oldest daughter Karis applied early decision to Davidson College. In a lot of ways, she was the ideal ED candidate. She had visited Davidson four times from spring of her sophomore year to fall of her senior year; she had lived on campus for three weeks during the summer; and she'd attended their multicultural visit program as well as a traditional open house. Karis had also visited over a dozen other colleges. She even did overnights at a few other colleges, and she had visited her second-choice school, Scripps College, twice. She knew at least ten Davidson students, and she had spoken with all of them at length.

I had done my homework too, as I had completed the net price calculator and spoken with David Gelinas, Davidson's Director of Financial Aid, about my tough questions. Karis is currently a senior at Davidson, and she has never regretted her decision–not even for a second.

Note: There is one thing that Franklin and Marshall College does that I wish every college that has an Early Decision process would do. F & M goes beyond the net price calculator by providing an early estimate of the need-based financial aid you will receive if you apply ED. Earlier today, Assistant Dean of Admission Emily Herbert was kind enough to spend some time talking to me about F & M's early estimate of need-based financial aid. Emily made it crystal clear that the estimate goes beyond the net price calculator projections. F & M will stand behind this projection as long as you supply accurate information. If you are considering applying early decision and are also applying for financial aid, I encourage you to ask if the college will provide a written early estimate of your aid award like some colleges are providing.

57

HOW CAN I SHOWCASE MY PASSIONS IN THE APPLICATION PROCESS?

- ℵ Don't panic if you aren't sure yet what your passions are.
- ℵ Ask questions about your areas of passion at school fairs and during information sessions.
- ℵ Take four years of math, English, and science, but you don't need to take four years of history or foreign language. You can take a fifth year of math or science, if that's your area of interest. You can also take a double language. In most states, you don't *have* to take four years of science, which gives you more flexibility to play to your strengths and interests.
- ℵ Use your electives to very carefully explore areas of interest.
- ℵ Take online classes in your areas of passion.

- Utilize your summers to develop your areas of interest and explore your extracurricular activities, but also consider taking a summer course in your area of interest.
- You can also use your personal statement or supplemental essays to articulate your passions, but be careful to only do this if you are also answering the question in the essay prompt. This is particularly true for supplemental essay questions. You miss a huge opportunity to let schools know what excites you and what you care about if you don't write about it when schools are practically screaming out for you to let them know what distinguishes you from the thousands of other applicants.
- Consider doing an independent study in an area of passion.
- Set up shadow opportunities or internships.
- Identify teachers who teach in your area of interest, and get to know them well outside the classroom. If it makes sense, have one of them write one of your recommendations.

Manny was a math guy, and he was out to prove it. He took his math skills up to Calculus BC and participated in Georgia Tech's summer engineering camps after tenth and eleventh grade. He took five math courses, and only three history courses. Manny asked one of his teachers in an advanced math course to write one of his recommendations, and he even discussed his passion for math in his personal statement. As a result of his efforts to show his passion, he had some excellent choices for college selection, including Howard University with a Presidential Scholarship, Case Western Reserve, the University of Pennsylvania, and Georgia Tech.

58

WHAT IS DEMONSTRATED INTEREST, AND WHY IS IT IMPORTANT?

Demonstrated interest is exactly what it sounds like: a student comports him or herself in a way that the college believes they are genuinely interested and seriously considering attending their college. For the rest of this chapter, I will refer to demonstrated interest as DI.

The opposite of DI is what's known in admission parlance as the "stealth applicant" or a "phantom applicant." A stealth applicant is a prospective student whose first recorded contact with a college is their submission of an application. Around 30 percent of applicants are stealth applicants, and at some schools the number is as high as 50 percent. You don't want to be a stealth applicant at a school that uses holistic admissions and considers DI. There's a good chance you'd be waitlisted or denied for this due to lack of expressed interest.

Colleges are businesses, and in order to pay all of their salaries and expenses, they have to enroll the right number of students. If they under-enroll, they can't pay their bills, and if they over-enroll, where will all of those students live? It isn't only a quantity challenge, but also a quality challenge. A school is expected to enroll quality applicants in a wide range of different ways.

In order to accurately forecast who will enroll, admissions offices rely on a number of strategies. They pay very close attention to what they refer to as their "yield." Yield is simply the percentage of admitted students who accept an admissions offer. If a college accepts 100 students and 40 of them choose to enroll, they have a 40 percent yield. The lower a school's yield is, the more likely DI is to be a factor in the decision process for schools that use holistic admissions. The opposite is also true. Schools with very high yields like Northwestern, MIT, Stanford, Princeton, and Harvard, don't factor DI into their decision making.

DI is also tracked more closely by private schools and smaller liberal arts schools.

The problem is that yields have been steadily declining. According to NACAC research, the average yield for colleges was close to one in two fifteen years ago, but now it is much closer to one in three. Figuring out which students will attend the school is one of the most important functions of an admission office.

Some schools use rolling admissions to help forecast yield, and some use early decision or ED2. But what about the schools that don't offer ED, which is nearly 90 percent of four-year colleges? Many of those schools turn to sophisticated approaches to studying human behavior to forecast which admitted students will attend.

NACAC Admissions Trend reports that about one in two colleges surveyed say that DI is either of considerable importance or moderate importance in determining who is admitted. From my experience, it is very rare for more selective private colleges to not factor DI into their decision making; it happens, but it is unusual. These more selective colleges are trying to have the lowest acceptance rate they can, and they don't like to waste an admission offer on someone they do not believe is going to come. So how does a school measure DI? If there is one metric that colleges pay particular attention to when it comes to DI, it is whether the student took an official visit to the school. By "official," I mean, did they sign up through the admission office so that there is a record of them having visited? If you attend your friend's party on campus and the admissions office doesn't know about it, this does not count.

- ℵ Visit the school's website and sign up for their mailing list. This will not only be noted, but may lead to you receiving special invitations to events both on campus and when the school has representatives traveling to your area.
- ℵ Do your homework and research a school. This will be very evident in the questions you ask and in your actual application. Study the "About Us" section of the website and ask very specific questions. Study the mission statement and the strategic plan.
- ℵ You'll need to write customized answers to any supplemental essays you are asked to write. Don't use a "one essay fits all" approach.
- ℵ If a representative from a college visits your school, attend the information session. Be genuinely engaged, either by asking great questions during the session or by spending some one-on-one time with the representative before or after the session. I strongly recommend doing *both* of these things. This same approach can be used if you attend an information session at a hotel or an event in the community. If you don't know any great questions to ask, look for an article I wrote on this. In your Internet search bar, type, "Excellent Questions to Ask in an Interview, School Match 4U." This article will show you how to design your own great questions for interviews, information sessions, or college fairs.
- ℵ I recommend finding out who the admissions counselor is for your school or your area. You may be able to get this from your high school counselor, from the college's website, by calling the college, by doing a "Meet the Admissions Staff" search, or by checking the faculty directory. Do a LinkedIn search on that person and see what you learn. Ultimately, you're trying to build rapport, and if you have any common interests, that only helps.

Interviews are another great way to show DI. Not every school offers interviews, but you should make every effort to find out if a school you're interested in does. Even if it's a non-evaluative interview with a trained student or an alumnus, it is absolutely worth it for you to do this for your top schools. I would just assume an interview is evaluative if you have any doubt whatsoever.

Visit the college you're interested in at a local college fair and make sure to ask meaningful questions when you interact with the representative. Be sure to fill out the information card. If you have a great conversation with an admissions representative, send them a thank you note afterward.

When you receive an email from one of the colleges you're interested in, open it up. If they have attached a video, watch the video. Believe it or not, these things can be tracked.

Ginger was one of those students for whom you just want the best. She was so courteous and hard-working that she deserved everything she received. I could not have been happier for her the day she received her acceptance letter from Brown University. Ginger had been attending informational sessions for Brown since tenth grade, and during Brown's annual visits to Westtown School, where Ginger was a student, she asked the most insightful questions. I would watch her speaking with the representative, and it was clear she had built rapport.

When the representative visited Westtown the year after Ginger was accepted, I thanked her for admitting Ginger. She said to me, "When Ginger's application came for me to read, I thought, *this is Ginger! I've been waiting to read this application for two years.*" Ginger knew how to demonstrate interest and build rapport, and it was all genuine.

If the school offers an opportunity for a virtual chat with a student ambassador or a college representative, sign up for one.

Keep in touch with the representative assigned to your school by asking them some very good questions two or three times a year. But here's an important warning: don't stalk them! If you stalk them, you become the weird stalker kid, and no one wants to accept the weird admissions stalker kid. It's like dating in that you want to show enough interest so that the college doesn't feel like they're wasting their time on someone who isn't serious, but if you throw yourself at someone on the first date, and then after the first date you call or write them all the time, that's going to be a major turnoff. Every admissions rep can tell you bizarre stories about admission stalker kids: not cool!

Apply early action or early decision, but please read this book's chapter on the pros and cons of applying ED before doing so.

DI only works if it's genuine. I was conflicted about writing this section, because there's always someone who has no interest in a school but will act disingenuously in order to try to get in. That's absolutely not what I'm advising here.

Your head may be spinning because this is a lot of work. This is why I recommend you go deep in your research and apply to two to four Reach schools, two to four Mid-range schools, and two to four Likely schools. Do you really want to be doing all the things I am recommending for 20-25 schools? The college process should be fun, and it shouldn't dominate your life.

Parents and students would be shocked to learn about all of the sophisticated methods schools use to predict which students will enroll. Some schools track how much time you spend on their website and which portions of the website you visit. Others, like High Point, pay big bucks to groups like NRCCUA to access their data and the complex metrics they use to predict who will come once admitted.

Just today I was talking with a director of admission at a highly selective college about all the ways an admissions office can use technology to track where a student goes on their websites, and whether they open emails.

She said to me, "There is something unseemly about this process. They are kids, and it's just creepy how we are tracking all their movements on our websites." She then said, "It is the easiest thing to track with Slate's admission software."

When the information session had ended, the Davidson College rep passed out contact cards and asked the students to please complete the information on the card and turn it in to her. Lamar spoke up and said, "That's okay, I already completed that same form when I visited the Davidson booth at a college fair."

The rep said, "It's in your best interest to complete it again anyway, because we track how many contacts a student makes with us."

About six months later, I had the same experience with Washington University St. Louis. Colleges really do keep track of this information.

59

WHAT DO I NEED TO KNOW ABOUT MY SOCIAL MEDIA PRESENCE AND THE ADMISSION PROCESS?

In a Kaplan Test Prep survey of almost 400 college admissions officers, 35 percent of officers reported that they looked at applicants' social media entries to learn more about them.

If you think about it, why do schools ask for recommendations? Do they really care about what Mr. Jones thinks? Actually, they're looking for social proof that you have the kind of character, academic preparation, skillset, and mentality they're looking for. Well, social media is another form of social proof. Colleges can learn a lot based on how you present yourself within your social media networks.

If I were still in admissions, I would absolutely be checking your social media presence if I was on the fence about admitting you. So much of the admissions process has the potential to have been put through the filters of a professional, but social media allows the admissions rep to see students as they truly present themselves in "real life."

So what are you going to do about this? First of all, don't use unprofessional email addresses like "sexymama2004@whatever.com." Secondly, Google your own name, and if you find anything disturbing, delete what you can and dilute what you can't by creating positive content that will push it down in the results rankings. Check your online photo galleries for obscene words and images. When I worked in boarding school admissions, I remember seeing party photos on social media pages of students drinking alcohol, and this was a quick trip to the denial pile. Avoid profanity and any scintilla of sexual or flirtatious expressiveness that could be deemed offensive.

I knew something was up when I checked my email and saw that several friends, clients, and coworkers had emailed me the same article. The article was titled, "Harvard Pulls Admission Offers After Explicit Posts," and discussed how Harvard had rescinded a minimum of ten admission offers from its fall freshman class when they learned that prospective students had exchanged sexually vulgar and offensive messages in an online Facebook chat. You don't want to be that kid!

Think of social media as another opportunity to shine. You can join great online groups that showcase your interests. You should create a LinkedIn profile and have a professional-looking photo. You can include your LinkedIn link in your application, and you should definitely fill out the section of LinkedIn that allows you to showcase your volunteerism and community service.

60

HOW DO COLLEGES VIEW HOMESCHOOLED APPLICANTS?

Homeschooled students are becoming increasingly more attractive to colleges for the following reasons:

- On average, they have higher ACT and SAT test scores.
- They matriculate to college at a higher rate.
- They have higher college GPAs.
- On average, they have higher graduation rates.
- With almost 2.5 million homeschool students in the United States, they're a rapidly-growing portion of the applicant pool.
- Many schools report that they're very innovative thinkers who are creative, independent, and entrepreneurial.
- Most schools value the diversity of thought that homeschool students bring to the classroom.

- א A lot of schools like Dartmouth, Amherst, and Brown, along with many others, actively recruit homeschool students.

Still, not every college is so receptive to homeschooled applicants. Many homeschooled students and parents report obstacles they face in the college application process. Some schools will not accept the fact that the student would not be coming in with an accredited diploma. Other schools are suspect of the dominant role often played by the parent, and they don't always trust the grades or comments. Others question what the social adjustment will be like for the student. Some schools are cynical and find it difficult to accurately evaluate the academic preparation of the student. This is sometimes even more apparent for out-of-state homeschool applicants.

In order to substantiate a homeschool student's academic, extracurricular, and social qualifications, it is highly recommended that the home school applicant do the following things:

- א Read any information the school's website posts about homeschooled applicants very carefully, because additional paperwork is often required.
- א Take SAT Subject Tests or AP tests, and have the scores sent to the schools you're applying to. Know that even more weight will be put on your ACT or SAT scores.
- א Have a minimum of three recommendations other than your parents'. Even when three are not required, except in cases where submitting extra recommendations is discouraged.
- א Pick up the phone and call the school if you have any questions about what should be submitted.
- א Seriously consider taking summer classes in a traditional high school or college setting, and/or online courses that are respected by the colleges to which you're applying.
- א Get involved in outside organizations like youth sports, volunteerism, theater, orchestra, etc.
- א Strongly consider having at least one recommendation from someone who knows you well outside your homeschooling context. This could be an employer, an outside coach, a performing arts leader, a clergy member, etc.

- Keep in mind that more scrutiny will be placed on how well you integrate with others, so you may even want to ask your outside recommendations to comment on this in their letter.
- Your personal statement may also be weightier in the review process.
- You should submit a detailed description of courses you took, including books you read in the courses.

When I worked with Malik, he was a lot like a typical home-school student. Both of his parents had master's degrees from prestigious colleges, and both had a profound commitment to education. They severely restricted Malik's use of television, and they had a strong Christian component to his educational grounding. Malik was an omnivorous reader, and he aced his SAT scores and his SAT Subject Tests. I wasn't surprised when Northwestern University admitted Malik, because he had done what was necessary to prove himself as a valuable student.

61

WHAT DO COLLEGE ADMISSION COUNSELORS LOOK FOR IN MY PERSONAL STATEMENT OR MAIN ESSAY?

If you've ever watched the political show *Hardball* with Chris Matthews, then you know he often ends with a panel of reporters and the quip, "Tell me something I don't know." The colleges who read your essay are asking the same thing: "Tell me something I can't find out from your transcript, teacher recommendations, extracurricular activities, and test scores." It's like a job interview, and they want to get to know the applicant beyond their application. For those colleges that don't have an interview as part of their admissions process, the essay acts as the substitute interview in the sense that the reader wants to learn something about you that they wouldn't know unless they heard it in your own voice.

Colleges don't want to hear about who you *want* them to think you are. They want to know who you *really* are. So genuineness is essential in your essay. For those who do have an evaluative interview, it is an opportunity to see how you express yourself in writing and what you choose to say about yourself when you have had time to prepare.

Let's say the admissions officer gets to know you and they don't like what they learn. Well, that's a very poor essay. The best essays contain an "Aha!" moment for the reader. This is the moment where the reader not only feels like they know you and how you're distinct from the other applicants, but they also like you, and they feel as if they need more students like you in their school. Likeability is very important, because college happens in the context of relationships. They should be thinking, "I'd like to have dinner with you and get to know you more." This means you can't come off as Generic Ginny or Boring Bob. Another greatly-valued character trait, in addition to genuineness and likeability, is being unique and interesting.

It has been said that everyone in the world listens to the same radio station: WIIFM. WIIFM stands for "What's in it for me?" A college admissions officer will be reading your application from the perspective of, "How will this student make our campus stronger?" When an admission officer reads your essay, this is what they're looking for:

- ℵ Who is the real you?
- ℵ How are you different from other applicants?
- ℵ Are we a good match for each other?

The University of Pennsylvania just changed its admission rating system. They now rank applicants on three different scales: Excellence of Mind, Impact In Your Space, and Fit With Penn. If you questioned how important the assessment is of Fit/Match, "Fit With Penn" is one of three categories that gets its own admission rating at UPenn.

How will you make the campus's academic, residential, and extracurricular life more vibrant? In short: What will you add?

Here is what Janet Rapelye, the Dean of Admissions at Princeton, says about the essay: "Please take time to work on your essays. We are looking for how well you write because it is a reflection of how you think. How you think is important to those of us on a college campus."

I had a great conversation with Will Torres, an admission officer from Pomona College, about the essay. Will said, "80 percent of the essays don't move the needle. They're pretty good, but they don't stand out." He said it's the other 20 percent that *do* stand out: 10 percent in a negative way, and 10 percent in a positive way that makes him feel like the essay was a game changer and he really wants that student on Pomona's campus. As an applicant, your goal should be to deliver *that* essay.

As if it was today, I remember the vivid details of Wagner's application essay to the Westtown School fifteen years ago. He talked about all of the obstacles his family had to overcome to leave Ecuador and come to America. He had me right there with him, experiencing the sounds, the smells, the sights, and fears, and the surprises. A strong essay pulls the reader in emotionally, like a powerful magnet.

62

WHAT ARE THE BIGGEST MISTAKES APPLICANTS MAKE WITH THEIR PERSONAL STATEMENTS/MAIN ESSAYS?

There are so many common mistakes, but these are the biggest offenders, in my experience:

א Too many students "tell" instead of "show." The mind is a picture gallery, not an encyclopedia of facts. The best essays usually take one instance and develop it into a powerful emotive story that captures the reader while effectively conveying the point the student is trying to make. The reader should be able to visualize what you are describing, just like a movie. This is sometimes referred to as "the slice of life" essay. It isn't the only way to "show and not tell," but it is a very effective way to do it.

- ℵ Many students pick the wrong starting point. Start with what you want to convey about yourself to the school (choose something genuine, unique, and compelling) and turn this into a story. Ask yourself these questions: Am I one piece of the puzzle in the class they are assembling? What will my unique contribution be? This could be a character trait or any area of strong passion, but if you stay focused on this, it will help you to stay focused on what you bring of value to the school.
- ℵ Don't get so caught up in the details of the story that you forget to make yourself the focal point of your essay: "what is it that makes me unique?" The personal statement is your billboard; your message should be clear.
- ℵ Make sure that your transitions between paragraphs have a natural flow.
- ℵ Don't try to take one of your term papers and make it your personal statement.
- ℵ Stop trying to impress the admissions officer with an inflated vocabulary. He or she knows you don't really speak that way, and it sounds unnatural in your essay. One admissions friend of mine refers to this as "pseudo-intellectual syndrome."
- ℵ You must be the central person in your essay. If you're telling an interesting story about your mom, don't make the admissions office want to admit your mom instead of you. When it comes down to it, your essay should always come back to a statement you're making about yourself.
- ℵ Don't be afraid to say that you're really good at something. Some applicants are too modest. When you confidently share what you're good at, hopefully through a story, it gives the admissions officer confidence in you. It is okay to be proud of what you have accomplished.
- ℵ You are not the greatest thing since sliced bread, so avoid the other extreme, too. You don't want to come off like an obnoxious braggart. If you are not likeable, you are not getting in at any selective school that uses holistic admissions.
- ℵ Professionalism matters. Don't submit an essay with poor grammar or typographical errors. Proofread your essay, ask someone you trust to proofread it for you, and then proofread it again yourself.

- ℵ Don't write like you are texting a friend. In other words, no LOLs and lower case 'i's.'
- ℵ Don't let someone edit your essay so heavily that you either lose your own voice or your writing quality and style doesn't match up with the writing sample they'll see elsewhere in the file. This often happens when a student has too many editors.
- ℵ Follow the directions. If the directions say don't go over 500 words, don't think the admissions office won't care if your essay is 530. They wouldn't have given a word limit if they didn't care. Now, for the Common App, you will have 650 words, but don't be lazy and stop at 270. Use the words allotted to you. You don't have to write the full 650, but use your words wisely to develop your theme. I ask my students to write at least 550 words for their personal statement.
- ℵ Remember, you don't want to be Generic Ginny or Boring Bob. Be interesting and distinctive, even entertaining, if you can do this in a natural way. Building rapport with the reader is an extremely important part of the personal statement and the supplemental essays and this often gets overlooked.
- ℵ The opening sentence needs to grab the reader, and the final sentence should end with some "pop." Don't open your essay by restating the question.
- ℵ Don't miss an opportunity to showcase your passion. It is called a personal statement for a reason! Your essay should reveal something important about you.
- ℵ There are certain topics that students write about so often that it's hard to stand out when your admissions officer is reading the same topic for the 100th time this year. One example is the "overseas trip that changed my life." Another example is how you went from being a very average athlete to scoring the winning goal and being the star.
- ℵ Don't procrastinate writing your essay.
- ℵ Read it out loud so you can hear how it sounds. Make sure it is your authentic voice. This is also a great way to catch grammatical errors.
- ℵ Don't try to be a comedian if you aren't naturally funny.
- ℵ Avoid addressing controversial subjects like your political views or your sexual experiences.

- א If you are sharing a tragic story, don't be so explicit that it is disturbing for the reader. You are trying to inspire, not evoke pity. I tell my students, "Don't be graphic with the gruesome." If you are writing about the gash over your eye, don't describe the pus that was comingled with the blood that gushed out.
- א Make sure that you are optimistic. It is okay to talk about difficulties and setbacks, but you never want to come off like you are depressed, embittered, or whiny. Avoid any scintilla of negativity. I cannot stress enough the importance of being positive.
- א Write and rewrite, write and rewrite.
- א Be the doer, not the receiver. Don't write in passive voice.
- א Too many "I" statements make you seem self-centered.
- א Don't exaggerate to try to impress; admissions counselors can see right through this.
- א I think one major thing students don't realize about the essay is how important likeability is. People make decisions on emotion and they justify them with logic. Another thing students and parents don't understand is how much admission counselors get emotionally attached to students from meeting them, reading what teachers say, and reading the personal statement. After reading your essay, if the readers of your file would not want to spend a lot of time with you because they do not find you interesting and likeable, you will not make it through the selective admissions process.

Alvin gave me a draft of an essay he'd written so I could review it. In the essay, he had basically excoriated people for being so upset that Donald Trump had won the election. He said, "The election is over, so get over it and move on with your life, and stop being a bunch of whiners." I had to tell Alvin that first of all, a lot of educators would have their own sore feelings about the election, and second, he was coming off as an unlikeable jerk, and this would fail to endear him to at least one (likely more than one) reader of his essay. It's very hard to share your political views without offending, so this is one topic I advise students against using in their essay.

63

HOW DO I DECIDE WHICH OF THE ESSAY PROMPTS I SHOULD CHOOSE FOR MY PERSONAL STATEMENT?

Let's start by looking at the 2018 Common Application choices from which students can select:

1. Some students have a background, identity, interest, or talent that is so meaningful they believe their application would be incomplete without it. If this sounds like you, then please share your story.
2. The lessons we take from *obstacles we encounter* can be fundamental to later success. Recount a time when you faced a *challenge, setback, or failure*. How did it affect you, and what did you learn from the experience?

3. Reflect on a time when you *questioned* or challenged a belief or idea. What prompted your *thinking*? What was *the outcome*?
4. Describe a problem you've solved or a problem you'd like to solve. It can be an intellectual challenge, a research query, an ethical dilemma—anything that is of personal importance, no matter the scale. Explain its significance to you and what steps you took or could be taken to identify a solution.
5. Discuss an accomplishment, event, or *realization* that *sparked* a period of personal growth and a new understanding of yourself and others.
6. Describe a topic, idea, or concept you find so engaging that it makes you lose all track of time. Why does it captivate you? What or who do you turn to when you want to learn more?
7. Share an essay on any topic of your choice. It can be one you've already written, one that responds to a different prompt, or one of your own design.

When you're ready to choose a prompt, start by brainstorming what character trait and/or passion you want the admission officers to know about you that they don't know already. Make sure it's something that is genuinely who you are, and that it's appealing to the school and something they want to see more of on their campus.

If you have writer's block, you should brainstorm a list of your most appealing and distinguishing character traits. If you are still stuck, ask those who know you the best to share what they believe are your most appealing and distinguishing characteristics.

Let's say that either through your own self-assessment or by consulting with those who know you best, you decide your most appealing and distinguishing trait that the admissions office doesn't already know is your resiliency; you just never quit.

Next, you'll want to go through a brainstorming session again and ask if there is any interest you have that explains who you are in a way your application doesn't already show. Let's say you conclude you are passionate about investing, and you want to manage people's money and help them plan their financial futures.

Now, you read the Common App essay options and see which one of them allows you to tell your story about your passion for studying finance, and how you combine your intellectual inquisitiveness about finance with your defining character trait (resiliency). This is critical, and so few people approach their essays this way. It really isn't hard to find a prompt that will fit what you want to share. The new Common App prompts give students maximum freedom to go where they need to go to tell the admissions office who they are.

You don't need to combine both your passion and your defining trait into your personal statement, but many of the best essays I have read do both. You also don't need to explicitly state the character trait or passion you're trying to showcase. You can *show it* instead. For example, you don't need to say, "I believe that I have grit because ..." Your story of how you have tried to climb a 10,000-foot mountain every year for the last four years is an example of showing that trait instead of telling it. You also don't have to always end with what you believe is a success. Sometimes the best essays say, "I still haven't made it up that 10,000-foot mountain, but I'll be back next year to try it again."

Nick had masterfully blended his defining traits (hard work and resiliency) by writing about how he loved playing basketball despite being heckled for his lack of coordination and dribbling skills. He shared how he had been cut from the ninth-grade team and again from JV, but he worked strenuously all summer amidst lots of resistance, waking up at 5:00 a.m. to practice. Normally, I tell students to avoid this common athletic story, but in Nick's case, you really can't understand Nick without understanding how he ate, slept, and breathed basketball, so this was something that worked for Nick.

Nick easily found a Common App topic that fit his story. His story had suspense; it was visual and multi-sensory. He then transitioned, saying, "I know a basketball career is not in my future, but now I'm turning my drive and zeal to my second passion, which is engineering." He talked about his fascination with Google, which he's had since he was nine, and how his goal is ultimately to work for Google. He knows there will be haters and doubters, but nothing will keep him from chasing his dreams. Nick and his family were happy when he received his acceptance to the University of Pennsylvania, aided by his excellent essay.

64

WHAT DO ADMISSIONS COUNSELORS LOOK FOR IN SUPPLEMENTAL ESSAYS?

A supplemental essay is a school-specific essay that the college requires you to respond to. For example, when my oldest daughter applied to Davidson College, she had to answer the question, "Why are you interested in Davidson College?" This is a very common essay for many colleges, and it's an extremely important essay.

Many students and parents think that admissions is all about your qualifications being stronger than those who you're competing with, and while that's important, colleges want to enroll students who will be happy and fit in well with their school culture. A great way to assess this is through the supplemental essay questions.

Stop for a moment and think about the admission process. The colleges you apply to don't control your transcript, your high school curriculum, or your grading scheme. They don't control the content and structure of the SAT or the ACT. They don't control the extracurricular activities you are involved in. They don't control the prompts for the Common App, the Coalition, the Universal App, or the QuestBridge application, but they do control the supplemental essays and short questions. This is the one place they get to design, and it is extremely important. These questions reveal personality. They show how well you think and write. They show how much you have prepared by learning about the college's unique culture. They greatly help assess whether you are a match and fit. You can't fool college admission officers as to whether you have done your homework on their school. Every question is asked for a very specific reason. Great time and thought went into selecting the question.

It is essential that a student answer these questions VERY specifically, with plenty of examples to show that you really know the school values and culture. You have to make the case for how the distinguishing characteristics of the school are what you're looking for, and where you will flourish. The best responses will answer the "how and why you're a match" question, and I can't stress this enough: they are very specific. In order to do this, you have to know what the school prides itself on and its cherished traditions, differentiating factors, and unique academic and non-academic culture that you genuinely value and appreciate.

The best way to learn this is to study the history, mission statement, and About Us sections of the website. I find it extremely helpful for students to study the college's strategic plan, and also look at their promotional material and definitely look at their admissions blog, if they have one. You can also ask multiple students, alumni, and faculty what makes this college different and special.

Let's give an example. A horrendous answer for why you like Davidson College would be that it has an Honor Code. Let's say you respond by saying you like self-proctored exams. That's still far too generic.

Here is a famous supplemental essay that Stanford asks every year: "Stanford students possess an intellectual vitality. Reflect on an idea or experience that has been important to your intellectual development (250 word limit)." You have to nail this essay if you want to get into Stanford. Remember, they are accepting 1 in 20 students, and their applicant pool is full of valedictorians. Stanford is assessing how much you love learning for learning's sake because those are the smart kids they admit. These essays can be hard, because 250 words forces you to be very efficient.

Some students think the personal statement is the main essay, and they don't put the time into these supplemental essays, but they are extremely important because grades, rigor, and test scores don't narrow down the applicant pool much at all at a place like Stanford. These essays are also hard because everyone is writing on the same subject and you want your essay to stand out.

There are other types of supplemental questions. There are the one-word-answer questions, like, "What is the biggest problem in the world today?" There are also questions that ask you to complete a statement, such as, "The one change I would recommend this college to make is __________." The list of creative questions is endless.

There are also questions designed to see how you think. You want to put some time into these questions, but don't overthink them. Hampton University asks students to write a 250-500- word essay addressing the following prompt: "If your name were an acronym, what would it stand for, and how would it address your strengths and personality?" Too many students approach these questions with the mindset, "What do they want me to say? Hmm, let me figure it out so I can tell them what they want to hear." This is the wrong approach. You should have the mindset of, "I am going to honestly answer the questions and let the college know who I am, and if a school doesn't want me for who I am, then it is not the right college for me."

To give examples of creative prompts you may have to answer, here are a couple of actual questions the University of Chicago has asked in the past:

- ℵ Joan of Arkansas. Queen Elizabeth Cady Stanton. Babe Ruth Bader Ginsburg. Mash up a historical figure with a new time period, environment, location, or occupation, and tell us their story.
- ℵ What's so odd about odd numbers?

A few years ago, I was talking to a few admissions counselors at Davidson College about Davidson's committee discussions about students. One said, "We often spend more time talking about how a student answered the 'Why Davidson?' question than we spend discussing their grades, rigor, recommendations, or extracurricular activities."

If you ever needed proof that many colleges are not only concerned with qualifications but also with who is really a good match for them, this statement should convince you.

65

WHAT ADVICE DO YOU HAVE FOR ME ABOUT MY COLLEGE ADMISSION RECOMMENDATIONS?

Read the recommendation requirements very carefully. I would only trust two sources here: the website itself, or if it's a Common App school, you can trust what is said there. There are schools that do not require recommendations, and they do not want them. They see them as just creating extra work for them to process when they aren't used as part of the admissions decision-making.

It is standard practice for a college that does a holistic review to require recommendations. One common requirement is for two teacher recommendations and a counselor recommendation, but there are many different variations of what schools want. In most instances, you will have the freedom to decide which teachers will write your recommendations. In these instances, I recommend you select teachers who meet the following criteria:

- ℵ They know you very well, ideally both in and outside the classroom.
- ℵ They hold you in high regard as a student and as a person.
- ℵ They taught you in eleventh or twelfth grade. If you choose a ninth-grade teacher, colleges will wonder if what they say about you reflects the way you are now. I like for students to ask for recommendations at the end of the eleventh grade, so that is really the ideal grade to use for selecting your recommenders.
- ℵ They taught you in math, science, English, history, or foreign language.
- ℵ If possible, they taught you in an advanced course.
- ℵ Ideally, one teacher would have taught you in math or science and the other in English, history, or foreign language, but you shouldn't prioritize this over selecting teachers who know you well and hold you in high regard.
- ℵ It should be someone who is known to write good recommendations. Your school counselor may know this if you ask them about their experiences with recommendations from that teacher.
- ℵ It should be someone who is genuine and reliable, who you won't have to repeatedly remind to submit your recommendation.

I recommend requesting your recommendations at the end of your junior year, to give your recommenders ample time. I recommend asking in person, and privately. Tell them you have a question for them, and you need them to be completely honest with you. Ask them if they could write an enthusiastic recommendation letter on your behalf. Watch their body language as well as what they say. If there is any hesitation, select someone else.

If they agree to write a letter, give them your résumé. The résumé will remind them of all that you have done, and they may incorporate some of this into their letter. When a teacher incorporates any of your out-of-the-classroom impact in their letter, it often really enhances your desirability to the college. If the college accepts the Common App or Naviance, you'll send them an email invitation through the Common App or the Naviance portal, but if a school needs a paper copy, you need to give your teacher an addressed, stamped envelope.

I love to have a minimum of two letters of recommendation in the file (even if they are not required), but no more than that. You must read each college's policy on this to see if they will consider these letters in the admission file or if they are truly not welcome. Other great sources for letters are coaches, anywhere you have volunteered, employers, clergy, and mentors. I love when one letter is outside the school community. But remember, your recommenders should know you well and genuinely be able to write about you enthusiastically. Don't fall into the trap of thinking colleges will be impressed by some celebrity who barely knows you.

Common mistakes students make with their recommendation letters:

- ℵ Asking a teacher within a few weeks of the deadline
- ℵ Asking a teacher who taught you in ninth or tenth grade
- ℵ Asking a teacher who didn't teach you in a core subject
- ℵ Asking a teacher who doesn't know you very well
- ℵ Asking a teacher who isn't a raving fan of yours
- ℵ Asking a teacher who is not reliable or responsible
- ℵ Asking any recommender who isn't going to share a perspective about you that is not already in your admission file
- ℵ Not reading the instructions very carefully about who to ask for your letters
- ℵ Not reading the instructions very carefully about how many recs they want
- ℵ Feeling as if you have to ask a teacher when a school administrator is better
- ℵ Asking a relative to write a letter on your behalf
- ℵ Asking a famous person who doesn't know you well
- ℵ Not asking for a rec from a source outside the school (coach, employer, clergy, etc.) if your college is open to receiving this
- ℵ Not giving your recommendation writers a résumé/activity sheet
- ℵ Making your résumé/activity sheet too vague; you should describe the activities you are passionate about in detail
- ℵ Not having a conversation with recommendation writers about the main contributions you would love them to mention if they

feel you have made a difference in this area; it helps to underscore your passions when your rec writers are mentioning your areas of impact

- ℵ Attempting to encourage your recommenders to discuss certain things if you do not have the trust and rapport with them to make such a request
- ℵ Feeling as if you have to ask a teacher in whose class you got an easy A
- ℵ Failing to ask your counselor which of the teachers you are considering asking will write the most honest and vivid recommendations, complete with anecdotes

Recommendations are extremely important at the most selective schools. The problem is that most teachers do not know how to write a good recommendation. One thing I have started doing this year is to have the students I coach privately give school counselors a great article titled "Writing Recommendations, A Guide To Writing Evaluations for MIT" and ask if he/she thinks it would be helpful to share this with the teachers. The article does a great job of explaining what makes a great letter of recommendation, but it also shares six letters and then it critiques the letters.

I am a school counselor at KIPP Metro Atlanta, and I have shared this with KIPP teachers; they absolute love it and find it to be immensely helpful. Most teachers really want to write great recs, but they need some guidance. I strongly encourage all teachers, administrators, students, and parents to Google this excellent article on recommendations by the MIT admissions department.

Here is what Janet Rapelye of Princeton says: "By far the most important part of your application is your transcript ... Tied with that are your teacher recommendations."

I agree 100 percent with Rapelye. If I was still in admissions and I could only have two things to judge an applicant on, I would select the transcript (with a School Profile) and the teacher recommendations. To be honest, no other part of the application (essays, test scores, interview, extracurricular activities) are even close. Having said that, each piece has tremendous value and sheds light on another aspect of who you are. This is only true when you know the feeder school well, though. They know their students well, and they write honest candid recommendations. In other words, they paint the picture with the warts.

Jim Miller, former Dean of Admissions at Brown, used to say to students, "Make sure you write a thank you after a teacher agrees to write a teacher rec for you." He also said, "Not only is it the polite thing to do, but chances are the teacher hasn't written it yet and nothing will motivate them to write the letter like that." Miller went on to say, "It worked on me every time it happened. I felt guilty that this student was thanking me and I had procrastinated and hadn't written the letter yet."

When I was working in boarding school admissions, I once read a letter of recommendation we received from a senator whose name anyone would recognize. The letter was vague, and it was very clear that the senator didn't know the student. The letter talked more about the student's dad than the student. One teacher on the committee said, "I feel like crumpling up this letter and throwing it in the trash." That teacher spoke for everyone in the room. We all felt offended that a family had insulted us by thinking that having a well-known person (who didn't know the student) write a letter would impress us, and that we wouldn't be able to see through that gimmick. Colleges feel the same way. That student was denied. It wasn't only because of the letter, but the letter certainly didn't help, because it spoke to the student's judgment.

66

WHAT DO VISUAL AND PERFORMING ART MAJORS NEED TO KNOW ABOUT HOW THEIR COLLEGE APPLICATION PROCESS IS UNIQUE?

If you are an arts major, I do recommend starting your process in ninth grade, because your process is distinct from other majors in that, in addition to all of the requirements other students must submit, you'll also have either an audition or a portfolio review. In ninth grade, you'll want to start researching any schools you may be remotely interested in to learn what their audition/portfolio requirements are. This applies to so many majors, including actors, filmmakers, singers, musicians, dancers, visual artists, designers, etc. If you aren't sure what schools you might be interested in, ask your teachers and mentors in that field about some of the most common schools students in your specialty have attended. Visit the websites of those schools to see what will be required of you.

Here are some unique things you'll need to do:

- ℵ Attend the closest NACAC arts fair in your area.
- ℵ Try to visit three different types of schools: an arts institute, a university with a College of Art, and a university with a strong arts department. If you end up liking the arts institute the most, just know that 1) their financial aid packages are not usually strong, and 2) if you decide to switch to a non-artistic field, you will likely have to transfer to another college. When you visit a school, ask if they deny more students due to their portfolio or being an academic mismatch. Some schools put more weight on the portfolio or audition, while others emphasize the traditional indices by which all students are evaluated, like grades, curriculum, testing, essays, recommendations, DI, etc.
- ℵ Plan on going to National Portfolio Day as a sophomore and junior. At this event, representatives from visual and performing arts schools from all over the country will take a look at your portfolio and give you honest feedback.
- ℵ Begin studying what career opportunities your arts interest can lead to. You can make a living as an arts major, but it requires a definitive plan and great networking; some fields are easier than others for finding sustainable jobs. Besides, you may have a huge battle on your hands telling your parents you want to be an arts major, so you'll want to have a plan for job sustainability.
- ℵ Find out early on if your parents will support you having an artistic major. You will likely need their financial resources, and if they aren't going to support this, it is better to know in tenth grade than in January of your senior year after you've worked hard on your portfolio or your audition talents for three and a half years.
- ℵ Be open to attending great schools and programs that may not be household names. In a recent admissions year, 164 applicants out of 2551 were admitted to Julliard. That is close to 1 out of every 17. You may be very talented, but the most popular schools are the most selective, so keep an open mind.

- ℵ Traveling around to auditions for arts programs can be expensive, so consider going to one of the national auditions held in places like Chicago, New York, and Los Angeles, where you can perform for multiple schools in the same trip.
- ℵ Trust the feedback of your arts teacher. You may want to be the next Picasso, but your teacher has seen hundreds of talented artists and will be able to put your gifts into perspective.
- ℵ Start thinking about how you can make your portfolio unique and distinctive. Be sure to showcase your creativity.
- ℵ Make sure you are taking the most rigorous courses your school offers.
- ℵ Read the requirements on the website very carefully. Is the portfolio submitted online, or in person? Do you have to meet with the head of the art department as part of the process? For music majors, is prescreening a requirement before you can even have an audition? Does the school encourage you to submit video to them of your artistic talent? Some schools like Princeton strongly encourage this, and they send it out to their faculty and have it rated. If you are going to add to their community because you are that talented, it will definitely help your chances if you are already a competitive applicant. Other schools do not have the manpower to accommodate a surge of more materials for them to evaluate.

Lorin faced a lot of criticism from other students when he said he wanted to be a graphic designer. Likewise, Lorin's mother Wendy faced as much criticism from other parents for being willing to spend the money she spent to send him to the California Institute of the Arts. But Lorin was an extremely talented artist, and he had won all kinds of school-based and regional design awards. No one was laughing when Lorin started picking up clients like *Bloomberg Businessweek*, *Good Magazine*, HUF, IKO, Nike, Stussy, The *New York Times*, and Urban Outfitters. They aren't laughing now that he owns the highly reputable One and Done Design firm in metro New York. Lorin chased his dream and caught it, but even from the tenth grade, he'd had a plan for making it work.

67

HOW IMPORTANT IS IT TO SHOW ACADEMIC PASSION, AND HOW DO I DO THIS?

Don't freak out if you don't know yet what your passions are. But if you do, here are several ways to develop and showcase them:

- Ask open-ended questions about your areas of passion at school fairs, during information sessions, and in an interview, if one is offered. You should be asking great questions in order to compare the various colleges on your list. The more information you have, the better the decision you will ultimately be able to make.
- You will probably be required to take four years of math and four of English, but you don't have to take four years of history, foreign language, or science in most states. You can take a fifth

year in your area of interest, and you can also take a double language.

- Use your electives carefully to explore areas of interest.
- Take online classes in your areas of passion. In the past, selective colleges would say, "We won't hold it against you if your high school doesn't offer a lot of advanced, AP, or IB classes," but the growth of online classes is making some schools now expect that you will have sought out these opportunities if your school isn't challenging you.
- Utilize your summers to develop your passions and extracurricular activities, and consider taking a summer course or doing research in your area of interest.
- You can also use your personal statement or supplemental essays to share your passions, but make sure you answer the question you are asked.
- Consider doing an independent study in an area of passion.
- Set up shadow opportunities and internships.
- Really get to know teachers in your area of passion outside the classroom, and if it makes sense, consider having them write one of your recommendations.

- I love when students send in a recommendation from outside the school from someone who can speak to their passions.

Mola is a student I'm working with right now, and he's doing a month-long unpaid internship with a doctor over the summer. I told Mola to ask the doctor if he'll write a letter on his behalf. I like that this would be an outside recommendation in contrast to a school teacher recommendation, but I also like that it's Mola's area of interest, which reinforces his passion. I like to have applicants weave a theme throughout their application, while still being unique.

Benny was passionate about volunteerism. He helped the homeless, he helped the elderly, and he worked with underserved teenagers. Service is something Benny's mom had instilled in him since elementary school. Benny submitted a résumé that really highlighted his community service, and the College of Wooster liked what they saw, so they offered Benny a $40,000 merit scholarship.

68

WHAT ARE THE BIGGEST MISTAKES STUDENTS MAKE WITH THEIR EXTRACURRICULAR ACTIVITIES?

Don't have extracurricular activities as your starting point, thinking that's what colleges want. This may be the biggest mistake students make. Your starting point should be, "What do I love? What am I curious about? What do I want to explore?"

- א Don't get involved in too many extracurricular activities. The problem with this is that your commitment and involvement will be too shallow, simply because there is only so much time in a day or week. Colleges would rather see a multi-year commitment to a handful of activities than a long laundry list. Colleges are looking for passion, and one way they'll evaluate this is by the activities you choose to get involved with, and your sustained commitment to those activities.

- ℵ Don't start and stop too many activities. Choose something you feel excited about and stick to it. Having said this, freshman year is the year of exploration, so use that year to try different things and figure out what the school offers that you can get involved in. A strong three-year or even two-and-a-half-year commitment to an activity is impressive.
- ℵ Don't always be a "joiner" and never an emerging leader. Leadership is one of the most valuable traits that a school using holistic admissions will be looking for on their campus.
- ℵ Avoid using abbreviations to list your activities, and don't assume people will know what your club or activity is unless you describe it. You don't need to explain if you're the head of the Peer Tutoring program and you list it as Peer Tutoring, but if the club is called "Empower," you can't say that you're the president of Empower and think the admissions counselor will know that Empower is peer tutoring.
- ℵ Don't select activities you don't really love or care about just because you think they'll improve your college application. A lot of applicants feel that there's this "magic activity" that they must be involved in or they'll fall behind the competition, but it's just not true.
- ℵ Don't feel as if you need to fill out all ten lines in the Common App activity list. Don't be like the Lafayette College applicant who felt he needed to complete all 10 lines so he wrote down that he gave blood once a year for an hour. The admission office will have a good laugh about this, but it will be at your expense. There is no magic number of activities, but you should stop and omit anything that didn't involve a reasonable time commitment.
- ℵ Colleges will be focusing on what was most important to you and what activity demanded the most time. You should make it easy for them by listing your activities in priority order. Colleges want to be able to use your listed activities as an indication of what you love.

- Don't make the mistake of not getting involved in anything until junior or senior year. This looks like résumé-padding, and admissions counselors can spot this a mile away. Activities, organizations, and clubs are one insight into what you truly love. Colleges know this isn't something mandatory like algebra or geometry: you could choose whatever you want here, so they're looking for clues as to where you'll contribute at their institution.

Felecia had been involved in the Pet Partners program since the sixth grade, well before I began working with her. Pet Partners takes trained dogs to visit the elderly. They find that the connection with a loving animal lifts the spirits of those who are bedridden and confined by their health restrictions. Felecia had increased her commitment to Pet Partners each year. First, she brought the organization to her private high school and recruited other students to join her. Then, she expanded Pet Partners by convincing another school to start a program as an extension of their community service. Felecia loved dogs, and she found a way to channel this love into serving others in need. She showed a sustained commitment as well as leadership.

69

WHAT DO I NEED TO KNOW ABOUT COLLEGE ADMISSIONS INTERVIEWS?

You need to know that most colleges don't have the manpower to give every student a college admission interview. You also need to know the difference between an informational interview and an evaluative interview. The informational interview is designed to answer your questions and make you feel that the school is warm, personable, and approachable. It's also a way to keep alumni involved in the school. Sometimes student ambassadors give these informational interviews; having alumni and student ambassadors do interviews can lighten the workload for the admissions office. Many colleges have extensive training programs and materials they send to their alumni, as it's very important that they accurately answer any questions they're asked.

The evaluative interview, on the other hand, is an important variable in how you as a student will be evaluated in the admission process. A college will usually be honest with you if you're not sure which type of interview they conduct. You also can't assume that an interview is informational just because it's given by an alumnus instead of an admissions representative. Many, and arguably the majority, of alumni interviews are evaluative interviews. The combination of the alumni knowing the school, coupled with the excellent training that the admission office provides, gives the admission office confidence that they can use the alumni feedback as part of their evaluation. Colleges can't afford to pay their admission team to do all of the interviews, so they partner with enthusiastic alumni and make them a part of their evaluators.

You should also know that some alumni interviewers who technically may be doing informational interviews may have such a good track record of having "spot on" write-ups that the admission counselors value their perspective on an applicant. In other words, sometimes the line is blurred between the informational and the evaluative interview.

There are some schools that are not clear on their website whether the interview is an informational or evaluative interview. Here are seven ways to determine this:

1. Just directly ask your admission rep if the interview is part of your admission evaluation.
2. Look carefully at what the website says about the value of the interview.
3. Ask your admission officer what is the acceptance rate for interviewers versus non-interviewers. MIT could not be clearer about this. Their acceptance rate for interviewers is around 10 percent, but it is under 1 percent for non-interviewers, and they will let you know that number has been consistent for several years. They are screaming at you and telling you it is evaluative.
4. Ask the percentage of students that have interviews. When Brown says that almost every one of their over 30,000 applicants has an alumni interview, you know it is evaluative.
5. If an admissions officer ever does interviews, that is often another giveaway that they are evaluative.
6. Normally when the school has an automatic process of them reaching out to you to schedule your interview after you submit your application, it is a tell-tale sign.

7. Look to see what lengths they go to in order to have most students have interviews. Harvard is not clear on their website about whether their interviews are evaluative by explicitly stating it, but when you see the lengths they go to in order to give international students in obscure countries an interview, it is crystal clear just from this alone that they are evaluative.

Usually the most selective and wealthiest schools in the country do evaluative interviews. Cornell is the only Ivy league school that does informational interviews. You should think of it is as a conversation, and that should help to relax you.

You'll need to pay attention to the basics, such as dressing appropriately, arriving on time, and giving a firm handshake with both eye contact and a smile at the beginning and end of the interview. You should follow up immediately with a thank you email or a handwritten note. However, I believe there are four things that ultimately make or break an interview:

1. Your research and preparation for the interview
2. The caliber of the questions you ask
3. Whether you are genuinely interested in the college and convey this well
4. Whether you display an engaging, genuine, and likeable personality. Are you comfortable in your own skin?

That last one is hard to fake; you are who you are. I strongly recommend you read our chapter on what to look for one a school's website (Chapter 17), and really learn what the college prides itself on as its most distinctive features. You should be prepared to discuss why you appreciate these features and why they make the college a good match for you. You must go beyond the surface. If a school has a requirement that all students live on campus for the first two years, don't just say you like this, but be specific with examples of how such a policy is beneficial to you. For examples of the types of questions you should be prepared to ask, do a Google search for "Excellent Questions to Ask During an Interview, School Match 4U" to find an article I wrote on this topic that you'll find to be helpful. These questions are designed to help you learn things about the college that really matter to you.

You should also request an interview, and request it early. The only exception to this is when a school lets you know that they will contact you to set it up. Many colleges use your request for an interview, or lack thereof, as a measure of your interest in them. If the interview is listed as optional, it's wise for you to treat it as if it's required. Online video interviews have become popular in the last decade or so, and these are great because you can do them without traveling.

When a school says an interview is optional, you should take that to mean that it is required in order for you to be competitive. The one exception is if you are a very poor interviewer. A poor performance in an interview will be held against you.

When Francis left her Georgetown interview, she just knew that she was in. She had felt so comfortable in the interview, and shared that the interviewer told her, "You're a very impressive young lady with a really bright future." Francis was taken aback when Georgetown denied her admission. Interviews are important, but remember that no matter how much you excel in the interview, the interview alone is never enough to get you in.

70

HOW CAN I KEEP A WEAKNESS IN MY APPLICATION FROM LEADING TO AUTOMATIC DENIAL?

Anything that appears in your application that could raise concerns about your desirability or qualifications should be of concern to you. The term used in admissions parlance for these negatives is a "red flag," which gives warning to the admissions office that there's a problem. The good news is that many times, by being proactive and taking the right steps, you can significantly mitigate the damage these red flags do to your applications. In my experience, there are four common red flags with the potential to sink your ship:

1. Serious disciplinary infractions like behavioral suspensions, expulsion, or probation
2. Poor grades for one or two semesters across the board, or in one or two classes

3. Lack of academic rigor in your overall curriculum choices
4. Confusing course selection, for example:
    a. You take Spanish 1 in ninth grade; Spanish 2 in tenth grade; Spanish 3 in eleventh grade; and then in your senior year you take a freshman-level French 1 course
    b. You only take two lab science courses
    c. You don't take a math course in your senior year
5. Lack of extracurricular activities with any evidence of impact in the ones you're involved in

How you respond to these red flags is the same three-step approach to any major problem in your application. There is an Additional Explanation section at the end of the Common Application, and that's your chance to tell your story. You would be surprised how gracious and understanding a college can be if there really is a legitimate explanation. Here are a few examples of very understandable circumstances you could share that might mean the difference between a denial and acceptance.

- Did your parents go through a divorce during the time of your poor grades? You need to share it.
- Did your grandmother, who you were close to, pass away?
- Did your family go through a difficult financial time involving home foreclosure or car repossession?
- Have you been through drug and alcohol counseling after your suspension, and you are so contrite about your past transgressions that you have matured and are determined not to go down that road again?
- Did your school not have a Latin teacher during your senior year, so you had to find another language to take instead of Latin 4?
- Were you wanting so badly to play volleyball, but your single mom had to work two jobs and you had to come home right after school to watch your baby sister? This makes your lack of involvement in school activities much more understandable.

Have other credible people include a letter in your application to substantiate your explanation. This could be a school counselor, a teacher, an employer, or a clergy member.

You have to be totally honest. This is not gamesmanship. Admissions officers have nonsense detectors, and if you're disingenuous in coming up with phony explanations, this is the worst thing you can do.

If you are not applying through the Common App or the Coalition, there usually will not be a prompt to add such an addendum. In these instances, you should let your admission counselor know that you would like to include a written explanation to explain a few things that may be misunderstood in your application. You can ask them if an email or a typed letter is better. Keep in mind that colleges that admit by the numbers will not likely be influenced by this. Schools that use a holistic approach will usually welcome anything that gives them a fuller picture of who you are.

Do not think that this approach guarantees that a red flag will not be a negative factor in your explanation. The more selective the school, the more likely anything will put you in the denial or waitlist pool. Let's say you have a job interview and you're going to be an hour late, then you show up late and say nothing. You are not getting the job unless it's a low-level job and they can't find any other employees. However, let's say there really is an 18-wheeler turned over on the highway, and you're not moving at all, so you call 30 minutes in advance to let the employer know. You suggest that you could either arrive an hour late, or you could reschedule. You now have a chance of receiving grace and still being considered, but there are no guarantees.

When I was at the Westtown School, I started a national college fair that also gave workshops on various subjects in college admissions. We put current college admission counselors on our panels and let them speak directly to students. Four college admission officers were on a panel titled "How to Get Into a Selective School," and it was time to wrap up the workshop and hear from the panelists with their final comments. One of the officers, Sarah, spoke up with passion and gusto.

She said, "If you have a red flag in your file that is understandable, please, please, please, explain to us what happened. We want to help you, but we can't read your mind, and if we don't have an explanation that makes sense we'll be forced to assume the worst–and you will almost assuredly be denied."

71

WHAT ARE 13 STEPS TO TAKE IF I'M WAIT-LISTED?

Students can be admitted, denied, or waitlisted. A waitlist is supposed to mean a student is an acceptable applicant, but others who were deemed more desirable were admitted and filled up the initial openings. Because a school knows not every admitted student will attend, some colleges use waitlists. According to NACAC, 39 percent of colleges surveyed in 2015 reported using waitlists, a number that's been on the rise in recent years. Every college must have a plan to ensure they are fully enrolled.

Some schools will admit students from the waitlist as early as April, while others wait until July or even August.

What should you do if you're on the waitlist?

- Attempt to find out of it is a courtesy waitlist or a genuine waitlist. Some schools use courtesy waitlists to avoid taking a public relations hit by denying a particular student. Let's say an applicant is a recruited athlete that the college is going to admit, but they know they are passing on another student from the same school with a much stronger academic profile. It is often just less of a headache for the college to waitlist the student with the stronger profile that they have no intention of taking; getting waitlisted instead of actually being denied always feels like less of a rejection (at least initially).
- With a courtesy waitlist, the college doesn't really intend to change a student's waitlisted status. The best way to discern this is to have your school counselor make a call and ask, but there's still no guarantee they'll get a straight answer: colleges like to keep this information close. This call is a chance for your counselor to verbally advocate for you.
- You'll also want to be realistic. Check out the waitlist statistics at places like the Common Data Set. Some schools take 1 percent off the waitlist. This link gives you a sense of how competitive waitlists can be: http://collegetransitions.com/waitlist-statistics

  You can also use the prestigious and highly-selective Haverford College's Common Data Information at https://www.haverford.edu/sites/default/files/Office/President/CDS2014_2015.pdf
- If you visit section C.2, you will see that Haverford waitlisted 831 students and 368 chose to remain on that waitlist, but only five students were admitted off the waitlist. This is less than 1 percent of the students initially waitlisted. When the odds are that stacked against you, it's important that you be realistic.
- Waitlists for highly selective schools are like insurance policies in case they have a poor yield one year. You also need to know, for instance, that if the yield is soft for freshman males from the Midwest, and you're a local female student, you can't expect to be one of the students admitted off the waitlist. This is why if you are waitlisted, you will not be told you are number three on the waitlist. Colleges honestly don't know where you are because

they don't know where their yield will be soft and what demographic they will need to admit to give them a balanced class.

- א Remember, forming a class is like selecting musicians for a symphony or assembling a football team. If it turns out you have five quarterbacks and only two linemen, you will pass on a sixth quarterback and select a lineman if that is what you need to strengthen your team.
- א Don't obsess over the school where you've been waitlisted. I tell students and parents, "What would you think if I told you I knew a person who would only be happy if they worked for one company? If you're only going to be happy at one school, the problem is not with the school, but with you."
- א If you have lost interest in a college that waitlisted you, write to withdraw your name from the waitlist and open up a spot for another student.
- א Don't forget to enroll at your second-choice college by submitting your non-refundable deposit before the deadline (which is usually May 1).
- א If you want to remain on the waitlist, formally notify the school by closely following their official process.
- א Write a powerful letter to the admissions officer with whom you have been communicating. I recommend copying the admission dean on this letter. In your letter, be very specific and share something new about why you are a great fit for the college, and share your enthusiasm. Make sure you are positive. If the college is your first-choice school and you will definitely attend if admitted, then share this. But ONLY say that if it's actually true.
- א Have one more recommendation sent on your behalf. This could be a senior year teacher, an employer, or someone else, but it should be someone new who is a raving fan of yours and will communicate enthusiastically. They should be adding something new, and I wouldn't recommend having more than this one additional letter.
- א Consider a second visit to the school. I would only do so if the college encourages this, and if they do, you want to try to get some face time with your admissions contact.
- א If you are waitlisted by a college that accepts less than 5 percent of students off their waitlist, seriously consider refusing to stay

on that waitlist and moving on. Hanging on emotionally often keeps you from accepting reality and appreciating the strengths of the colleges that did accept you.

- Don't be desperate. Remember how we were talking about being the weird admissions stalker kid? That warning applies here as well.
- Keep up your grades, because for waitlist applicants, your entire senior year's grades will count. If any new grades come out, share these with the college.
- Submit any new test score information, like AP test scores or SAT Subject Tests.
- If you applied for financial aid and are willing to pay in full, have your counselor call and let the school know. The truth is that a lot of the time schools are out of aid, and the only students who will come off the waitlist are those who don't need any aid.
- According to the 2015 NACAC State of College Admissions report: "For the Fall 2015 admission cycle, 39 percent of institutions reported using a waitlist. Institutions accepted an average of 32 percent of all students who chose to remain on waitlists."

Throughout the whole year, Abby had one school she desired above all others: Columbia University. However, when Columbia waitlisted her, she accepted it and moved on. She had four other outstanding choices, and she declined to remain on Columbia's waitlist so she could focus on visiting her top choices of the other schools. Abby eventually settled on Washington University in St. Louis, and she couldn't be happier with her decision. This approach isn't for everyone, but it shows that Abby understood that there was more than one college where she could be happy. I was happy, too, because the chances of being admitted off the waitlist at a highly selective college like Columbia are very, very slim.

72

WHAT ADVICE DO YOU HAVE FOR UNDOCUMENTED STUDENTS?

First of all, what is an undocumented student?

According to the National Immigration Law Center (online at http://nilc.org), undocumented persons are defined as foreign nationals who entered the US:

- ℵ Without inspection;
- ℵ With fraudulent documents; or
- ℵ Legally as nonimmigrants, who then violated the terms of their status by letting their visas expire

The dilemma that they face is that by remaining in the United States without authorization, they are in violation of the law. However, the children of undocumented immigrants didn't make the decision to enter or remain in the United States unlawfully. In most instances, their parents came to the United States when they were very young. These undocumented students have grown up in the United States, their friends are American, and they see themselves as American. According to the CollegeBoard.org report "Young Lives on Hold," only 5-10 percent of high school graduates who are undocumented students go on to college. This is partly due to fear of deportation, and partly due to financial barriers they face for attending college.

Here's my advice for undocumented students:

- Know the federal and state policies. Undocumented students are not citizens or permanent residents, and therefore are not eligible for federal grants or loans. State policies vary widely and students and parents need to know them.
- Consider moving to an undocumented-friendly state. I know this is a herculean task and not even possible in many, or perhaps even most, instances, but if you have multiple students in a K-12 school and you value education, the value of going from an anti-undocumented state to a state with receptive policies is priceless. The NCLS provides the following statistics about undocumented-friendly states, available in detail at http://www.ncsl.org/research/immigration/tuition-benefits-for-immigrants.aspx

Currently, 20 states offer in-state tuition to unauthorized immigrant students, 16 by state legislative action, and four by state university systems. Sixteen state legislatures–California, Colorado, Connecticut, Florida, Illinois, Kansas, Maryland, Minnesota, Nebraska, New Jersey, New Mexico, New York, Oregon, Texas, Utah, and Washington–enacted laws to allow in-state tuition benefits for certain unauthorized immigrant students. These laws typically require attendance and graduation at state high schools, acceptance at a state college or university, and promising to apply for legal status as soon as eligible. At least four state university systems–the University of Hawaii Board of Regents, University of Michigan Board of Regents, Oklahoma State Regents for Higher Education, and Rhode Island's Board of Governors for Higher Education–established policies to offer in-state tuition rates to unauthorized immigrant students.

Know the various policies that private colleges have. The biggest distinction is whether they treat an undocumented student like a domestic student or like an international student from an admission standpoint. Examples of some of the most generous colleges in this group include Macalester, Amherst, Bates, Bowdoin, Brown, Bryn Mawr, Colby, Columbia, Cornell, Dartmouth, Duke, Franklin & Marshall, Haverford, Oberlin, Princeton, Rice, Swarthmore, Tufts, U Chicago, UPenn, Williams, Yale, and Pomona. These schools treat undocumented students the same way as they treat domestic students in terms of admissions.

Examples of colleges that treat undocumented students as international students include Carleton, Wellesley, Harvard, Kalamazoo, Kenyon, Lafayette, Lehigh, MIT, Reed, Claremont McKenna, Harvey Mudd, Occidental, and Pepperdine. This doesn't mean there is no money for international students, but it is an incredibly competitive pool with limited resources, and all of these schools are already extremely competitive.

- Excel in school and follow this section's advice about getting in, so you can be a competitive applicant and make yourself potentially eligible for a generous aid award.
- Stay positive and try not to be discouraged.
- Look closely at our chapter on private scholarships and target your private scholarship search to organizations that give money to undocumented students.
- Stay in touch with the news, because laws are changing. I recommend the following source for admission news for undocumented students and those who care about undocumented students: http://bigfuture.collegeboard.org/get-started/for-undocumented-students

President Trump recently ordered an end to the Obama-era DACA program that protects young undocumented immigrants from being deported. He called it an "amnesty-first approach" and he implored Congress to pass a replacement before he begins phasing out its protections in six months. Things are really in flux for undocumented students these days. I am expecting a lot of changes in 2018.

Eliana was as extraordinary as any student I have ever worked with, but she was undocumented, making her college placement challenging. Exactly how exceptional was Eliana? On one occasion, she was riding the train in her home state of New Jersey and a businessman struck up a conversation with her. He was so impressed with her that he asked for the address of the New Jersey Seeds Program that had recruited her and aided in her development. Eliana gave the address, and the businessman wrote to New Jersey Seeds with a $50,000 check and a powerful letter that said, "If you are developing extraordinary young women like this, here are some more resources to help you do what you are doing."

Eliana ended up at Yale University, but I can't help but reflect on the fact that due to Georgia state law, someone like Eliana, who inspires everyone she meets, couldn't even have attended the University of Georgia or Georgia Tech.

73

WHAT QUESTIONS SHOULD STUDENTS WITH DISABILITIES BE ASKING?

The Americans with Disabilities Act (ADA) requires colleges to support students with disabilities, but the quality of that support varies greatly.

Families are encouraged to write to the Disability Support office at the colleges that they're considering to learn more about their support resources. Of course, a campus visit is essential.

Disabilities can be physical, including speech, hearing, vision, mobility, diabetes, multiple sclerosis, cancer, heart disease, cerebral palsy, asthma, etc. They can also be learning impairments in areas such as listening, reading, math, writing, focus, speaking, and social interaction.

So, what questions should you ask? I have been impressed with the tips of two disability experts, Joy App, and Micah Goldfus.

Joy App, from Houston, recommends you ask the following questions:

1. How current must my testing be to apply for accommodations?
2. How many students use your services?
3. What Assistive Technology (AT) services do you offer? Do you have an AT expert on staff?
4. What accommodations do you offer? What are the procedures and timelines to receive them?
5. How many Disabilities Support counselors do you have on your staff? Do they act as liaisons?
6. If a professor is not in compliance regarding the student's needed accommodations, how is the situation resolved?
7. What is the procedure to get extended time on exams? How much notice is required? Do students arrange extended time with professors or through the Disabilities Services Office?
8. Where do students take exams? Who proctors?
9. What do you consider the most difficult majors/classes for Disabilities Support students on this campus?
10. Will I have both an advisor in the Disabilities Services Office and a regular academic advisor? If both, how will the two advisors work with each other?
11. What is the four-year graduation rate for students with learning disabilities similar to mine?
12. Do you track students who have used your services after graduation? If so, what do your findings show?

Joy also says to be on the lookout for two red flags when evaluating campus disability service. Based on her advice and Lynn O'Shaughnessy's August 24, 2012, article "How to Judge College Learning Disability Programs," these are two questions you should ask:

1. Is the personality of the director of staff off-putting? This is paramount, since he/she represents the personality of the department.
2. Is the Disability Services website of the college user-friendly and simple to navigate?

Joy is an expert in this field, and she can be reached at http://appeducationalconsulting.com/about-us

Micah Goldfus, the national program director of Eye to Eye, is also an expert at assessing the quality of the disability services that a college offers. In a Noodle article on April 29, 2015, "Three Questions to Ask About College Disability Services," Micah recommended that you ask the following three questions:

- How does the disability service office collaborate with other parts of the school?
- Does the disability service office provide mentorship opportunities?
- How does the disability service office train and communicate with the university's staff, professors, and administrators?

Harold was a student I worked with who was absolutely brilliant, but who struggled with Asperger's Syndrome. This led to some awkward social interactions, as Harold had a very hard time reading nonverbal behavioral and other social cues. Fortunately for Harold, Tulane University admitted him, and they provided outstanding support through their Goldman Center for Student Accessibility. Studies show that between 15 and 25 percent of students with disabilities utilize the resources that are on campus. If you have a disability, follow Harold's example and access all the support resources on campus.

74

What is an admission hook, and what are some of the main hooks?

Hooks are occasionally referred to as "tags"; they are tipping factors that add weight to the scales, much like how we described how a weighted GPA differs from a non-weighted GPA. Hooks are institutional priorities, meaning they are factors that some students bring that the college has identified as desirable traits to make them more effective at carrying out their mission.

Not all hooks are of equal weight. The more they help the college, the more valuable they are, and the more valuable they are, the more the student who has these hooks will leapfrog over other applicants with stronger academic profiles. In general, schools that practice holistic admissions will be much more likely to look at a wide range of hooks and factor them into their admission decisions, but even the schools that admit by the numbers make huge allowances for varsity athletes, especially when they are in revenue-producing sports.

Here are some of the hooks that can be an asset in the admission process:

- ℵ Being a recruited athlete in a revenue-producing sport like football or basketball
- ℵ Being a recruited varsity athlete in a non-revenue producing sport
- ℵ Being the child of an alumnus
- ℵ Being the child of a faculty member
- ℵ Being the child of a member of the Board of Trustees
- ℵ Being the child of a celebrity
- ℵ Being a "development admit," or the child of someone likely to give a gift that could change the college for years to come
- ℵ Being an underrepresented student of color
- ℵ Being a woman applying to a major in which women are underrepresented
- ℵ Being a man, for most schools, as schools want gender balance and women tend to be the students with stronger GPAs and greater academic focus
- ℵ Applying to an underrepresented major
- ℵ Being a full-pay student to a need-aware college (See Chapter 143 on Need-Blind vs Need-Aware in the Paying for College section)
- ℵ Applying early decision
- ℵ Having a unique talent in the arts, such as singing, dancing, instrumental music, or acting
- ℵ Coming from a unique geographical location from which the college lacks applicants (could be domestic or international)

Sometimes the same hook at one school will carry either less weight or more weight at another school. This is often a result of the mission of the school or the institutional priorities that will vary from one school to another.

It is helpful to know if you have any hooks, and if you do, are they minor hooks or major ones? This can impact not only your list-building, but also your follow-up strategy for getting in. It is the one danger of scattergrams. If you have a hook of substance and you are looking at graphs full of students that don't have a hook, it is an apples to oranges comparison.

Getting into the University of Virginia as an out-of-state applicant is tough, but I was not surprised when Kathleen applied and was admitted. Kathleen was obviously an excellent student, but she also had two hooks in her favor that I thought would help her. As a woman, she was applying as an engineering major, and that major is dominated by men, so that was a hook for her. Second, in the state of Virginia, most of the engineering majors gravitate to Virginia Tech, so in general UVA could use more engineering applicants. Kathleen also had that working for her.

75

WILL A COLLEGE EVER RESCIND AN ADMISSION ACCEPTANCE?

Absolutely, they will do this, which is one reason why senioritis (the tendency to slack off in your senior year because you are already accepted to a college and/or are burned out on high school) is a high-risk game.

There are four reasons I have seen admission decisions rescinded. The first reason is because the final grades at the end of year transcripts are significantly worse than the grades that were on your transcript when your admission decision was rendered. Usually the grades have to drop quite a bit, as in more than a letter grade, but a school reserves the right to rescind your acceptance even if you only drop a letter grade (from A student to B student), so don't push it. If you read the language in your admissions contract, you will see that the acceptance is contingent on your continual strong performance. Lee Coffin, Dean of Admissions at Dartmouth, calls this the escape clause, and he is clear with all students that this language appears with every acceptance offer.

The second reason I have seen admission decisions rescinded is because of an egregious moral lapse in behavior. This is the most common reason I have experienced an admission reversal, but other counselors I know have seen more acceptances rescinded for grade slippage. When I use the words "moral lapse," I am talking about things like expulsions and suspensions for drugs, alcohol, stealing, fighting, plagiarism, bullying, inappropriate sexual misconduct, etc.

The third reason I have seen this is when a student drops several courses after they are admitted. The rigor and workload of the senior year really matters, especially to rigorous and selective colleges.

Decisions can also be rescinded for a failure to send in your deposit by the due date, and because of a failure to meet orientation and registration obligations. Schools are usually incredibly patient with these deadlines before they rescind, but there are families that just have not been able to come up with the money; usually when this happens, it's because a family or student is having cold feet about their decision.

I was at the University of Georgia and an admission counselor was walking me around campus while we were just talking, and the subject turned to students who had had their acceptances revoked this year. The admission officer shared a disturbing story about a student who was arrested for shoplifting, and UGA felt they had no choice but to rescind their initial acceptance. Don't slip in your senior year, or you could find yourself in a much different situation than you expected.

Parents need to allow their kids to ask questions during information sessions.

76

WHAT ARE SOME MISTAKES PARENTS MAKE IN THE COLLEGE APPLICATION PROCESS?

They attempt to vicariously live through their child. They see their child's college choice and their choice of a major as their opportunity as a parent to do what they wish they had done. Don't tell your child what they need to major in and where they need to go. Loving and caring parents make this mistake all the time, and they are in denial that they are doing this.

- ℵ They write their child's essays. Don't be naïve: admission reps can detect the adult voice and it can be a quick move into the denial pile.
- ℵ They complete their child's applications.

- ℵ They dominate all of the questions at the information session, on the tour, and in the follow-up communication with the college.
- ℵ They refuse to accept a denial or a waitlist decision, and they approach the school counselor or the college for an explanation of what happened.
- ℵ They tell a student that they can go to their dream school no matter what the cost is, and then they sacrifice their retirement savings to make it happen.
- ℵ They refuse to pay their EFC (Expected Family Contribution), which is the parents' responsibility, and is based on the parents' resources 99 percent of the time.
- ℵ They do not set expectations early on about what they can afford and what they expect the student to contribute in the way of loans and summer earnings.
- ℵ They do not start a 529 plan early enough to build up a college savings account.
- ℵ They live above their means and enter into their child's college years with credit card debt and car payments. You can get a very good used car for under $15,000 or even under $10,000. If you have a car note and credit card debt, I can all but assure you that you will not feel as if you can pay your EFC.
- ℵ They brag nonstop to anyone within a football field's range of where their child got in and all of the scholarships they received.
- ℵ They call and contact the admission office too often during the application process. Colleges expect parents to call and set up visits and interviews, but here is a word of advice I hope you heed: Colleges know the *student* is coming, not the parent, and it is the student they want to hear from.
- ℵ They make their child feel as if they are not proud of where they get in and where they choose to go to college.

I had to pull Carl aside and have a firm conversation with him. I had attended an information session with Carl, and he not only wouldn't let his son Jack ask a question, but it was incredibly difficult for anyone else to get a question in either. As soon as there was a moment of silence, he would blurt out his next question. The admissions counselor didn't manage the situation very well. She should have required that hands were raised, or she should have said, "I am going to let someone who hasn't asked a question get their chance," but regardless, Carl didn't do Jack any favors. Admission counselors want to know that the student is driving the process, and their antenna is up for helicopter parents.

77

HOW DO ADMISSION OFFICES EVALUATE APPLICANTS WHO ARE TRANSFERRING FROM ANOTHER COLLEGE?

You may recall me saying that only about 1 percent of students I work with glean all of the information from the college's website that they should. Well, nowhere is the 1 percent rule more applicable than with transfer admissions. There are a few policies that are similar across the board, and others that differ greatly.

Similarities in Transfer Policies:

- The longer you are in college, the more weight your college GPA will carry in the process and the less weight your high school transcript and testing will factor into the college's decision.

- ℵ If an essay is required (and not all schools require this), the reason why you want to transfer is important, and how you state this in your essay will carry weight.
- ℵ You should emphasize the opportunities that the school you want to transfer to offers you in a positive way, and in no way, shape, or form disparage the school you want to leave. The antenna will be up for whether you are a positive person in general, or a chronic malcontent, so be aware of this. Don't even talk about what you don't like about your current school. Focus instead on what the new school can do for you and what you can do for them.
- ℵ If recommendations are required from college teachers, they are going to be a very important part of the evaluation process.
- ℵ Start planning well in advance. Part of this planning involves getting to know some teachers so they can write about you with conviction.
- ℵ Be extremely attentive to deadlines, because they are often different than the deadlines for freshman applicants.
- ℵ Usually large public universities have higher acceptance rates for transfer applicants than selective private schools. Usually large public state schools will have Articulation Agreements with certain community colleges that will, for the most part, accept their core classes as transfer credit.

You should Google "Common Data Set" and the college you are considering transferring to. If they provide this data, you can go to Section C and see what the transfer acceptance rate is. It is often very low.

- ℵ Usually the pool of financial aid from the college itself for transfer applicants is not as large as the pool of money that is reserved for freshman applicants and returning students. Some schools have merit money for transfer students, and others do not. Federal money will transfer, and there is no difference here.
- ℵ It is important that your full legal name is on all of your admission materials. This is also important for any applicant to college, not only transfer applicants.

Differences in Transfer Policies:

- א Some schools will accept the Common Application Transfer Application, while others will not.
- א Some will have clearly-established policies of the minimum number of credits you will have to have completed in college to even begin the transfer process.
- א Some schools have a minimum GPA that you need to transfer, and they will state what that is.
- א Some schools will only accept applications for the fall, while others accept applications for any semester.
- א Some colleges will have interviews, and others won't.
- א A Transfer Mid-Term Report may be required.
- א ACT or SAT scores may be required, or they may not.
- א A college may or may not be able to definitely tell you which courses will transfer before you apply.
- א Some colleges put significant weight on the college you are transferring from, whereas others do not factor this into their evaluation.
- א Some schools have a transfer coordinator, and some colleges have a special orientation for transfer students.

My roommate in my sophomore year at Michigan State was named KC. KC started out at Sienna College in Loudonville, NY. KC had more friends at the end of three weeks at MSU than most freshmen had; he was like a fish *in* water at Michigan State. In asking KC why he transferred, he said, "Sienna only had 3000 students; it was just too small." Sometimes a student needs to learn to stick it out, because they can't just quit when life gets tough. But other times, a school just isn't working out, and it is best to move on.

78

SHOULD I HIRE AN INDEPENDENT COUNSELOR TO ASSIST ME WITH THE COLLEGE APPLICATION PROCESS?

Some of you are thinking, "Mark, you *are* a private college coach, so of course you are going to say yes." Well, that is not what I am going to say. I'm going to say, "Some people would find it to be extremely beneficial, and for others it is absolutely not necessary or advisable." I am also going to say that just like mechanics, school teachers, doctors, and any other profession, there are good independent counselors and there are bad ones. I am also on the other side of the fence. I work as a counselor on the KIPP Through College team, and I have students I am helping right now with the college process. As a counselor working in a school, I once had a family seek outside consulting assistance. It is a blow to the ego when this happens, but you have to humble yourself and work collaboratively together with the outside consultant in order to get the best result for the student.

Let's start by talking about your school counselor. They will always be your primary counselor from the perspective of the college. They are the one who has access to the official records of the school. They complete the Secondary School Report. They are the one who must write the official counselor recommendation. Colleges will not accept this from a private counselor. The school counselor is relied upon by the college to place the applicant in the context of the school. I strongly recommend to every student that I work with that they make getting to know their school counselor a top priority.

If the school counselor is most important, why did one study find that 26 percent of families whose child scored 1150 or higher on the SAT admit to hiring a private college counselor? Part of it is because the college process has become very complicated and stressful. Just building the right college list alone is challenging, with over 4500 two- and four-year colleges. The biggest reason families hire an outside college coach is because the ratio of school counselors to students usually ranges from 1:200 to 1:1000 in public schools. Many times students don't feel as if they can get enough face time with their public school counselor to get their questions answered. The ratios are usually better at private schools, but there is a wide range here as well.

In some instances, private counselors are hired because they have more knowledge of the college admissions process than school counselors, but there are many instances where school counselors (especially at selective private schools) have college admissions experience on top of their counseling experience, and they know more than the private counselors. Most master's programs in school counseling give very little time to college counseling, so this is often not an area of expertise for public school counselors. One of the primary reasons I wrote this book was so public school counselors could use it as a reference book with their students.

There are times when a family just wants a voice outside of the bubble of their school to give them a new perspective on matters. Other times, a family just feels a rapport with a particular private focus.

There is also an expense with private counselors that may not be in your budget. The national average is over $4000, according to a 2014 IECA study, and in places like New York it will cost you considerably more. There are many that are a lot less, and those who have their heart in their work almost always do some pro bono work, but in general, it is a considerable expense.

Colleges have mixed feelings about private college coaches. Some love us and will fly us out to see their school because they want us to send them applications, and they want us to really understand their culture and unique offerings. Others feel like we are advantaging the already-advantaged by giving the wealthy another leg up in the process. Some colleges feel like they are less likely to see the true authentic voice of the applicant because they have been so pre-packaged. I've personally found colleges to be very receptive to the good private college coach if we build a relationship with them. I discussed this subject with a counselor from one of the Claremont colleges, and she said to me, "I feel like I am a good judge of character as to which ones can be trusted."

To be honest, I understand why there is resistance from some colleges to working with us. The truth is, some consultants violate the authenticity of the application process because their focus is not on matching, but rather on getting kids into prestigious schools. An example of this would be taking a student who wants to major in an oversubscribed major, telling them they should instead apply to a major the consultant knows the college is prioritizing in admissions, and telling them to position their entire application as someone who cares about this undersubscribed major. Then, the consultant tells the student to switch to the major they actually care about after they are admitted. I have a big problem with this, and unfortunately, it is not that uncommon in the private consulting profession.

I also wish that the colleges that won't communicate with private college coaches would have the mindset that there are good school counselors and there are those who pre-package applicants and are not honest in their recommendation writing. The same is true for school counselors. The key is not the school counselor (perceived as the good guy) versus the private college coach (perceived as the one who went to the dark side) but rather, the motivation, honesty, and character of any counselor, be they a private coach or a school-based counselor. It can be self-righteous for a college to say they won't communicate with private college coaches. There are some great private coaches who love kids and believe in education and would be a huge asset to colleges looking for more quality applicants.

Private counselors should agree to adhere to the Principles of Good Practice outlined by organizations like HECA, IECA, and NACAC. They cannot write essays for students, take money from colleges, promise families they can get their child into a specific school, and many other guidelines.

I am going to be totally candid with you. This is the hardest chapter in this book for me to write, because there is a lot of friction between school counselors and private counselors. The biggest challenge I face as a private college coach is how I will communicate with the school counselor at the high school. I love collaborating with school counselors, but it is not always possible. On one hand, in HECA's Standards and Ethics statement it says the private counselor should work 'collaboratively' with the high school counselor, but this same Ethics statement also says you can only confer with a high school counselor about the student in matters related to college admission if you have written permission from the family.

I have partnered with outstanding school counselors who believe that two minds are better than one and that it is great to have me on their team, and I've attempted to work with others who are offended and resentful, and they interpret the family decision to hire me as their college coach as a personal rejection of their competence. I recently had a school counselor in California say that, "If I was in admissions and I found out someone hired a private consultant, that would be reason enough for me to deny their kid admission."

> Working with Alice and Dr. Jackson was a perfect example of how a private counselor and a school counselor should work together. Alice was a student at a private Atlanta day school, and Dr. Jackson (Alice's mom) gave me permission to let her school counselor know I was helping her. He was so supportive and encouraging to work with. He had the mindset that two heads are better than one, and after all, it wasn't about either of us, but about what was best for Alice. We worked together very well, and Alice is currently very happy at LSU.

If I represented a client from his school, there is no way the family could be honest about having hired me. Some school counselors have a tendency of letting their ego cloud their judgment. Their starting point is not, "This is clearly something my student wants, let's give them the benefit of having two minds collaborate together for their best interest." Too often their reaction is, "I'm insulted that you don't think I am adequate to be the only source that you need."

Many times this backlash is warranted, because there are unprofessional private counselors out there who disparage the school counselor. There are also a lot of private consultants who are slick at sales and marketing, and they actually know less than the good school counselors, so this has to be frustrating. A lot of families know that their school counselor is going to be offended and they do not want to give me written permission to confer with their school counselor.

On the other hand, a lot of school counselors don't acknowledge that there is any value to working with a good college coach, and good private counselors know they bring tremendous value, so this mindset from some school counselors creates a barrier. It is very hard for either counselor to do their job as effectively as they can do it if the private college coach and the school counselor are not on the same page.

79

WHAT ROLE DOES MY SCHOOL COUNSELOR PLAY IN THE PROCESS?

School counselors are extremely important, because colleges rely on the counselor to describe the student in the context of the entire class. This is so important that there is a question on the Common Application that asks the counselor to rank the academic rigor of the student according to the following options: *most demanding, very demanding, demanding, average, or below average curriculum offered.* This assessment is invaluable to the college, and for the most selective schools, a rating other than most demanding or very demanding is almost always the kiss of death.

School counselors are also important because many colleges that do a holistic review require a counselor letter of recommendation. The counselor can write a prose description of the student, and if they describe the student as having character traits that they find extremely valuable on their campus, such as leadership, amicability, intellectual curiosity, work ethic, resilience, being well-liked and respected, having a positive attitude, and modeling personal integrity, it is going to really matter a lot at the selective schools that use a holistic review.

The counselor is also the official link between the student and the college, so if the college has a question about anything, they aren't going to call a teacher or an independent consultant. They are going to call the school counselor.

The school counselor may help you build your college list, select appropriate courses, make schedule changes, assist with the Common Application and financial paperwork, assist with getting test score and application waivers if you qualify for them, and help answer your questions about the college process. They will also send the official transcript and School Profile. I strongly encourage students to take the initiative to build a relationship with their school counselor very early in their high school career and take advantage of this invaluable resource.

Jennifer is great friends with my daughter Joy. I was so happy for Jennifer at graduation when she was recognized for receiving an $80,000 Dell scholarship. When I asked her where she heard about the scholarship, I was especially pleased when she said, "From my school counselor."

80

What are some common mistakes made by black and Latino applicants?

Many students of color are first-generation college students, and they don't have parents who have been to college to mentor them, so all of this is new and mistakes are understandable. Here are the most common mistakes I see from black and Latino families.

- ℵ Some are unwilling to take out student loans. I am a big fan of the Federal Direct subsidized and unsubsidized loans. Of course, having *no loans* is better than even this loan, but I am constantly challenging parents of color on their refusal to even entertain taking out a reasonable loan when they are okay with a car loan or a home loan. An investment in your child's education is priceless.

- Some don't read closely about the application requirements.
- Missing admission deadlines and priority scholarship deadlines is always bad. In general, submitting applications late is a more widespread problem in the black and Latino community, from my experience.
- Starting the whole college process too late is a mistake. This includes school research, essays, applications, test prep, college visits, etc.
- According to a June 27, 2016, article by Tanzina Vega of CNN entitled "Blacks Still Far Behind Whites in Wealth and Income," "In 2014, the median household income for whites was $71,300 compared to$43,300 for blacks." That works out to blacks making 60.7% of what whites make in annual household income.
- Parents having too much credit card debt and having car loans makes it extremely hard for parents to pay the EFC. I know it is hard. According to a September 28, 2017, article by Tracy Jan in the *Washington Post* entitled "White Families Have Nearly 10 Times the Net Worth of Black Families. And the Gap is Growing" black net worth is 1/10th that of white families, so things are much tougher and families have to be more frugal.
- They may not start college saving accounts early enough to have any money saved for college.
- Expecting that they will get a full ride and not have to pay anything for college. Financial aid guru Mark Kantrowitz says that only .3 percent of students (that is 1 in every 333) go to college on a full scholarship.
- Making mistakes on the FAFSA is a big one. Too many parents of color let their child complete the FAFSA, and there are not many 17-year-olds that will not make mistakes on this paperwork without a parent or an advisor looking over this very carefully.
- Not completing the FAFSA at all is a major problem. Research by NerdWallet in 2016 revealed that 2.7 billion dollars in aid is lost by students not completing the FAFSA.

- They select for-profit colleges that are often a colossal waste of time.
- They may take on too much loan debt, especially with Parent PLUS loans and private loans.
- They don't read the fine print and get stuck in bad private loans.
- Parents sometimes feel as if they are being bad parents if they don't let their child go to their dream school, and therefore incur an unsustainable amount of debt. You need to establish early with your child what you can afford to pay and what you expect the student to pay.
- They try to get their child to major in what you want them to major in. This is a form of living vicariously through the life of your child.
- They automatically assume that because students can't compare aid awards that applying as an early decision applicant is imprudent, but for certain wealthy schools, applying ED may be the best financial move.
- They select a college because their friends are going there.
- Under-matching refers to when a student is a desirable applicant at a much more selective school than the college they end up attending. This is a major problem for low-income students of all races. This was the impetus behind why the extraordinary organization QuestBridge was formed. Here is what QuestBridge says on their website: "Annually, approximately 30,000 talented low-income students nationally are academically qualified to attend the nation's best colleges, but the majority of them don't even apply to one selective college."
- There are a lot times when under-matching is absolutely the right decision, but all too often, students of color receive bad counsel as to which schools they are actually competitive for, so they don't apply to colleges that would love to have them.
- There are a growing number of wealthy black families with incomes over $250,000 and net worths of over one million dollars. One of the biggest mistakes I see some of these families make is that they spend so much money on cars,

homes, clothes, hair, travel, and restaurants that they don't have the money saved that they should for college. Most families don't feel they can afford to contribute what the Department of Education's FAFSA formula says they can contribute; these families often feel they cannot even pay half of what they are projected to be able to afford.

Patrice was a black mom I worked with, and both she and her husband worked for a church where they were not paid much money. They had three children that were each four years apart in age. They moved into a good school district to give their kids a great public education, but the mortgage and the taxes were high. We were talking about college savings and I turned to Patrice and said, "Do you have any money saved in a college fund?"

Her voice got louder and her brow was furrowed; she looked at me like I had just asked the most preposterous question and then she said emphatically, "College fund? The college fund is the Now Fund!"

We both laughed, but I did get it. Sometimes it's really hard just to keep your head above water when bills are coming at you now. As much as some people would love to have a college fund, the mortgage, utilities, and feeding the kids (the Now Fund) have to be the priority.

81

What are some common mistakes made by international students applying to United States colleges?

- ℵ Overlooking sections of the college website, like the contact information for an international admissions counselor provided by some colleges
- ℵ Starting the I-20 visa or passport requirements too late with the American embassy in your area
- ℵ Not realizing you can chat with a current international student from your cultural background to help determine if the college is a good match for you
- ℵ Not connecting with the university's international education office or an international student group on campus

- Not adequately showing what you can contribute to the class in both academic and non-academic ways, or not presenting yourself as well-rounded
- Not valuing liberal arts colleges (I understand that in some cultures anything with the word "college" behind it is seen as second tier to "university," but many international students overlook the attractive acceptance rates at, say, medical schools within highly selective liberal arts schools.)
- Focusing only on the most prestigious schools and not realizing the other gems that are there
- Insisting on going to a school in the Northeast
- Refusing to consider more rural schools
- Missing important details about things that are strongly recommended; for example, Georgia Tech says on their website, "We recommend that applicants who are non-native English speakers participate in a third-party, unscripted interview" (many don't even know this, let alone actually do it)
- Not including anything you've done outside of classes, from volunteering to working part time, or playing the cello; there should be passion for what you love to do outside of class; it is not only an academic evaluation
- Many colleges mandate that international students turn in the certification of finances along with applications; don't neglect this
- Know how many students from your country are applying and being admitted: it's basic supply and demand, so go where your culture is under-represented (According to independent educational consultant Ellen Richards, 10 years ago, 17 Chinese students applied to the University of Virginia; three years ago, 177 students applied, and this year 800 applied. Three years ago, 16 Chinese students applied to Brown, but this year 500 applied.)
- More and more colleges are becoming aware of the difficulties in confirming the accuracy of information on international applications, so there is intense scrutiny for some applications in certain parts of Asia; students need to be writing their own essays

When I worked at the Westtown School, Haverford College had a 99 percent medical school acceptance rate for several years in a row. It was the highest medical school acceptance rate in the nation, but I was never able to get any international students to consider it. I tried really hard to get this really charismatic student named Juan, who wanted to stay in the United States and go to medical school, to visit, and he would not even step on campus because Haverford ended with the word "college" and not "university."

82

WHAT IS A "GAP YEAR," AND SHOULD I TAKE ONE?

A gap year occurs when instead of going from high school straight to college, you decide to delay your college entrance for a year. They are sometimes referred to as "bridge years." Gap years are on the rise, and are becoming much more popular, especially at selective schools. I think it is the Malia Obama Effect.

To take a gap year, you have to request in writing that the college hold your accepted spot for a year. Before you request anything in writing, read the website to learn what their gap year process is. You cannot approach this with an attitude of entitlement, because some colleges do not accept gap years, and even those that do accept them on a case-by-case basis. You should go to the school's website and consult the policies of the school you plan on attending the following year before you request a gap year. You should expect to state in writing why you want a gap year and how it will benefit you.

The reason so many colleges are receptive to this bridge year is because usually their research shows that these students come in with more focus and more maturity when they enroll the following year.

The most common reasons for gap years are the following:

- א To find your passion and discover a major or a career of interest
- א To travel and be exposed to other cultures
- א To work and save money to be in a better financial situation
- א To pursue a passion project, i.e. write a book, learn how to build websites, etc.
- א To commit to a year of community service
- א To improve your desirability to other colleges that you want to apply to for the following year, if you plan to defer applying altogether
- א To learn a foreign language
- א To address a health concern in your life
- א To spend time with a relative who is having major health concerns and may be near death

There are some fears associated with gap years. The biggest fear that parents have is that their student may just decide they don't want to go to college after all. Perhaps they end up addicted to the money they are making and forgo college. Parents can also worry that their child will be a non-productive coach potato during this year. Students and parents can both worry that the financial aid they receive will not be as good the following year, or that any money the student makes during their gap year may have a drastic effect on the aid they receive. Colleges sometimes lose the students that deferred, and while they factor in some attrition, there is always a concern that they did not project the number accurately.

There are a lot of outstanding gap year programs out there that allow students to go into inner cities and help in under-resourced schools. City Year is one example.

Troy is a student I worked with who was a great candidate for a gap year. He had graduated from high school when he had just turned 17, and the gap year would allow him to gain maturity and be the same age as the other freshmen in his class, but he also was passionate about filmmaking and he had a film he wanted to complete. Taking a gap year allowed him to do that. Northwestern University in Evanston honored his request, and Troy and his parents will tell you that the gap year really helped Troy mature.

83

WHAT SHOULD I INCLUDE ON A COLLEGE RÉSUMÉ?

There are four different uses for a college résumé that you'll want to be aware of.

1. They are great to give to recommendation writers, because they remind them of all that you have been involved in and they will often incorporate this into what they say about you. This can really help show a school how you have impacted your community. I worked with an eighth-grade science teacher, Larry Hampton, at KIPP in Atlanta who would not fill out a recommendation for a student unless they gave him a résumé. He wasn't being cruel, he just wanted to know them better and talk about them outside of class.

2. They can be used as a handout during a college admission interview.
3. They may be included as an attachment to a scholarship application.
4. Sometimes it is wise to include your résumé in your college application itself.

What makes a great college résumé?

- ℵ I often have my students use two categories on their résumé: activities they are passionate about, and activities they have been involved in. Colleges will care about the passion category, and it is one more way to underscore what excites you. This makes it easy for the areas you are most likely to contribute on the college campus you attend to emerge at a glance. For the activities you were not passionate about, you can just list them, but for the two to four areas you were involved in and you really cared about, you should provide more detail about what you actually did. This is how Karis submitted her résumé to Davidson.
- ℵ Do not just repeat what is in the activity section of the Common App. You should add more detail in describing what you did in your activities that you really cared about.
- ℵ Do not exceed two pages in your résumé length. Remember, you don't have to list everything, only the most important things. There are colleges that like résumés, but they are sticklers for the one-page résumé. I have heard admission officers say, "You are 18 years old; your résumé should not be longer than mine is." Ask your college if a two-page résumé is okay or if they would prefer just one page.
- ℵ Don't use abbreviations for activities, and explain what any obscure activities are.
- ℵ Read and re-read, and have another set of eyes proofread your résumé.
- ℵ Some colleges that like résumés prefer them grouped by common activity. For example, rather than having four musicals you were in listed chronologically, having them under a theater section is something some admissions reps who welcome résumés recommend.

א Make sure to include work experience, volunteer experience, and your honors and awards. If you are putting in significant hours with household chores, you should list this with your number of hours so colleges can see how you are spending time.

א Make sure you only send a résumé to colleges that like résumés. You need to ask, because schools tend to have strong opinions on whether they like résumés. There are people like Eric Furda, Dean of Admissions at UPenn, who hate résumés. When you ask, you have to let them know that there is additional information on your résumé that there wasn't room for in your Common App activity section with the 150-character limit. The University of Virginia will tell you they do not want to see a résumé, but the University of Texas will tell you that they strongly encourage you to submit a résumé.

> About five years ago, I wanted to know exactly what current college admission officers thought of the college résumé. I went to a local college fair on a Saturday in Atlanta with the purpose of asking the admission officers this question. I got mixed responses; there were the schools that use numerical admissions that said they are a waste of time and they'd rather students not send them, and there were those who really liked them. But the most common response I got from the smaller private colleges that practice holistic admissions was this: "If you're just going to repeat what is in the Common App activity section, then don't waste your time or our time by sending it. But if the résumé is going to add something new that is important to you, then I encourage students to send it."

א You can see if the résumé policy is on the admission web page. You can easily check for the 700+ schools who take the Common App. If they encourage résumés, they will do what Boston College, Carnegie Mellon, Brown, and many others do; they will allow you to upload a résumé from their portal.

84

WHAT IS AN HONORS COLLEGE, AND HOW WILL IT BENEFIT ME?

Honors Colleges have become an effective way for public colleges to compete with private schools for the top students. While the details of what each Honors College offers can vary, they all have significantly higher entrance requirements than for the school in general. For some Honors Colleges, students with very strong transcripts and test scores are automatically admitted, and for others, there is a separate application that may involve separate essays and an interview. Almost all Honors Colleges provide an opportunity for high-achieving freshmen to be admitted once they are at the college.

Here are some of the common benefits that Honors Colleges provide that are similar to what a student would receive at an elite private school:

- small classes

- ℵ rigorous advanced classes that are more discussion-based
- ℵ classes taught by the school's leading faculty
- ℵ an opportunity to live in Honors housing with the top students
- ℵ unique research opportunities
- ℵ priority registration and course selection
- ℵ unique study abroad opportunities
- ℵ guest speakers that come speak to the Honors students
- ℵ prestige, and
- ℵ interdisciplinary study.

Where public colleges really get aggressive with their Honors Colleges is by claiming that they can also offer some of the following benefits that a student would *not* receive at a small, elite private school, such as lower tuition, possible merit scholarships, big-time athletics, a more "real world" experience that is more socio-economically diverse, and opportunities to major in professional degree programs like engineering, business, and architecture that a lot of liberal arts schools don't provide.

In my opinion, Honors Colleges are some of the absolute best bargains in America when it comes to higher education. I think that the stronger programs are fantastic, and most others are very good. I would caution students to do their research. One Honors College I recently visited only offered a total of six honors courses for a student to take in four years. You'll want to see how many honors courses are available to take per year, and what these courses are. Are they appealing to you? Really study the academic opportunities. You'll also want to make sure students feel they fit in the entire school.

I recommend talking to Honors College students that the admission office did not assign to you. Sit in on classes, and see if an overnight visit is possible. You also need to make sure you fit into the culture of the entire college. If the Honors College has 200 students and the college has 20,000, 99 percent of students are not in the HC; would you be better off at a smaller private school where the entire school is like the Honors College? These are decisions that you must make.

There are Honors Colleges at private schools like Howard, Tulane, George Washington, and American, but they are much more prevalent at large public schools.

There are some entire colleges that are Honors Colleges like St. Mary's for Maryland and the New College for Florida. There are some well-established Honors Colleges, like Schreyer at Penn State and Barrett at Arizona State, but there are also dozens of lesser-known but equally as impressive choices. I want to encourage you to visit the website http://publicuniversityhonors.com/ and check out the book *A Review of Fifty Public University Honors Programs* if you want to research these opportunities.

Sometimes you will see that a school offers an Honors Program and not an Honors College. Sometimes this difference is significant, and sometimes it is semantics. In general, Honors Colleges have a college dean assigned to them, and they offer more campus-wide resources and opportunities.

Marge had a really tough decision to make, and I felt for her. She had gotten into her top choice, which was John Hopkins University, and she was so excited about it. Marge was a top student. She had an A-average with an extremely rigorous curriculum; she attended a highly-respected private school; and she had scored 1480 on her SAT. There was one problem, though. John Hopkins was going to cost her family $40,000 more per year than Penn State's Schreyer Honors College. Her family income was above average, but not enough so that they could absorb a $160,000 hit over four years without a significant burden on the family. They also had to think about her sister, who was two years younger. Marge chose Schreyer, and once she made her decision, she embraced it and never looked back. Marge and her parents had made a financially-sound decision for their family.

Vince wanted to get in Valdosta State's Honors College and he wanted it badly, but his test scores and GPA weren't high enough. When he got to VSU, he emailed the Honors College dean, Mike Savoie, asking what he needed to do to get in. After posting a 4.0, Vince was admitted, and he has a 4.0 still as a rising senior. He has emerged as powerful leader on campus and VSU has even flown him around the country to represent them at VIP events. He has also earned several department scholarships. Vince understood that even though he was originally denied admittance, he could still get in by excelling once he got to college.

85

WHAT CAN I DO NOW TO SET UP OPPORTUNITIES FOR MY CHILD IF HE/SHE IS 12 OR UNDER?

In a way, you could say that the process begins at birth. Parents are encouraged to start college savings plans right away, to read to their kids frequently, and to encourage a wide range of different types reading once children can read on their own. Parents should select the best schools they can find for their children and expose them to a wide range of activities that develop critical thinking skills. Parents should allow their children to be exposed to a wide range of extracurricular opportunities. There should be exposure to as many different cultures as possible, to broaden their horizons. If you can afford to travel, this is a great education.

Parents should also be looking for the best summer enrichment opportunities within their budget, and should be looking for those areas where their child is gifted and passionate so that these can be cultivated. Is important that a student still lives a balanced life. Families have to work within the constraints of their own budgets and their other work and family obligations.

I want to recommend a great book to help with this. The book is called *Love That Boy: What Two Presidents, Eight Road Trips, and My Son Taught Me About Parent Expectations* by Ron Fournier.

Instead of saying parents should start college savings plans right away, I'd like to add that parents should become very knowledgeable about 529 plans. I recommend going to savingforcollege.com and studying the different state plans to select the one that is best for your family, and then start putting money away; the earlier, the better.

I also recommend parents read the book *The Childhood Roots of Adult Happiness* by Dr. Hallowell.

- א Watch how your child plays, listen to what they love, and then tailor your enrichment to their interests.
- א Be honest with yourself about whether you are vicariously living through your child in an unhealthy way.
- א Educate yourself on the college process.
- א Understand your child's unique learning style.
- א I said exposure to different cultures above, but let's be more explicit. Kids should be exposed to different races, ethnicities, international students, and kids of all incomes and religions.
- א I'm a huge believer in summer residential experiences.
- א Give your kids plenty of household chores so they can learn responsibility and learn not to expect everything to be handed to them.
- א Give your kids opportunities for paid jobs at a younger age, so they learn responsibility and the value of money.
- א Get actively involved in your child's school. Meet regularly with your child's teachers and constantly ask your child's teachers what your child's strengths and areas for growth are. Listen to what they say, and don't be defensive.

- ℵ Expose your child to outstanding role models for them to emulate.
- ℵ Start getting your child in volunteering in an area of interest to them. This will teach them to be a giver and not a self-centered taker. They will experience the joy of service. Secondarily, it is going to really help their outside scholarship applications.
- ℵ Parents should accept their child for who they are and love them unconditionally.

> One of the best things my parents did for me growing up was to send me to sleep away camps every summer. I attended these camps from ages seven to 17, and in some summers, I attended multiple camps for up to six weeks of my summer. I know this may not be affordable, but if it is, what it did for me was it provided exposure to kids of all races, cultures, personalities, incomes, and it broadened my horizons. It also taught me independence and responsibility. You have to do enrichment within your budget, but exposure to kids who are different from your kid will benefit them for the rest of their life.

86

WHEN SHOULD I START THE COLLEGE ADMISSION PROCESS?

As far as the formal process is concerned, it starts out really light and builds up. In middle school, you want to map out a curriculum if you are at a school that offers choices. If your child can handle advanced math, they should be encouraged to take that or any honors classes that they can excel in while still having balance in their lives. Continue to expose them to a wide range of extracurricular activities to see where their passions and gifts lie. If they are open to applying to some private scholarships, have them apply to a few each year in middle school; there are quite a few scholarships for college for middle school students. If they are receptive to college visits in middle school, take a drive to a few different campuses when you are already in the area to inspire them to the kind of opportunities that are there for them if they do well in high school. It would be a good idea to take a PSAT 8/9 or a PreACT by ninth grade to see how they are as test takers. Do they have any gaps, and do they need any subject tutoring?

Between the summer of eighth and ninth grade, you'll definitely want to map out a four-year curriculum plan that will consist of at least four years of math, English, and science, and most likely, four years of a foreign language. You should decide whether your child will take any summer school. If they like math, you may want them to take a for-credit math course at a school that your high school will accept credits from. This can be the difference between getting to Calculus AB or even Calculus BC. If they are a language person, this can be a great opportunity to enhance their foreign language proficiency. Don't push it if your child detests this. You have to know your child.

Summers are great opportunities for your child to develop their athletic or artistic passions and gifts. Use your summers very wisely, and play to your child's gifts and interests and their need to explore cultures outside of their own in order to be a better-rounded person and develop their cross-cultural critical thinking skills.

There is no need to start full-blown college counseling in the ninth grade or even the fall of tenth grade, but every effort should be made for your student to take the most rigorous classes in which they can excel academically while maintaining a healthy balance between their mind, body, social, and spiritual development so as to be a well-rounded person. For students that are really curious and really want to get ahead, I am okay with them starting the fall of tenth, but it absolutely has to come from the student and not the parent.

If you have a child that is intellectually curious, they can visit a wide range of campuses in ninth and tenth just to get a sense of the kind of college they are looking for. Listen to your child; you may go on formal tours and info sessions, or you may just do campus drive-arounds where you casually talk to students.

Students should explore all of the online college courses available at colleges they are interested in or by using the Guide to Online colleges. Taking online courses is a great way to take courses that are of interest to them while simultaneously showcasing interests and their ability to handle rigor to the colleges that they will eventually apply to.

I believe the full process should start between April of tenth grade and July after tenth grade. Most high schools start their process too late, if they have a formal process at all. If your child is going to apply early action, early decision, or file a priority application, this may be due as early as late September of their senior year. If you start in April, you have 17 months, and if you start in July, you have 14 months to solidify your student's college list, research schools, visit colleges, complete quality applications and essays, get test scores, and build relationships with admissions officers at various colleges.

Test prep should start in the summer between tenth and eleventh grade, or in the fall of eleventh grade at the latest. If going into senior year, your student's list is built, their applications are completed, and their test scores are behind them, they will enjoy that year with much less stress on their plate. If your student is are a poor test taker, he or she may want to start 12 months earlier.

I had placed Heather at a Northeast boarding school in the eighth grade. Three weeks later, Heather's mom was calling me to start the college process. I had to tell her, "Let's pump the brakes a little here." I said, "I will do one session of curriculum planning and school orientation and we can do one or two sessions at the end of ninth grade, but we are two years away from starting full-blown college counseling. Our kids are under a lot of pressure, and at some point we need to let them get off the treadmill, smell the roses, and live in the moment."

Phillip was a student who came up to me and said, "Those who told me the eleventh grade was going to be the hardest year in high school lied to me. The twelfth grade is by far the most stressful, because trying to manage the college process is like having two more major classes." Phillip started the college process too late. This is why I recommend starting in the spring of tenth or the summer between tenth and eleventh. The senior year is so much more relaxing and enjoyable when the college process is already well underway, and the "hard stuff" is finished.

87

HOW DOES THE ADMISSIONS COMMITTEE MAKE DECISIONS?

That is a complicated question, and there are a lot of models out there. When I worked in boarding school admissions, I was given the task of revamping our admissions decision-making process, so I studied seven college models and we ended up using one that worked for us. We had sub-committees that were comprised of admission officers and faculty members, with an admissions rep who was responsible for that geographic territory present on the committee.

We used a 1-9 rating system for academics, character, and extracurricular impact. We spent anywhere from 15-30 minutes reading a file on our own time, and then we would discuss a file for anywhere from 90 seconds to 10 minutes. Clear acceptances and clear denials occurred when everyone on the committee agreed; these were the 90-second decisions and if we reached consensus, our decision was final. If we did not agree, we would refer a file to a big committee meeting where a number of sub-committees would read the file and discuss the applicant. We could have nine to eleven readers read the file for these difficult decisions.

I served as a chair of one of our sub-committees for five years and it was one of the best experiences of my career. I really got to see how people look for people like themselves. We had to intentionally make sure that we had committee members from different races, cultures, socio-economic statuses, and interests. We all had our biases, and we would have to check each other to make sure our biases didn't impact who we were admitting. The committee members who aced standardized testing wanted high scores. The college athletes wanted athletes, and the artists wanted artists.

Interviewing comes naturally to me, and I could be really harsh on students who had poor interview scores. The one difference between our model and what most colleges use is that we had three readers on every file where the college model is usually two readers per file and you usually only see three for certain applicants, i.e. alumni kids.

There are so many different rating systems out there that I can't list them all, and candidly, I don't know all of them. At some colleges, everyone goes to committee. At other colleges, no one goes to committee. At some colleges, the territorial manager (regional rep) has the most weight because they know the schools and possibly have interacted with the applicant. At many schools, the dean of admissions or the VP of enrollment makes the call. At many schools, the committee members vote and the majority prevails. Some schools require a number of "accept votes" that is above the majority and less than consensus, i.e. two-thirds or three-quarters. At other colleges, the committee reaches consensus as opposed to voting.

At some colleges, there is an extra reader who is an admissions staffer but *not* the regional rep, who serves as the first reader. Some colleges hire readers who exclusively read files, but they don't travel, attend fairs, recruit students, or manage a territory. At some schools, the territorial manager/regional representative presents the applicant to the admissions committee, and at other schools a senior member of the staff is in this role as the initiator.

I recently listened to four seasoned admission officers who were on a panel. They were discussing which part of the application they read first.

All four of them started with something different. One started with the academic information. Another started with the family info. A third veteran just read the Common App in order. A fourth member liked to go to the School Profile first. Other admission reps like to read the essays first.

There is a new method that is being used to read admission files that has me very excited. I first learned of this after hearing Yvonne Romero DaSilva, Vice Dean and Director of Admissions at UPenn, describe what is known as Committee-Based Evaluation (CBE). UPenn and DaSilva are the pioneers of CBE, but it is getting rave reviews. Instead of relying on the territory manager to be the primary expert to the rest of the committee, with CBE there are two first readers; one reads to focus on the academic evaluation and the other reader focuses on the non-academic evaluation. This is only possible because readers are now reading online instead of having physical folders like I had to read when I did admissions.

Yesterday, I had a meeting with Sam Rosenbaum of Amherst, and he expressed his enthusiasm for CBE, helping me to understand three major advantages to CBE:

1. With two readers, there is less bias and less reliance on the territory manager.
2. For clear denials, the two readers can reach this conclusion quicker and this allows them to spend much more time at committee discussing the applicants that are truly under consideration.
3. Admission offices can handle the growing surge of applications without having to hire a lot more staff.
4. According to Rosenbaum, UPenn and Swarthmore have been leaders in the rollout of CBE, but a number of highly selective colleges are using it and everyone he talks to is finding it to be very helpful.
5. I met with the talented admissions counselor Jade Sims of Georgia Tech last week and she expressed her enthusiasm about the fact that Georgia Tech is going to be using CBE this year and she can't wait to read files with this new innovative approach.
6. A huge problem for AOs is the lack of work-life balance during reading season. Reading season are the months AOs spend long

hours reading applications. AOs are often under great pressure to keep up a very challenging schedule to read, review, and rate applicants. One of the benefits of CBE is that AOs can work from 8:00 a.m. to 5:00 p.m. instead of working 12-hour days.

7. Having said that, CBE is not for everyone. I have talked to admissions counselors who claim it was taking them too long to read a file. Others say that they have too many other responsibilities and juggling CBE meetings didn't work for their office. Some I have spoken to say that they already were checking biases with multiple readers and others say that so little time is being spent on a file that students are not getting the full and fair read they deserve. You can see that when it comes to admissions committees, there are so many different approaches.

I was talking to an admissions officer from a large state school about her role in decisions and she said, "I am just a PR person; I travel, I recruit, but I don't read files. We have the number crunchers in the back who make those decisions." It just shows how many different models are out there.

88

DO COLLEGES EVALUATE THE HIGH SCHOOL I ATTENDED?

Absolutely, they do! Some colleges have "experience ratings" that track the success of how graduates from your high school have done at their colleges, and they factor this into their admission decisions. Many more colleges read all of the applications from the same high school in the same school grouping, so they can figure out the context and see trends like grade inflation, an unusually hard-grading teacher, etc.

The overwhelming majority of high schools have official School Profiles, aka college profiles, that they submit along with each transcript to every college that a student from their high school applies to. With around 40,000 high schools across the country, many selective high schools rely on this profile to learn about how your high school is different from the other high schools they are receiving applications from, but they also use it to assess how well you are prepared for the rigors of their program. They use it to help them to interpret your transcript in the context of your high school.

All of these School Profiles are very different, but some of the things that colleges find valuable on a profile are:

- School mission statement.
- What percentage of students are going to four-year colleges?
- What is the size of your graduating class?
- How many AP or IB courses, or dual enrollment courses, does your school offer, and in which subjects are they offered?
- What are the average SAT, SAT Subject Test, ACT, AP, or IB scores for your school or for your specific class?
- What is the racial, ethnic, and socio-economic (free and reduced lunch numbers or Pell Grant recipients) make-up of the school?
- What is your grading scale? They cannot assume that a 90 is an A and an 80 is a B, etc., because there are dozens of different grading scales.
- Is there a grade distribution? This is extremely helpful because it lets a college know how many students got a particular grade in a specific course
- Does your school have any distinguishing curriculum features like "winterims" or block scheduling, etc.?
- A five-year record of which colleges students from your high school were admitted to and where they matriculated is of great value to a college that practices holistic admissions. Keep in mind that large numbers of schools do their admissions by the numbers, and for those schools, this assessment of your high school will not occur.
- Test scores and/or colleges by quartile or quintile.
- Number of students receiving special awards.

I was talking with Caroline, the Director of Admissions at the Paidea school in Atlanta. I asked her how she'd ended up at Paidea. Caroline said, "For five years in a row when I was in admissions at Harvard and I visited Atlanta, the Paidea kids were so interesting and they asked me the most thought-provoking questions. When an opening occurred, I said to myself, I want to work at that school." It is awfully naïve to think that colleges don't notice differences between schools–they do, and it matters.

89

WHAT IS THE DIFFERENCE BETWEEN ADVANCED PLACEMENT (AP) COURSES AND THE INTERNATIONAL BACCALAUREATE (IB) DIPLOMA?

I am often asked how Advanced Placement (AP) and International Baccalaureate (IB) classes are different, and which curriculum colleges value more. The similarities are as follows:

- Both programs offer advanced, college-level rigorous work for the most able students in the student body.
- Both programs have year-end exams that are respected by the colleges. Colleges generally feel that a strong score, usually 4/5 on an AP or 6/7 on an IB, is a positive reflection of the student's

ability to handle higher-level college work. Note that some colleges feel this way about a 3 on an AP exam or a 5 on an IB exam, and in many instances, this variation depends more on the actual course the score was in rather than the specific college to which you are applying.

There are quite a few differences between the programs, including:

- AP is an American-based program that was founded in 1955 with American students and American universities in mind.
- IB was founded in 1968 in Switzerland with the entire world in mind, and with an intentional focus on international-mindedness.
- The AP was designed to be an a-la-carte program that allows a student to showcase their rigor in whatever subject matter they feel they can excel in.
- While most IB programs allow students to take the occasional IB course, the heart of the IB is the IB diploma program, which is an interdisciplinary program that demands rigor in language and literature, individuals and societies, language acquisition, science, math, and the arts.
- There are no required courses for a student to be an AP student, but in order to be an IB diploma candidate, students must take a philosophy course called the Theory of Knowledge (TOK). They must write an extended 4000-word essay (EE) that is a serious research paper, and they must engage in a Creativity Activity and Service (CAS) 150-hour project.
- The IB is a more writing-intensive program.
- The IB demands more critical thinking in its curriculum.
- The AP only has one level, but IB has two levels: higher level courses and standard level courses.
- IB exams cost more to take, and they have required registration fees.
- AP courses cover more content, but IB goes into more depth in the content they cover.
- AP courses are college-level courses for high school students, but IB covers ages 3-19; they have a Primary Years Programme,

a Middle Years Programme, the Diploma Programme for high school, and a Career-Related Programme.

- א AP courses are offered at almost 15,000 United States high schools. While IB is growing, it is currently offered at less than 1000 high schools.

There are not enough high schools offering the IB for colleges to penalize students for not taking the IB diploma. Colleges will evaluate your rigor in light of your options, but most selective colleges love the IB diploma. In my opinion, it is a superior option to the AP if you are a student who is capable of handling that level of academic rigor and an IB program is available to you. However, if you have some subjects in which you are not particularly strong, the flexibility of the AP may make this a better way to showcase your strengths.

You have to decide if you are looking at this from the admissions angle, or the quality of education perspective. The reality is that students don't get to choose their curriculum, and colleges know this and won't hold that against them. When I was at Westtown, we dropped all our APs and designed our own advanced courses that had more depth and creativity, and the colleges we consulted with loved this and it didn't hurt our college acceptances.

Brenda and her husband did not feel they could afford a private middle school for their daughter, Ginger, but when we met, they said they were willing to sell their home and move into the area with the best public school they could find. I recommended a school district that had a very good IB Middle Years Programme and that fed students into a high school that offered the IB Diploma Programme. This was a great way to showcase Ginger's abilities in a way her family could afford.

90

DO THE COLLEGES I APPLY TO KNOW WHERE ELSE I APPLIED?

Not unless you, your counselor, or your parents tell them. When a college signs an agreement with the National Student Clearinghouse, they receive a report telling them where every applicant who applied for financial aid eventually enrolled, but this is well after admission decisions are made. The Clearinghouse Report allows them to see which colleges enrolled the students they admitted, so it is very helpful for them, but the report does not let them see where applicants who did not request financial aid enrolled.

Colleges do use surveys for new enrollees to find out where else they were admitted. Most admission counselors I have talked to feel very confident that they are getting accurate data, but you control what you share and when you share it. It is considered an ethical breach for a college to ask you in an interview on their application or through casual chitchat, "Where else are you applying?"

One of the myths that I hear occasionally is that the Common App lets colleges know where else students are applying, but this is not true.

Some of you may be thinking, "This isn't true. Colleges can not only see where else you applied via the FAFSA, but they can see the order that you listed the schools on the FAFSA, and they can use this information to impact their aid awards." This was correct in 2015 and before then, but as of 2016, colleges can no longer see who else receives your FAFSA.

Raymond was perplexed when a letter arrived in the mail from Williams College and he had been denied. He had been the number one ranked student at his large public school for ninth and tenth grade before he transferred to Westtown School for eleventh grade. I was counseling Ray through the situation when he asked me, "Do you think me not getting in might have had something to do with a casual conversation I had with the Williams rep where I told him that I really like Williams, and the only school I like more is Dartmouth?"

Ray was very smart, but that was a very dumb move. No one wants to be anyone's backup school.

91

Why is there so much buzz about the new Coalition College Application?

The Common App has dominated college applications, with more than 700 schools accepting the Common App. There have been competitors, like the Black Common App, the Cappex App, the College Greenlight App, the UC (University of California) App, the QuestBridge App, and the Universal App, but none have really enrolled the colleges the Coalition has. Out of nowhere, the Coalition emerged with around 100 colleges signing up, and what really has eyebrows raised is that they have convinced the most prestigious schools in the country to join them. The Coalition is being polite and diplomatic, but they are taking on the almighty Common App.

Why was the Coalition founded? The full name is the Coalition for Access and Affordability (http://coalitionforcollegeaccess.org) and every word in there is meaningful. They believe the process of higher education is supposed to provide quality education for all, but that lower income and under-resourced students are falling behind and not enough is being done to provide access to knowledge about the college process, an affordable application process, affordable college options, and college options that lead to graduation and opportunities.

How are they attempting to address this? By forming an organization that only lets colleges in who meet full demonstrated financial need and have a track record of being committed to recruiting and enrolling under-resourced students and providing support so that they graduate. They implicitly put pressure on other colleges and politicians to make these same commitments. The Coalition aims to make fee waivers for college apps easier to obtain, to simplify the application process, and to partner with community-based organizations (CBOs) that help under-resourced students. The Coalition also provides a tool called the Locker, where kids can save things like awards, essays, class projects, art, and videos in private online storage beginning in ninth grade. This is based on research that if under-resourced students start planning for college earlier, they will not fall through the cracks.

If the Coalition is going to make further inroads, it is going to have to improve its communication and its user friendliness. According to a 2016 Inside Higher Ed survey, only 8 percent of admissions directors agree or strongly agree that the Coalition has done a good job of explaining its process to colleges and their applicants, compared to 68 percent who disagree or strongly disagree. Last week I talked to an admissions rep at a school that uses the Coalition and he said, “I sure hope they have made it more user friendly for us to read applications this year.”

No one I have talked to is questioning the motives behind the Coalition. The confusion and the disappointment have come from the execution, but people are giving them a mulligan for year one. I expect them to make strides and get it together. Only time will tell if they get hot and really cut into the Common App’s market share.

I personally think the Coalition is here to stay, and I think it is going to really take off. The application is very sensitive to the needs of low- and moderate-income families and I have seen over and over how there are always kinks when something is new in admissions, but they usually get the kinks worked out. I was talking to a senior admissions rep at the University of Florida last week and she raved about the Coalition and said that their rollout could not have been smoother. She also talked about how many more low and moderate applications they had gotten last year and she credited the Coalition for that. UF exclusively accepts the Coalition and she felt that was a great decision on their part.

Two days ago I was working on the Coalition with Nick Brown, one of the students I am coaching. Nick was going to complete UGA's online app but he liked the Coalition application so much more. The Coalition's approach to the personal statement is something students like. Their main essay is shorter and they give the student tremendous flexibility in their choice of a topic. Students also like the fact that there is more flexibility with the word length of the personal statement than the Common App allows. I can see the Coalition vs. Common App battle resembling the SAT vs. ACT battle over the next decade for those schools that take the Coalition.

The other day, I met with a client named James, and his mom. They had just returned from visiting a bunch of schools on the West Coast. James's mom spoke up and said, "When we went to Stanford they would talk about the Coalition, and then we went to Cal-Berkeley and parents asked about the Coalition, and then we went to Cal-Tech and we heard about the Coalition again. What's up with this Coalition?"

Many parents and students may still be unfamiliar with the Coalition, but it's creating a buzz that will continue attracting attention.

92

WHAT'S THE SECRET ABOUT COLLEGE ADMISSIONS THAT THE MEDIA ISN'T TELLING ME?

We are always hearing the hype about how hard college is to get into. We hear about how UCLA received almost 120,000 applications for their class of 2021. We hear about how Stanford and Harvard are accepting 5 percent of their applicants and how Yale, Columbia, Princeton, and the University of Chicago are right on their heels. We hear about how UPenn accepted 41 percent of their applicants in 1990, but now they are only taking 10 percent, and parents and students are freaking out.

These schools have gotten much more selective for the following reasons:

1. There are more high-school-age kids now.

2. More kids are applying to college and enrolling in college than 30 years ago.
3. Applying is easier through the Common Application.
4. It's easy to apply online in general; four-year schools received an average of 94 percent of their applications online in the fall of 2013, up from 49 percent in 2005, according to NACAC.
5. International applications had been on the rise until the 2016 election.
6. The college rankings industry has grown in the last 35 years, putting a fixation on prestige.
7. The college's own marketing often purports how selective they are because they know that families value this.

There are 100 colleges that admit one-third or fewer of their applicants, and they gobble up more than 95 percent of the publicity about college selectivity. These stories are sexy and they generate buzz, sell magazines and newspapers, and generate clicks on websites.

What the media is not telling you is that there are more than 3000 degree-granting four-year colleges in the United States, and only about 200 of them are selective. This is about one out of every 15 four-year schools that are selective. Let me put this in real-estate terms: the media makes you think that the college admissions process is a sellers' market, but in reality it is a buyers' market. According to NACAC research, the average college accepts two-thirds of its applicants.

It is true that for 7 percent, college has gotten harder to get into, and about 100 colleges are only admitting anywhere from 1 in 20 to one out of every three applicants, but that is only 3.5 percent of all of the four-year schools that take one in three. There are far more colleges and universities that accept 80 percent of their applicants than there are colleges that take less than one in three applicants.

A lot of colleges are really, really struggling just to have enough students to pay their bills and keep from closing. I encourage you to Google a June 29, 2017, *Business Week* article titled, "College Enrollment Has Plummeted, and Private Universities are Scrambling."

In September 2017, Inside Higher Ed revealed survey results that came from the answers of 453 admissions directors or officials with equivalent titles. What did the survey reveal? "Only 34 percent of colleges met new student enrollment targets this year by May 1, the traditional date by which most institutions hope to have a class set."

That is a key finding of the *2017 Survey of College and University Admissions Directors,* released today by Inside Higher Ed, in collaboration with Gallup.

The 34 percent figure is down from 37 percent a year ago and 42 percent two years ago. These numbers depict a different story than the media narrative about how hard it is to get into college these days.

When I sat down to meet with Pat and her son Chris, Pat was concerned. Pat said to me, "Chris is a good kid, but he is a B student; he has to step up his game because the way things are going these days, there aren't any schools that he is going to be eligible for."

I corrected her immediately and told her how she can't believe the media hype about how hard college is to get into. The most selective schools are much harder to get into, but I told her the average school accepts two out of every three students who apply.

93

HOW DO I KEEP FROM GOING CRAZY FROM THE COLLEGE ADMISSIONS PROCESS?

In writing this book, I faced a real dilemma.

On the one hand, I wanted to answer a lot of the questions that students and parents frequently ask me about the college process. A lot of those questions revolve around how to get in or how to get your child in. I wanted to answer those questions, because these questions were stressing out families and I wanted to relieve some of the stress from the college process.

On the other hand, what I did not want to do is imply in the slightest of ways that where you go defines who you are. I have attempted to address that dilemma in a few ways. I have emphasized the importance of character throughout the book. I have rallied against the college ranking guides that say with precision that X school is ranked number four in the country. I have also used a definition for success that does not involve fame, fortune, or prestige, but is based on making a difference in the lives of others by doing what you are gifted and passionate about, an approach where we all can be winners without being the valedictorians.

However, my biggest fear for this book is that this alone is inadequate and that I have just contributed more to all of the noise that makes kids feel as if they need to go to a highly selective college to be considered winners and to have futures that are full of opportunity. That is a bunch of malarkey! I am trying to turn down the temperature, not ratchet it up.

I have an idea, and I am convinced that if you will take my advice it will abrogate my concern. After you complete this book, please, and I implore you, I beseech you as vociferously as I know how: purchase, read, and imbibe Frank Bruni's bestselling book, *Where You Go Is Not Who You'll Be: An Antidote to the College Admissions Mania*. In my opinion, this is the most profound and most desperately needed book that has been written about college admissions in my lifetime. You can get it for $10 on Amazon, as of my last check. It complements this book like a hand in a glove.

When I am asked to speak to a group of middle school students or high school students, I almost always have them engage in a chant. I start by saying, "Students, it is not where you go, it is what you do when you get there." Pretty soon they get it and when I say, "It is not where you go ..." I pause, and they complete it by saying "... it is what you do when you get there."

After we collectively repeat this three or four times, I can see their faces light up. I can see them thinking, "You mean I can be a winner too?" The truth is that it is not only what you do when you get to college that matters, but what you do when you get there and when you get *out* of there that will matter one thousand times more than where you go to college. If you forget everything you have read in this book, I hope you will remember this.

SECTION 4

PAYING FOR COLLEGE WITHOUT GOING BROKE

94

WHAT IS COST OF ATTENDANCE, AND WHY IS IT IMPORTANT?

Cost of attendance (COA) is the total projected cost for all expenses that a student will incur if they attend a particular college. In reality, there are multiple costs of attendance that will vary based on factors such as whether the student lives on or off campus, whether the student is from out of state, and more.

COA is important because a family needs to know all of the costs when they are deciding which college to attend. It is also important because federal, state, and college aid cannot exceed the total cost of attendance, so this figure becomes the starting point for financial calculations.

It is important that you divide COA into two categories: direct costs and indirect costs. Direct costs are costs you pay directly to the college. There are four expenses that comprise direct costs: tuition, fees, room, and board (for on-campus students), and there are three indirect costs: transportation, books and supplies, and spending money. Sometimes these two categories are called billable and non-billable costs. In some instances, students are required to pay for medical insurance. This would be paid right to the school, so it would be considered a billable or direct cost that would be classified under the student fee category.

It is important when you look at projected COA that you note what the school is listing as their COA, but what is extremely important is that you create your own customized COA to get your true costs. The COA figures are based on averages but every situation is unique. Let's look at the four direct costs:

1. Tuition will vary based on how many credit hours you take
2. Room will not only vary based on if you live on campus, but also whether you are in a single, suite style, or traditional-style dorm because usually the costs of dorms will vary
3. Board (meals) will vary based on which meal plan you select; and
4. Fees will vary as well. Some colleges will have set fees for things like use of the Wellness Center or technology, but other fees like an art or chemistry class you may or may not take often charge fees for materials and studio or lab use.

For the three indirect fees:

1. Books will vary significantly based on where you get them, what classes you are taking, and whether you rent textbooks or buy new or pre-owned
2. Transportation from halfway around the world will differ drastically from someone who stays close to home
3. Spending money: a five-star restaurant vs. ramen noodles is not the same, nor is shopping at Neiman Marcus vs. Goodwill.

I use the term *spending money* as a catch-all category for all other expenses. Sometimes it is a small expense, like a movie or pizza, but spending money could be a computer or childcare expenses for students that have children while they are in college.

You can get COA information on each website, but each school lists it differently, and it can be confusing. I recommend using bigfuture.org to do a search for the college and clicking the "Paying" tab. This is the College Board's website, and they list current figures in the same format for all colleges.

Another great source for this information is the Department of Education's College scorecard: https://collegescorecard.ed.gov/.

My oldest daughter Karis is a senior at Davidson College. Davidson has a charge of over $2100 per semester for health care for a student who is not covered on their parents' plan. My Blue Cross plan covers Karis, but Karis's classmates who aren't on their parents' plans are out over $4200 for both semesters. This just shows how COA can vary so much from one student to the next.

I was talking to Mr. and Mrs. Thompson and their son Peter two days ago about COA. Peter is a client from Philadelphia. He wants a gorgeous campus in a more liberal community, and one school of interest for him is the University of Colorado at Boulder. I was explaining COA to Peter's family, and I had to point out that while the college is listing $936 for transportation expenses, there is no way that figure is accurate for their family. I said to Mr. Thompson, "If you and Mrs. Thompson each fly out twice a year and Peter flies there four times, that is eight airline tickets, so you are probably looking at closer to $3400, so you should add $2500 to the COA figures that are published."

95

WHAT ARE THE FIVE MAIN REASONS WHY COLLEGE COSTS ARE SKYROCKETING?

According to ttlearning.com, "Between 2003 and 2013, the overall consumer price index in the United States went up by 26.7 percent, but the price index for college tuition went up by 79. percent—far more than even the notoriously inefficient health care system, which saw a price index increase of 43.1 percent."

There is great debate in Higher Ed circles about why this is happening. Almost everyone agrees that the five factors I am revealing are contributors, but the variance is over which of these factors are the *biggest* contributors.

א **The "facilities arms race":** Any parent who graduated from college and is now taking their child on college tours sees the money that is being spent on extravagant facilities that would not even have been imaginable when they went to college. For example, the University of Colorado is spending 143 million on athletic upgrades. I asked Scott Jaschik, founder of Inside Higher Ed, how big of a factor the facilities arms race is to the cost of college. Jaschik said the athletic facilities arms race is a definite contributor, and it is something of a sacred cow, but he said some of the other posh facilities you see like lazy rivers are paid for by adding surcharges to those students who elect to use them and therefore are not a significant factor in the rise of college costs.

Colleges are caught up in an extravagant arms race with their competitors for dorms, dining halls, recreation centers, athletic facilities, etc. From a January 5, 2016, article by ThinkTank Learning: "The college campus arms race is a sort of higher-education version of 'keeping up with the Joneses,' where colleges find themselves forced to spend more and more on shiny new facilities and amenities just to stay in step with their competitors."

- א **Administrative bloat:** In an October 2011 *Washington Monthly* article titled, "Administrators Ate My Tuition," Benjamin Ginsberg makes the case that the blame largely lies on the excessive expansion of more administrative jobs on campus. According to *Bloomberg*, colleges added administrative positions at ten times the rate they added tenured faculty jobs between 1993 and 2009. From 1993 to 2007, they increased spending on administration at more than double the rate they increased research funding.
- א **Health-care hikes:** On average, 75 percent of an expense a college incurs are faculty and administrators' salaries and benefits, and health care has been a huge part of that for several decades.
- א **Increased access to student loans:** Lucca, Nadauld, and Shen studied student loans for over a decade, and they found that loans grew from 53 billion to 120 billion from 2001 to 2012. That same January 5 ThinkTank Learning article states, "It seems clear that giving schools access to a bottomless cookie jar of federal student lending enables the cycle of rising tuition costs and rising debt."

- ℵ **Decreased support from federal and state governments:** Shortly after Eric Greitens became the Governor of Missouri in January 2017, he cut 68 million dollars from the colleges and universities in Missouri, and the worst part is that he plans on cutting more money from colleges and universities next year. From an outstanding Demos article titled, "Pulling Up the Higher-Ed Ladder: Myth and Reality in the Crisis of College Affordability":

  > We find that declining state appropriations for higher education is indeed the primary driver of rising tuition, responsible for 79 percent of tuition hikes at public research universities between 2001 and 2011 and 78 percent of tuition hikes at public master's and bachelor's universities over the same decade.

State and Federal government took great pride in the past about supporting educational initiatives like the GI Bill, but now education is labeled as "big government" that needs a severe trimming.

My roommate during grad school was named Troy. Troy shared with me on several occasions how he was really enjoying his undergraduate experience in college in Cleveland Ohio as an engineering student at Cleveland State, and then cutbacks came in his Federal Aid in the 1980s out of nowhere, causing him to have to drop out and work part time for a few years before he could save enough to re-enroll and graduate. My wife Anitra had almost an identical experience in the same year in Detroit.

96

WHO IS ELIGIBLE FOR FEDERAL FINANCIAL AID (GRANTS OR LOANS)?

This is the largest source of all available money (40 percent of all money or over 120 billion dollars). Here are several factors and tips that can affect your eligibility.

- Have a high school diploma, GED, or completion of a state-approved homeschool program.
- Be enrolled at or accepted at an eligible degree or certificate program.
- Males must register with the Selective Service between the ages of 18-25.
- Have a valid social security number (there are very few exceptions for students born in some unique countries).

- ℵ Complete the FAFSA for every year you need or would like to be considered for federal aid.
- ℵ Agree on the FAFSA that you are not in default on any federal student loan.
- ℵ Agree on the FAFSA that you do not owe a refund on federal grant.
- ℵ Agree on the FAFSA that any federal aid you receive will only be used for your education.
- ℵ Satisfactory Academic Progress (SAP) standards ensure that you are successfully completing your coursework and can continue to receive financial aid. All students receiving any federal money are required to meet SAP standards. Federal regulations mandate that the university establishes, publishes, and applies standards to monitor your progress toward completing your degree program. If you fail to meet the SAP standards, you will be placed on financial aid warning or suspension.
- ℵ Be a United States citizen, national, or permanent resident (very few exceptions).
- ℵ You must have a financial need.
- ℵ If you are incarcerated, you cannot receive a Pell Grant or any federal loan, and while technically you are still eligible for FSEOG and Federal Work-Study, it is highly unlikely you will receive this either.
- ℵ Even if you are no longer incarcerated, there are certain drug-related offenses and sexual offenses that will severely limit your ability to receive federal aid.
- ℵ High school graduates missed out on as much as $2.7 billion in free federal grant money in the past academic year, according to a January 27, 2016, article from *NerdWallet.* This money went unclaimed mainly because of incomplete or unsubmitted FAFSA forms. From the article:

> Our analysis shows that in 2014, a total of 1,445,732 high school graduates didn't fill out a FAFSA application. Of those, we believe 747,579 of them would have been Pell eligible: Submitting the FAFSA could have earned them federal Pell Grant money. The average amount of money left

on the table per eligible high school graduate who didn't apply was $1,861. The two places with the most unclaimed funds were Mississippi at $2,639 per grad and Washington, D.C., at $2,513. High school graduates also left on the table an average of $2,000 or more in Pell Grant money per grad in Alabama, Arizona, Arkansas, California, Florida, Idaho, Kentucky, New Mexico, New York, North Carolina, Tennessee, and Texas.

Those of us in education are really moved by students who do all of the right things and are so deserving. Yocelin was one of those students. When a local private school had a fire, the community service club that she started raised money to help a fellow school, but when it came time for college, Yocelin wasn't a citizen and she wasn't a permanent resident, and she wasn't eligible for financial aid. It was really disappointing to see that someone so deserving couldn't benefit from financial aid.

97

WHAT IS EFC, AND WHY IS IT SO IMPORTANT?

In order to fully understand EFC, I recommend you read the preceding chapter on Cost of Attendance (COA) first.

EFC is an acronym that stands for Expected Family Contribution. It is the amount of money that the Federal Government's formula or Individual College's formula (for colleges that use the CSS PROFILE) expects a family should be able to annually contribute for college expenses. It is based on need. The EFC will not vary based on how expensive a college is. The EFC *may* vary from one sibling to the next, based on that sibling's assets and income.

There are over 4500 degree-granting two- and four-year not-for-profit colleges in the United States, and they require that the FAFSA to be completed if a student is going to be eligible for federal financial aid.

The United States Department of Education oversees the FAFSA, and when a FAFSA is completed, a student receives their EFC based on what is known as the Federal Methodology (FM). The EFC arrives on a form called the Student Aid Report (SAR).

There are also around 180 private schools and a few highly selective public schools that require an additional financial aid form known as the College Scholarship Search (CSS) PROFILE. Organizations that use the PROFILE will generate a different EFC than the EFC that the FAFSA generates, because the PROFILE uses a different approach to calculating EFC.

In the case of the FAFSA, each school just accepts whatever EFC the FAFSA generates and uses this to derive a financial aid award. For the 180 schools that require the PROFILE in addition to the FAFSA, they take the information they learn when families complete the PROFILE, put it through their own value system, and determine their own EFC (see Chapter 108 on the CSS PROFILE and Chapter 109, called, "Why are my financial aid awards completely different between colleges?")

The basic college formula is COA - EFC=Family Financial Need. It is imperative that you know this formula. For example: $50,000 (COA) - $20,000 (EFC) = $30,000 of family need. A college cannot give you an aid award that exceeds your need, and they are not obligated to meet your need, but knowing the EFC is essential to know the maximum aid you are eligible for in a needs-based assessment.

For the rest of this chapter, I am only speaking of the EFC-based version of the FAFSA, as more than 95 percent of colleges do not require the PROFILE. There are eight factors that determine what your EFC will be:

1. Whether you are classified as a dependent or independent student (substantial impact)
2. Parental income from the custodial parent or parents (if married, remarried or cohabitating) (substantial impact)
3. Number of students from the household in college at the same time (substantial impact)
4. Student income (if it is high, it will be substantial, but most students don't make much money)
5. Parent assets (for about 1/20 this is substantial)
6. Student assets (usually modest impact)

7. Number of dependents in the home (modest impact)
8. Age of the oldest parent (modest impact)

The following assets count in the EFC asset formula:

- savings
- checking
- money market
- CDs
- brokerage accounts
- investment real estate
- mutual funds
- stocks
- bonds
- ETFs
- commodities
- 529 college prepaid and savings plans.

There are two simple versions used to assess the EFC. If the adjusted gross income (AGI) for the family is $25,000 or less, then the dependent student automatically has a zero EFC. If the AGI is $50,000 or less, then student and parent assets are disregarded in the FAFSA formula. This is known as the "Simplified Needs Test."

There are four reasons why assets don't have a substantial impact for most people with the FAFSA EFC formula:

1. Money in your primary residency is excluded from the FAFSA EFC formula
2. Money in your retirement accounts is excluded as well, and it is in retirement accounts and homes where most families have their assets
3. Businesses with fewer than 100 employees are sheltered
4. Assets above the Asset Protection Allowance (see Chapter 117 called, "How can I increase my need-based aid?") in the parent's name count toward the EFC formula, but only at 5 percent

   Assets in the student's name are computed at 20 percent

If a family had $100,000 in assets outside of the protected categories and after the Asset Protection Allowance was met, this would add $5640 to the student's EFC.

Vanessa was a student I worked with this year who I was expecting to have a low EFC. She was a strong student, so I expected she would qualify for a lot of need-based aid based on her EFC, and based on her desirability as an applicant. I asked and learned the family had modest resources when it came to savings, checking, money market, CDs, brokerage accounts, mutual funds, stocks, bonds, ETFs, commodities, and 529 college prepaid and savings plans. I was shocked when I saw how high her EFC was. I had forgotten to ask about rental properties; they had several of them, and these can greatly increase your EFC.

98

WHY DOES MY EFC SAY I CAN PAY SUCH AN OUTRAGEOUS AMOUNT OF MONEY?

EFC is an acronym for Expected Family Contribution. Let's suppose that your family and mine are great friends, and we are planning on going on a trip together from New York to Disney in Orlando. I say to you, "I've done the research and your expected family contribution is $3000." Wouldn't you think I meant that the whole trip would cost you $3000? What if what I really meant was that $3000 is the minimum you will pay, and the chances of that being *all* you will pay are highly unlikely? Wouldn't the $3000 mean something different?

EFC is not what you are *going* to pay, EFC is the *minimum* you will pay (unless you get scholarships/merit money), so EFC should be MPFC (minimum possible family contribution) if you are extremely fortunate.

It is critical that you understand the basic financial formula:

COST OF ATTENDANCE (COA) – EFC = FAMILY FINANCIAL NEED

The problem is that very few colleges will meet your family financial need. Colleges are not obligated to meet this need, and the vast majority of them will leave you with a large amount of unmet need. This is what we call a "gap," and it is so prevalent that there is a name for being left with an unmet need. It is known as "gapping."

It isn't that colleges are being unethical or insensitive to your finances. The reality is, very few colleges are not really struggling to meet the fiscal demands of salaries, benefits, facilities, and other expenses while providing you with the financial aid that you are eligible for. You may be the most generous person in the world, but if you only have $50 in your bank account, how generous can you really be?

In 2014, Inside Higher Ed had Gallup administer a survey to admissions directors about gapping and here is what they learned:

> More than half (55 percent) say they practice gapping at their institution, but private college directors are much more likely (72 percent) to say they use this practice than are public college admissions directors (39 percent). Almost 6 in 10 directors (58 percent) say that gapping is a necessary practice for institutions like their own, although again, there is a wide difference in opinion between admissions directors at private (76 percent) and public institutions (38 percent). However, overall, 61 percent say the practice is ethical, with private sector directors (75 percent) much more likely than their public sector peers (46 percent) to say so.

In reality, I am convinced the numbers are higher than what was admitted in this survey.

According to the 2011-2012 National Postsecondary Student Aid Study (NPSAS), the net price on average is $7,000 more than the EFC for undergraduate students at four-year colleges. The difference between the net price and EFC is about $4,000 at four-year public colleges, but it is more than $10,000 at four-year private non-profit colleges. Net price is what you pay after you receive grants and scholarships.

The actual formula used for calculating the EFC is flawed. According to financial aid maven Mark Kantrowitz:

> It is based on a budget for a family living a 'lower standard of living' in 1967. That budget has been adjusted for inflation every year, but not for changes in family spending patterns. Thus, there's no room in the budget for HBO, cellphones, Internet access, Nintendo Wiis, or other modern luxuries. Nor has it been adjusted for more necessary expenditures, such as the dramatic increase in health-care costs.

If you are thinking, "I will just get low-interest loans to cover my gap," that won't work, because colleges almost always put a federal loan into your aid package, but that loan does not go to cover your gap (unmet need). The federal loan actually goes to help meet your actual need. An aid award will often also include giving you a campus job, but this also goes to your need and not your unmet need.

Example: A college has a $65,000 COA, and your EFC is $20,000, leaving you with $45,000 in need. A college gives you a $15,000 need-based grant and a $15,000 scholarship, neither of which has to be repaid, but they give you a $5500 loan and a $2500 campus job. You still have a gap (unmet need of $7000) and that is *with* the loan and a weekly job.

Then there are other bizarre things that the FAFSA EFC calculation does, such as not looking at the cost of living where you live in assessing your need. The EFC for the PROFILE can look at cost of living, but that doesn't mean a college will choose to do this, and remember, only about 180 of 4500 colleges use the PROFILE to calculate a different EFC. The median price of a one-bedroom apartment in Manhattan is $710,000. That would get you a mansion in Fairburn, Georgia, where I live.

Any money saved for college in your name, as opposed to your parents' names, will go to your EFC at almost five times the rate for the PROFILE version of the EFC and almost four times the rate for the FAFSA version of the EFC.

In their EFC calculations, both the FAFSA version and the PROFILE version of the EFC punish laudable decisions like adding retirement contributions for the year, health saving contributions for the year, tithing, and other charitable giving.

Almost without exception, when a family makes more money, they are going to spend more money on things like restaurants, cars, homes, vacations, and shopping, but the formula takes such a high percentage of a family's disposable income and expects it will go to EFC that when 95 percent of families with a high five-figure income or higher see their EFC, their reaction is, "there is no way I can pay that EFC."

In many instances, for every $10,000 of increased adjusted gross income from $100,000 and above, the EFC formula will expect that 45-47 percent of that after-tax money to be used for college. Remember, the EFC is really the BMFC (bare minimum family contribution), so it is highly probable that you are going to be asked to pay much more than your EFC. I'm not trying to be the Grinch that stole Christmas, but I am trying to keep it real.

Vincent Robinson was a very talented kid. His family reached out to me for help after he was admitted to some prestigious colleges and their EFC was just not making these college options possible. The Robinsons' family income was almost $190,000, but they lived in New York; they had two other kids in private school; and Vincent's parents were devout Christians who gave $20,000 of that $190,000 to the Lord through tithing. The family thought it would be a stretch, but they could pay $20,000 for college. Still, some private schools asked them to pay almost $50,000. I had to have a tough conversation with the Robinsons. I told them, unfortunately, these schools you are admitted to do not take the tithing, the cost of living in New York, or the tuition you are paying for Vincent's siblings into account.

99

WHAT DO I NEED TO KNOW ABOUT THE VERY-IMPORTANT FAFSA?

The Department of Education takes the *Free Application for Federal Student Aid* (*FAFSA*®) form and processes approximately 20 million FAFSA submissions each year. Here's what you need to know.

- ℵ The FAFSA is required for access to 120 billion in federal grants, loans, and Federal Work-Study.
- ℵ Many states and colleges themselves require the FAFSA to be completed in order to be eligible for need-based (usually referred to as grants) or merit-based (usually referred to as scholarships) money.

- ℵ You need to create a FSA (Federal Student Aid) ID that creates a username and password in order to sign the FAFSA electronically, and if you are a dependent student, your parents will also need to create their own FSA ID. Even though FAFSA gives you the option to do this at the end, it is much better to do this when you are just starting. You can do this on FAFSA.gov and you create your ID before October 1. Save this in a secure location.
- ℵ In addition to using your FSA ID to electronically sign the FAFSA, you can use your FSA ID to access your federal loans you have taken in the past and to see what you need to repay. Many people call the FSA ID the FAFSA ID. The FSA ID/FAFSA ID replaced the old Federal Student Aid Pin in May 2015.
- ℵ You file the FAFSA online at FAFSA.gov.
- ℵ Use a permanent email address, not a high school one that you can't use anymore once you leave high school.
- ℵ You have to fill out FAFSA annually because financial situations almost always change to some degree from one year to the next. It will take about 45 minutes to one hour in year one and about 35-45 minutes in subsequent years. The Renewal FAFSA is quicker, partially because you have already completed it once, but also because some of the information will automatically prefill for you the second time you are completing it. You don't have to complete it in one sitting. You can log out and then use your FSA ID to log back in.
- ℵ FAFSA is easier than ever to complete, because you can use the IRS Data Retrieval tool, which lets you sync your filed taxes to your FAFSA application.
- ℵ It is best to file the FAFSA early because some of the funds that states and colleges control are available on a first-come, first-served basis. For the 2018-19 year, you can file the FAFSA as early as October 1, 2017, and you have until June 30, 2019, to be in compliance with the federal date, but state deadlines can be much, much earlier. You can see what the state deadlines are by going to https://fafsa.ed.gov/deadlines.htm Each state sets its own FAFSA deadlines. Now that early FAFSA is here, some states have moved their deadlines back. According to the De-

partment of Education's records, 10 states (Alaska, Illinois, Kentucky, Nevada, North Carolina, North Dakota, Oklahoma, South Carolina, Vermont, and Washington) changed their deadline this year for most grants to: "As soon as possible after October 1, [year]. Awards made until funds are depleted."

ℵ Completing the FAFSA is the basis for determining your EFC (see Chapter 97).

ℵ If you need to make a change on the FAFSA, you can always come back and log in and make changes. When you set up the FAFSA, you create a four to eight digit save key and this is used for returning to the FAFSA in case you need to make changes.

ℵ You can select up to 10 colleges where you want your SAR sent. If you are applying to more than 10, wait five days and delete some schools and then add new ones. Deleting schools after you have allowed them to process does not keep them from receiving your ISIR (college version they receive electronically of your SAR). If it helps your peace of mind, you can call your colleges you are about to delete to make sure they received your ISIR first. Once you have received your SAR, the colleges should have received their ISIR.

ℵ You should have your W2s, taxes, bank statements, and investment records, and social security card ready before sitting down to complete your FAFSA. It will ask about your driver's license, but this is optional. If you are not a citizen but you have a green card, you will use your Alien Registration Number.

ℵ A major overhaul of the FAFSA occurred for the 2017-18 school year. Before this year, students applied with the previous year's tax information, but that often led to students missing deadlines and not completing the FAFSA. Now you apply with the tax returns for the year before the year you are currently in. For example, for 2018-19 your EFC will be based on the 2016 tax returns. This is known as "Prior Prior Year," Early FAFSA, or PPY. With Prior Prior, the FAFSA is now available to be filed on October 1, three months earlier than the traditional January 1. You submit your tax returns for two years before you are enrolling in school. For example, for students starting school in the 2019-2020 year, the FAFSA will involve submitting your income and tax returns for 2017.

- ℵ There is a paper FAFSA, but I strongly recommend you complete the FAFSA online at FAFSA.gov.
- ℵ Once the Department of Education's Department of Federal Student Aid processes your FAFSA, the colleges you listed will be notified and you will receive a Student Aid Report (aka SAR) within days if you file the FAFSA online, and within weeks if you file the paper FAFSA. Your SAR will summarize what you submitted on the FAFSA but it will contain your EFC. You can access your SAR at FAFSA.gov by using your FSA ID. You should go over your SAR with a fine-toothed comb to make sure there are no errors.
- ℵ If you realize you made a mistake with your FAFSA, go to fafsa.gov and use your FSA ID to log in and make changes.
- ℵ Once your college receives your FAFSA, they will send you an aid award if you are accepted at that respective college.

The FAFSA is necessary if you want federal aid, and federal aid comes with benefits that private aid doesn't come with. I received a very encouraging phone call today. Sharon called to tell me that both she and her dad just received public service loan forgiveness. Sharon had $12,000 erased and her dad had $100,000 erased. Private loans don't offer loan forgiveness. Sadly, in some states, less than 50% of college students complete the FAFSA. Just think what the situation would be if Sharon and her dad had selected private instead of federal loans.

100

WHAT IS FAFSA4CASTER, AND HOW CAN IT HELP ME?

Let's say you are a parent of a sixth grader and you just want to get a fairly accurate sense of what the federal government's formula thinks you should be able to afford for college. You can do this by completing the FAFSA4caster. Instead of taking 45 minutes to an hour to complete an actual FAFSA, you can take 15 minutes to complete the FAFSA4caster and get a fairly reliable estimate of your EFC. Here is how https://studentaid.ed.gov/sa/ describes FAFSA4caster:

> FAFSA4caster is an early eligibility estimator that can help you plan ahead when it comes to paying for college. FAFSA4caster is a free financial aid calculator that gives you an early estimate of your eligibility for federal student aid.

What is great about FAFSA4caster is that because it is not an official process (like the real FAFSA), a parent can estimate and experiment with different incomes to see what they will be asked to pay at a minimum if their income changes. Let's say you are a parent and your oldest child is in the ninth grade, and you anticipate getting a $20,000 raise in the next three years. Maybe you want to know what the federal formula thinks you can pay; you can plug those numbers in.

It isn't just income, either. You can estimate various projections to see how they impact your aid eligibility, such as other important variables like number of dependents, number of kids in college, parent and student assets, and being an independent versus a dependent student. FAFSA4caster gives you a worksheet to complete, and it is linked to the government's premier website for college information: College Navigator. This is important because of our core financial aid formula: Cost of Attendance – EFC = Family Financial Need. College Navigator will give you access to the Cost of Attendance for virtually every accredited college in the nation.

When completing the FAFSA4caster, you will need to have your tax returns on hand and your bank account information available. This is important because the real FAFSA relies heavily on these factors to generate your EFC.

Here is how https://studentaid.ed.gov/sa/ describes what is next:

> A number of sources of college funding are listed. FAFSA4caster indicates your estimated Federal Pell Grant amount (if any), Federal Work-Study amount (based on the average nationally), and maximum Direct Subsidized Loan and Direct Unsubsidized Loan eligibility. There are fields where you can fill in the amounts of state and college aid and private scholarships you expect (or hope) to get. Once you click on "Calculate," FAFSA4caster summarizes the cost, the total aid entered, and the difference (the net cost of attending college). Your estimated Expected Family Contribution (EFC) also appears. You can compare schools by changing cost of attendance, deleting state aid if you will be an out of state student at a particular school,

amending the amount of aid available from the school, and so on.

It is important to remember that about 180 colleges that are usually selective private colleges use the CSS PROFILE, which uses a different method of calculating an EFC.

The FAFSA is necessary if you want federal aid, and federal aid comes with benefits that private aid doesn't come with. I received a very encouraging phone call today. Sharon called to tell me that both she and her dad just received public service loan forgiveness. Sharon had $12,000 erased and her dad had $100,000 erased. Private loans don't offer loan forgiveness. Sadly, in some states, less than 50% of college students complete the FAFSA. Just think what the situation would be if Sharon and her dad had selected private instead of federal loans.

101

HOW DO I KNOW WHETHER I AM CONSIDERED AN INDEPENDENT OR DEPENDENT STUDENT?

On the FAFSA, you are asked several questions that determine if you are a dependent or independent student.

If you are a dependent student, you will be required to provide the income and asset information for both yourself and your parents. An independent student only has to provide their own income and asset information. It is therefore much better to be an independent student, because you are going to have lower income and fewer assets and are therefore much more likely to qualify for the Pell Grant, the SEOG grant, need-based institutional aid from the college itself, Federal Work-Study, and a subsidized federal loan.

The big myth is that a student can declare themselves as an independent student simply by doing one of the following things: 1) living on their own; 2) being responsible for their own bills; and 3) saying their parents refuse to pay for college. In other words, students think of the literal word "independent," and they feel that if they meet the traditional definition of the word, this corresponds to the FAFSA definition. They also think that being classified as an independent student for financial aid is similar to being an independent student on your taxes, and it is not. The problem with this approach is that it would simply be too easy for a student to cheat the federal government and colleges who grant need-based financial aid.

All you need to do is answer "yes" to any one of the questions listed below on the FAFSA, and you will be considered an independent student. You will see these questions listed below on net price calculators, FAFSA4caster, the FAFSA, CSS PROFILE, and any other institutional aid form you may be asked to complete. The reason this must be asked in any EFC estimator is because being labeled an independent student can have a colossal impact on your aid award eligibility.

- Are you a graduate student? Students who start school young or who have a lot of IB, AP, or dual enrollment credits can often easily be grad students before the age of 24. Professional school, i.e. law or medical school, also counts here.
- Are you married?
- Are you on active duty in the armed forces?
- Are you a military veteran?
- Are you 24 or older? (They don't ask the question this way. You are asked what your age will be by Dec. 31 of that award year.)
- Do you have children and provide at least 50 percent of their support? You can have seven kids, but if a grandparent or someone else is handling most of their expenses, then you are still a dependent student based on this question. A grandparent counts as a dependent if, in fact, they live with you and depend primarily on you for taking care of them.
- Are you an emancipated minor? (When you were a child, were you emancipated in a court of law?)
- Is your legal guardian not one of your parents? Earlier today, I met with John Leach, Director of Financial Aid at Emory, about

this. John said, "This is one of the more common ways students are classified as independent students. If your aunt or uncle or one of your grandparents are your legal guardian and you are 18, you are classified as an independent student."

- ℵ Are you an orphan, in foster care, or a ward of the court since age 13?
- ℵ Are you homeless or at risk of homelessness? (It is too easy to exploit this by just saying you are homeless, so you will need to get documentation by a having a homeless shelter write a letter on your behalf, or your school liaison can also provide a letter stating this.)
- ℵ Do you have an incarcerated parent?
- ℵ There are times when your status is not crystal clear, and you will need to contact your college. They have been empowered by the federal government in these very subjective cases to make the decision. Their verdict is final and cannot be appealed. The most common case of subjective analysis is when someone has no idea where their parents are even though they are not homeless. The financial aid office has their antenna up for fraudulent claims, and they have their ways of seeking to confirm the legitimacy of such a claim.

I was explaining to Jimmy how different the financial aid formula is for a dependent student compared to an independent student. Once Jimmy found out that if he was an independent student, his dad's income wasn't going to count and he would be eligible for a large need-based award, he replied, "I guess it is time for me to move out of the house." This is a common misconception. Being independent in life doesn't make you independent in the eyes of the federal government.

102

SHOULD I COMPLETE THE FAFSA IF I'M WEALTHY?

Yes, and here are the reasons why.

- FAFSA is often used for many private scholarships.
- FAFSA is often a requirement for institutional aid from the college itself for automatic scholarships. It's often a requirement for state-based aid, and not just need-based aid, but merit-based aid. For example, the FAFSA is used as a validator of the HOPE Scholarship in Georgia.
- You may want a student loan. Some people take loans even though they do not need them, because the interest rates are so good with the Federal Direct Loan Program. Some people see

value to building credit with this loan, and they feel they can invest and get a better return than what they pay in interest in the loan. The FAFSA is required to get this loan.

- ℵ Furthermore, there are public loan forgiveness programs available for students who work in non-profit sectors, so a large portion of the loan could be converted to a grant.
- ℵ FAFSA completion is a sign of demonstrated interest in that school you list. Colleges that are looking for clues that you are interested in them before they offer you a spot may use this as one of their factors they are using to assess your interest in them.
- ℵ FAFSA may lead to a small award for schools that use their aid to target wealthy families who are looking for some merit money when the school is need-aware and they are looking for families to whom they do not need to give much aid. In a January 6, 2016, in an article in the money section of *TIME*, here is how admission veteran Robert Massey describes it: "You can qualify with a much higher income than you realize depending on how expensive the college is and how many kids you have in college. You could earn $500,000 in some instances and still qualify for a grant if there are two other kids in expensive colleges simultaneously."

The state of Louisiana had only a 50% FAFSA completion rate, so they got aggressive in 2015 by requiring that a student must complete a FAFSA or they do not get their diploma.

One of the wealthiest families I worked with in 2017 had an income of close to a million a year. Their son received close to a full tuition scholarship from an out-of-state school because of strong academics, but the scholarship required the submission of the FAFSA. Just think if this family had said, "We make too much money; we are not completing the FAFSA."

103

HOW CAN I GET OUTSTANDING FREE ASSISTANCE IN COMPLETING THE FAFSA?

College Goal Sunday has helped millions of students complete the FAFSA. Each state sets its own date for College Goal Sunday, and the date comes well before that state's FAFSA deadline. Here is how College Goal Georgia describes their mission on their website: "The College Goal Georgia (CGG) FAFSA Completion initiative is sponsored by the Georgia Student Finance Commission (GSFC). It is a FREE event where selected schools and volunteers help students and families who need assistance." Locations all around the state dispatch professionals to help students complete the FAFSA. Some states have been hosting these events for less than ten years, and other states have been doing it for thirty years.

Each state has their own College Goal Sunday website where you will find some very helpful resources. In order to find out where to go for free resources for your state, visit http://formyourfuture.org and you will see a dropdown box where you can locate your state. The hashtag "#formyourfuture" also has a great Twitter feed.

Here are a few other tips:

- ℵ You can find a preparation worksheet on fafsa.gov that will assist you in getting your tax returns and your W-2, bank statements, driver's license, and social security car ready for completing the FAFSA.
- ℵ https://fastweb.com has great resources, but there is no substitute for https://studentaid.ed.gov/sa/
- ℵ 1-800-4-Fed Aid is fantastic and I have used it many times. When you have a question and you need an answer, this site is staffed with professionals whose job is to answer your FAFSA questions. If you have a scintilla of doubt that you are filling out the FAFSA correctly, call this number and seek assistance.
- ℵ For great Twitter chats, try @FAFSA, where you can post questions and get answers. This information is as current as it gets.
- ℵ Find great online supports at fafsa.gov by using the Help and Hints box after each question. I find these answers to questions people are often thinking to be invaluable.
- ℵ Step Up to Higher Education Utah does a great FAFSA walkthrough every year and they put it up on YouTube. Here is the 2017-18 one, and I have found this to be an extremely helpful tool for parents and students: https://www.youtube.com/watch?v=voo6FOr15Gs

I strongly encourage you to go through this tutorial and share it with others.

Virginia called me from New York City. She wanted to pay me to help her with completing the FAFSA. In good conscience, I just couldn't take her money. I explained to her the "help and hints" that are on the right side of virtually every page of the FAFSA. I told her about the worksheet and about 1-800-4-FED-AID, and I shared with her the 2018 full walkthrough that is on YouTube. I got a text a few days later saying, "Thank you, we are all set."

104

WHY DID I RECEIVE A LETTER SAYING MY FAFSA INFORMATION NEEDS TO BE VERIFIED?

Should you need to be verified by your college or by the Department of Education, your college will inform you of your verification request and they will tell you what you need to do. A verification request means they want to check to see if what you submitted was accurate.

Being selected does not imply that you did anything wrong. It doesn't mean there are legitimate grounds for skepticism of the accuracy of your information. Some students are randomly selected for verification, but families sometimes think that they are being punished, penalized, or audited, which is not correct. The Department of Education selects between 30-33 percent of all students who file a FAFSA, and those students are required to verify that a portion of the information they submitted was accurate.

Verification can occur both for new students and returning students.

Different colleges use different methods for notification of verification requests. Some put this in the student portal, others send emails or letters, and others call. There is nothing wrong with you calling the financial aid office just to make sure you have not been selected for verification, but it is their job to communicate with you if you have been selected. You will also see the request for verification on your Student Aid Report (SAR).

If changes are made to your EFC after you complete verification, you will get a new SAR. If no change occurs you may get a letter, but usually you will get an email.

You will often have to use the US data retrieval tool, or you may need to request tax return transcript documents from the IRS, because as of 2012-2013, copies of your tax returns will not be accepted because they are too easy to fabricate. A tax return transcript is a line-by-line accounting of your tax return as it was originally filed with the IRS and can be used instead of the data retrieval tool.

Some of the common requests for verification are for:

- Federal tax data
- Number of family members in college
- High school completion information
- Household size
- Another common mistake that may trigger verification is for parents to include themselves on the FAFSA

In some cases, you will need to use a notary to verify your information.

You want to complete the verification process as soon as possible, because your FAFSA application is not considered complete until this is resolved, and your college will not be able to complete any grants or scholarships for which you may be eligible.

You can expect it to take anywhere from three days to four weeks for a school to resolve the matter once you have completed the requested information. The length of time will vary based on the nature of the request, the amount of staff your college has, and how busy a time of the year it is. You may be asked to submit verification information by multiple colleges in the same year, and for different reasons.

Both of my daughters were verified for the FAFSA, but I will talk about Joy's because it was this year. Joy had to complete the verification process to prove that she did not file a 1040, a 1040A, or a 1040EZ under her social security number, but the request was made in such an arcane manner that I don't know how students without adult guidance know how to handle these requests.

A stepparent is treated like a biological parent; their income counts in EFC.

105

WHAT KINDS OF FINANCIAL AID QUESTIONS MIGHT SINGLE, DIVORCED, AND REMARRIED PARENTS HAVE?

Q: If one of my parents is divorced and remarried, which parents are responsible for submitting their financial information?

A: If the student lives with the divorced and remarried parent, then the biological parent and the stepparent must complete the FAFSA. If they live with the biological parent who has not remarried, then it is only the custodial parent who has to complete the FAFSA. For the PROFILE, it is going to depend on the policy of the individual college, but four options are possible:

1. Only the two biological parents

2. Only the biological parent and the stepparent (most common option)
3. Both biological parents and the stepparent
4. Custodial parent only, like the FAFSA. There are only around 40 schools that require the PROFILE and do *not* require the noncustodial parent to complete the PROFILE. For schools that take the FAFSA, there is no such thing as a noncustodial parent profile.

Q: What happens if the two parents never were married?

A: They are treated just like divorced parents. If the noncustodial parent has paid alimony or child support, this must be submitted on the FAFSA.

Q: If both parents have joint custody, who is the custodial parent?

A: It's the parent the child has lived with the most for the 12 months prior to October 1, the first day you can file the FAFSA or the PROFILE. If it still is not clear, the tiebreaker is which parent provided the most financial support for the 12 months before the first day you can file the FAFSA or PROFILE. The term "custodial parent" is confusing. It is not the legal definition of custody, nor is it the tax filing definition of custody.

Q: Are you trying to tell me that if the student lives mostly with one parent who makes $30,000, and the noncustodial parent makes $300,000, then that $300,000 will not even be reported for schools that only require the FAFSA?

A: Yes, that is exactly what I am saying. It is why the overwhelming majority of colleges that require the PROFILE require the non-custodial PROFILE. It is one of the many reasons why the PROFILE is indisputably a more accurate picture of your family finances. One family I worked with legally separated when they learned this, with the full intention of getting back together after their child was through college. I did not encourage this, but even if I had tried to stop them, they had made up their minds.

Q: We signed a prenuptial agreement absolving the stepparent from any obligation around college support, so why is the stepparent being required to submit their income and asset information?

A: Prenuptial agreements are irrelevant to the financial aid process. Prenuptial agreements are state agreements. Two people cannot bind a third party (the federal government or the college).

Q: My two parents live together, but they never were married. How do we handle this?

A: They are treated just like they are married for financial aid purposes (FAFSA or PROFILE).

Q: My parents separated, but it isn't a legal separation; they are just not in the same home. How do we handle this?

A: This is treated just like a legal separation. For the FAFSA only, the custodial parent will have to submit information, and for the PROFILE, both parents will have to submit information, unless it is one of about 20 percent of PROFILE schools that exempt the noncustodial parent from submitting their financial information.

Q: What if my parents are in a same-sex marriage?

A: This is treated just like a marriage between a man and a woman. In fact, the FAFSA uses the gender-neutral terms Parent 1 and Parent 2, not father and mother.

Q: What if my parents are divorced or legally separated, but they still live together?

A: Both parents must complete the FAFSA or the PROFILE.

Q: Are there ever any times I may be able to submit a FAFSA without my parents' financial information?

A: There are four possibilities here:

1. Parents are incarcerated
2. Parents are abusive
3. You are between 21-23 and are homeless
4. You have no idea where your parents are. Should any of these situations describe you, here is how the federal government's

website (https://studentaid.ed.gov/sa/) says you should handle this:

- ℵ Although your FAFSA will be submitted, it will not be fully processed. You will not receive an Expected Family Contribution (EFC) and must immediately contact the financial aid office at the college or career school you plan to attend.
- ℵ The financial aid staff may ask for additional information to determine whether you can be considered independent and have an EFC calculated without parent data. Gather as much written evidence of your situation as you can. Written evidence may include court or law enforcement documents; letters from a clergy member, school counselor or social worker; and/or any other relevant data that explains your special circumstance.
- ℵ The financial aid office's decision about your *dependency status* is final and cannot be appealed to the United States Department of Education.

When Juanita called me, she was bewildered. She could have easily paid for her daughter to attend the University of Miami when she was a single mom, but then she got married, and she couldn't believe how much more Miami was asking her to pay. Miami is not alone; almost every college requires the stepparent to submit their financial information, and they factor that into the EFC.

Any parent who won't complete the FAFSA is making it really hard on their child.

106

What happens if a parent refuses to complete the FAFSA?

- ℵ The student will probably only be eligible for a direct unsubsidized loan, and this is not guaranteed. The student will not be eligible for a Pell Grant or subsidized loans.
- ℵ If a parent won't sign the FAFSA, no EFC is generated.
- ℵ Sometimes a parent refuses to give you any of their tax information. Sometimes parents are so private, they just do not want their children to know this information, or they don't want the school to have this information.

- ℵ This can sometimes occur when parents are going through a divorce. It can also happen because a stepparent refuses to complete the FAFSA, feeling as if it is the biological parent who should be completing this information (see previous chapter on single, divorced, and remarried families).
- ℵ Parents sometimes refuse if they are not documented themselves and they fear deportation. Parents should know that if their children are citizens, permanent residents, or eligible noncitizens, the child will not be kept from aid because of their parents' undocumented status. This is an area where people should check to make sure this policy doesn't change, because our nation's response to Hispanic immigrants in particular is undergoing significant scrutiny at the time this book is being written. DACA was revoked by President Trump, and we are all waiting for the Congress to act.
- ℵ Sometimes parents refuse because they didn't complete their tax returns. This is another advantage to Early FAFSA, aka Prior Prior Year, because a parent may not have filed their taxes last year but it is now tax information two years ago that is being asked about on the FAFSA.
- ℵ Maybe it is a small town, and the people at the college who work in financial aid know your parents. Your parents should know that it is the Department of Education which will be scrutinizing the responses and using their formula to assess your need for schools that rely on the FAFSA. I am not saying local colleges don't have access to your information, but they see the ISIR (school version of the Student Aid Report without all of the tax information on it).
- ℵ Usually when parents refuse, it is because they are convinced that a student will get more money from the federal government, state government, or the college themselves without the parents' information. If your parents refuse to complete the FAFSA, it is important that you let them know that completing the FAFSA does not obligate them to pay for college, but it will prevent you from important free sources of money from the government and from the college itself. A lot of times this information will be better received if it is not coming from you. Have your parents read this chapter. Have your school counselor or a rep from the

college explain to your parents that completing this information doesn't obligate them to pay a certain amount.

One of the parents I once worked with said to her son, "I am not paying for college and I'm not completing the FAFSA; it's on you, so figure it out." This happened quite some time ago, and her son never went to college. He worked some minimum wage jobs and did quite a bit of job-hopping. I am all for tough love, but I'm not for walking away from free and very low-interest money.

Parents, don't let your child complete the FAFSA without you!

107

WHAT ARE THE MOST COMMON MISTAKES STUDENTS AND PARENTS MAKE ON THE FAFSA?

- One of the most common mistakes is not writing your legally registered name exactly the same as your name is listed on the social security card. Your FAFSA will be rejected right away. No abbreviations and nicknames.
- Forgetting to include social security.
- Forgetting to include your birthday.
- Thinking FAFSA is a family form and not an individual student form; a separate FAFSA must be completed for every student in the family.
- Confusing the custodial parent with the noncustodial parent.

ℵ Simple typos like putting 93,000 instead of 39,000 for income; watch out for transposing numbers.

ℵ Not accurately reporting your financial picture is a very serious federal offense.

ℵ If you have dual enrollment courses or AP credits, you should still select "never attended college/1 year" when it asks about this.

ℵ Make sure you use FAFSA.gov. You should never have to pay anything to fill out the FAFSA, and if the website asks you to pay, you are on the wrong website. There are lots of fraudulent websites hoping to trick you.

ℵ Mixing up parent and student assets; parent assets are assessed at 5 percent and student assets are assessed at 20 percent.

ℵ Procrastination causes you to lose out on dollars; lots of money is first come, first served.

ℵ Missing deadlines.

ℵ When asked about assets you own, DO NOT include home, car, and possessions like boats or jewelry.

ℵ Don't misinterpret investments with retirement. Your retirement is not included and should not be included, such as a 401K, 403B, IRA, SEP IRA, etc.

ℵ Using your definition of who is in the household and not the FAFSA definition (read carefully).

ℵ Using your definition of who is in college and not the FAFSA definition.

ℵ Not getting your zeroes right; for example, amount in savings: $200,000 instead of $20,000.

ℵ Mistakes can be fixed, but they slow down the process and can make you lose out on state aid, institutional money from the college itself, and private scholarships.

ℵ Not completing the FAFSA itself.

ℵ Not getting a parent signature.

ℵ Before you submit, sleep on it and review the next day with fresh eyes to make sure you made no mistakes. If you complete on the web, you can print out the results before you hit submit.

ℵ Lack of parental involvement is the biggest mistake. Don't trust your child to get all of your financial information correct. A lot of people make this mistake and I can understand why. The

Federal Direct Student Loans are student loans in the student's name, so a lot parents think, "this is their loan and they can complete it," but I have seen so many problems when this occurs. The biggest factor is parent income, and the form requires properly answering parent income and asset questions. This is just too high-stakes to put in the hands of an 18-year-old. Parents/guardians are used to completing these types of forms, and kids are not. Ideally, the FAFSA should be filled out with the student and the parent working together, but the parent is absolutely essential or you are asking for major errors. The student has to sign it. The student has to get their own FAFSA ID, but the fact that both student and parent signatures are required tells you they both need to be involved in the process.

- א Not using the free resources we discuss in Chapter 23.

Colleges don't give away their own money without making sure you really need it.

108

WHAT IS THE CSS PROFILE, AND AM I REQUIRED TO FILL IT OUT?

The CSS PROFILE (College Scholarship Service Profile, which I will refer to as PROFILE) is an online financial aid application administered by College Board. It's an in-depth assessment of your financial profile that is significantly more comprehensive than the FAFSA; it is used to allocate aid from the college's resources, whereas the FAFSA is used for disbursing federal and state aid. Colleges guard their resources very carefully, so if they are going to give them up, they are going to go to great lengths to make sure that you really can't pay.

Around 180 colleges (over 95 percent are private colleges) and over 100 scholarship organizations use this in-depth and, at times, very intrusive look at your financial picture in order to truly see who needs money. Most private colleges don't require the PROFILE, but the wealthier and more-selective private schools usually do.

Private and public schools that don't use the PROFILE use the FAFSA to decide how they will dispense their own college resources.

As of 2018, only six public schools among the 180, the University of Virginia, North Carolina, Michigan, William and Mary, Colorado State, and Georgia Tech, require the PROFILE.

Some require it for international and domestic students and some just for domestic.

Like FAFSA, the PROFILE is available on October 1 and you will be asked about 2016 information for the 2018-2019 year. Find it at student.collegeboard.org/PROFILE or using a Google search. Check with the PROFILE website to see the link to see which colleges you are applying to require it.

You can also go to the financial aid sections of your college's websites to see if they require the FAFSA and the PROFILE or just the FAFSA. I have noticed that when a college adds the PROFILE or drops the PROFILE, the update occurs on the college's website before it is on the College Board's website.

The PROFILE is never a substitute for the FAFSA; it's like comparing apples and oranges as it's federal aid vs. institutional aid. The PROFILE will always be required in addition to the FAFSA.

The FAFSA is free, but PROFILE is $25 for the first college and $16 for each additional college that requires it. Because it is administered by the College Board, if you took the SAT and received a fee waiver for the SAT, you will automatically be eligible for a fee waiver for the PROFILE. If you took the ACT, there is no automatic qualification when you sign up for the PROFILE to see if you are fee waiver eligible.

There are a number of areas where the PROFILE assesses your need differently than the FAFSA (see the next chapter to learn about those areas) but I will share one area in this chapter. If you live with only one of your parents, it is only that parent's income that is included in the FAFSA. Most schools that require the PROFILE will require you to submit a noncustodial PROFILE application, which is as deep a dive into the noncustodial parent's finances as the PROFILE is into the custodial spouse's finances. The noncustodial parent's income and assets will be factored into your aid award.

You will find an extensive Help Desk and a frequently asked question session to help you. You can also call 844-202-0524 if you are still not clear how to answer a question. You can also send an email to help@cssPROFILE.org.

Before completing the PROFILE, I recommend completing the PROFILE worksheet. You will need your tax returns, bank account information, social security number, business or farm records, and housing information. There is no way in the world a student should do this without a parent with them making sure everything is correct.

Tax returns are the great leveler when it comes to accurately assessing your income and assets. If you are thinking, "I still don't see how you can go from income and assets to an EFC," here is a simplified overview of how the process works. Start with line 37 (adjusted gross income or AGI) on your tax returns. Then you have to add nontaxable income like child custody, retirement contributions for the year, health savings contributions, charitable giving, a percentage of your assets, and in some instances, business expenses that you wrote off that the aid office feels should not lower your EFC. Other non-taxable income can include veterans' non-education benefits such as disability, workers' compensation, disability benefits, etc. See Chapter 94 on the FAFSA for a complete list of factors that constitute untaxed income.

Then you have to add back factors like: taxes paid, income protection allowance, cost of living adjustment. Now you have a number, but it will still be adjusted based on number of kids in college, number of dependents in the home, business losses, rental property losses, real estate losses, etc.

The PROFILE generates its own EFC, which is different than the FAFSA EFC. The FAFSA is based on Bureau of Labor data. The PROFILE is based on the consumer price index, which is more current and up to date.

Colleges that require the FAFSA can use the IRS Data Retrieval Tool (aka DRT) to make sure that accurate information is being submitted. Submitting DRT for verifying your income information on the PROFILE is not an option. The College Board has its own system for income verification. It is referred to as IDOC. Here is how the College Board's website describes IDOC:

> Through the Institutional Documentation Service (IDOC), the College Board collects families' federal tax re-

> turns and other documents on behalf of participating colleges and programs. The College Board notifies students selected by participating institutions when to submit the required documents. IDOC also distributes these important documents to the college on behalf of the student. These important documents include tax returns with all schedules, W2s and other pertinent financial information. You should be expecting that sometime in late January or early February you will receive an email requesting an IDOC submission of a lot of financial information on behalf of any college that requires that IDOC gather financial information for them.

Here is where it can get confusing. Some PROFILE schools require IDOC, but a school can require IDOC without requiring the PROFILE. The IDOC is very thorough, and this is why some colleges use it even if they don't use the PROFILE. It is also a pain to complete. Davidson is an IDOC school, so I have completed this form all four years for Karis.

At the end of the PROFILE, it asks you if you have any special circumstances. This is your opportunity to talk about questions that were not directly asked to you in a formulaic manner, which is something the FAFSA doesn't provide. If you want to know the kind of things you can write about in this section, see Chapter 154 on how to appeal an aid award. There is a webinar on the home page for the College Board that will help you to fill out this complex form.

Ms. Peters called me in a state of panic. She had just gotten her daughter's SAR back, and her EFC was more than $20,000 more than what she was expected it would be. She had completed the FAFSA4caster. She had completed the cost calculator on the University of San Francisco's website. Her daughter Victoria really wanted to go to USF, and Ms. Peters was prepared to pay, but not if her EFC was $20,000 higher than she expected. I had told her that the EFC was the absolute minimum she would pay but she should expect to pay more than this. The problem was that Victoria had completed the FAFSA and she had put her mom's retirement as an investment and the home as an asset, neither of which is correct. I have seen this mistake far too often. Do not let your 18-year-old complete the FAFSA without your oversight!

109

WHY ARE MY FINANCIAL AID AWARDS COMPLETELY DIFFERENT BETWEEN COLLEGES?

- Some schools gap, and some don't (see Chapter 98 on why your EFC says you can pay so much for college).
- FSEOG: Some schools offer this grant, which may lead to fewer loans, and some don't (see Chapter 119).
- Some colleges meet the remaining need, (remember the basic financial aid formula: Cost of Attendance – EFC = Family Financial Need) with loans and some without loans.
- Merit scholarships will vary from school to school, and whether you get one, or how big it is, will substantially impact what you are asked to pay.
- Preferential packaging is when a school gives you a much better package in terms of gift money (grants and scholarships) because

they want you more, and most private schools utilize preferential packaging in some form.

- ℵ Costs of Attendance can vary. If a school is only asking you to pay your EFC and your income is modest, then you want a high Cost of Attendance, because that means they have factored in all of your expenses into their formula. For example, how much is built in for things like transportation, books, spending money, and the other indirect costs?
- ℵ There is a very big difference between how the FAFSA and how the PROFILE impact your aid award. The FAFSA generates an EFC that is the same across the board for all schools. The PROFILE is like a smorgasbord in that it gives a college access to hundreds of pieces of information about your assets and income, but instead of generating one number like the FAFSA does, it lets the college develop its own policy about which items on the smorgasbord they will use in their own individual calculation of your financial need.
- ℵ Here is how John Leach, Director of Financial Aid at Emory, put it in a presentation he did in Atlanta that I attended on September 9, 2017: "We get to turn the knob with the CSS." The following areas are where you will see significant divergence from one PROFILE school to another in terms of which items they are going to use and how they are going to use them.

1. A noncustodial spouse is factored into the PROFILE for 80 percent of PROFILE schools, but the FAFSA only looks at the income from the parent the student lives with in the case of divorced or single parents. This can result in a swing of over

$65,000 per year, depending on the COA of the colleges you are interested in and the income and assets of the noncustodial spouse vs. the income and assets of the custodial spouse.

2. **Home equity policy:** FAFSA doesn't even look at this at all for your primary dwelling (additional rental or vacation properties are included) because the government feels you shouldn't have to mortgage your house for college, but when colleges that use the PROFILE see a large amount of home equity, they feel you should be able to tap into that to pay for college. Home equity policies are all over the place for colleges that require the PROFILE. They range from counting all of your home equity in their formula to not counting any of it, and everything in between, but this is a major reason why packages vary with PROFILE schools.
3. The PROFILE uses 5 percent of your family's assets in calculating your EFC. Let's say your parents' home is worth $600,000 and they only owe $100,000 on it. This means they have $500,000 in home equity. Five percent of $500,000 is $25,000, so if one college counts all of your home equity in their college and another one counts none of it, then just off of this factor alone your EFC will be $25,000 higher with one college vs. another one. The worst part is that this $25,000 is an annual amount, so that is an extra $100,000 over four years.
4. Few PROFILE schools do not count home equity or count all of it; most have a cap on your home equity that ranges between 1.2 times your adjusted gross income (line 37 on your tax return) and three times your AGI. Let's look at our example of $500,000 in home equity and apply that to a family with an AGI of $133,333. If a college applies a 1.2 cap on your home equity, the formula would be AGI X 1.2 x .05 or $133,333 x 1.2=$160,000 x .05=$8000. In this instance, every year $8000 would be added to your EFC based just on your home equity. Now let's use the college that caps equity at 3 times the income for someone with the same income. $133,333 x 3.0=$400,000 x .05=$20,000. In this instance, $20,000 will be expected from you every year from college just based off of home equity.
5. **Non-working spouse:** the easiest way to lower your EFC is to have one spouse quit work to lower their income, but colleges know this, and they will impute a certain amount of income they

feel is reasonable for a spouse that chooses not to work. Policies are all over the place as to how or if a college does this.

6. **Remarriage situations:** some schools will require and factor into their EFC formula the stepparent, the biological parent you live with, and the other biological parent that may even be remarried with their own family, into what they expect from you. Other PROFILE colleges will follow the FAFSA and only count the biological parent you live with and the stepparent they are married to, but they will exempt the biological divorced parent you don't live with from their formula.
7. **Summer earnings:** are they factored in or not, and if so, is it a $500-dollar expectation or a $3500 expectation? The FAFSA does not project a student's summer earnings into their EFC, but most PROFILE schools expect a student to make money that goes toward their EFC. How much they expect varies tremendously.
8. Outside scholarship policies vary widely (see Chapter 130).
9. Schools that use the FAFSA rely on the AGI and untaxed income, but PROFILE schools look at business losses, rental property losses, and real estate losses.
10. **The college's K-12 tuition paying policy:** Some PROFILE schools will see the tuition your parents pay for your siblings to go to a private school as a legitimate expense, and they will reduce your EFC accordingly. Other colleges will see this as an unnecessary lifestyle decision that you made, and they will not lower your EFC based on this. Imagine if a parent has two children in boarding school at $60,000 a year, and their student applies to one PROFILE school that will reduce their income by $120,000 and another one that doesn't do this. This alone could result in a swing of over $30,000 in your EFC. Many PROFILE schools will let you count a portion of your child's private K-12 costs, usually between $6000-$12000, but that is often only a fraction of what you are paying.
11. **Business income:** PROFILE will look at all business equity, and the FAFSA will not look at business equity if there are fewer than 100 employees and the family owns 50 percent or more of the business, so the EFC will vary significantly based on this alone.

12. **Farm income:** PROFILE will look at all of it. For FAFSA, if a family lives on the farm and the family participates in the operation of the farm, then this money is excluded. Some PROFILE schools are very sympathetic to the fact that a family can't tap the value of their farm that easily.
13. How are gifts from a relative factored into the EFC? Policies vary here.
14. Does a college factor in COLA (Cost of Living Adjustment) for expensive locations like Santa Barbara, San Francisco, Chicago, and New York? If they do, how much of an adjustment is being made? This is often factored in by PROFILE schools, but it is not in the FAFSA formula.
15. There are differences in how a college handles the various concerns that get raised in the special circumstances section of the PROFILE, i.e. reduced wages, high medical costs, elderly care, etc. Now that Early FAFSA is here, a very common special circumstance is how a school will factor in whether your income goes down in the year after your taxes are submitted or in your current year. For example, if you are applying for aid in 2018-19, you will submit your 2018 PROFILE or FAFSA based on your 2016 tax returns, but what if your income goes down in 2017 or 2018? This is now a very common special circumstance and policies will be all over the place on this issue.
16. I knew about the 13 factors I just listed, but I learned of another factor from the book *Admission Matters*. Here is how author Sally P. Springer describes another variable: "The PROFILE includes additional child tax credit, earned income credit, untaxed Social Security benefits received for all family members except the student applicant, tuition and fees deduction, and the amount of foreign income exclusion. The FAFSA does not include these amounts."

Colleges have different policies on whether they will match or adjust their offer based on what a competitor offers in their aid award.

In 2016, I had a great conversation with Michael J. Runiewicz, the very personable and knowledgeable Director of Student Financial Services at Washington University in St. Louis. I was telling Michael that the PROFILE can be brutal to fill out. Michael said the reason for this is because when all of the Financial Aid Directors meet with the College Board, they all have different questions they want answered. The PROFILE amasses all of these questions, even though each school will pick and choose which answers they want to use.

Michael was very sympathetic to how onerous completing the PROFILE is. He went on to say that it is precisely because the PROFILE asks so many questions not relevant to the school that they developed their own Washington University Family Financial PROFILE (FFP). Michael said it is not only easier to complete, but it usually yields a result that is more favorable to the family. Wash U gives the family a choice between their own PROFILE and the CSS PROFILE. I didn't dedicate a whole chapter to it, but a number of schools (like Wash U) have developed their own financial aid forms.

A major difference between FAFSA and PROFILE is how they treat a non-custodial parent.

110

WHAT ARE THE ANSWERS TO THE MOST-ASKED QUESTIONS ABOUT THE REQUIREMENT TO SUBMIT THE NONCUSTODIAL PARENT PROFILE APPLICATION?

The FAFSA will not ask any information about the noncustodial parent's income and assets, but the PROFILE usually will require the noncustodial PROFILE. This can cause a lot of angst for the custodial parent and for the student applicant.

The College Board's website has an excellent frequently asked question section about the noncustodial parent and I am sharing verbatim five of their answers that the college applicant and the custodial parent frequently have:

Q: Will my child and his custodial parent have access to my information from the Noncustodial PROFILE?

A: The College Board separates processing of the custodial and noncustodial parent's applications. Neither parent is given access to the other parent's information. Colleges that collect noncustodial parent information are careful to protect the confidentiality of each parent's information unless the parent clearly indicated that it can be shared with the other parent or the student.

Q: Why does my daughter's college require the Noncustodial PROFILE?

A: Colleges that award institutionally funded need-based aid support a basic principle that holds the family responsible for college expenses, to the extent of its financial ability. Colleges that require noncustodial parent information have an inclusive definition of family and believe that both parents share that responsibility, even if they are no longer living with or married to one another. The Noncustodial PROFILE application service is designed to support efficient, confidential, and consistent transmission of noncustodial parent information by providing one central point of processing.

Q: How do I know if I need to complete the Noncustodial PROFILE Application?

A: Your son or daughter will be notified of the requirement as part of the PROFILE Application process. He or she will be notified online within the PROFILE Application, and your child will receive an email outlining the requirement. You may also receive an email notification directly from the College Board.

Q: My ex-spouse and I have a court order that states that I am not responsible for my child's college expenses. Why must I complete the Noncustodial PROFILE?

A: Each college that awards institutionally funded need-based financial aid has the right to request the information it wants to determine eligibility for funding, regardless of what an individual divorce decree mandates in terms of support. If your child has filed an application for financial aid, the school has the right to request your information even if you are not required by the court to provide educational support. Failure to provide your information may cause your child to be denied institutionally funded aid on the basis of an incomplete application.

Q: If I give estimated financial information on my Noncustodial PROFILE, will I be required to send in a completed tax form at a later date?

A: Many colleges and programs will ask families to submit copies of their completed income tax returns and other financial documents. Your colleges and programs will let you know if tax return copies are required. Follow institutional instructions about where to send these documents. Some institutions require that documents be sent directly to the financial aid office. Other institutions participate in the College Board's Institutional Documentation Service (IDOC) and instruct applicants to forward documents to a College Board address.

As helpful as those answers were, the College Board does not answer the most frequently asked question that I get about the noncustodial PROFILE. That question is, "What happens if I don't know where my dad (from my experience it is the dad who can't be located over 98 percent of the time) is?" Here is Cornell's policy, found on their website:

> If the whereabouts of your noncustodial parent are unknown, or if you have extenuating circumstances regarding your situation, complete the Noncustodial Parent Waiver Petition. Note that third party supporting documentation is required. Refusal of your noncustodial parent to provide information or support does not constitute a waiver.

Every college has a different policy. You can expect to really have to document this with credible adults who know your situation, and there are many schools that will receive this favorably.

If the noncustodial parent's whereabouts are known but they just refuse to complete the form, most PROFILE schools will not consider an appeal under the rationale that it is too easy for one parent to hide money by claiming that the other parent is not accessible. One of the most talented students I ever worked with fell in this category in 2007, and he was admitted to some of the most selective schools in the nation, but shut out over and over for aid. I found an outstanding PROFILE school that aided him, but it was only one of the half a dozen that admitted him, and we had excellent substantiation for his situation. If you find yourself in this situation, you would be advised to have several FAFSA-only schools and schools that do not require the noncustodial PROFILE on your college list.

111

WHAT IS A MERIT SCHOLARSHIP FROM THE COLLEGE?

There are only two ways you can qualify for money for college. You can qualify because an assessment is done of your family resources and you are determined to have a financial need, or you can qualify because you have gifts and talents that the college wants, so they offer you a merit scholarship. The money you receive in the latter case has nothing to do with your family's financial need. The way I explain merit scholarships to my students and parents is by saying, "If Bill Gates' kid could get free money for college, then it is a merit scholarship."

Merit scholarships can be athletic. FBS football schools have 85 football scholarships they can offer at one time, and FCS (formerly Division I-AA) can have 63 scholarship players on the roster. Merit aid can also be for special talents in areas such as debate, instrumental music, dance, art, singing, and theater, or it can be in the form of academic-based merit scholarships.

One of the biggest shifts in college admissions in the last 25 years has been the shift from colleges giving money away based on need to allocating their resources based on merit. A July 20, 2016, article in the *Huffington Post* said the following:

> A landmark 2011 United States Department of Education study found that the portion of students receiving merit-based scholarships grew dramatically (133 percent) between the 1995/96 and 2007/08 school years. By 2007/08, more students were receiving merit-based aid than need-based aid in both public universities (18 percent vs. 16 percent) and private colleges (44 percent vs. 42 percent).
> One key turning point in the trend toward merit aid occurred in 1993, when Georgia created its entirely "merit-based" HOPE Scholarship program. By 2012, 27 states had followed Georgia's lead to create merit-based programs, and 29 percent of state scholarships were merit-based. Today in Georgia, students from zip codes above state median income are three times as likely to receive a full HOPE scholarship than students from lower-income neighborhoods.

Merit scholarships are often referred to as merit aid or tuition discounting. Merit aid is very attractive to families, because the EFC formula is flawed, and most colleges practice gapping (see Chapter 97 on EFC and Chapter 98 on gapping), but it is also attractive to colleges because they need more money with the federal and state cutbacks. The same *Huffington Post* article says, "Many colleges and universities view merit aid as a way to compete in the higher education marketplace, using small awards as a tactic to attract higher income students who can afford higher tuition prices."

One of the biggest debates in college admissions is how much (if any) money should be given away based on merit vs. need.

My daughter Joy was attracted to Florida colleges; she is a beach girl who loves the palm trees, the architecture, the beaches, and the multicultural vibe of Florida. She loved Nova Southeastern in Fort Lauderdale, the University of Tampa, and Southeastern in Lakeland, but I set a maximum price and those Florida schools all exceeded our budget. Joy was thrilled that Valdosta State was 16 miles from Florida and it had the Florida beauty, but she also received the HOPE merit scholarship and half a year of dual enrollment credit, making Valdosta extremely affordable.

112

HOW DO I GET A MERIT SCHOLARSHIP FROM A PUBLIC COLLEGE?

Historically, private schools gave merit aid (a synonym for merit scholarship) and public schools didn't, but that trend is changing quickly. On October 17, 2017, I had a great conversation with Andrew Morrison and Melanie Lorick, two regional recruiters with Georgia territories who work for the University of Alabama. They were telling me about how they have increased the generosity of their Capstone merit scholarships. I asked them who their biggest competition is. They listed several schools, but they both said Mississippi State is getting really aggressive with their tuition discounting (merit scholarships), so they are definitely a competitor. The days where public colleges rarely give merit scholarships away are over.

For most families that do not qualify for the free and reduced lunch program, money from the college itself will be by far and away your best chance to get a large aid award, because you are unlikely to qualify for much (if any) free federal money. In addition to this, most students who get outside scholarships get less than $3,000. Check with your school counselor about state-based merit aid programs. You can also look up the details about merit aid for in-state students from your state's Higher Educational Agency. Just do a Google search. This is good for in-state aid, but it is also important because the trend is for states to give away more of their aid to in-state students based on merit.

If you want to get a substantial merit award, you need to be in the top 5-10 percent of the applicant pool for that college. If are okay with a lesser award, you should still be in the top quarter to top third of the applicant pool. This means you have to know how you stack up compared to other applicants.

Every state has at least one, and sometimes two, flagship colleges. There is no official definition of a flagship college, but flagship colleges almost always have the following traits:

1. They are large
2. They are prestigious
3. They offer a wide range of doctorate programs
4. They participate in D-1 sports
5. They are older
6. They are more expensive than the other in-state schools
7. They are more selective than the other in-state schools. In Michigan, you have the University of Michigan and Michigan State. In Texas, you have Texas and Texas A & M, and in Arizona, you have Arizona and Arizona State. Most states, however, are like Kentucky, Ohio, and Illinois where you only have one flagship: UK, Ohio State, and University of Illinois.

Flagships tend to fall in two categories: those who give away a lot of merit awards, and those who don't. In the first category, they are very competitive, and they are usually small awards compared to their out-of-state sticker price. Included on this first list would be schools such as Clemson, Ohio State, Colorado, Alabama, Vermont, Delaware, Iowa, and

Maryland. Flagships that just don't give out that many merit awards of any size to out-of-state students, no matter how strong the student is, include Georgia Tech, Michigan State, NC State, North Carolina, Penn State, UCLA, Florida, Georgia, Texas, Virginia, Washington, and Wisconsin.

It is much harder to get large aid awards and at times, even small merit aid awards, from flagships because they are in demand and they don't need to throw money at students in order to convince them to enroll.

I was not surprised when I found out that Bowling Green in Ohio and Louisiana Lafayette give away a lot of merit money, because they are not flagship public colleges. This is quite common with non-flagship public colleges. There are also some states that give away more merit aid in general than other states. Mississippi, Ohio, and Louisiana are known for their merit aid. Focus on non-flagships if you are looking for a large award and start with your in-state schools, because out-of-state schools often charge three times what in-state schools charge for tuition.

Flagships are aggressively recruiting out-of-state students (who pay much higher tuition) through merit aid to offset the cutbacks they are getting from their state legislature, but they often give a modest merit offer. If you get modest merit from Alabama, Colorado, Cal-Berkeley, or Michigan, how much will it really help when each school's respective tuition is around 30k for Alabama, over 35K for Colorado, over 40K for Cal-Berkeley, and over 45K for Michigan? I encourage you to Google the following outstanding article by Stephen Burd called "The Out-of-State Arms Race: How Public Universities Use Merit Aid to Recruit Nonresident Students."

Julie really wanted to go to either Ohio State, Michigan State, or the University of Michigan, and she was in the top 5 percent of her class at Cherokee High School in Canton, Georgia. She had almost a 30 on her ACT. But the best offer she got was from Michigan State, and all she got was a $5000 merit scholarship, which may sound good, but tuition alone is close to $40,000 at Michigan State for out-of-state students. Julie received the Zell Miller full in-state tuition scholarship and she ended up enrolling at the University of Georgia.

113

How do I get a merit scholarship from a private college?

I do a fair amount of private boarding school placement, and last year I called a boarding school that was asking a student to pay far more than they could afford. I just wanted to get a sense of how they came up with their aid award. The director of admissions told me, "Mark, we use financial aid strategically to enroll the students that will help our school the most; we don't just give it out willy-nilly because a student qualifies for it."

Private and public colleges function the same way, and it is imperative that you understand this. If you want to get a substantial merit award you need to be in the top 5-10 percent of the applicant pool for that college. If you are okay with a lesser award, you should still be in the top quarter to third of the applicant pool, and at some schools you will still qualify for a very small award if you are not in the top third.

Merit aid is used by some colleges on the frontend for recruitment, and for others it is used on the backend for yielding the students they admitted. Most colleges use it for both recruitment and for yield.

Private colleges differ from public colleges in that their sticker price is often substantially higher. This is partly because they aren't getting the same government assistance, and partly because they usually have smaller classes and just smaller overall populations to share the financial burden for all of their salary, facility, and other expenses.

A major reason their sticker price is so high is because they usually utilize a practice of tuition discounting (another term for merit aid). The way this works is that the bottom of the class effectively pays the sticker price so that the top kids can get merit scholarships. Let's look at a couple examples from Ohio, a state known for its merit aid, so we can see how this works. Both the College of Wooster and Denison College give merit aid or non-need based aid to over one-third of the students that didn't qualify for aid based on need. They also each charge around $50,000 for tuition and well over $60,000 for the total Cost of Attendance. They give aid to these students for two reasons: They are either the strongest applicants in their applicant pool and they are trying to entice them to enroll (Denison and Wooster), or they are an admissible student who will pay the full sticker price and Wooster fears they may not select Wooster, but they want their tuition revenue. I only mentioned Wooster here because this school admits it looks at the ability to pay when it makes admission decisions, while Denison claims that it doesn't do this. The point is that these decisions are not arbitrarily made. They aren't picking straws or saying, "Eeny, meeny, miny, moe." Very few students pay full sticker price. The weaker students pay for the stronger students.

There are even a sizable number of colleges that automatically give everyone a small tuition discount in order to make them feel special so they will increase their chances of enrolling, but these awards are small for students that aren't standouts in the applicant pool.

The more prestigious and the more in-demand a college is, the less likely they are to give merit aid away at all, and if they do give merit aid away, it is usually to a small percentage of their student body and the qualifications you will need to receive it are very difficult to achieve. Take a look at the acceptance rate of a college and it will usually give you a clue as to how hard it will be to qualify for merit aid.

Here are some of the colleges that have such strong brand strength that they can give all of their money away based on need and still generate a strong applicant pool: Amherst, Barnard, Bates, Cal Tech, Colgate, Franklin and Marshall, Georgetown, Hamilton, Haverford, Middlebury, MIT, Pomona, Skidmore, Stanford, Swarthmore, and all eight Ivy league schools.

Here are some others that give merit aid away to less than 1 in 20 applicants and it doesn't stop them from enrolling a high-powered group of applicants: Boston College, Bowdoin, Brandeis, Carleton, Colby, Claremont-McKenna, Connecticut College, Davidson, Duke, Emory, Johns Hopkins, Lehigh, NYU, Northwestern, Pitzer, Trinity (CT), Tufts, Notre Dame, Wake Forest, and Wesleyan.

Unless you are an exceptionally strong applicant, you are wise to target colleges that are not in the super-selective group if getting merit money is a priority for you in your college search. Here are a few examples of the many private schools that give large aid awards to large numbers of students: Agnes Scott, Allegheny, Baylor, Brigham Young, Catholic University, Centre College, Clark, Wooster, DePaul, Eckerd, Hendrix, Hobart William and Smith, Hollins, Hope, Illinois Wesleyan, Lawrence, Marquette, Rhodes, Sewanee, SMU, Texas Christian, and the University of Denver. These are excellent schools, but their acceptance rates are noticeably higher than the no-merit and the low-merit colleges listed above.

There's one thing that catches a lot of families off guard. If you are admitted to a school that gives away based on need *and* merit, they will almost always use a merit award to decrease what they give you in need-based aid. For example, the Cost of Attendance of the private college is $70,000, and your EFC says you can pay $20,000, and the school promises to meet your full demonstrated need, so you are expecting $50,000, mostly in a need-based grant, but you also receive a $10,000 merit award. Now you think you only have to pay $10,000 (20K-10K), but most schools will take the 10K in merit and apply it to the 50K they were going to give you, still leaving you with $20,000 to pay the college.

Because many people find the EFC is not realistic (see Chapter 98) and they have not been able to save enough for college, here are the other choices:

- ℵ Go into exorbitant debt for college (not advisable)
- ℵ Go to a community college
- ℵ Take courses online

- ℵ Live at home and go to a local public college
- ℵ Find an affordable in-state college
- ℵ Have modest resources, and qualify for one of the few schools that gives generous need-based aid
- ℵ Find a college where you are strong enough to qualify for merit aid. For a lot of families, this merit aid approach is a game changer. For example, Sewanee: The University of the South gives away $14,000 in renewable Wilkins Merit scholarships to 100 of their 450 freshman every year. This is not just $56,000 over four years but that is after tax money, so it may be close to $80,000 in real money.

I was having a conversation with the director of admission at a school that if I mentioned the name, you all would know it. I asked him, "Why are you charging so much when you have the billion-dollar endowment and you could afford to charge less?"

He responded honestly, "We charge it because we can get away it and we would rather have the money in our coffers to implement our mission."

This was another way of saying, "There are enough wealthy families who will pay our $65,000 cost, and we can use that to pay our faculty well and provide financial aid for the lower-income gifted students who can't afford to pay but make our school better if we enroll them." When it comes to merit money, the average student is subsidizing the amazing student.

114

WHERE CAN I FIND MERIT SCHOLARSHIPS?

There are six places where you can find merit scholarships:

1. You can scour the financial aid and scholarship section of each college that you are interested in. This is the best way by far, but it is also the most time-consuming way. It is the one method that is absolutely imperative even if you also use the other methods. This is where information will be most current, most thorough, and most accurate. You will find extremely important information here like criteria for selection, application process, criteria for renewal, and deadlines.
2. You can learn about school-based merit scholarships from surfing other college admission websites. Many sites list merit-based scholarships, but I still want you to go to the college's own website to learn more.

3. You can sign up for an account on websites like https://www.cappex.com/ or https://www.collegegreenlight.com/ and if the details in your account match a scholarship in their database, you will either receive an email or see the scholarship listed in your Cappex or College Greenlight inbox.
4. You can visit your state's Higher Educational Agency and learn about the scholarships for your state. Here is a link to help you access the state agency for your state: https://www.petersons.com/college-search/financial-aid-state-agencies.aspx#/sweeps-modal
5. You can choose to opt in when you sign up for the PSAT, PreACT, SAT, ACT, AP, and IB exams, and colleges can purchase lists of students who match certain criteria (see Chapter 25 on why you're receiving so many mailers). The colleges can then inform you about certain merit scholarships.
6. You can work with your school counselor and/or your private college coach to help you identify appropriate merit-based scholarships. You should definitely be working with your school counselor. I am part of the KIPP Metro Atlanta college team, where I am a school counselor. Just yesterday I had a meeting with Elle Jackson and her mom Carla to help Elle find merit scholarships. I am also a private college coach for School Match 4U, and I do the same thing in that capacity. School counselors and private counselors alike can really help you through this process.
7. Note: Many colleges also factor an applicant's need into who they award their merit scholarships to. Usually the way this works is you first need to be a standout throughout their merit criteria (usually test scores and GPA and sometimes other factors), but they will prioritize who will be the award recipients. Last month I had a conversation with the very talented Allyson Smith, the Assistant Director of Admissions at Spelman College, about their merit money. Allyson made it clear that, "First we look at merit criteria and then

we see who needs the money the most." When you are looking at merit money, check the website to see if financial needs is one of the factors under consideration.

Lemar called me about his daughter Anita. He had just completed the net price calculator at the schools Anita was interested in, and he said, "Mark, I don't know how we are going to afford this without going into substantial debt."

I recommended Anita for the John B. Ervin scholarship at Washington University in St. Louis, and I was so happy for her when she sent me a text message that said, "I got it!"

Anita was awarded this renewable scholarship valued at well over $50,000 a year only after Anita and Lemar had diligently studied the website for the John B. Ervin scholarship. You can choose to utilize the second through fifth approaches listed above, but you MUST study the information on the website.

115

HOW WILL I BE ASSESSED BY A COLLEGE FOR A MERIT SCHOLARSHIP?

Assessment can refer to the criteria that will determine what award you receive, or it can refer to the process that is used to determine if you will receive a merit scholarship at all. We have thoroughly covered how you get admitted to colleges in Section 3, and it is these same factors that determine who receives merit aid, so I encourage you to read those chapters. For a quick overview, visit Chapter 11 about holistic admissions vs. admissions by the numbers.

Here are the seven most common processes that are used for your assessment based on the students I have worked with:

1. **Automatic inclusion based on holistic review:** At Duke University, all undergraduate students who apply are automatically considered for all merit scholarships, with exception of

the Robertson Scholars Leadership program. I absolutely love it when colleges include every applicant in the scholarship search. There is so much for students to do in this college process that it really helps to have one thing taken care of already, and it is one way to ensure everyone is considered for a merit scholarship. A common variation of this process is what Agnes Scott does. They automatically consider anyone for a \$15,000-\$22,000 award who applies through their early action or early decision process. Some schools automatically consider anyone who applies through the regular process, but by a priority admission date.

2. **Automatic inclusion based only on your GPA and test scores:** Calvin College in Michigan automatically grants academic scholarships for incoming students ranging from \$8,000 to \$18,000. These scholarships are awarded automatically based on Grade Point Average and ACT or SAT scores. Calvin claims that over 85 percent of students get one of their scholarships. They have six levels: National Merit, Trustee, President's, Provost, Dean's, and Faculty's. Merit scholarships based solely on GPA and test scores are very common, so keep that GPA up and put in the work to get your scores as high as you can. Even schools that do a holistic review invariably put a lot of weight on test scores and GPA. One simple way to know if a school is giving merit aid based just on test scores is to complete their net price calculator, and if it asks for your test scores and GPA, that is a telltale sign.
3. **Separate application requesting additional information:** Vanderbilt gives away 250 full-tuition awards plus summer stipends for study abroad, research, or service projects through their Ingram Scholars, Cornelius Vanderbilt Scholars, and Chancellor's scholarships. The application requires additional essays and two more recommendations, and the Ingram Scholars application requires an onsite interview. Sometimes the additional application is the only additional requirement.

4. **School nomination required:** The University of Virginia Jefferson Scholars' stipend includes tuition, fees, books, supplies, room, board, and personal expenses, but your school has to nominate you. North Carolina's equally generous Morehead-Cain scholarship would prefer a school recommendation, but they will let you self-nominate.
5. **Audition or portfolio review required:** See Chapter 66 on what visual and performing art majors need to know about how their college application process is unique.
6. **Athletic scholarships:** See Chapter 131 that discusses things athletes can do to get athletic scholarship.
7. **Interview Weekend:** Here, students come in for multiple days of activities including things like private interviews, group activities, faculty meetings, VIP meetings, fun activities, dinners, and special parent programming. An example of this is the University of Miami's Stamp Scholarship. The John B. Ervin scholarship I mentioned in the last chapter has a four-day mandatory weekend program requirement. The great thing about the scholarship weekends is that the students who are invited are the top priorities for the colleges, and, almost always, the students who do not win are still awarded a smaller merit scholarship (usually at least $8000/year), making the weekend well worth your time.

John really wanted to go to Tuskegee University. He was the oldest of five kids, and had triplet siblings, so all of the kids were pretty close in age and a scholarship was really going to take so much financial stress off of the family. John was burned out on school. AP Chemistry had taken its toll him, but he was determined to get the University Merit Scholarship at Tuskegee. The scholarship required a 1310 on the SAT or a 28 on the ACT and a 3.5 GPA in order to get full tuition and an $800 stipend. John's mom hired a great test prep instructor and John put in the hard work and accomplished his goal to receive the full tuition scholarship.

116

WHAT IS NEED-BASED COLLEGE AID, AND HOW DO I GET IT?

The only two ways financial aid is allocated are through merit or need. Need-based aid college aid is money that is given from the college's own resources because an objective analysis of your family's resources indicates that there is a gap between the Cost of Attendance and what you can afford to pay.

Usually, colleges that give away the most need-based money use the CSS PROFILE (see chapter 108) to assess what you can afford.

Colleges that are committed to need-based aid do so because they believe that they help their own school and society when they make sure that their resources are not only going to upper-middle class and upper-class students. Here is how Yale describes their rationale for their commitment to need-based financial aid: "Need-based aid allows us to direct our institutional resources to the students who truly require and will benefit the most from them, and it helps maintain socio-economic diversity at Yale."

As Seth Allen, the Director of Pomona, likes to say, "Need-based aid is not want-based aid." You are not the one who determines the need: an outside formula does that.

Most colleges that offer need-based aid also offer merit aid. Many colleges that do not offer significant amounts of need-based aid wish that they could, but they either lack significant resources in their coffers, or they feel they will not be fully enrolled with quality students if they don't dangle merit scholarships out there to entice families. The colleges with the most need-based aid are usually among the most selective and wealthiest colleges in the country. Because they are so selective, need-based aid is really a de facto form of merit aid, in the sense that only the students with the strongest qualifications will be able to compete.

Trevor was being courted by Yale. He had the grades, test scores, and rigor that Yale likes. He was also a recruited athlete, and the basketball coach wanted him to play at Yale. But Trevor's dad (Dr. Jones) had a successful medical practice as a surgeon. Trevor could go to Yale, but Dr. Jones was going to have to pay the full tuition because Trevor didn't qualify for any need-based aid and that is the only type of aid Yale gives.

Courtney was in the top 3 percent of her graduating class at Westlake High School in Atlanta. She took AP courses and she had the test scores and the GPA. A lot of her classmates were telling her she should stay in state, get the Zell Miller scholarship, and only have to pay room and board, but Courtney was one of four siblings and her mom was a single parent. Vanderbilt's generous need-based aid, coupled with her family's financial need, made Vanderbilt a better financial opportunity than staying in state and paying for room and board. Need-based aid really benefits talented kids who qualify for a lot of money.

117

HOW CAN I INCREASE MY NEED-BASED AID?

My answer to this question is mainly for parents. The single biggest way to increase need-based aid is to decrease your parental income. Parental income is the biggest factor, by far, in determining EFC for students who are classified as dependent students. The problem is that many people either are living check to check and they need all of their income just to make ends meet, or they have other expenses to which that income needs to go. And anyway, are you really going to approach your employer and ask them to lower your salary? Of course not. But here are some ways you can ethically keep your income from adversely impacting your EFC:

1. If you have a bonus from work coming and it can be deferred until after the last year, aid will be calculated for your student in college without that bonus, and it will lead to a lower EFC.

2. Try not to take a withdrawal from your retirement plan, because a distribution will count as income. For families with an adjusted gross income of $100,000, almost half of what you receive on every additional $10,000 will be expected to go to your EFC. If you take a $20,000 retirement withdrawal, the EFC formula will say the college should get almost $10,000 of this withdrawal (ouch!)
3. Try not to take capital gains unless you are going to offset those gains with capital losses, because that will count as income. The same almost-50 percent rule applies here that we just discussed.
4. If you don't have any kids yet and you are reading this, having two kids in college at once simultaneously substantially decreases your EFC, virtually cutting it in half for most colleges. If you can plan to have multiple kids in college at the same time, it is going to significantly lower your EFC and make you eligible for a lot more aid. For those of you who have twins, you just hit the lottery from an EFC standpoint. After parent income, the number of kids you have in college simultaneously is the second-biggest factor in determining your EFC.
5. If you have two kids who are two years apart and the oldest one takes a gap year, leaving them one year apart when it comes to college, this could save you over $30,000 a year for college for that extra year that they will both be college students. This will depend on where your kids are admitted and what your EFC is (see EFC Chapters 97 and 98).
6. Don't save money in the child's name, because the EFC formula counts money in the child's name at 20-25 percent vs. 5-5.64 percent if it is in the parents' name.
7. Don't have a grandparent save money in a 529 in the grandparent's name and make a distribution to the child. This is classified as untaxed income, and could be taxed at 50 percent rather than the 20-25 percent rate I just mentioned. If a grandparent has a 529 for a grandchild, they need to look into switching it to the parent.

Assets don't impact EFC as much as income, but the following assets are included in the EFC formula unless they're in retirement accounts:

- ℵ amount in the bank (savings, checking, money market, CDs)
- ℵ brokerage accounts
- ℵ investment real estate
- ℵ mutual funds
- ℵ stocks
- ℵ bonds
- ℵ ETFs
- ℵ commodities, and 529 college prepaid and savings plans.

Some assets are protected, because the EFC formula understands not all money can go to college. This is called the Asset Protection Allowance, and it is based on the age of the oldest parent and whether you are in a single parent or a two-parent family. Asset Protection, though, is on the verge of extinction. For a 50-year-old two-parent family, the Asset Protection Allowance is around $20,000, but seven years ago it was around $50,000. For a single parent, it is closer to $11,000. This means that for any assets over $20,000, 5-5.64 percent (and usually it is 5.64 percent) of those assets will go to the EFC. If you can lower your assets, your EFC will be lower and you will be more eligible for need-based aid. So what are a few ways you can do this?

Let's say that a two-parent household had $50,000 in assets. A 50K-20K Asset Protection Allowance means 30K is currently being multiplied by 5.64 percent (or $1692) to go to the EFC, but if you won $100,000 in the lottery or put it in the bank, or you bought Amazon stock in a non-retirement account, $5640 every year would go to your EFC. Let's say it took your child five years to graduate. That would be $5640 x 5=$28,200 you would have paid by having an increased EFC. However, if you used the $100,000 to pay down your mortgage and your child went to a school that only requires the FAFSA, none of that money would go to your EFC, because your primary home is protected under the FAFSA calculation.

Pay off consumer debt like credit cards or auto loans, because you will have less money in the bank and therefore less assets.

If you were planning on buying a car or finishing your basement, consider doing it in cash to keep your assets down (cars or your primary home don't impact EFC).

Go through the financial aid appeals process if it makes sense (see Chapter 154).

If your student gets into one of the few schools that offers no loans, this could save you $27,000 over four years.

My cousin Janice was very fortunate. Out of the blue, she got an email saying that she had inherited $110,000 from an aunt. She thought it was a scam, but it turned out to be legitimate. I knew Janice had one college student with two more on the way, so I immediately told her, "Janice, don't put this money in the bank or buy a stock, because it will noticeably impact your kids' EFC." Janice put about $15,000 in an emergency account, but she mostly paid off debt, made some home upgrades, and made a big payment on their mortgage.

118

WHAT IS A PELL GRANT, AND HOW DO I GET IT?

A Pell Grant is the largest federal grant administered by the United States Department of Education. The government gives away over 30 billion dollars every year to almost 10 million students who receive Pell Grants. Lyndon Johnson's Higher Educational Act of 1965 was revised in 1972 to include Pell Grants. The name Pell Grant comes from six-time Democratic Senator Claiborne Pell of Rhode Island, who originally proposed the Pell Grant.

One myth about the Pell Grant is that it is only for low-income students. Actually, the grant is for low and moderate-income families. When a family has multiple kids in college at the same time, they can have an income above the national average and still be Pell Grant-eligible.

In order to receive a Pell Grant, a student must complete the FAFSA and they must be working on their undergraduate degree or certificate program or in a teacher certification program.

Pell Grant awards range from a few hundred dollars to around $6000 a year, and are based on the EFC formula. This is a grant that does not have to be repaid. If a family has an EFC of $4995 or less, they will be Pell Grant-eligible. Evaluation is done on a year-by-year basis.

Typically, the college first applies the grant toward a student's tuition, fees, and (if the student lives on campus) room and board. Any money remaining is paid to the student for other expenses like books, off-campus rent, and transportation.

Once you have earned a baccalaureate degree or your first professional degree, or have used up all 12 semesters of your eligibility, you are no longer eligible to receive a federal Pell Grant. There are a few exceptions for post-baccalaureate teacher certification.

Most incarcerations and convictions for sex crimes and drug crimes will result in the loss of Pell Grant eligibility.

When I met with Maya and her grandma, they were really worried about how Maya was going to afford college. Maya's grandma was her official guardian, and she was about to retire and they had no college savings. Ms. Thompson (Maya's grandma) called me one evening and I could hear the joy immediately in her voice. Maya had received a $5000 Pell Grant, and she starts at Georgia State this fall.

119

What is FSEOG, and how can I get it?

The Federal Supplemental Educational Opportunity Grant (FSEOG) is the other main federal grant for students.

<u>Similarities to the Pell Grant</u>

- ℵ As a grant, it does not have to be repaid
- ℵ The student must file the FAFSA to be eligible
- ℵ It is a need-based grant that also has a range for the award based on income
- ℵ Usually your student aid is credited first before any disbursement to you occurs

Differences from the Pell Grant

- ℵ Total amount awarded nationally is closer to 1 billion than 30 billion
- ℵ Total recipient number is closer to 1.5 million than 10 million
- ℵ Award range is from $100-$4000
- ℵ Average award is well under $1000
- ℵ Not every college participates
- ℵ Partnership between the federal government and the college, with the government paying three-quarters and the college paying one-quarter of the award
- ℵ The money must be given out to the poorest students who qualify for the largest Pell Grants
- ℵ This is exclusively a low-income program and not a low- and moderate-low income grant
- ℵ Money is often given out to the first students who submit the FAFSA and enroll
- ℵ The aid award is initiated and managed by the college's financial aid office and not the federal government
- ℵ Each college sets its own FSEOG deadline
- ℵ If the college does not use its entire share of the FSEOG money, the Department of Education will not disburse as much money to that college for the next school year.

FSEOG is currently on life support. A March 17, 2017 *USA Today* article discusses how there is "Bad news ahead for low-income students." The proposed budget in Washington wants to reduce 3.9 billion from Pell Grants, and the budget also proposes totally eliminating the Federal Supplemental Educational Opportunity Grant (FSEOG) program. The article states that killing this program will "save $732 million."

120

WHAT IS THE TEACH GRANT, AND HOW CAN I GET IT?

The TEACH Grant is a clever acronym that stands for Teacher Education Assistance for College and Higher Education. The maximum amount of the grant is $4000 per year, but for the 2017-18 year the maximum is $3736.

For eligibility, you must:

- Complete the FAFSA
- Be eligible for Federal Student Aid
- Have SAT, ACT, or GRE scores in the 75th percentile in at least one portion of these tests, or your GPA must be a 3.25 or higher

- ℵ Commit to teaching low-income students in elementary or high school for four years within eight years of graduating. Medical leave or a call to active duty can extend the eight years. If you want to know if a school qualifies, the annual Teacher Cancellation Low Income Directory is the authoritative source. If you fail to complete your required four years, your grant will be converted to a direct unsubsidized federal loan, and you will be responsible for the interest on the loan from the date that the grant was disbursed. This is why I say the TEACH Grant is really a forgivable loan more than a grant.
- ℵ Teach a subject where there is a shortage of quality teachers. Math, science, foreign languages, bi-lingual education, reading specialists, and special education almost always qualify, but other subjects are eligible if they are listed in the annual Teacher Shortage Area Nationwide Listing.
- ℵ The college you attend must participate in the TEACH Grant program. You need to talk to the financial aid department to see if the program of study you are signing up for is approved for the TEACH Grant for your state and for your college.
- ℵ Complete the TEACH Grant counseling session every year.
- ℵ Sign the TEACH Grant Willingness to Serve form.

I am a member of the KIPP Through College team in Metro Atlanta, and our school is approved as a low-income school where teachers can serve and receive the TEACH Grant. I was talking to Dr. Shannon, one of my amazing colleagues, about the fact that we lost a few teachers I didn't think we would lose last year.

Dr. Shannon replied, "I honestly believe one or two of those teachers were just here for their four years so the TEACH Grant would reduce their college loan burden."

121

HOW DO I KNOW HOW MUCH LOAN DEBT TO TAKE OUT FOR COLLEGE?

My clients usually come to me with two extreme views on college loans. Either they say they'll do whatever it takes when it comes to loans, or they talk about the 'L word' like it is a four-letter word. In other words, "we are not going there."

A great college education is precious, but that doesn't mean you should imperil your future and/or your parents' future with an onerous debt load. Student loan debt is now up to 1.3 trillion dollars, and it has surpassed both car loans and credit card debt.

I encounter the other extreme more frequently. There is a growing tendency to think that no college debt is ever worth taking on. I could not disagree more vehemently. When I hear this from a parent, I say, "Are you against taking out a car loan or mortgage in any circumstance?"

I then say, "A car is a depreciable asset and a house will usually appreciate modestly, but your return on your investment in your education will exceed your return on a car or a house in financial and in non-financial ways."

The average student is graduating with a tad more than $37,000 in debt according to an August 7, 2017, report on https://studentloanhero.com/ titled, "A Look at the Shocking Student Loan Statistics for 2017." This is $10,000 over the Federal Direct loan limits for a student who spends four years in college. It is also $10,000 more than what I recommend for a student who is not sure what they will major in.

If this is the best loan (see Chapter 124), then $27,000 in loans will result in a payment of about $270 a year for ten years at the current interest rates. Here is a great loan calculator to use to crunch your own numbers:
https://bigfuture.collegeboard.org/pay-for-college/loans/student-loan-calculator#

Is this too much or about right? The answer is, "It depends." A dime to one person is a dollar to someone else. I am telling you what I tell my clients:

1. Figure out what your entry level salary is going to be by doing research on first year pay at Payscale.com or the Occupational Outlook Handbook.
2. Multiply your first year pay by 80 percent.
3. This is the maximum amount of student debt that you can incur for your entire undergraduate education.

Is less debt better than more debt? Absolutely, but education is not a commodity, and oftentimes it is worth it to take on a manageable of debt to get a better education.

Example using real data from Payscale:

1. First-year pay for a social worker in Houston is $32,760.
2. Multiply this by 80 percent.
3. Your maximum loan total for four years is $26,208.

And for a second example:

1. First-year pay for a chemical engineer in Houston is $58,853.
2. Multiply this by 80 percent.
3. Your maximum four-year loan amount is $47,082.

If you are doing these calculations with high-paying majors, you can't start out as chemical engineer and switch to social work. You also have to have a plan so you are not an unemployed or underemployed college grad.

If you are not sure what you are going to major in, use the four-year Federal Stafford Loan maximum of $27,000 as your ceiling. The maximum was wisely set at this amount.

I serve on the board of a stupendous organization called Go to College NYC (http://gotocollegenyc.org/). We help gifted and talented under-resourced kids find the right college. Every once in a while, we get carried away with focusing too much on how we have to find "no loan" colleges for our students, but on three different occasions in the last 18 months a really sharp member of our board, Angel, has spoken up and said, "A lot of times your return on your investment for making a better college choice, even though you incur a manageable load amount, is well worth it." Angel is correct.

122

WHAT IS THE PLUS LOAN?

PLUS was originally an acronym (Parent Loan for Undergraduate Student), but now it is also a graduate student loan, so often you will hear it referred to as a Parent Plus in order to not confuse it with the PLUS graduate student loan.

The loan can be as much as the full Cost of Attendance minus any other aid you are receiving. The college you are accepted at determines the COA.

A parent has to have a credit check and qualify for the loan, but they don't need to have a 700 credit score. You will be denied if you have any of the following problems with your credit: $2085 or more in 90-days delinquent, written off, or in collections. Secondly, in the last five years any of the following on your credit report will cause problems:

1. bankruptcy

2. foreclosure
3. repossession
4. tax lien
5. wage garnishment, and
6. debt in default.

Here are a few other facts to know:

- The lender is the Department of Education.
- You must file the FAFSA.
- Most schools use http://studentloans.gov as your source to start your application. You should confirm with your school which system they use.
- You must be the biological or adoptive parent (stepparents are rarely approved).
- The student must be at least half-time status, which is usually six credit hours in semester system.
- You must meet federal standards for aid (see Chapter 96).
- The interest rate is 7 percent with a 4.264 loan origination fee for 2017-2018, but this rate usually changes slightly ever year. The new rates come out in June. This is a fixed loan.
- Repayment options are either 10 years or 25 years.
- You can cancel the loan, but you can't transfer it to your child. This is a parent loan and the parent is responsible for payments.
- Payment goes directly to your college to cover your direct costs, but if there is still a balance you can receive a check to be used for other educational expenses.

Payments begin right after the loan is disbursed to your college. There is an option to defer payments if your school is using studentloans.gov, but you need to know that interest is still accruing should you take this option.

Ms. Walker and her daughter Tameka met with me to see if I had any ideas that could help them pay for college without so many loans. As I started to review their finances, I was surprised that instead of Tameka having any Stafford Loans, Ms. Walker had taken out PLUS loans instead. I said, "Ms. Walker, why are you paying for PLUS loans when Tameka could save thousands of dollars over the years with the Stafford Loan?"

Ms. Walker replied, "I really don't want Tameka to have any debt when she graduates."

I said. "Why don't you have Tameka take out the Stafford Loan and you pay it back at the much lower interest rate?"

She hadn't thought of that, and she isn't the only one who is making that mistake.

123

Mark, tell me what you really think of the PLUS Loan.

- PLUS loans cause parents to borrow far more than they can afford to repay. It is so easy to get a lot of money if you don't have adverse credit that it really can put parents in financial bondage over the long haul.
- They seriously jeopardize your retirement. Here is what Liz Weston of Reuters said in her excellent Aug 10, 2015, article titled, "Parent Education Loans Can Ruin Your Retirement":

> College graduates presumably will benefit from higher incomes as the result of their education. Their parents will not. Parents also have fewer working

> years ahead of them, which means any financial setback such as a layoff can make a heavy debt load overwhelming and kill any shot at a comfortable retirement.

- ℵ It is not unusual for colleges to inflate the Cost of Attendance, causing parents to borrow more than they even need. It is not uncommon for me to see a PLUS loan in a student aid award for over $50,000 for one year.
- ℵ Some colleges are deceitful in how they present the PLUS loan on the aid award. It can be confused with a grant. There is often little explanation of the PLUS loan from the college, giving an uninformed parent a false sense of the affordability of the college.
- ℵ PLUS loans permit parents to take out enormous loans without a responsible assessment of whether the borrower has the income or ability to repay the loans. It is outrageous.
- ℵ Weston's article said that filed financial disclosure forms "revealed that former Maryland governor Martin O'Malley and his wife borrowed $339,200 to educate the first two of their four children."
- ℵ These loans are particularly hard on low-income families. According to Weston, "An analysis by financial aid expert Mark Kantrowitz in 2012 found that monthly PLUS loan payments ate up an average 38% of monthly income for borrowers in the lowest 10% of incomes."
- ℵ There is a lobbying effort in place from colleges to keep the money coming, because a lot of colleges rely on parents who really can't afford these PLUS loans to take them out. The lobbying effort doesn't focus on parents' long-term financial health. Here is how a September 19, 2013, article by SBLA titled, "The Problem with Parent Plus Loans" described the conduct of presidents and other college leaders who met with the Department of Education to lobby for leniency in not making it harder for parents to get PLUS loans:

> The school officials talked about the devastating impact on enrollment at their schools. This is understandable, given their interest in keeping their doors open, but one would also expect the officials to at least mention the need for relief for struggling borrowers. This didn't happen much. For example, only a few school officials raised concerns about the limited repayment options available to parent PLUS loan borrowers.

- ℵ There are no loan forgiveness options for PLUS loans, like Federal Stafford Loans have.
- ℵ Income-based repayment options are not nearly as gracious as the Stafford Loans. Here is how that same SBLA article puts it: "If the borrowers decide to separate their PLUS loans and non-PLUS loans and apply for IBR only for the non-PLUS loans, they will find that their often significant PLUS loan debt is not considered in determining the IBR payment because PLUS loans are not eligible loans."
- ℵ A parent can select a 25-year repayment option, which amounts to an inordinate amount of interest and often, long-term financial bondage. It can be the equivalent of a second mortgage.
- ℵ The deferment option is too tempting for some families who are not great with money.
- ℵ Student loans lack protection from bankruptcy, and that is also true for PLUS loans. Here is how Weston puts it,

> As with student loans, parent PLUS loans are extremely difficult to erase in bankruptcy and the government has extraordinary powers to collect, seizing tax refunds, getting wage garnishments without going to court, and taking a portion of defaulted borrowers' Social Security checks, which are off-limits to other creditors.

- ℵ There is some good news here, and it is much better than before. It is harder to get PLUS loans since 2011. According to the Student Borrower Loan Assistance (SBLA),

> The Department tightened the credit standards for parent PLUS loans by deciding to go back five years instead of just 90 days in looking at a borrower's delinquent accounts and charge-offs. The decision stemmed at least in part from concerns about increased PLUS loan borrowing, very high PLUS loan acceptance rates and increased default rates.

א There are some people in the black community who cried foul because black families and HBCUs were hurt by the higher qualifications for approval, but I supported this Obama initiative because many black parents were taking on PLUS loans that were putting them in bondage. Here is how SBLA put it:

> PLUS loan denials increase by 50 percent for parents of students at historically black colleges and universities (HBCUs), costing the institutions about $50 million in enrollment revenue. The *Huffington Post* even reported that at least some HBCUs were considering suing the administration over the changes. Affected schools and their allies pushed the department to reconsider the restrictions. The department responded first by making some changes to the borrower appeals process and then in August 2013, agreeing to review the rules in upcoming negotiated rulemaking sessions and in the meantime taking steps to make it easier for parents who were initially denied PLUS loans to receive loans on appeal. There is no question that the changes harmed many colleges' bottom lines, which also harms students. The real question is about a system of higher education that is dependent on parents taking out relatively expensive loans with limited flexible repayment options.

Note: There is one thing I love about the PLUS loan. If you have adverse credit history (bankruptcy, repossession, 90-day delinquency, foreclosure in the last five years) and you apply for a PLUS loan, you will be denied, but you can get $4000 in unsubsidized Stafford loans in its place.

Here is what a borrower that NCLC ended up helping said about her experience with Parent Plus Loans: "I am a parent of two boys who borrowed what FAFSA would let them borrow and then I had to take out PLUS loans. I have $157,000 in PLUS loan debt. My payments are $1864 per month. That is 53 percent of my total net pay. I cannot afford the payments."

124

WHAT ARE THE 15 REASONS WHY THERE IS ONE LOAN THAT IS UNQUESTIONABLY THE BEST LOAN THAT ALMOST ALL STUDENTS ARE ELIGIBLE FOR?

The United States Department of Education offers both subsidized and unsubsidized loans. They are sometimes called Direct Stafford Loans, and other times they are called Direct Subsidized or Direct Unsubsidized Loans. Other times they are called Subsidized or Unsubsidized Loans, but I will usually refer them to as Stafford Loans because it is shorter and simpler.

These two loans are the best two loans that a student can take and they are the ONLY loans I like to see students take. I realize there will inevitably be some exceptions (i.e. jobs that are in high demand with high starting salaries).

The four differences between the Subsidized and Unsubsidized Direct loans are:

1. Subsidized loans are only for undergraduate students, but unsubsidized loans can be used for graduate or professional school.
2. Subsidized loans are based on financial need, whereas unsubsidized are not income-dependent.
3. For subsidized loans, the government pays the interest as long as certain conditions are met (see below).
4. The maximum eligibility for subsidized loans is only good for up to 150 percent of the length of your academic program. For example, for a two-year program, 150 percent would be three years, and for bachelors' programs, you can take the loan for up to six years. In order to be eligible for either loan, you must complete the FAFSA.

Here are 15 reasons why I love both the subsidized and the unsubsidized loans:

1. Low interest rates of currently under 5 percent. Private loans are credit score dependent and are often more than two times higher.
2. Low origination fee, just over 1 percent, whereas it is over 4 percent for PLUS loans.
3. Government pays the interest until one of three things happens: you move to less than half-time status, you drop out of college, or until six months after graduation.
4. Fixed-, not variable-rate loans, allow you to know what you are going to pay. Private loans often are variable-rate loans that go up when the Federal Reserve has a hike.
5. No co-signer is necessary. The government is trusting you even though you have either no credit history, very little credit history, or even a poor credit score. This protects your parents or other adults from having to risk their financial health by having to co-sign your loans and be liable if you default.

6. Loan forgiveness options are possible for certain forms of public service.
7. Flexible repayment plans (see Chapter 126 on private vs. federal loans to learn about seven repayment options).
8. Deferment allows you to postpone or reduce your payments due to economic difficulty for a total of three years.
9. Forbearance lets you put your payments on hold for up to a year at a time.
10. No prepayment penalties.
11. Safeguards against over-borrowing are in place based on the reasonable caps of $5500 for freshman year, $6500 for sophomore year, and $7500 for junior and senior year, for a total of $27,000. If you need more than four years, there is another $4000 for a possible maximum of $31,000 for a dependent student and considerably more for an independent student.
12. Loan balances are expunged should you die. I know this may seem obvious, but it is not true for so many private loans. If you read the fine print, there are some private student loans that go into "auto default" should a student die, meaning the co-signer must pay the total balance right away.
13. Loan balances can often be expunged should you become severely disabled.
14. **Delinquency and default:** Private loans almost always go into delinquency or default much sooner than federal loans. There are private loans that go into default the day you are late; federal loans are much more patient if you fall behind. You have to miss three consecutive payments for your loans to be "delinquent," and your missed payments won't be reported to the credit bureaus unless you miss three straight months of payments. In order for your loans to go into default, you have to miss nine months of payments
15. It is very easy to consolidate your loans, and you don't have to have great credit to do this.

As much as I like these Stafford Loans, students need to realize how serious it is to default on their loans. I was teaching a college admissions class two days ago and a student said, "If I don't pay back my loan, they can't do anything to me other than lower my credit score, can they?"

Over four million students are in default on their student loans right now, and it is a national crisis. If you default on a loan, you can have your tax returns seized and your wages garnished. You can fail an employer verification screening and you are likely to be rejected for a car loan or mortgage.

125

WHY ARE FEDERAL LOANS BETTER THAN PRIVATE STUDENT LOANS?

Private loans are nonfederal loans that are made by a lender such as a bank, credit union, state agency, or the college itself. Federal student loans are loans made or guaranteed by the Department of Education. For the last 15 years, I have called Mark Kantrowitz, the most knowledgeable person in the world when it comes to grants, loans, scholarships, and college money matters. According to Kantrowitz, about 1.5 million undergraduate and graduate students borrow private student loans each year, typically about $5,000 to $10,000 each on average.

- ℵ Private loans are dangerous, and they often have small print in the loans that would be shocking if the student actually realized how much power the lending institution has.

- ℵ Private loans do sneaky things that give a false impression that the student is getting a good deal. One example of this is advertising low teaser rates that few people qualify for, or they may give you that rate initially as a teaser rate and then an expensive variable loan kicks in. A 2012 survey by the Washington, D.C., youth advocacy group Young Invincibles found that 70 percent of students who took out private student loans were not told by the lender about other options.
- ℵ They almost always will cost the student more than the federal Stafford Loans.
- ℵ They require a credit check and because students usually have not established sufficient credit, this means that a co-signer is required. The co-signer is at risk for covering all of the expenses if the student defaults.
- ℵ Federal loans offer a lot more flexible repayment options, including income-based repayment.
- ℵ Private loans are more complex. They can even vary with some lenders, based on the college you attend and what you major in.
- ℵ Federal loans are much more likely to offer to suspend or reduce your loans if you encounter tough times. This is called forbearance.
- ℵ Federal loans offer some generous loan forgiveness programs for various forms of public service, but this is very rare to find in a private loan.
- ℵ There are fixed private loans, but there are a lot more variable loans. Federal loans are fixed and allow you to know what you are going to pay.
- ℵ Federal loans offer no prepayment fees if you want to get ahead on your payments. Some private loans offer this, but many others do not.
- ℵ Federal loans are abrogated if the student dies, but many private loans have fine print indicating that the co-signer is responsible for payment even if the student dies.
- ℵ In some cases, federal loans can be annulled if a student has a permanent disability, but I have never seen this in a private student loan.

- ℵ Federal loans can be combined with other federal loans to offer much simpler repayment options for students. This is referred to as consolidation, and it is not something that a private loan can do with a federal loan.

One of the best features of the federal subsidized loan and the federal Perkins loan is that the government is paying your interest until you either drop out of school, go to less than half-time status, or at least six months have passed since you graduated. This can save you over $5000. Private loans may agree to have you defer payments, but the interest is accruing.

The federal Stafford Loans have loan limits to discourage irresponsible lending, but private loans can be up to the cost of attendance if the co-signer has good enough credit.

Another thing I don't like is that if you are taking out a private loan, you are usually over-borrowing. There is no reason to take out a private loan instead of a Stafford Loan, and if you also need one to cover your unmet need, you are probably borrowing too much.

Five years ago, I would have said, "Never, in any circumstance, get a private student loan." But a conversation I had with Kenny, a Director of Financial Aid at a large public school, changed my mind. Kenny said, "Now that PLUS loans are at 7 percent with an origination fee over 4 percent, a lot of times savvy parents who have very high credit scores and read the fine print carefully will get a better interest rate with a private loan than a PLUS loan."

I have come to agree with Kenny, but you have to read the fine print, and it is best if there is no prepayment penalty and you know you have the resources coming in to pay it off soon.

I can always spot the private student loan lenders at college fairs or career fairs. They are well dressed. They hire very attractive, well-spoken, and gregarious sales people. They usually have the nicest treats, including both food and nifty giveaways that make you want to come by their table, grab the goodies, and tell your friends to head over there. Buyers beware. They may be friendly, but trust me, they are not the friend of your wallet.

126

WHAT ARE MY REPAYMENT OPTIONS FOR FEDERAL STUDENT LOANS?

If you drop out, are enrolled at less than half-time enrollment (fewer than six credit hours on semester systems), or graduate, it is time to start to repay your loan. When I say "Stafford Loan," that refers to both subsidized and unsubsidized direct loans.

For Stafford Loans, you must begin payment within six months of graduating. For Perkins it is nine months, and for PLUS loans, repayment begins shortly after the funds are disbursed from the Department of Education to your school.

For PLUS loans, you can usually postpone payments, but know that interest is accruing.

A loan servicer manages loans and collects payments on behalf of the lender. Your loan servicer will contact you when it is time to repay your loan. They can help you to select which repayment plan is best for you.

If you have a Stafford Loan or a PLUS loan, you will use the loan servicer selected by the Department of Education.

If you have a Perkins loan, you will make payments either directly to your college or to the loan servicer that your college has decided to use. You will need to contact your college to find out whether you are paying the school directly or paying their loan servicer.

There are different repayment options depending on which type of loan you selected. Some of the possible repayment options include:

- A standard repayment plan, which is fixed payments over a 10-year period that stay the same until the loan balance is paid off.
- Graduated payment, which starts out low and increases every two years (the thinking is that you should make more money a few years later and you will be able to handle the increase in payments).
- An extended repayment plan in which you may select a 25-year plan instead of a 10-year plan if you qualify. You should know that while your payment is lower, the overall amount of interest you will pay is noticeably more.
- Income-based repayment, which varies depending on what you are making.
- You may be able to postpone or defer your payments for a while, with these deferrals usually being granted for one of the following reasons: a return to college for more education, entry into military service, or unemployment/underemployment.
- If you are having a hard time repaying your loans due to unemployment or underemployment but you do not qualify for a deferment, you may qualify for forbearance. This will result in either a reduced payment for you, or a temporary deferment of your payments.
- Consolidating your loans is often in your best interest, and if you have multiple federal loans, this can usually be done. This allows you to pay one payment and keep track of one loan. Consolidation may also reduce the rate of some of your loans. Remember, every year you take out a Stafford Loan, it is a separate loan with different loan terms.

Note: not every loan will offer all of these options! Your loan servicer can go into more detail with you about all of your options.

For questions about your loan, such as who your loan servicer is, where you can find their contact information, or the details of your loan, go to nslds.ed.gov. This is the website for the National Student Loan Data System and there you will get answers to your questions.

If you want to estimate what your loan payment, here are a few of the many great repayment calculators:

- ℵ The federal student loan calculator is located at: https://studentloans.gov/myDirectLoan/mobile/repayment/repaymentEstimator.action
- ℵ The College Board also has one: https://bigfuture.collegeboard.org/pay-for-college/loans/student-loan-calculator
- ℵ For students and parents: https://bigfuture.collegeboard.org/pay-for-college/loans/parent-loan-repayment
- ℵ For consolidation, it is best to use the federal loan consolidation over other options. Find information here: https://studentloans.gov. You will save money in the long term over other options, and you will have more flexibility and grace should you get into a bind.

When you take out a consolidation loan, you can exempt certain loans.

One out of every three students default on their loan, and it is very serious. It will destroy your credit and student loans cannot be written off in bankruptcy. If you default on a loan, you will not be able to get financial aid again for graduate school.

It is important that you do a pulse check on your loan once a year to make sure that you are in the right payment plan.

The best way to avoid default is to set up an auto-draft with your loan service company.

It can be challenging to pay student loans because you are also trying to get six months in your emergency savings account, pay down credit cards, and save for retirement.

One of the nice things about federal loans is that loan forgiveness is a possibility. There are many possible ways to be eligible for loan forgiveness. Most states have loan forgiveness options for students who go into careers like nursing, where there is clearly a shortage of workers. The most common loan service option is the public service loan forgiveness option, which applies to workers who work for the federal, state, and local governments; schools; and non-profits. The Public Service Loan Forgiveness (PSLF) Program forgives the remaining balance on your Direct Loans after you have made 120 qualifying monthly payments under a qualifying repayment plan while working full-time for a qualifying employer.

One of the people I loved to talk to when I worked at Westtown was Mary Jo. She was the sweetest lady, but she also had the job of collecting the money from students who were late on their tuition and room and board payments. She used to say, "Mark, I will be so gracious and creative in working with any family that is struggling to make their payments, but they need to respond to my calls, emails, and letters. Sometimes they are embarrassed so they avoid returning my calls and notices, and it is the worst thing they can do, because then we have no choice but to take drastic measures."

When it comes to real estate, we often hear the same thing: Location, Location, Location. But when it comes to working with loan servicing companies, the three most important words are: Communication, Communication, Communication.

127

IS PAYING FOR COLLEGE THE STUDENT'S RESPONSIBILITY, OR THE PARENTS' RESPONSIBILITY?

The answer is both. This will be the perspective of the colleges you apply to.

It is also the perspective of the federal government. For example, the EFC is largely based on parent income in most instances. This is because the government and the colleges expect parents to pay their fair share. However, the majority of times, a college will also give a student a student loan in the student's name, showing that they expect the student to also contribute. The student will often get a work-study job or a campus job. Colleges that require the PROFILE will usually factor in around \$2000-\$2500 of summer earnings that will increase your EFC, once again showing that they expect the student to be contributing to the college expenses. This makes sense for two reasons:

1. We are not talking about kids anymore; when you are 18, you can go to war for the country, so you should be able to pay a portion of your college expenses.
2. You are the one who is going to benefit from your education, both personally and financially. It also makes sense that the parent should contribute, because the cost of college is just too onerous for a student to take on by themselves unless they stay at home and attend a community college.

I have known quite a few parents who have said to their kids, "You better work or get a full scholarship, because we are not paying for college." I've seen this work and I've seen this backfire. I've seen students step up their game and get full scholarships because it was all on them and they better make it happen. I've also seen kids feel like abject failures because this standard was established, they never achieved it, and they felt like they never measured up. Remember, Mark Kantrowitz's research indicates that only three out of every 1000 students get a full scholarship. That is a lot of pressure to put on a student, especially one that may not be exceptionally gifted and talented.

You may be thinking, "That is a very middle-class perspective to think a parent should help with college expenses." My perspective is not that every parent needs to pay X amount of dollars. I believe every parent should pay the EFC, because it is mostly their income that creates the EFC. The nice thing about the EFC is that if a family makes under $25,000, their EFC is zero, and in that instance, the parent cannot contribute and the student will get a Pell Grant and maybe FSEOG, but the rest is on them.

Let's say you make more than $25,000, but things are still real tight. The EFC takes family size into consideration. There is also something called the "Income Protection Allowance" (IPA) that helps here. The IPA is the amount of money the government calculates you need just to survive. It is based on family size and the number of kids in college and it factors in things like food, housing, transportation, medical expenses, clothing and personal care, and miscellaneous expenses. It is around $30,000 for a family of four with one student in college. The way IPA impacts aid is that no money is expected to go to college at all until your IPA threshold is reached.

The other extreme I often see is the parent who says, "I don't want my child to have to pay for college. I don't want them to have any debt, and I don't want them to have to work. I just want them to focus on getting good grades." People don't appreciate things when they are given to them anywhere near how they appreciate them when they have some skin in the game. Skin in the game is requiring your child to pay a portion of their college expenses.

When I was meeting with Ms. Alexander and her daughter Maya, she was having a hard time with my belief that every child should pay something for college to truly value it and not squander the opportunity. I said to Ms. Alexander, "Let Maya take out the full $5000 loan, and you can tell her that for every semester Maya gets a 3.5 GPA or higher, than you can match her dollar for dollar in paying off the subsidized and unsubsidized loans she will have." Ms. Alexander loved this idea!

128

HOW DO I STAND OUT FROM THE COMPETITION AND WIN PRIVATE SCHOLARSHIPS?

Make a list of all of the activities you are involved in. Focus on areas where you have demonstrated leadership, or areas where you showed a high level of community service. Also make a list of any academic areas where you have demonstrated passion or longevity, or received any awards. Did you get the top chemistry award for tenth grade students?

You can start in middle school and just apply to three or four every year in middle school, and as you learn more about scholarships, it will really help you in high school when you apply to more scholarships. There are scholarships for elementary students and there are scholarships for adults who want to go back to school. You can start at any time. It is never too early or too late to start.

Brainstorm and come up with all of the ways you think someone could search for a scholarship in one of these top two areas. Think of other words that could be used to describe the same area. For example, if it is debate, don't just look under debate, but also search under public speaking.

Remember the three words when looking for private scholarships: Local, Local, Local! Start with a search in your city, then your county, and then your state.

For example, if you are in Atlanta and you complete the list of activities, and it turns out that your top two activities are robotics and debate, then your list of ways someone could search for scholarships would look like this: start with Atlanta, then Georgia, then the nation.

You then start doing a Google search for cash awards, foundations, scholarships, and organizations. When an organization pops up, try searching the company website for scholarships, or pick up the phone and call.

Focus on scholarships between $250 and $5000; these have less competition.

Don't neglect the large national competitions like Dell, Horatio Alger, Jack Kent Cooke, etc., if you are very talented and you meet the qualifications to compete in a nationally-competitive field. You are unlikely to know this, so you should ask your school counselor, CBO counselor, or independent counselor.

Visit Cappex.com and use their indicator of how much work is involved and how much competition is involved.

Thoroughly fill out the scholarship PROFILEs, even the optional questions. You may think these questions are irrelevant, but they are there because they are targeting scholarships.

Read the scholarship applications very clearly. I can't stress this enough.

Be honest with yourself. Do you meet the criteria for this scholarship?

Write down what they are looking for in a few words, i.e. "outstanding leadership in scientific research."

Write down your past, current, and future experiences that line up with what the scholarship is targeting. Write down your awards in this area as well.

Start volunteering early and often and make sure you're volunteering in any area that excites you.

Build very good relationships with the people who oversee your volunteering roles and keep in touch with those adults. Many scholarship applications will rely heavily on your recommendation letters. Master the content in Chapter 65 on recommendation letters.

Ask your recommenders to give you twenty to thirty copies of the recommendations they write. They should be signed and sealed, but you will need recommendation letters and you don't want to have to keep going back to your recommender for another letter.

Writing about your passions and showing longevity, commitment, and depth of involvement is often the best compelling narrative. Donors invest in passionate people who they believe will make a difference in the world.

Reach out to the contact for the scholarship and ask one or two questions. This is a great way to put you on their mind. Even if you do not have a question, find a question. For example, "I know this scholarship is targeting students who have done community service to MS patients. I have a lot of community service with MS patients, but also with other auto-immune diseases. Should I include this in my background for this scholarship?"

Really think hard at developing your compelling narrative. This has to be something that is genuinely you, but it also has to be something that would generate enthusiasm for a donor. Your compelling narrative cannot be that you love playing video games if you want to win scholarships.

A compelling narrative can be an obstacle that you have to overcome. Let's say you were homeless for a month. That is a compelling narrative. Let's say your single mom lost her job and you had to work 30 hours a week while maintaining good grades. That could be a compelling narrative. Let's say you were 60 pounds overweight but you lost that weight through a rigorous exercise and diet program; that could also be a compelling narrative, but compelling narratives don't *always* have to be obstacles you have overcome.

You have to produce very strong and emotionally compelling essays. Master the content in Chapters 61-64 and apply the tips from those chapters on required scholarship essays. Essays are a major factor in determining who wins outside scholarships.

Keep your GPA high; lots of donors and scholarship judges will want you to be a good student

Look at organizations you have worked for or that your parents have worked for. You should also focus on organizations where you have done volunteer work.

Get your applications in at least 72 hours before the deadlines. Take deadlines very seriously.

Velanie was a Woodward Academy student who is also my next-door neighbor. She received two private scholarships and this allowed her to attend the University of Miami. She was very smart in how she applied and where she applied. Velanie had learned about workplace scholarships, and she researched and found a scholarship at United Airlines where her mom worked. She applied and got the scholarship, but Velanie didn't limit herself to that one: she reached out to a local Chick-fil-A, wrote an essay, and won that scholarship as well.

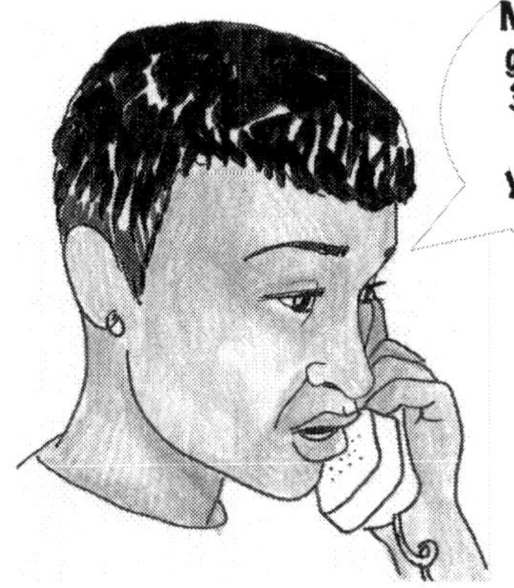

129

WHERE DO I FIND THESE OUTSIDE PRIVATE SCHOLARSHIPS?

Your local guidance counselor at your high school can help. Scholarship information is often sent there with the hope that it will be disseminated to the students. Dr. Corey Sheffield serves as the Director of College Advisement at KIPP Through College for our Metro Atlanta region. Dr. Sheffield will tell you that the students that were the most successful in getting private scholarships focused on the local scholarships where organizations reached out to us to inform us about their scholarships and encouraged us to have our students apply to them. KIPP Metro Atlanta hired Laura Sims as our scholarship specialist, and we saw a substantial increase in our private scholarship award winners under Laura's leadership. This was mostly because Laura focused even more on local scholarships than we had done in the previous year.

There is no question that the source of scholarships that has the most momentum is the scholarship App known as Scholly https://myscholly.com/. Three admission officers have recommended it at information sessions I have attended in this month alone.

Scholly was founded by Christopher Gray in 2014. Gray is a black male who grew up in poverty in Birmingham, Alabama. No one in his family had graduated from college and he didn't even have a computer at home. His app is so popular that it was the number one app in the Apple store and in Google Play for three straight weeks. Scholly has been featured on the following news outlets: CNN, *The Wall Street Journal, Forbes,* BET, Fox News, *USA Today,* and the *Huffington Post.* Oprah lists Gray among her favorite people. Gray won the Smithsonian American Ingenuity award for creating Scholly.

Scholly is a disruptor, just like Uber. Before Scholly, the conventional wisdom was that no one should ever pay to have someone find them scholarships, but Scholly isn't free. It will cost you about $3 a month, but they have over two million users and they have delivered over 100 million in scholarships in three years. What makes Scholly unique is the sophistication of the algorithm that they use to match you with personalized scholarships tailored to who you are. These scholarships are delivered very quickly to your dashboard. They have a mobile and a web platform. Scholly gets rave reviews for its ease of use. Our KIPP Through College team is impressed with Scholly. Some high schools are taking out Scholly accounts for all of their students. What I love about Scholly is that they have lots of scholarships for current undergraduate and graduate students in addition to those targeting high school students.

Other places to look for outside private scholarships:

- Other local high schools besides the one you attend. Check to see if they list them on their website, or use your parent network to have another parent whose student attends that high school tap into their resources. Ask the guidance counselor at your high school which other schools in the area have a strong college counseling department.
- Local civic organizations like fraternities, sororities, Kiwanis and Rotary clubs, Knights of Columbus, etc.

- ℵ Current college students should check in with the financial aid department at their college to see what resources they can provide.
- ℵ *The Ultimate Scholarship Book* is updated annually by the College Board; this is the one physical book worth having. Many books are outdated, but this one updates its contacts and addresses every year. My second favorite scholarship book is *How To Win College Scholarships* by Monica Matthews. You can get around 200 great free scholarship tips from Monica by going to http://smartcollegevisit.com/author/mmathews/
- ℵ The Internet is loaded with private scholarships. My go-to scholarship databases have been Google (go past the first three pages and do VERY specific searches) and Cappex. Fastweb, Scholarships.com, scholarshippoints.com, and Bigfuture.org are others I like. Bigfuture.org has some outstanding articles and tips for applying for scholarships. Each scholarship database will have unique scholarships. I recommend using at least three different databases.
- ℵ Social media sites like Twitter, Facebook, and LinkedIn.

Jasmine, a student I had recently worked with, was discouraged. Her mom called to say that Jasmine had applied for 30 scholarships, and had been rejected by all thirty. I knew exactly what had happened. I knew she had not applied to *local* scholarships. I said to Jasmine's mom, "How many of the 30 were local scholarships?"

Her mom said, "Jasmine couldn't find any local scholarships."

There's always something, so really scour your resources!

130

IS IT TRUE THAT SOME COLLEGES WILL REDUCE MY GRANTS IF I RECEIVE A PRIVATE SCHOLARSHIP?

In order to fully understand this hotly-debated subject, let's take a more detailed look at our financial aid formula:

Cost of Attendance-EFC=Family Financial Need

Example: COA (40k) - EFC (10k) = 30k of need

Let's say a college addressed the 30k of need in the following way: a $5500 Stafford Loan, a $2500 work-study assignment, a $5000 need-based grant, and a $5000 merit scholarship, leaving $12,000 in unmet need that they address by giving your parents a PLUS loan of $12,000.

Now you want to reduce either your $5500 loan, your $2500 in work-study, or the $12,000 in PLUS loans by applying to some outside private scholarships. Let's say you are awarded three $1000 local scholarships. Most families just assume that this $3000 is going to go to your unmet need, reducing your net price (the amount you have to pay out of your own pocket), but different schools will handle this differently.

Most schools will take the $3000 and reduce the self-help portion (loan or work-study) of your award, in effect leading you to have to pay less out of pocket money. But there are some schools—perhaps as many as one in five—that will take that $3000 and reduce your $5000 need-based aid award down to $2000 under the rationale that you now have $3000 more dollars and your need is not as great originally expected.

Those that support this rationale often use the lottery argument. It goes like this: if you were getting financial aid from us and you won three million in the lottery, wouldn't it be fair for us to reduce your aid award and give the money to someone with a greater need? They then say that whether it is three million or three thousand, the principle is the same.

Those who oppose this (including me) are extremely passionate. They say that the student worked extremely hard to win the scholarship; often they wrote essays and sometimes even interviewed to gain money so that they would pay less, and now they still have to pay the same amount because the school has taken the money and allocated it elsewhere. They also argue that when the donor gave the money, they gave it with the intention of helping the award winner, not another student the college chose to help. They argue vehemently that this is a moral issue and an integrity issue.

The most common name for this practice is "scholarship displacement." In the summer of 2017, Maryland was the first state to prohibit colleges from displacing scholarships. This measure has been wildly popular.

It isn't as simple as colleges either reducing the self-help portion or reducing the unmet portion when you get an outside private scholarship. There are plenty of hybrid positions in between these extremes. Some colleges will shelter the first X number of dollars, and then after that is received, they will apply 50 percent to reduce the grant and 50 percent to reduce the loan or work-study portion. For example, if the shelter was a $2000 shelter, and you had $3000 in private scholarships, then the first $2000 of private scholarships would go directly to the loans or work-study (often it is your choice which one they apply it to) and the remaining $1000 would be split into a $500 reduction in your self-help and a $500 reduction in your grant.

According to research by my primary financial aid teacher, Mark Kantrowitz:

> About four out of every five colleges will reduce unmet need and the student's loans and employment first, thereby replacing loans with the scholarship. This reduces the student's net price, making the college more affordable. About one out of every five colleges will reduce the college's own grants first, replacing a grant with the scholarship. The student derives no net financial gain from winning the private scholarship, and the student's net price remains unchanged. The federal Pell Grant is never reduced, not even if the student is over-awarded. Colleges are also not required to reduce campus-based aid, such as the Federal Supplemental Educational Opportunity Grant (FSEOG), Federal Perkins Loan, and Federal Work-Study (FWS), unless the student is over-awarded by $300 or more.

To complicate matters further, colleges cannot give an aid award where the EFC plus the need-based aid award exceeds the Cost of Attendance; this is considered an over-award and colleges can get in trouble with the federal government for this.

What are you to do about this? You have to research your college's outside scholarship policy, which should be on their website, and if it is not there, you must talk to someone in the financial aid department to find out what their policy is.

If you find you are about to receive an over-award, which is impermissible by federal law, there are still possible things you can do. See if your financial aid office will let you present your real Cost of Attendance and not the average figures they are using. If your indirect costs allow the Cost of Attendance to go up another $2000 over their average projections because of travel or other expenses, they may be able to apply your private scholarship to reduce your net price. The other option is to see if your college and your scholarship provider will allow you to apply your private scholarship to the following year, so that you don't have an over-award and a reduction in your college grant.

I knew from my research that Davidson College was one about 16 colleges in the country that met the full demonstrated need of their students without any loans for students of any income level. I also knew that they would displace private outside scholarships by reducing their institutional grant, so I set up a meeting to talk to David Gelinas, their Director of Financial Aid and one of the most knowledgeable financial aid directors in the country. I wanted to see if there was any way it would make sense for my daughter Karis to apply for private scholarships, or if she was just going to be working for Davidson by reducing her grant, because they would displace any scholarship she won.

David said, "We would get in major trouble if we gave an over-award, because we meet full need without loans, so we don't have loans to eliminate. When it comes to scholarship displacement, do your homework, read the policy, talk with the financial staff, and get anything you learn in writing."

131

33 Things Athletes Should Do to Get a Scholarship

1. You have to get an honest assessment of your skill level to discern if you are Division 1 (D1), Division 2 (D2), Division 3 (D3), or NAIA. The best evaluators are current college coaches. Once you know what division you can play at, you then need to find out if you are a High Major, a Mid-Major, or a Low Major.
2. Be careful about relying too much on summer travel coaches, because many of them have a tendency to inflate their evaluation of you. If they tell you that you are a D3 prospect, but you or (especially) your parents think you are a D1 prospect, you may conclude that this coach doesn't believe in you, and you may take your money and your talents elsewhere.

3. All of your games should be recorded and saved on a cloud-based storage system or on an external hard drive. This is a great project for a dad or another caring adult to take on.
4. You have to have great film available for coaches. You should have a professional two-to-four minute highlight film as well as a half game and a full game available. This should be against strong competition, and obviously, you'll need to show a game in which you excelled. Ideally, you should pull the highlight video from no more than four different games.
5. You should load your quality highlight clips up on websites like YouTube, MaxPreps, Captain U, NCSA, Berecruited, Huddle, and more.
6. For sports like track, cross country, and swimming, your times tell most of the story. I have worked with a number of track and field recruits, and most colleges will publish their performance standards right on their websites. They will list their required times or distances for scholarship money and for preferred walk-on status. But for sports like football, baseball, lacrosse, softball, wrestling, and volleyball, you will need to be seen in person or on film.

7. Know the specific process for your sport. For some sports, like football, it is mostly about going to the showcase camps. For basketball, it is usually about playing on a travel team where coaches come to see your team play. You need to know which showcases

you should be going to if your sport is one like baseball, soccer, and lacrosse, which are big showcase sports. Showcases can be for teams or for individuals. A showcase is an opportunity to play a lot of games in front of college coaches. It differs from a camp, where there is a lot of teaching and coaching.

8. If your sport is one like basketball, where most of the action occurs on AAU summer teams, then you need to be very careful about the summer teams you pick. You should select a team with great coaching, ample playing time, and a great reputation, and your coaches should have contacts with colleges that are at the level you can play at.
9. Don't make the mistake of thinking, "Either I go play D1, or I am a failure." It is not fun being on the bench when you could be playing the sport you love. Take a look at the list of D1 transfers every year to D2 or D3, and it is ridiculously long. Go where you will get playing time and a great education.
10. Don't overlook Division 3. Sure, D3 won't give you an athletic scholarship (they are not allowed to) like D1, D2, or NAIA, but you can earn an academic scholarship with superlative academics, and sometimes the colleges' need-based aid packages can make these schools extremely affordable. D3 is a very high level, and you can still have more of the typical college experience, so consider D3 as a first-choice option. Some examples of great D3 schools are Emory, Washington University in St. Louis, John Hopkins, Case Western Reserve, NYU, Amherst, Pomona, Williams, Haverford, and Wellesley.
11. Put together an athletic résumé that showcases your awards and the teams you have played for, has basic contact information, and includes your high school, GPA, test scores, and class rank if it is available. You should also have contact information for a few references.
12. Put together a quality cover letter that is customized to each school. Almost every admission office has an athletic liaison as one of the admissions reps. This is someone you want to establish a relationship with. The athletic résumé, cover letter, and film can go to both the athletic liaison and the head coach as well as any assistant coach who may be recruiting you.

13. You need to reach out and recruit the colleges; don't just sit back and wait for them to recruit you. For one, you know what you like, but also, colleges want students who want to come there, so if you do this and you send your cover letter, athletic résumé, links to your video clips and full game, and if you are good enough to play, it will get noticed. Be persistent, but not obnoxious. Write a handwritten letter and follow up with a phone call.
14. Complete the athlete questionnaires on the college website in ninth or ninth grade to get on their radar.
15. When you get an email or letter from a coach, respond right away. Your manners can go a long way.
16. None of us who had seen Latasha play basketball doubted for one minute that she would go to college on a full basketball scholarship. She made second team All-State and went to a major showcase event, where she was ranked the number one player at the event. When I heard she never got a scholarship, I reached out to her AAU coach who I knew personally to find out what is going on. He told me, "No matter how many times I tell her that she has to respond to all of the letters and emails that she gets, she just won't listen to me." He went on to say, "Coaches are talking to each other out there about her lack of responsiveness, and it isn't good."
17. Know the NCAA calendar and the rules about when and how you can contact coaches and when they can contact you. All of this is listed at http://ncaa.com
18. The student, not the parent, needs to be the initiator with colleges; this is very important. Coaches like to get verbal commitments early, so you need to start earlier than a student that doesn't want to be a varsity athlete. I recommend the spring of ninth grade as a starting point for athletes.
19. Get the best personal trainer you can afford. A great trainer is priceless. Listen to what they say about nutrition in addition to their skill acquisition drills.
20. Choose a school you would love to attend even if you couldn't play your sport.
21. While you probably won't go somewhere if you dislike the coach or philosophy, don't select a school because you love the

coach, because there is a great chance the coach won't be there in two years, let alone four years.

22. Make sure you register with the NCAA Eligibility Center well in advance. This is a requirement for D1 and D2. Find it at https://web3.ncaa.org/ecwr3/
23. Understand that this is big business, and coaches will try to recruit over you no matter what they promised you. Consider positioning yourself to get around this; one way is to go to a school in the division one level below where you can play. There are lots of benefits to being a core player and not a reserve that the coaches simply see as insurance in case players get hurt or transfer.
24. When you are on a visit to the school, you may be hosted by other players on the team. Be on your best behavior, because the coaches will likely probe them for information about how you behaved and what you are like when they were not around.
25. Like I said, sports is big business at this next level. The coach who you thought was the nicest guy in the world when he recruited you will probably be much different when he is under pressure to win or get fired.
26. Consider working with a recruiting service like NCSA. I have worked closely with NCSA and have found them to be extremely professional and knowledgeable at helping you identify the right level and the right college. I recommend their bronze package. At a minimum, go through their free evaluation and get your film, statistics, and contacts on their free portal. I worked with them for my daughter Joy, and it led to her getting far more offers to play basketball from coaches who found her there than she got from playing AAU for ten years. Joy decided she wanted the normal student experience, but they more than delivered on my investment with them.
27. Don't neglect your academics. A lot of sports give partial athletic and partial academic scholarships, and your test scores and grades are going to matter. Keep your GPA high, and a $1500 investment in quality test prep may get you $10,000 or more per year for four years.

28. Don't neglect developing your character. Teams are like families, and your work ethic, integrity, ability to get along with teammates, and catchability could often be the difference between who gets offered a spot and who doesn't.
29. The most valuable thing a coach has is their time. Don't get excited about mass recruiting mailers. If they are serious about you, they will invest their time. This means they will do things like visit your school, call you, text you regularly, and write you handwritten letters. If you are not having a school invest a lot of time in recruiting you by your junior year after you have reached out to them, they are not interested. You have to figure out if it is because you can't play at their level and you should be looking at a lower level of competition.
30. Don't be afraid to ask coaches the tough questions. You are evaluating them as much as they are evaluating you. You should ask, "Where am I on your recruiting list?" and "How many students have transferred in the last three years, and what were the reasons?"
31. Build a relationship with someone in the financial aid office at the schools that are interested in you.
32. Don't get so caught up in your travel team that you don't give it your all with a great attitude for your local high school team. Your high school coach will assuredly be contacted, and they can make or break you based on what your attitude has been like on your high school team.
33. You don't control your God-given talent, but you do control your attitude and work ethic. Be the most positive person on the team and the hardest worker.

Note for parents: Don't live vicariously through your child with sports. You can't want it for them more than they want it for themselves. Accept your child for who they are.

When Patrick and his parents came to me, they were frustrated. Patrick loved football, and he was going to all of the college football camps, but no one was offering him a scholarship. He was watching his friends get offers and he didn't know what to do. He had the highlight video and the personal trainer, and he was keeping his grades up, and those who knew him all gave him raving character reviews. I explained to Patrick and his family that it was obvious what the problem was: he was going to camps at high D1 schools like Georgia, but they were not sold on his ability to play at their level. I told them he needed to have some honest conversations with college coaches about what level he could play at.

I got the nicest letter from Patrick's mom two months later telling me that they had listened, gone down a level, and Patrick would be attending Savannah State on a full football scholarship in the fall. I see this tendency to target schools above the level you can play at far too often. I call it ESPN Syndrome: let's face it, very few of us will ever be on SportsCenter, so let's stop only aiming at schools we see on TV over the weekend.

132

WHAT IS A DEPARTMENT SCHOLARSHIP, AND HOW DO I GET ONE?

Department scholarships are given out by specific academic departments at a college to award passion and excellence in that respective field.

They are not given out by the admissions office to high-achieving high school seniors.

They are not given out by the athletic department.

They are not given out by a private scholarship fund or foundation.

One of the great things about department scholarships is that current students and even transfer students can often win them. Some of them are only for current students who have excelled while they are at the college. What's so exciting about this is that the lion's share of aid awards are targeting high school seniors, but students that get to a college are often overwhelmed by expenses. In many instances, they are maxing out their federal loans, but they wisely don't want to turn to private loans. They are working as much as they can work, and their parents are contributing all they can contribute. Where is the money to come from?

In order to understand department scholarships more, let's take an actual look at the department scholarships Iowa State is offering for 2018 by college.

Application Timeframes	Freshman	Current Student	Transfer Student
Agriculture & Life Sciences	Sep. 1 – Dec. 1	Dec. 1 – Feb. 1	Sep. 1 – Feb. 1
Business	Oct. 1 – Dec. 1	Dec. 1 – Feb. 1	Dec. 1 – Feb. 1
Design	Varies by scholarship	Varies by scholarship	TBD
Engineering	Invites sent by College of Engineering	Jan. 2 – Feb. 1	Jan. 1 – Aug. 1
Human Sciences	Deadline: Dec. 5 at 11:59 p.m. CST	Deadline: Dec. 5 at 11:59 p.m. CST	Deadline: Dec. 5 at 11:59 p.m. CST
Liberal Arts & Sciences	Oct. 1 – Dec. 1	Dec. 5 – Feb. 1	Dec. 5 – Feb. 1
Graduate	Contact the college	Contact the college	Contact the college
Veterinary Medicine	Contact the college	Contact the college	Contact the college

At Iowa State, the College of Liberal Arts and Sciences even has a study-abroad Department scholarship.

When it comes to department scholarships, the department is in charge, and they dictate the rules. Here is how the University of North Texas describes the process on their website:

> Please note that departments administer their own scholarship processes for donor-funded scholarships. The department awarding the scholarship is always the first point of contact regarding any scholarship-related inquires. If there are questions that need assistance from Student Financial Aid and Scholarships (SFAS), the department will make contact with SFAS regarding the information needed. Once scholarship awards are made, the department notifies SFAS of the award, so that it can be posted to your student account.

A lot of people care about what others are doing, but what really matters is what you can afford.

133

HOW DOES THE TYPICAL FAMILY PAY FOR COLLEGE?

Your family may be different, but I thought you would want to know how the average family is paying for college. Fortunately, we have Sallie Mae and Ipsos to thank, because they have done a fantastic survey for ten straight years that lets us know this. Sallie Mae is a national saving, planning, and paying for college company, and Ipsos is a reputable national independent global market research company. They surveyed 1600 people: 800 parents of undergraduate students, and 800 undergraduate students between the ages of 18 and 24.

Breakdown by percentages:

Scholarships and grants (includes Pell Grants)	35%
Parent income and savings	23%
Student borrowing	19%
Student income and savings	11%
Parent borrowing	8%
Relatives and friends	4%

Breakdown by dollars:

Scholarships and grants (includes Pell Grants)	$8390
Parent income and savings	$5527
Student borrowing	$4551
Student income and savings	$2569
Parent borrowing	$1819
Relatives and friends	$901

Changes from 2013:

- Scholarships and grants are up 32%
- Parent income and savings is down 3.6%
- Student borrowing is up 16.2%
- Student income and savings is up 12.5%
- Parent borrowing is virtually unchanged
- Gifts from relatives and friends is down 16.9%

Interesting findings:

- 87% of the scholarships or grants come from the colleges themselves.
- 49% of students received a merit-based scholarship.
- 47% received a need-based grant.
- $35,431 is the average amount spent from families in the Northeast. This region has a much higher percentage of students selecting private schools.
- $20,953 is the average amount spent for college from students from the south. Southerners attend college in their own home state at a higher rate than any other region.

- א $21,577 is the average amount spent by students in the Midwest. Midwesterners work more hours than students from other regions.
- א $19,181 is the average amount spent from students from the west. Westerners attend college on a part-time basis at a higher rate than the other regions.
- א 69% of respondents said they ruled out a college they were interested in because of cost.
- א 86% of parents said they always knew their child would go to college, but only 39% said they had a plan to pay for

When I meet with a family, I always ask them, "If you are blown away by a college, what is the most you are willing and able to pay?"
I am always taken aback by how many people respond by saying, "What do most people say?"

My response is always, "That is irrelevant." I go on to say, "I hate to compare education to buying a car, but let's say you walked on the car lot and I asked you, 'Should we look at $15,000, $25,000, or $40,000 cars?' and you said, 'What do most people say?' All that matters is what you can afford." Still, I have learned that what others do really does matter to people.

134

WHAT ARE THE AREAS WHERE ADMISSIONS COUNSELORS ARE OFTEN NOT TOTALLY HONEST WITH ME WHEN IT COMES TO MONEY?

College personnel are not snake oil salespeople. They almost always go into education because they love students, they love their schools, and they want to help people. I hold the profession in the highest regard and I think it is such a rewarding and impactful career that goes overlooked. I am overjoyed when my former students become AOs (admission officers.) But they also need to pay their bills, and that creates a tension between how transparent they can be with you about certain matters.

Colleges are businesses, and a lot of decisions they make have to do with them making money. They may be visiting your school every year because they have done in-depth research on the average income in your area and they want students who can pay, which explains why they are visiting your school but not the school ten minutes away. But they can't tell you this. They have to emphasize how great the students are at your school. They just can't say, "We visit this school every year because you have a lot of rich kids who can help us pay our bills."

Very few colleges are not influenced by money in where they travel to recruit, how they prioritize certain affluent schools, and who they admit. This weekend, I had a candid conversation with a college admission rep at a highly selective northeast school. He totally acknowledged this.

He said, "We talk about how we want people of all incomes, but look at where they ask us to travel to recruit—who is kidding who?"

Lots of colleges that say they are need-blind are really need-aware. Who wants to explain to an 18 year-old that you are looking at how much they can pay and using it to decide who gets in? Even if it is for a small portion of their applicant pool, this goes against the concept that college admission is a meritocracy. However, when Wesleyan admitted in 2012 that they are no longer need-blind for a portion of their applicants and Haverford followed suit in 2015, I commended their honesty. I have had two very senior college admission officers tell me, "Mark, the number of true need-blind schools can be counted on one hand."

Lots of schools that say they meet full demonstrated/calculated need may factor in one of a number of unreasonable measures, like having a summer earnings expectation of $4000 built into your aid award, to be able to make this claim. There is a lot of prestige in being able to say you meet full demonstrated financial need; you join a list of very prestigious schools that any college would want to be associated with. Some schools will give you a different aid package if you apply early decision because they feel they have you and you will pay more because of your zeal. They know that it will be tougher to yield students in the regular round and they may need to get aggressive with money to make it happen.

A lot of schools practice preferential packaging. They give more money to those students they want the most, even if it is masked as a need-based award.

Some colleges will frontload your grant and then the cost will go up in subsequent years. This practice is more common that people realize. You can do a little digging by using https://nces.ed.gov/collegenavigator/ to find out who is overpromising to freshmen and then pulling back the award in subsequent years.

First go to the website and use the Search Bar to put in the college you want to research. When you have it up, click the "Expand All" tab. Next, you want to compare the amount of institutional (from the college) aid freshmen receive with the section under this, which will list the amount of grants and scholarships all students receive. Now, keep in mind, freshmen are in the "all undergraduates" category, so you will need to subtract out the freshman numbers to compare freshman aid to the other years. The data is here to make the comparison for the percentage of students receiving free money from the college as well as the average aid award.

I just ran the numbers for Drexel University in Philadelphia. Try it for yourself and see what you learn. Mark Kantrowitz is as knowledgeable as anyone in the country on college money, and he thinks as many as half of all colleges may frontload their grants.

The website my clients tend to find the easiest for looking at frontloading of grants and a wide range of money related matters is CollegeData.com. Their Money Matters section is extremely helpful and user-friendly. Here's where you can find their money Matters tab for Drexel:

https://www.collegedata.com/cs/data/college/college_pg03_tmpl.jhtml?schoolId=407

Compare this to College Navigator and Bigfuture's financial aid by the numbers:

https://bigfuture.collegeboard.org/college-university-search/drexel-university

All three are excellent.

Some colleges will adjust your aid award if you make more money, but if your income goes down, your aid award will never be more than it was during your freshman year. Other colleges will not adjust your need-based award to take tuition raises into consideration.

For selective schools that use holistic admissions, the deck is really stacked against poor students. They can't afford consultants, subject tutors, or the best test prep tutors, etc. They don't have the money to develop and refine their athletic or artistic hooks over 15 years. They are adversely impacted by demonstrated interest because they can't afford to visit, attend summer camps, or attend the schools where the reps visit on an annual basis. On top of this, not only are states walking away from need-based aid, but so are the colleges.

Some colleges will give you better packages your second year if you did very well in and out of the classroom when you were actually at the school.

The CSS PROFILE methodology for calculating aid when a family has two kids in college at the same time assumes you can pay 120 percent of EFC for two kids.

Mandatory meal plans are usually more for the college than they are for your health. They are a revenue producer. Google the following article: "Cornell Students Erupt Over Health Care Fee." If you read the article, you will learn how in 2015 the President of Cornell, David Skorton, announced in a memo that students were going to be billed $350 if they opted out of Cornell's health care coverage because they already had coverage.

If a venerated Ivy league school like Cornell is squeezing its students like this, don't you think others are as well? The poor admission counselor who just loves kids and loves his school is in a bind. How honest can the Cornell rep be? Can they throw President David Skorton under the bus if a prospective student asks, "Why is Cornell gouging its students?"

Some colleges that displace private scholarships by reducing grants claim they are using this money to have more need-based aid, but some of them are using this to give more merit money away, often to kids who have less need than the student whose scholarship displaced a portion of their grant (see Chapter 130 on outside scholarships displacing grants).

A lot of merit awards are masked as merit awards based on high performance, but more often than not, you realize they are clever attempts to attract students that can help them pay their bills (see Chapter 161 on affirmative action for rich kids).

In fairness to colleges, there are some things that colleges just can't tell you. Let's say a college is starting a new nursing program. Internally, priority for admissions and scholarships is being given to students who declare nursing as a major. Let's say you are an admissions counselor doing an information session and a student asks you, "Are there any majors that if I select them, my application will be prioritized for a scholarship?"

This presents a dilemma. If the admission officer says, "We are giving more money to nursing majors this year," guess what happens? Word gets out, and students who have no interest in nursing will start pretending they are interested in nursing to get the extra money.

The best I could do in that instance is say, "if there were, I could get fired if I told you something like that." Most counselors love kids and that is what drives them to work as hard as they do for a fairly modest income.

I was having a conversation with a director of financial aid, and she was venting to me. She was particularly perturbed about students who don't request financial aid the first year and then ask for aid in year two. She said to me, "That was not the deal we accepted you with."

I could not help but think, "Did you tell them you expect them to be a full-pay family for the next three years?" But I didn't have to ask that because I knew the answer was NO.

135

WHAT ARE YOUR TEN BEST COST-SAVING TIPS FOR UNDER-RESOURCED STUDENTS?

I have had the opportunity to do college counseling with many families that make under $30,000 a year, as well as a lot of families that make over $500,000 a year, and I never cease to be amazed by all of the ways that the college admissions process is biased toward the wealthy. When I was at Westtown School, there was one junior I was assisting with the college process who was already on her third flight to California to visit colleges, but I was also working with a student who had no way of getting to Princeton even though it was only 69 miles away from West Chester, Pennsylvania, where Westtown School is located.

According to the *New York Times* the *Upshot* (blog) on January 17, 2017, 38 selective colleges have more students from the top 1 percent of income earners than they have from the bottom 60 percent of income earners. The title of the blog article was, "Some Colleges Have More

Students from the Top 1% than the Bottom 60%." You can Google the article to see who makes the list, but more than half of the Ivy leagues were among the 38 colleges. I blame *US News and World Report* for this. Their rankings incentivize colleges to target the wealthy. I am not alone in this conclusion. In an article in Politico on September 10, 2017, entitled "How *U.S. News* College Rankings Promote Economic Inequality on Campus," the president of LSU said, "I think *U.S. News* has done more damage to the higher education marketplace than any single enterprise that's out there."

The hurdles under-resourced students face are at times almost insurmountable. An outstanding Inside Higher Education article from January 12, 2016, titled "Poverty and Merit," quotes Harold Levy, the Executive Director of Jack Kent Cooke Foundation, a stupendous organization that attempts to level the playing field by helping gifted and talented under-resourced students: "The college admissions system is rigged against low-income applicants in many ways," said Levy, "from the test prep wealthy students get, to legacy admissions and so-called merit aid, which is frequently an attempt to attract middle- and upper-class students to attend one college instead of another. Even so, most top colleges claim they are committed to economic diversity on their campuses. That's so much blather," said Levy.

The numbers back him up.

"Students from households in the bottom income quartile make up just 3 percent of enrollment at the nation's most competitive colleges," the report said. "But 72 percent of enrollment at these colleges is comprised of students from the wealthiest quartile."

In the recommended resources section of this book, I will highlight a number of organizations like Jack Kent Cook, Go To College NYC, and Questbridge, which are doing outstanding work at assisting under-resourced students with the college process.

This chapter will focus on opportunities that exist to make the college process affordable for under-resourced students, but before we look at those resources, here is another great quote from that same Inside Higher Education article:

> Hidden within these numbers are thousands of students from economically disadvantaged households who, despite attending less-resourced schools and growing up with less

intellectual stimulation and advantages, do extremely well in school, love learning, are extraordinarily bright and capable, and would do very well at selective institutions if offered admissions. They are just being ignored.

1. ACT AND SAT FEE WAIVERS:

According to the Fee Waiver Eligibility Requirements document for the ACT 2017-2018, "ACT Fee Waivers cover the ACT with writing or without writing. The waiver will cover a report to the high school and up to four college choices. A student is limited to a maximum of two separate fee waivers." In order to qualify for a fee waiver, **ALL** of the following eligibility requirements must be met:

- ℵ Be currently enrolled in high school in the eleventh or twelfth grade
- ℵ Be a United States citizen or testing in the United States, United States territories, or Puerto Rico
- ℵ Meet one or more of the indicators of economic need listed below
- ℵ Enrolled in a federal free or reduced-price lunch program at school
- ℵ Enrolled in a program for the economically disadvantaged (i.e. GEAR UP or Upward Bound)
- ℵ Residing in a foster home, a ward of the state, or homeless
- ℵ Family receiving low-income public assistance or living in federally subsidize public housing.
- ℵ Family's total annual income is at or below USDA levels for free or reduced-price lunches (see table below)

Number in Household (including the student)	Total annual income before taxes (last calendar yr)
1	$22,311
2	$30,044
3	$37,777
4	$45,510
4	$53,243
6	$60,976

Each additional plus $7733 each

The ACT relies on the integrity of the school counselor to make sure all of these conditions are met.

The SAT also has a few waiver program, and it is significantly more generous than the ACT's program. The ACT explicitly puts the word ALL in caps and in BOLD, meaning that all of the criteria must be must. The SAT uses almost the exact criteria that one must meet to be eligible (i.e income cutoffs are the same), but for the SAT, you only need to meet **one** (not ALL) of the criteria. Here is what the College Board says in their 2017-18 document, "SAT and SAT Subject Fee Waiver Service Counselors Guide:" "Fee waivers are available to high school students who meet **at least one** of the eligibility criteria listed here."

In addition to this, because the College Board administers the PROFILE and the SAT, you automatically get 8 PROFILE waivers, which is a savings of around $150.

2. Book Scholarships

There are many book scholarships, and they usually prioritize students who really need the financial assistance to pay for books. My favorite scholarship search sites for book scholarships are Google, Cappex, Fast Web, Scholarships.com, and Collegescholarships.org.

3. College Application Fee Waivers

College application fees are a substantial barrier to access for under-resourced families. The application fees of Stanford, Duke, and Columbia are close to $100 each, so if you can get those fees waived, those three schools alone are the equivalent of a plane ticket. The application fee to a specialized school like the Berklee College of Music or the Curtis Institute of Music is $150 according to a March 22, 2017, Cappex article titled, "Most Expensive Application Fees."

One of the great things about the SAT waiver is that it automatically qualifies you for four college application waivers. You get these fee waivers from your school counselor or your CBO (Community Based Organization) counselor.

In Rebecca Safier's excellent Dec 18, 2015, article entitled, "How to Get a College Application Fee Waiver: 3 Approaches," Safier eloquently articulates several ways a student can get their application fees waived:

The ACT, Inc. Fee Waiver

Unlike College Board, ACT, Inc. doesn't automatically grant its test fee-waiving students with application fee waivers. In fact, it doesn't advertise its fee waivers anywhere I can see on its website.

However, it does have one that students and counselors can use—somewhat buried on page 39 of the *ACT User Handbook for Educators.*

The NACAC Fee Waiver

NACAC provides a useful fee waiver request form, as well as a page of FAQs to help students. It's similar to the Common App page and the ACT waiver. It asks for your basic info and asks you to **specify an indicator of economic need.** You'll also need your counselor or designated school official to sign it. Any student can use this form, regardless of the admission test you took, but remember that **NACAC recommends limiting your use of its fee waiver requests to four colleges.** Don't miss the words 'request form.' The truth of the matter is, even for the four application waivers that come with an SAT waiver, a college is not obligated to honor this waiver. Most colleges will honor this request, but many will not.

The Realize Your College Potential Fee Waiver

The *Realize Your College Potential* fee waiver, which comes from College Board, is a bit less accessible than the other two. Students who are in the top 10-15 percent of their class and the bottom 33 percent of the income distribution (roughly $40K–$50K and below) will **receive *Realize Your College Potential* packets from College Board** with college planning, scholarship, and fee waiver information.

For more information about this fee waiver that few know about, use the following contact information:

Email: collegepotential@collegeboard.org

Phone: 866-444-4025

Common Application Fee Waivers

Here is how Big Future's FAQ document about Common App fee waivers answers question about whether fee waivers can be used for the Common Applications.

Q: If I am applying to colleges using the Coalition, Common, or Universal Applications, can I still use a college application fee waiver?

A: Each of these applications has a specific process for students who apply with a fee waiver. If you have received (or are eligible to receive) an SAT fee waiver, you may apply to any Coalition, Common, or Universal Application college without a fee.

I encourage you to read the document for more details: https://bigfuture.collegeboard.org/get-in/applying-101/college-application-fee-waivers

Ask the College Directly

I think you would be surprised how many colleges will respond favorably if a student or a counselor writes a polite letter indicating the student's interest in a particular college, explaining that the application fee is cost prohibitive and asking to see if there is any way it can be waived. I encourage you to very specifically state why you are interested in the college, should you choose to write this letter. No school will be interested in granting this request if they feel your interest in them is tepid at best.

4. COLLEGE GREENLIGHT & COLLEGE RESULTS

I am listing these websites separately from the other organizations I list at the end of the book, because these websites are dedicated to serving the needs of all under-resourced students and not just those who are members of their organization. Check out https://www.collegegreenlight.com/ and College Results http://www.collegeresults.org/

5. COLLEGE FLY-IN PROGRAMS

Thankfully, a lot of colleges know that the cost of an airline ticket, transportation, and lodging make visits cost prohibitive for some students. There are a lot of college fly-in programs that target students of color of all incomes, and if you are a gifted and talented student of color, you should be in touch with the person at the college who has responsibilities with diversity recruitment or student of color recruitment. There are other programs that specifically target women in STEM and under-resourced students of all races (socio-economic diversity), and they assist with the transportation costs to their colleges.

You are going to have to be extremely talented to get a school to pay for your airfare; even the need-based programs target what is sometimes called "need within merit." Read the fine print, because the process will vary by school, but in general, you can expect that if a school is going to pay that much to fly you out and assist with your other transportation costs, you are going to need to be a competitive applicant. You can expect you should have to submit your transcript and your test scores, and it is also not uncommon for a recommendation letter and a mini essay or a series of short questions to be part of the application requirement. There are a lot of lists of colleges that offer these fly-in programs, but I like the one offered by College Greenlight: http://blog.collegegreenlight.com/blog/college-fly-in-diversity-programs/

6. FREE FAFSA ASSISTANCE

See Chapter 103.

7. FREE TEST PREP

Khan Academy offers outstanding free online test prep for SAT takers of all incomes. They have an official partnership with the College Board that administers the SAT. They even have some free group sessions they offer for students, found at https://www.khanacademy.org/sat Their brilliant software engineers sync your PSAT or SAT scores to their proprietary software, and they will give you customized questions that target the areas were your skills needs to be bolstered. There is no free ACT test prep equivalent, but Kaplan has a partnership with the

ACT to offer test prep at a reduced price. They also offer free opportunities to take a practice ACT or SAT in a group setting. You'll receive an excellent detailed report that breaks down your areas of strengths and weaknesses: https://www.kaptest.com/college-prep/free-resources/free-events

8. NEED-BASED FINANCIAL AID

See Chapters 116 and 117.

9. CBOS

Community Based Organizations that comprehensively help under-resourced students with the college process (see Recommended Resources for a list of some of the leading national CBOs)

10. PRIVATE SCHOLARSHIPS

A lot of merit scholarships also consider financial need. In other words, you need to be a strong applicant, but priority will be given to students who have a real financial need. See Chapters 128 and 129 about private scholarships.

I was having a conversation with a mom in our first meeting about some of the access opportunities that exist for under-resourced students. I didn't know the family's income, and I was telling the mom she might or might not qualify. The mom responded, "How low does our income need to be? Because I can get poor very fast."

Don't be that mom. If you don't qualify for these programs, leave these resources for those who truly do qualify.

You can save a lot on room and board.

136

How do I lower my costs if I am already enrolled at a college?

CLEP: The College Level Examination Program is a group of standardized tests that are both created and administered by the College Board. There are thirty-six tests in various academic subject areas that assess your college-level knowledge and provide a mechanism for earning college credits without having to take an actual college course. For more information, see https://clep.collegeboard.org/exams

Room & board changes: There are some colleges that are approaching $20,000 a year for room and board. As states have cut back their funding to colleges, the colleges have turned to other sources of revenue, and room and board fees are a place where a college can get thousands more dollars out of each student. I don't mean to imply that every college is gouging every student, because running a quality residential program is expensive, but I am saying that you can usually save a lot of money if you select a leaner meal plan.

I encourage families to take a look at the cost of a full meal plan; now subtract all the times your child comes home, eats out, or sleeps in and doesn't have a full meal. Now divide the number of actual meals they eat from the plan by the semester charge from the college. I did this recently for a Virginia school and the average meal was costing $18! Most colleges have a variety of meal plans to choose from, and you can save money by choosing a plan that won't have you wasting meals and wasting money.

Become a Resident Assistant (RA): Compensation for being an RA varies so much that I encourage the families I work with to ask this question, because you can potentially save thousands. There are colleges that offer free room and board for being an RA, and many still offer a free room even if you still must pay board. Some schools also offer a stipend. Do some research to figure out how exactly you can become an RA at your school and what responsibilities are included. There are schools where you can be an RA in the second semester of your freshman year and there are schools where you must be a junior or a senior.

Become a school ambassador: Not every school pays for doing tours and panels for colleges, but a lot of schools do. Two days ago, I met with Ebony of Nova Southeastern University in Fort Lauderdale, and she shared with me how students get a free dorm room if they are an ambassador at Nova Southeastern. There are a lot of colleges like Nova that value this role and will compensate it generously.

Move off campus: There is a lot to consider before you move off campus. In general, students who live on campus graduate at a noticeably higher rate than those who move off. I like to see students who move off campus live very close to campus (preferably within walking distance). I also like to see students live with multiple other roommates, but they need to be positive academic and character influences on you. If you can't find this kind of roommate, then any cost-saving effect is simply not worth it.

Textbooks: You can save over a thousand dollars on your books over four years by being wise about your textbooks. Talk to other students who have taken the same course (with the same professor) to see which books are required versus recommended. You can always borrow books or buy a book from a friend. If cost is a concern, you should look at used books, online books, or book rentals. Here are my top choices for book purchases.

1. Amazon.com
2. Chegg.com
3. Dorksbooks.com

See if the on-campus bookstore matches competitor's prices. If they do this, I'd get all your books here. It will be convenient, and often they will allow you to use your aid for book purchases. More and more campus bookstores are matching the prices of their competitors. Valdosta State matched most of Amazon's prices for my daughter Joy.

You can also check with your professors to find out if an older (and therefore cheaper) edition of the textbook will work for the course. Many professors will let you know if that's the case if you explain that acquiring all new books is a hardship for you.

Department scholarships: (see Chapter 132)

Utilize your gifts and talents as an on-campus entrepreneur: I have seen students make a lot of money doing things like hair, nails, repairing cracked screens on cell phones, detailing cars, selling baked goods, tutoring, and dog watching. In fact, Joy called me two days ago to say that one student on her dorm floor is an amazing cook and she makes full meals and sells them to other students at reasonable prices.

Set a maximum budget on how much you will spend on restaurants and at coffee shops: eating out adds up! I strongly recommend using a financial tracking tool like Mint.com to track your expenses. My daughter Joy knew she liked quality coffee, so she bought a coffee maker instead of blowing $5-6 dollars a day on gourmet coffee.

Share your car expenses with your friends: A lot of financial planners will tell you to sell your car, but I know that is not always realistic. Instead, I am going to challenge you to split your car expenses with those that you transport. I am not talking about just getting $10 for gas. You also pay for the cost of the car, insurance, repairs, maintenance, parking, etc., in exchange for extra generosity with your vehicle. If you are taking a two-hour trip to the beach, or if you are transporting some friends home for the weekend, charge a fair price that is commensurate with your expenses.

One way I saved a lot of money on Karis's college was by switching her from Davidson's full-service 21 Meal plan, which costs around $7000, to their bare bones meal plan of 75 meals a semester. This plan costs under $2000 a year. Of course, 75 meals a semester is not enough to live off, so I send Karis $250 a month via the Cash App and she mostly uses this for groceries. This costs me another $2000 for 8 months, but it still saves $3000 a year. If Karis wants more meals at college, she uses this money to pay after her 75 meals have been used, but if she wants to cook or go to restaurants, she has the freedom to do that.

One great way Karis and her Davidson college friends used to make extra money was by dog watching. They could make $350 a week to stay in local homes while residents went on vacation. If you are in an upscale neighborhood and you like dogs or pets in general, look into this.

137

What do I need to know about state-based aid?

Every state has a different policy when it comes to how they distribute aid. It is essential that you are aware of what the protocol is for your state. Fortunately, there is help for you through NASFAA, the National Association of Student Financial Aid Administrators (NASFAA), which has provided a link to every single state's information so you can learn what the policies are for state-based aid for your state:
https://www.nasfaa.org/State_Financial_Aid_Programs This link is as valuable as any link in this book.

In an excellent *US News* article on October 31, 2016, titled "4 Need-to-Know Facts about State Aid for College," author Farran Powell points out how you need to know whether an individual special aid application is required in your state. Powell says, "[In] Pennsylvania, for example, families who are interested in-state aid have to submit the Pennsylvania State Grant Form."

"'Federal financial aid has very generous deadlines, but states often have deadlines that are several months prior—they're usually earlier than federal deadlines,'" says Kathy Ruby, director of college finance at College Coach.

According to the Department of Education's records, 10 states—Alaska, Illinois, Kentucky, Nevada, North Carolina, North Dakota, Oklahoma, South Carolina, Vermont, and Washington—changed their deadline this year for most grants to: "As soon as possible after October 1, 2016. Awards made until funds are depleted."

The earlier you apply, the better your chances, even if you're a stellar student. "Usually, it's first come, first served," says Maria C. Torres, director of communications and outreach at the Maryland Higher Education Commission.

For most states, the FAFSA is the only application that you will need to submit.

People have a tendency to overlook state-based aid: "I've definitely seen families that haven't received much in the way of the federal Pell Grant who received a larger award through the state," says Blaine Blontz, a financial consultant at Financial Aid Coach, who advises parents and grad students on how to maximize financial aid awards. "The amount can be from a few hundred dollars to the $5,000 range."

Most states offer some form of need-based aid, but there are some states that only offer need-based grants, such as Texas. "Our state programs are need-based, but some of them are need-based with merit," says Chad Puls, deputy assistant commissioner.

Many states offer merit aid either in addition to need-based aid, or, in some cases, exclusively. "Most states usually offer both," says Ruby from College Coach. "Understand if your state offers any merit-based aid to students."

The number of states that offer merit-based aid is growing. From a Hechinger Report article by Meredith Kolodner on June 22, 2015, titled, "States Moving College Scholarship Money Away From the Poor to the Wealthy and Middle Class": "Twelve states plus Washington, D.C., now spend more on merit-based aid than need-based aid, and many others have increased funding for scholarships based on academic achievement instead of need." Kolodner adds, "Georgia eliminated all of its need-based tuition aid in 2012."

Merit aid is extremely controversial, because research shows that merit aid benefits students who were already likely to graduate from college, while simultaneously taking money away from the neediest students who are oftentimes unlikely to attend, let alone graduate, from a college without the help of need-based aid. According to the Hechinger Report, "310,000 eligible low-income students were denied state tuition aid in Florida, Tennessee and Kentucky last year."

There is only one pot of money, so money that is given away based on merit takes money away from those who can't afford college without it. Here is another quote from the Hechinger Report: "Are we okay giving money to kids who are already going to go to college, or do we really want to make college change the trajectory of a kid who wouldn't have had that in his life?"

These issues are complex; the argument for merit money is that you keep the most talented kids in your state. Before Georgia launched its HOPE scholarship almost 25 years ago, the state was losing 75 percent of high school graduates who scored over 1400 on the SAT to out-of-state colleges. Almost 25 years later, three-quarters of the highest test takers now stay in-state. Georgia feels that giving money away based on merit and not need has accomplished exactly what it was intended to do.

Most state grants can only be used at an in-state college or university, public or private, according to Powell.

I sat down and started to rack my brain. I was trying to think of the last time someone other than a Georgia or Florida resident had asked me about state-based aid. I am constantly asked about outside private scholarships. I have a consultation tomorrow with a student about these. I am constantly asked about school based merit scholarships, federal grants, and federal student and parent loans. I am regularly asked about private loans. But state-based money (need or merit-based) is just not on students' or parents' radars.

Follow the guidelines carefully about getting in-state status.

138

How do I get in-state tuition when I am an out-of-state student?

The Cost of Attendance difference between in-state and out-of-state is around $15,000 on average, and it is over $25,000 at some colleges. Out-of-state tuition alone is often three times the in-state rate. What are you to do if you want to go to an out-of-state school but you can't afford what in some cases is a $100,000 decision over four years?

Look for regional college tuition discounts (see the next chapter).

Find out if your state has a reciprocity agreement with another state the way that Wisconsin and Minnesota or Colorado and New Mexico have.

If you live close to the border of your state, find out if there is a tuition reciprocity agreement for specific counties that are close to border states.

You want to start by asking someone who works in the Financial Aid department, or you can also try asking at the registrar's office.

In a *KIPLINGER* article on September 22, 2016, author Kaitlin Pittsker talks about the special circumstances that some colleges create to attract desirable out-of-state applicants:

> For example, the University of Maine at Orono recently began offering students from California, Connecticut, Illinois, Massachusetts, New Hampshire, New Jersey, Pennsylvania, Rhode Island, and Vermont its education at the same sticker price (tuition and fees) as that of the public flagship in the student's home state. To qualify for the best deal, students must earn at least a 3.0 grade-point average and score a combined 1120 on the SAT. Students from other states who meet the academic standards can receive $13,200 off the University of Maine's out-of-state tuition and fees ($29,480 for 2016-17). At Texas A&M University, non-Texans who earn a competitive scholarship of at least $1,000 also qualify to pay in-state tuition and fees. For 2016-17, that's a savings of more than $20,000 for out-of-state students. Similarly, the University of Arkansas will waive 70% to 90% of the difference between in-state and out-of-state tuition for students from Kansas, Louisiana, Mississippi, Missouri, Oklahoma, Tennessee, and Texas who earn at least a 3.2 GPA and score at least 1160 on the SAT.

An outstanding article published on July 18, 2017, by Kelsey Sheehy of *U.S. News & World Report* mentions "Eastern Oregon University, where there is no such thing as out-of-state tuition. The regional university sets tuition at $7,046 for all students, regardless of residency."

> Suzanne McCray, the Vice Provost for enrollment for the University of Arkansas, discusses how their program targets both states that are close by and high achievers. "The University of Arkansas also waives a portion of out-of-state fees for some scholarship winners," McCray says. "This 'New Arkansan' award is also available for students from neighboring states who excel academically. Students from

> neighboring states—Texas, Louisiana, Mississippi, Tennessee, Missouri, Kansas, and Oklahoma—who achieve at least a 3.25 GPA and an ACT score of 24 (1090 for the SAT) can get up 80 to 90 percent off nonresident tuition."

Financial aid scholar Mark Kantrowitz is quoted in this article, and he mentions more ways students can sometimes get in-state tuition: Schools make many kinds of exceptions, he says. "If your parents are in the military, but you are out-of-state, sometimes they will waive residency requirements. Sometimes if parents are policemen or firemen, they waive it. Sometimes there are exceptions for teachers."

The other way to get in-state tuition is to establish in-state residency, but this is not as easy as it used to be, because colleges are increasingly relying on out-of-state tuition to pay their bills, so they have beefed up their screening process to detect those who are just moving to the state to claim in-state tuition.

It is challenging, because all 50 states have their own policy on what they require in order to be classified as an in-state resident. Oftentimes, policies can vary from one college to another within the same state.

In a March 26, 2016, *Her Campus* article by Winnie Ma, Mark Kantrowitz and Jake Wells discuss getting in-state residency:

> In-state residency requires first and foremost a true intent to become a permanent resident of a new state, according to Wells. This entails establishing ties to the new state, like opening a local bank account, severing ties to the former state, and establishing a varying degree of financial independence (demonstrated through tax independence from parents who live in the state, employment, loans, etc.) depending on the state and university in question.

Jake Wells is the founder of In-State Angels, a company that provides resources for students who are trying to establish in-state status. Wells groups all 50 states into five categories, from those where it is the easiest to establish in-state residency (Arkansas, Nevada, New Mexico, North Dakota, South Dakota, and Utah) to a list of 19 states (Alaska, Arizona, Colorado, Delaware, Georgia, Illinois, Indiana, Kentucky, Maine, Massachusetts, New Hampshire, New Jersey, New York, North Carolina,

Pennsylvania, Rhode Island, West Virginia, Wisconsin, and Wyoming) where in-state tuition is the hardest to get.

"If it were a piece of cake, then there wouldn't be around two million out-of-state college students," Wells says. "In general, it's an intensive and paperwork-heavy process commonly spanning over a year or more. It's a process that you either take seriously and do 100 percent, or you might as well not even try—doing a halfway job is a waste of time."

Kantrowitz says:

> A student is more likely to qualify for in-state tuition if the student (or parent, if the student is a dependent student) moved to the state for a job; has strong ties to family living in the state; pays taxes as a state resident; gets a library card in the state; gets a state driver's license in the state; registers his/her cars in the state; votes in the state; graduated from a high school in the state [and], if the student/parent has hunting and fishing licenses, gets them in the state, etc.

Finaid.org has a section to learn about each state's residency's requirements are:

http://www.finaid.org/otheraid/stateresidency.phtml

Janice was determined to go to college in North Carolina. She attended a North Carolina boarding school, but that was irrelevant as her parents lived in Georgia and she was a dependent student, considered a Georgian for college admissions. But Janice did something that was very smart; she studied North Carolina's in-state policy and she followed the guidelines meticulously. She was awarded in-state status and saved herself and her family over $70,000 for college.

Regional tuition discounts can make out-of-state schools affordable.

139

HOW DO REGIONAL COLLEGE TUITION DISCOUNTS WORK?

I could have included the information in this chapter on the section on how to get in-state aid, but I felt that this information was so important that I wanted to give it its own chapter.

Regional college tuition discounts are sometimes referred to as educational compacts, regional exchanges, or tuition exchanges. There are four regional exchanges and one national exchange. These are agreements that allow students in a particular region to attend an out-of-state school at a rate that is less than the published out-of-state tuition rate, as long as certain conditions are met.

Two of the regional educational compacts require a student to be interested in a unique major that is not offered in their home state in order to qualify, and two of the regional college discounts do not require a unique major, but they offer a rate that is between the in-state rate and the out-of-state rate. There are lots of exceptions, so read the fine print.

Here is how NASFAA describes the four regional compacts:

SOUTHERN REGION

http://msep.mhec.org/

The Southern Regional Education Board Academic Common Marketprovides tuition discounts for more than 1900 academic programs in Alabama, Arkansas, Delaware, Florida, Georgia, Kentucky, Louisiana, Maryland, Mississippi, Oklahoma, South Carolina, Tennessee, Texas, Virginia, and West Virginia.

The Regional Contract Program enables students to pursue a professional health degree at out-of-state institutions, but pay in-state tuition at public institutions or reduced tuition at private institutions.

MIDWESTERN REGION

http://msep.mhec.org/

Students from Illinois, Indiana, Kansas, Michigan, Minnesota, Missouri, Nebraska, North Dakota, and Wisconsin may be eligible for tuition reductions at certain Midwest public and private schools through the Midwest Student Exchange.

WESTERN REGION

http://www.wiche.edu/wue

The Western Interstate Commission for Higher Education offers the Western Undergraduate Exchange for students in Alaska, Arizona, California, Colorado, Hawaii, Idaho, Montana, Nevada, New Mexico, North Dakota, Oregon, South Dakota, Utah, Washington, Wyoming, and the Commonwealth of the Northern Mariana Islands.

The Western Regional Graduate Program enables residents to enroll in available graduate programs outside of their home state at resident tuition rates.

The Professional Student Exchange Program enables students majoring in the health care professions to enroll in selected out-of-state professional programs.

NEW ENGLAND

http://www.nebhe.org/programs-overview/rsp-tuition-break/overview/

The New England Regional Student Program enables New England residents to enroll at out-of-state New England public colleges and universities at a discount. Students are eligible when they enroll in an approved major that is not offered by the public colleges and universities in their home state. More than 700 undergraduate and graduate degree programs are offered. Participating states are Connecticut, Maine, Massachusetts, New Hampshire, Rhode Island, and Vermont

"Many of these programs fly under the radar for families," says Tom Harnisch, director of state relations and policy analysis at the Association of State Colleges and Universities. "But students who meet the eligibility requirements can save hundreds or even thousands of dollars."

Here is how In-State Angels describes the one national tuition discount:

> There is a special reciprocity-esque arrangement for residents of the District of Columbia known as the D.C. Tuition Assistance Grant. Instead of leaving residents of D.C. hanging (who are United States citizens but residents of no official state), D.C. residents are offered up to $10,000/year toward the cost of any public university outside of D.C. Alternatively, $2,500/year is offered to study at certain district colleges, historically black colleges and universities (HBCU's) nationwide, and 2-year colleges nationwide. This grant has eligibility requirements and is awarded on a first come first served basis.

As great as these compacts are, there are states and schools that don't participate, or they do participate, but with severe restrictions. For example, in the Academic Common Market, North Carolina refuses to participate, and Florida will only participate for grad school.

An April 8, 2015, article by In-State Angels titled "Tuition Reciprocity Agreements Overpromise & Under-Deliver" points out the following limitations of these regional tuition discounts:

- ℵ Lots of popular universities opt out
- ℵ Some exchanges require certain majors are selected
- ℵ Some exchanges are geared to higher achievers
- ℵ Most universities limit their openings to a fixed number of students
- ℵ A separate application is often required
- ℵ Some of the discounts are only good for four years
- ℵ Some of the tuition discounts remove the benefits if your major changes
- ℵ Some of the exchanges will remove the benefit if your home state changes

From my experience, these exchanges often make the difference between whether a student can afford to go out-of-state. I hear the concerns In-State Angels raises, but these exchanges are extremely beneficial to a lot of students. Some colleges are much more receptive to giving out-of-state students from the region a discount. One school I have had a lot of success with is sending kids from Georgia to LSU. They have multiple pages on their website that make it crystal clear which majors qualify from the 12 states in the southern region. Here is a list of the majors they say will qualify from the state of Georgia for in-state tuition at LSU.

Eligible States & Undergraduate Programs for ACM

Georgia

- ℵ Coastal Environmental Science: Applied Coastal Environmental Science
- ℵ Coastal Environmental Science: Environmental Science and Research
- ℵ Environmental Management Systems
- ℵ Information Systems & Decision Sciences
- ℵ Interior Design
- ℵ Mass Communication: Political Communication
- ℵ Natural Resource Ecology & Management: Fisheries & Aquaculture
- ℵ Natural Resource Ecology & Management: Wildlife Ecology
- ℵ Natural Resource Ecology & Management: Wildlife Habitat Conservation & Management
- ℵ Petroleum Engineering
- ℵ Sport Administration: Sport Commerce
- ℵ Sport Administration: Sport Leadership
- ℵ Studio Art: Digital Art
- ℵ Textiles, Apparel, & Merchandising: Merchandising

Ariel Jones is a student that I worked with who graduated from Woodward Academy. Ariel knew she wanted to go to LSU. She was approved through the Academic Common Market, and this will save her about $80,000. Ariel is flourishing at LSU; she is doing well socially and academically and was just admitted to the Honors College for her sophomore year.

140

What is Federal Work-study?

Work-study is a job that some students who complete the FAFSA are offered as a means of helping them pay for college. It is available to undergraduate, graduate, or professional students who qualify.

Students can work in three different areas: on campus, off campus at a non-profit organization, and according to studentaid.gov, "some schools might have agreements with private for-profit employers for work-study jobs. These jobs must be relevant to your course of study (to the maximum extent possible)."

According to a 2016 study by Sallie Mae, the average work-study award in 2016 was $2649.

Students generally work between 10 and 20 hours a week, and while some jobs are mundane, The Department of Education encourages schools to try hard to find jobs for students that are consistent with their major. However, according to Homeroom, the government's education blog, this doesn't often work out, "some schools may match students to jobs, but most schools require the student to find, apply, and interview for positions on their own, just like any other job."

When you apply is important, because each college has a certain amount of work-study money, and funds are often given out to the first qualified students to apply.

Work-study money is managed by the college, but they have certain policies they must follow. They must pay students at least once a month. Most jobs range from minimum wage to $10 hour, and students are paid hourly.

According to studentaid.gov, your total work-study award depends on

- when you apply
- your level of financial need, and
- your school's funding level.

Unlike other types of federal aid, work-study money is paid directly to the student and not directly to your tuition bill. Students can use it to pay for any of their expenses.

One of the things that few students realize is that if they earn more than $6420 in a calendar year (as of 2017-18; the number changes a little every year), 50 percent of any additional money that they make will be added to their EFC. This is why the one of the best benefits of work-study money is that it is not counted for EFC calculations. Here is how the official education blog of the federal government, Homeroom, puts it: "One of the benefits of earning income through a Federal Work-Study position is that those earnings do not count against you when you complete the next year's FAFSA. Be sure to answer the question regarding how much was earned through work-study on your FAFSA accurately."

Some colleges don't offer the Federal Work-Study program, but they will offer a campus employment in their aid awards.

When Courtney got to Vanderbilt, she didn't want to use her work-study job to serve meals in the dining hall. She wanted to get a job in an area where she had career interest. She sought out career related work-study jobs and she got a job in the medical center as a research assistant as a freshman.

Courtney worked in public health for one year and in sports medicine for three years. She earned $10 an hour, and she told me that by the time she graduated, she was training other employees. Courtney listed this at the top of her résumé and as a 21-year-old, she landed a position with a software company as a data analyst. She told me she knows her professional experience at Vanderbilt and her internship at Emory landed her the job she has today. Follow Courtney's example and use work-study not only as a source of money but also as an opportunity to advance your career.

141

How does a school's endowment impact my education and what I have to pay?

Endowment is extremely important for private colleges, because they get very little government funding, so their primary sources of income are tuition-paying parents, fundraising, and endowment. Endowment is a pool of money the college has been given through philanthropy, managed by professionals in such a way that the principal is kept and preserved, but around 5 percent of the principal can be invested in the operating budget and used for things like faculty salaries, benefits, financial aid.

The American Council of Education aptly describes how endowments work in a document titled, "Facts About College and University Endowments." They say, "Endowments are very complex. They usually consist of many—sometimes thousands—of different funds. Most of these funds are subject to restrictions that donors impose and that institutions are legally required to uphold."

Suppose you have a twin brother; you are both married with two kids, and you both make $50,000. You are also both incredibly committed to using your resources to give your two kids the absolute best education possible. However, you have $500 in the bank, and your twin brother has 10 million in the bank. Let's say you each withdraw a 5 percent annual return on your savings (similar to most college endowments). Five percent of $500 gives you $25 a year, but 5 percent of 10 million gives your twin brother $500,000 to invest in his children's education.

As much as you love your kids, you have other bills to pay (like a mortgage, car, food, health care, etc.) so there is only so much you can do with your $50,025, but your twin brother can do all kinds of things to educate his two children with his $550,000. The bottom line is that colleges with large endowments can invest more on educating each student.

This is the situation the wealthiest schools find themselves in. I advise people not to neglect endowments when evaluating schools. The larger the endowment per student, the more the school can invest in you, just like in the twin brother analogy. Schools with larger endowments can attract the top faculty by paying them generously, and they can give out the most financial aid, because they have the resources to do so.

	Endowment Student($)	**Endowment ($million)**	**# of Students**
Princeton	2,707,860	22,153	8,181
Yale	2,063,759	25,409	12,312
Harvard	1,644,857	34,542	21,000
Stanford	1,410,720	22,398	15,877
Pomona	1,193,626	1,985	1,663
MIT	1,164,591	13,182	11,319
Swarthmore	1,104,997	1,747	1,581
Amherst	1,098,972	2,032	1,849
Olin Coll. of Engin.	1,005,714	352	350
Williams	1,004,900	2,256	2,245
Cal Tech	940,625	2,107	2,240

	Endowment Student($)	Endow-ment ($million)	# of Students
Grinnell	967,155	1,649	1,705
Rice	803,865	5,324	6,623
Bowdoin	744,858	1,340	1,799
Wellesley	721,099	1,784	2,474
Dartmouth	701,144	4,474	6,381
Notre Dame	687,577	8,374	12,179
Washington & Lee	650,177	1,472	2,264
Smith	566,110	1,627	2,874
U of Richmond	530,138	2,190	4,131
Claremont McKenna	525,574	709	1,349
Duke	461,165	6,840	14,832
Northwestern	454,923	9,648	21,208
Bryn Mawr	450,028	797	1,771
Univ. of Chicago	445,186	7,001	15,726
Hamilton	441,622	817	1,850
Washington U in St. Louis	435,386	6,462	14,842
UPenn	430,736	10,715	24,876
Emory	429,290	6,402	14,913
Middlebury	396,279	1,001	2,526
Colby	389,589	711	1,825
Vassar	379,184	929	2,450
Carleton	366,435	738	2,014
Haverford	365,891	472	1,290
Reed	356,528	497	1,394
Davidson	339,487	662	1,950
Macalaster	337,675	700	2,073
Harvey Mudd	338,290	273	807
Denison	333,023	716	2,150
Brown	326,573	2,963	9,073

These universities and colleges listed on the table above, from Reach-HighScholars.org, are the forty colleges and universities ranked from 1 to 40th according to the highest endowment per student. It isn't fair to compare an endowment of a college of 20,000 students to one of 1000, because obviously a school of 20,000 requires more money for salaries, benefits, financial aid, facilities, etc., so the true way to measure the financial strength of a college is by dividing their endowment by their number of students. The first column gives you this number.

Endowment per student is not a perfect metric for measuring wealth for major research universities, because some schools on this list like Harvard, Emory, and Vanderbilt have a considerable portion of their endowment tied up in money that is designated and restricted for their expensive medical schools. In reality, schools like Yale, Princeton, and the liberal arts schools on the list are even wealthier in comparison to the other schools listed above in the top 40 than they appear here. Having said that, it is still the best metric that I know of, and it effectively shows who has money and who doesn't.

Is there a correlation between endowment and salary? Take a look at how many of the colleges that pay their teachers the most show up on the list of the 40 colleges with the highest endowments per student:

Highest Associate Professor Pay for colleges that educate undergraduates:

Harvard	$230,292
Stanford	$227, 259
Chicago	$225,229
Columbia	$209,475
MIT	$204,138
University of Pennsylvania	$201,978
Princeton	$200,403
Yale	$198,369
NYU	$195,939
Cal Tech	$193,949
Northwestern	$192, 897
Duke	$187,731
Georgetown	$186, 750
Rice	$185,247
Vanderbilt	$179,172
Washington U-St. Louis	$175, 734
Dartmouth	$175,239

This data comes from the *Chronicle of Higher Education* 2015-16.

We see how wealthy schools can pay teachers the most, but they also offer the most generous need-based financial aid packages. Twenty-eight schools that are committed to exceptional generosity in helping students afford college got together and formed an organization called the 568 Presidents' Group. These schools all use the PROFILE, but they use a consensus methodology in assessing need that is more student-centered. For example, all of these schools limit how much home equity they use toward the EFC by capping home equity at 1.2 times income. Colleges with low endowments that use the PROFILE could never afford this unless they became need-aware.

Here are the 28 members of the Presidents' Group. Notice how many of them are in the top 40 of endowment per student:

Amherst College
Boston College
Claremont McKenna College
College of the Holy Cross
Columbia University
Cornell University
Dartmouth College
Davidson College
Duke University
Georgetown University
Grinnell College
Massachusetts Institute of Technology
Middlebury College
Northwestern University
Pomona College
Rice University
St. John's College
Swarthmore College
University of Notre Dame
University of Pennsylvania
Vanderbilt University
Wellesley College
Williams College

I had two interesting conversations yesterday. The first was with Joyce, one of the students I worked with last year, who is a freshman at Grinnell. I was telling Joyce, "Grinnell's large endowment is going to benefit you in ways you haven't even thought of."

Joyce replied, "I get it. I was looking at their summer study abroad opportunities, and many of them are free."

I told Joyce, "This is an example of how their endowment benefits you."

A few hours later, I was having dinner with my wife Anitra and my daughter Karis, a senior at Davidson College. Karis said, "You know, I thought it was bad that Davidson charges me $50 to have a car on campus for the year, but then I met students who have to pay $300 and even $500 a year for their car."

I said to Karis the same thing I said to Joyce: schools with large endowments can afford to be generous, but schools that are almost totally tuition-dependent often have lots of expenses they have to pass onto their students. The money just isn't there.

142

WHAT ARE PRIORITY DEADLINES, AND WHY ARE THEY IMPORTANT?

Priority deadlines are dates on the calendar that serve as watershed dates; those who meet the deadlines are treated differently than those who do not meet the deadlines.

Colleges can have priority deadlines for admissions, for financial aid, for housing, for course selection, etc. A priority deadline for admission means that your chances of being admitted are better if your application is submitted by a particular date. It is most common for these dates to be in the fall, and sometimes *early* in the fall. Why would a college have a priority admission deadline? They want to incentivize students to apply early in order to help them manage the reading of the application files. Reading thousands or tens of thousands of files that all come at once is a herculean task for any admission office. If these can be more evenly spread out throughout the application season, this significantly helps the admission office.

The other admission advantage to this is that it gives the admission office an early read on who is applying in a given year. If they notice that their applicants are soft from a particular area, there is still time to take this into consideration in their recruitment or in their decision-making. Having a priority deadline can also encourage applicants who would not otherwise apply. Sometimes there are incentives, i.e. waiving the application fee, etc.

What I find most common is a priority deadline for financial aid and scholarships. In other words, if you meet this priority deadline, you will be considered for merit scholarships. If you don't, you will still be eligible for certain forms of financial aid, but often not the very best and most lucrative awards.

Students should pay particular attention to admission deadlines. I strongly recommended that you create a master calendar with all of your admission and financial aid deadlines on it. I'm not just talking about your priority deadlines, but all your deadlines! Of course, you definitely don't want to be missing your priority deadlines. Priority deadlines are moving up earlier and earlier every year.

Earlier today, I had a lengthy meeting with Elsie Miles, a Senior Admission Counselor at Mercer University. One thing Elsie really emphasized was to make sure our students apply before October 15 because that is our priority deadline. Elsie went on to say that students are not eligible for Mercer's Presidential Scholarship if they miss this deadline. Like a lot of schools, Mercer has a scholarship weekend on Dec. 1 and 2 and the October 15 deadline gives the admission team time to read the thousands of applications they receive early and invite those who qualify for scholarship weekend with enough time to get it on their calendars.

Two days ago I listened to a Georgia Tech information session and they emphasized their priority deadlines. Georgia Tech said if students want to live in a living-learning community, or if they want to be considered for merit scholarships, they need to apply by Georgia Tech's October 15 early action deadline.

Need Blind vs. Need Aware admissions is a very difficult decision for colleges.

143

WHAT IS THE DIFFERENCE BETWEEN NEED-BLIND AND NEED-AWARE ADMISSIONS?

Need-aware is also known as need-sensitive, and occasionally you will hear it called "need-conscious admissions."

When we talk about need-blind versus need-aware, what we are asking is whether the admissions process is completely separate from an applicant's ability to pay, or if ability to pay is considered during the admission decision-making process.

Union College is a need-aware college, and one thing Matt Malatesta of Union points out on their website in an excellent article titled, "Need-blind vs. Need-aware" is that many of the schools that claim they are need-blind and meet full need "are not able to meet applicants' need without adding unrealistic work-study or loan options." Malatesta also says, "Maybe 20 institutions in the country can meet the full need of all of the applicants they accept."

I think that is high. I'm not convinced there are ten schools in the country that are truly need-blind, and there may not even be five. The majority of need-blind schools have to make wealthy schools a priority in their recruitment to attract students who can pay.

Malatesta also says, "But here is our perspective: once we admit you to Union, we will find a way for you to attend. We will put together a realistic financial aid package based on your family's ability to pay."

Most colleges don't agree with Union. The majority of colleges are need-blind, but they gap their applicants, leaving them with a significant amount of unmet need. This is one major reason students drop out, because they can't sustain their financial gap year after year.

A Penn State study by their Center for Higher Ed found that, "On need-blind status ... 93 percent of public institutions and 81 percent of private institutions say that they are entirely need blind."

I realize that many colleges could not fill their beds if they didn't admit students, gap them, and trust that they will find a way to come up with the resources to attend. I'm sympathetic to how a lack of resources constrains even the best of intentions.

The need-blind vs. need-aware argument is one people are very passionate about on both sides. Malatesta said two things that I think we all can agree on: "It's a controversial subject, but worth engaging." He also said, "I'm not convinced either is entirely right."

When I did boarding school admissions, we really wrestled with this subject. We actually changed our policy in my time from being need-aware to need-blind and back to need-aware again. The associate director took the position that it is immoral for us to not be need-blind. She argued that it isn't right for an applicant to be judged by whether they can pay. Secondly, she argued, "What message does this send to applicants to know that their lack of money may be why we didn't admit them?" She went on to passionately say that applicants have a right to know whether they met the admission standard, and if they are denied because they can't pay, we are depriving them of something they have a right to know. Finally, she said, "Who are we to play God? We don't know what other sources of money a family may have."

I acknowledged that my colleague had some good points, but I felt just as strongly that being need-aware was a better approach than being need-blind and gapping students, and we both knew there wasn't money to be need-blind and not gap, even though we had almost an 85-million-dollar endowment. Of course, if you can be need-blind and truly meet the calculated needs of a family, then being need-blind is the superior option; that is indisputable. But so few schools have the resources for that.

I argued that it gives people false hope to accept them and not aid them, and it leads to irresponsible decisions, like taking out unreasonable amounts of loans when parents feel guilty if they don't find a way to let their child attend their dream school even though they don't have the resources. I argued that our aid could be targeted to our strongest applicants, and we would have more resources to yield the students that could help our school the most. I argued that to admit a student and not give them the resources to come is cruel and immoral in a different way.

I was also persuaded by our business office, which felt that students who are admitted but lack the resources are more likely to go into default, and I knew that gapping a student leads to a higher dropout rate. It was "truth in advertising" not to pretend we were need-blind when we *were* conscious of whether a family could pay. We didn't need to be need-sensitive for all of our applicants, but only for a smaller number of our borderline applicants when we were about to be out of money. This same argument has been made by colleges like Macalester, Haverford, and Wesleyan. Colleges are having the same need-blind vs. need-aware debate, and there are strong arguments in favor and against both approaches.

Colleges that meet full need are wealthy and able to give a lot of aid to students

144

WHAT DOES IT MEAN IF A COLLEGE MEETS "FULL DEMONSTRATED NEED?"

This term is so confusing to most people. It does not mean you are getting a full scholarship. It also does not mean that the school is only going to ask you to pay what you believe you can pay. However, for schools that have enough resources (this requires a large endowment) to meet full demonstrated need, the student is getting something of great value. You will hear the terms "full calculated need" and "full demonstrated need" used interchangeably. Sometimes it is just called meeting "full need." I prefer the term full calculated need because it implies there is an outside calculation (which is true) that determines this, but I will use the terms interchangeably as well.

In order to understand this subject, we must return to our basic financial formula of Cost of Attendance - EFC = Family Financial Need.

Schools that meet full calculated need will give you enough money through a combination of grants, scholarships, work-study/campus jobs, Stafford Loans, and summer earnings (PROFILE schools only) to meet your financial need without gapping you or leaving you with unmet need.

You may be thinking that sounds like they are adding a lot besides grants and loans (free money), but the great news is that the other things they are adding all have reasonable caps.

- ℵ Work-study is unlikely to be over $3500
- ℵ The Stafford Loan will be $5500-$7500
- ℵ The summer earnings component will probably not be more than $3000

Let's see how a school that meets full calculated need will differ in their aid award versus a school that doesn't, and you will see why schools that meet full calculated/demonstrated need make a real point of emphasizing this in all of their marketing materials. There is prestige in being on the list of schools that meet full need, but there is also value.

$70,000 (COA) - $10,000 (EFC)
= $60,000 (Family Financial Need)
$60,000- $2500 in (WS) - $5500 (Stafford Loan) - $3000 (summer work job)
= $49,000

$49,000 that the school will give to the student because they will meet this need with grants and scholarships if the college meets full calculated need.

The wealthiest and most generous colleges will replace the Stafford Loan with more need-based aid for all students, or for families below a certain income. The poorest schools will not give any of that $49,000 in gift aid, but will leave $49,000 in unmet need. If a school has a $49,000 PLUS loan, that is unmet need that the family has to pay. Most schools will meet some of the $49,000 with scholarships and grants and leave a large amount of unmet need.

From Kim Clark's March 16, 2015, article in *TIME*, "The 10 Colleges With the Most Generous Financial Aid": "In all, only 64 colleges in the country say they hand out enough aid to meet the full demonstrated financial need of every regularly admitted undergraduate, according to Peterson's data."

This week I sat down with a mom and her daughter who have an automatic zero EFC. I knew Emory was a great match for her, but I wanted them to see how generous Emory would be, because they meet full calculated need without loans at her income. We completed the net price calculator, and even though Emory has a COA of around $67,000, this family would have to pay under $3000. The challenge is that schools that meet full need are not only rare, but they are competitive.

145

HOW DO I UNDERSTAND AND COMPARE FINANCIAL AID AWARDS?

If you apply for financial aid and you are accepted, the college will send you an aid award letter. The letters are supposed to list the expenses of the college, the resources you are receiving to help with the costs, and your financial obligations. These letters can be very confusing, because there is no standard format that they all follow. Fortunately, the Department of Education came up with a standard format known as the Shopping Sheet, and most colleges have adopted this format.

This is how the government's website (https://www2.ed.gov/policy/highered/guid/aid-offer/index.html) describes the Shopping Sheet:

> The Financial Aid Shopping Sheet (PDF) is a consumer tool that participating institutions use to notify students

> about their financial aid package. It is a standardized form that is designed to simplify the information that prospective students receive about costs and financial aid so that they can easily compare institutions and make informed decisions about where to attend school. The Shopping Sheet became available for use beginning in the 2013-2014 award year.

In July 2012, the Department of Education unveiled the 2013-2014 version of the Shopping Sheet. You can use the link above to see the colleges that use the Shopping Sheet, and this list is updated regularly.

You can also send an email if you have questions:

> As of April 2015, over 2,900 institutions have voluntarily adopted the Shopping Sheet, representing institutions nationwide from all sectors of higher education. Institutions may contact ShoppingSheet@ed.gov to indicate their commitment to use the Shopping Sheet. Students, parents, and institutions may also direct questions about the Shopping Sheet to that e-mail address.

The following link will take you to what is known as the Annotated Shopping Sheet. It not only will show you the standard format for aid awards, but it explains each component: https://www2.ed.gov/policy/highered/guid/aid-offer/shoppingsheettemplate20172018annotated.pdf

Aid awards sometimes come with offers of admissions, and sometimes they are sent shortly after admissions offers. At the latest, they should arrive in late March or early April.

I do not want to give the impression that the Shopping Sheet has fixed the problems of confusing aid awards. In an excellent article by Mark Kantrowitz on Edvisors titled, "How to Read Financial Aid Award Letters," Kantrowitz discusses some of the biggest areas where aid awards confuse families. Below, I have paraphrased his comments.

Nearly a third of financial aid award letters do not mention the college's Cost of Attendance. Of those that do, many do not list all college costs. Many list only the direct costs, such as tuition, fees, room and board (if the student lives on campus), which are paid to the college. (Note that financial aid is not based on or restricted to just direct costs.) About half of all public college costs are indirect costs, such as textbooks and supplies, transportation, computers, student health insurance, dependent care and other living expenses. This forces the student to search on the college's website and course catalog to get information about all college costs. Even when colleges provide information about all college costs, many do not provide realistic information about textbook, transportation and other living costs. Financial aid award letters also often blur the distinction between grants and loans. More than half of award letters do not include basic information about loan terms and conditions, such as interest rates, monthly payments and total payments. The award letters often list loans with just an award name and award amount, without any signals that the loan is an amount that must be repaid, usually with interest. Award letters rarely use the word 'loan' as part of the name of a loan, and sometimes use cryptic labels like 'L' or 'LN.' Loans and grants are mixed together, further confusing families as to what is a loan and what is a grant. Award letters sometimes use language that treats loans as though they reduce college costs.

What are you to do if one of your colleges does not subscribe to the Shopping Sheet? What are you to do if you find the Shopping Sheet confusing? There are a number of excellent Aid Award calculators online. My favorite one is the College Board's Aid Award calculator: https://bigfuture.collegeboard.org/pay-for-college/financial-aid-awards/compare-aid-calculator

Before using this calculator, be sure to follow the College Board's recommended tips. You will see a link to click that I strongly recommend you read carefully. The purpose of the calculator is to allow you to compare different aid awards to truly see which one is the best for you.

Rochelle and her mom called me because they were confused. Rochelle had applied to ten schools and was admitted to eight of them, but the eight colleges all had aid awards that were all very different. I explained the differences in the awards to them, but the College Board's Aid Award calculator is what really made it clear. I can't recommend this tool enthusiastically enough.

Get to know the FAO and treat them well!

146

WHAT DO I NEED TO KNOW ABOUT YOUR FINANCIAL AID OFFICER?

You need to know that they are a very important person that you need to build a relationship with. There are a lot of unique special circumstances when money is involved, and the Financial Aid Officer (FAO) has a lot of power to help you if you have a legitimate case.

There is a widespread perception that anyone who works as an FAO is a cold pawn of the institution and is determined to squeeze every penny out of you in order to help the bottom line of the college. Another stereotype is that FAOs are impersonal accounting types who lack people skills, but they enjoy working with numbers. Both of these stereotypes are inaccurate. In reality, most FAOs love students, and they are motivated by trying to assist parents and students by helping to answer their questions and by taking the stress out of the process.

Most people will encounter some complex financial question that is confusing or stressful. If you have a relationship with your FAO, they are going to go out of the way to help you in a fuller way than if you are a stranger to them. This is just human nature.

I can assure you that if you have an amicable relationship with your FAO, this can make the difference between how certain subjective matters are resolved if you need to appeal an aid award. I am not saying that FAOs are unprofessional; in fact, I am saying the opposite. I would say the same thing about your banker, your principal, your teachers, etc. Relationships matter, and they matter a lot with FAOs who have a lot of influence.

If you are struggling to pay for college and you let your FAO know this, and he/she knows of several internal scholarships and has a relationship with you, they may do more than mention a scholarship to you. They may describe the scholarship, tell you who to contact, and even make a call and recommend you. It has benefited me many times to know at least one FAO at each of my daughter's colleges.

In May, my 78-year-old mom was flying from Buffalo to Atlanta. It was the first time she had flown to the busiest airport in the world without my dad, her husband of 57 years. This was stressful to her, so she asked me if I could meet her at the gate. Well, ever since 9/11, it isn't that easy to meet someone at the gate when you don't have a ticket. I met with a customer service person at Delta and asked him how I could meet my mom at the gate.

The Delta employee told me who to talk to, saying, "You never know if they will approve your request." But then he said, "Remember these three words: nice gets nice." When it comes to working with your FAO, remember, "nice gets nice."

147

DO I NEED TO PAY ALL AT ONCE OR DO COLLEGES OFFER PAYMENT PLANS?

I do not know of a single college that does not offer a payment plan. Colleges know that if they required everyone to come up with the money all at once, they wouldn't have many students.

The payment options vary tremendously. Some schools have payment plans that are only for the semester, while most offer payment plans over the whole year.

The payment plans can be an outstanding way for a family to constrain their borrowing and to knock off a substantial portion of their net price by setting up a systematic pay plan that forces them to prioritize the college bills in the same way they'd need to prioritize a mortgage. The simple fact is that most families do not have a lump sum sitting there that they can use to cover the college costs in the fall.

These installment plans can be a great deterrent to the easy temptation to take out a PLUS or a private loan.

This process is very individualized; some schools get really creative in the payment options they provide. Remember, financial aid offices are really experts on consumer spending patterns, and they often tailor their plans to the various saving and spending habits of their families.

There is no standard number of months over which payments are split. It is very common to find an eight-month or a 10-month option, and there are schools that have 12-month options. You should be willing to sit down with the financial aid office to see if there is anything creative they can do if none of the options are that attractive to you, but don't expect that to lead to you paying a lower amount.

You should also not expect for this to be a way for you to rack up frequent flyer miles by using your credit card. Most schools will accept a credit card payment option with a hefty 2.7 percent to 3 percent surcharge, and some won't accept credit cards at all.

Just remember to keep in mind that these plans are only good for the billable costs, which is another term for the direct costs. You will still have to pay for the non-billable (indirect) expenses, so be sure to budget for these.

There is almost always a modest fee to set up a payment plan, but it is usually less than $100, and this makes sense because some people could just keep their money in their financial institution and earn interest.

Every year when Karis's Davidson College tuition bill was due, it would look formidable, but I always signed up for their eight-month installment option, and breaking it up into bite-sized pieces allowed us to avoid the extra interest and risk that comes with PLUS loans or private loans.

A high sticker price can also be affordable

148

IF I AM JUST FLAT BROKE, WHAT IS THE CHEAPEST WAY TO GO TO COLLEGE?

This is an important question, but there are quite a few different answers. If you only want to go to college for two years, you can still support a family well by getting an associate's degree in the right field. Too many people focus far too much on which college they attend as opposed to whether their major leads to jobs that the market is clamoring for. Air traffic controllers, for example, make over $120,000, and they only need an associate's degree. Radiologic technologists and nuclear technicians make over $80,000 on average, and you only need an associate's degree. I am absolutely not advocating selecting a career based only on money, but I share this to show that an associate's degree can lead to a salary that can support a family.

Another great move if you just don't have any money is to attend your local community college for two years and then transfer to a four-year college. The important thing here is to make sure that a strong articulation agreement is in place so that your credits transfer. The average community college is under $4000 a year. If you are in an upper-middle class school where most kids go to four-year colleges, this unusual path may earn you some strange looks. But if you can stay focused and disciplined, you will end up where your classmates end up, except with considerably less debt. This option isn't for most students, but it is an under-utilized option for families that are flat broke.

A third great option is to attend an in-state school close to home and be a commuter. Now, this won't help you if you are in a rural area and no colleges are close by, but the vast majority of readers likely have access to a college they can commute to. I know that it is a vision of almost every middle class American to have your child go off to college and experience life in the dorm, but if it isn't affordable, there are ways to get a degree without spending the extra $8,000-$18,000 to live on campus and incur related expenses, such as a meal plan.

Other options:

- Take online classes (see Chapter 162)
- Come from a low- or moderately-low income family, be an amazing student and citizen, and get into one of the most generous schools in the country.

Here is a list of 16 colleges that meet full demonstrated need without loans **for all incomes:**

> Amherst, Bowdoin, Claremont-McKenna, Colby, Columbia, Davidson, Haverford, Harvard, Pomona, Princeton, Stanford, Swarthmore, UPenn, Vanderbilt, Washington & Lee, and Yale.

The following 21 colleges offer no loans for students **with modest incomes:**

> Brown, Connecticut College, Cornell, Dartmouth, Duke, Emory, Kenyon, Lafayette, Lehigh, MIT, Northwestern, Oberlin, Rice, Tufts, Chicago, North Carolina, Vassar, Washington U-St. Louis, Wellesley, Wesleyan, and Williams.

Courtney was a very talented student I worked with from Westlake High School. She told me, "All my friends were saying I should stay in-state and attend Georgia or Georgia Tech and get the Zell Miller Scholarship, but that only covers tuition and not room and board." Courtney attended Vanderbilt, one of the no-loan schools on the list. She paid very little to go to college. I attended her college graduation party and she said to me, "Most of my friends have lots of loans, but I graduated with zero debt."

149

WHAT IS "NET PRICE," AND WHAT IS A NET PRICE CALCULATOR?

As of October 2011, the Obama administration required colleges to include a calculator on each college's website that reveals what you can expect to have to pay for college. These calculators are frequently referred to as net price calculators, NPCs, and cost calculators.

Prior to this requirement, colleges would list their Cost of Attendance figures, but you wouldn't have a clue as to what you would pay. Net price is what you pay out of pocket. You recall our basic college financial formula is:

Prior to this requirement, colleges would list their Cost of Attendance figures, but you wouldn't have a clue as to what you would pay. Net price is what you pay out of pocket. You recall our basic college financial formula is:

Cost of Attendance – EFC = Family Financial Need

Well, it is time for our second formula:

Cost of Attendance – Need-Based Grants – merit-based scholarships = Net Price, or Out-of-Pocket Price (excluding loans)

Notice that net price is not COA – Grants – Scholarships - LOANS. This is something that people frequently confuse.

It is great that the cost calculators are required, but unfortunately, the Department of Education gave colleges very minimalistic requirements as to what the calculator needs to include, and there are a lot of bad calculators out there. In an excellent article from January 26, 2016, by YourCollegeConcierge, titled, “What is a Net Cost calculator, and How Good are the Calculators on the Web?” three of the deficiencies of these calculators are explained particularly well.

Not all calculators are created equal. Some colleges are using the template created by the United States Department of Education. It asks only nine questions, including how many children the family has in college, family income, and whether the student is married or has dependents. Problem: these nine questions are all that the government is requiring colleges to ask, but there are 100 questions on the FAFSA and dozens of other factors that can seriously affect a family’s expected contribution (EFC). Those inputs can be as benign as your highest level education to as complex as how to value your business, personal and student assets. There are at least 575 colleges that engage Student Aid Services, a private company, to provide them with much more involved versions of the calculator.

The results are not guaranteed for four years. The calculators will give you an ‘estimate’ of what you might pay for the first year ONLY. Your circumstances, the school’s, and the federal government’s change year-to-year. Some schools will ‘frontload’ grants to induce a prospect to come.

They do not really account for merit discounts. The calculators work best when determining need-based financial aid awards, but they are less accurate when factoring how merit scholarships (awarded by the institution) can reduce the cost of college.

I don't entirely agree with the last statement. I find when a school gives merit awards based on academic GPA and test scores (which is a sizable number of colleges), the merit scholarships on the NPCs are quite accurate, but if a school is holistically determining merit, then I completely agree.

I was meeting with Ellen and her mom Mary when Mary asked me a great question. "I get it that these calculators have some value, but I'm not an expert, so how am I to know which of these cost calculators are good and which ones are bad?"

I told Mary, "The best calculators will ask you a lot of very detailed questions." I told her to have access to her tax records and bank statements. I told her that she could tell the ones that give merit awards based on test scores, because they will ask for this information, and you can actually change your numbers and you will see your awards change. Some of them will allow you to email the results to yourself. I told her that usually private colleges that require the PROFILE and offer early decision or early action have the best NPCs.

These schools want families to complete their net price calculators in order to feel comfortable knowing what they will have to pay before they apply early. It is not in their best interest to mislead a family, because if you apply ED and get an aid award that is less than what the NPC said, you can get out of your commitment, and then you are going to tell 50 family members and friends all about your terrible experience you had with the college. I told Mary that she should ask the financial aid person she was working with how accurate their NPC is.

There are a number of schools that do not require the PROFILE and do not offer early decision, but have excellent NPCs. I told Mary to fill out all of these cost calculators for any school Ellen is remotely thinking about, and she will become aware of who has the better cost calculator. A great place to access a basic NPC is on the Big Future website: https://bigfuture.collegeboard.org/pay-for-college/paying-your-share/focus-on-net-price-not-sticker-price

I told her that College Reality check (https://collegerealitycheck.com/en//) is another great place to find NPCs in one place. Finally, I stressed to Mary that if the colleges Ellen was looking at give merit-based scholarships through a holistic evaluation, she should not expect any calculator to be able to factor this into their projected net price.

150

TELL ME 18 REASONS WHY A 529 PLAN IS THE BEST COLLEGE SAVINGS VEHICLE.

The 529 is unquestionably the best way to save for college for the vast majority of people. In this chapter, you will see all of the reasons why I feel so passionately that the 529 is in its own tier for long-term college savings.

According to the IRS, a 529 Plan is "a plan operated by a state or educational institution, with tax advantages and potentially other incentives to make it easier to save for college and other post-secondary training for a designated beneficiary, such as a child or grandchild."

The plan takes its name from its section of the IRS code. 529 plans began in 1996.

Why do you need a savings plan? Jamie Hopkins tells us in the *Forbes* article, "Understanding the Tax Benefits of 529 Plans," that "the increasing cost of a college education has significantly outpaced national inflation by an average of 3.4% per year since 2005, according to CollegeBoard.org."

BENEFITS OF A 529 PLAN

1. Tax-deferred growth and tax-free withdrawals. If you invest $25,000 in a 529 and it grows to $75,000, you do not pay taxes on the $50,000 growth in your investment.
2. There are no income limits as to who can invest. Educational Savings Accounts (aka Coverdell ESA) and Roth IRAs have income caps, preventing some people from utilizing these savings vehicles.
3. You can put a lot of money away each year. The limit for a married family that files jointly is $28,000 per year per child.
4. The lifetime limits for savings are very high. These vary by state, but they can be as high as half a million dollars.
5. Most states offer state tax deductions. More than two-thirds of states offer tax breaks, and in some cases the tax breaks are significant. For instance, in Pennsylvania, taxpayers can deduct up to $14,000 of contributions to a Pennsylvania 529 plan per year, per beneficiary, from their Pennsylvania taxable income. With a current state income tax rate of 3.07 percent, a Pennsylvania resident could save roughly $430 per year in taxes by contributing $14,000 to a 529 plan, according to Hopkins' article in Forbes.
6. They can be used for so many different education expenses. Things like computers, printers, Internet service, and educational software are deemed valid Qualified Higher Education Expenses by the IRS.
7. You can have many different plans without being forced to consolidate: You can open multiple accounts in multiple states without ever having to combine or consolidate them, according to Jessica Dickler's CNBC-10 article "Hidden Benefits of 529s."
8. Some states go beyond a tax deduction and offer a state tax credit. Utah, Indiana, and Vermont fall in this category.
9. Dickler's article states that friends and family can contribute to a 529 and designate you as a beneficiary.

10. If you don't need to use all of the money you've saved in a 529, it is easy to redirect it without onerous taxes impacting you.
11. You have a substantial amount of investment vehicles to select from. You have mutual funds, ETFs, Fund of Fund, etc.
12. You have such a variety of 529 plans to choose from. Virtually every state has their own state plan, and while it is true that you often will get the best tax breaks from your own state's plan, there are plenty of exceptions. You need to shop around and you have a tremendous variety of options.
13. It is relatively easy to change your beneficiary from one person to another person. If the change is to a family member, the process is even easier.
14. An adult can save money for themselves through a 529 if they want to go back to college or just take some classes.
15. According to Dickler's article, 529s can be used for a wide range of different schooling options. "529 plans can be used for undergraduate or graduate school, technical or trade schools, even cooking schools or golf schools in the United States, and some accredited schools abroad," she writes.
16. Wealth can be transferred through 529s: According to Merrill Edge's "5 Things You May Not Know About 529 College Savings Plans," "contributing to a 529 plan also can help grandparents or others reduce the size of their taxable estates. It's even possible to accelerate your gifting timetable by contributing five years' worth of 529 plan contributions per beneficiary–as much as $140,000 for couples."
17. The donor gets to stay in control. Per the article "Name the Top 7 Benefits of 529 Plans," most recently updated July 29, 2016, "With few exceptions, the named beneficiary has no legal rights to the funds, so you can assure the money will be used for its intended purpose. This differs from custodial accounts under UGMA/UTMA, where the child takes control of the assets once he or she reaches legal age."
18. There is no age limit on when you can contribute, and there is no minimum age limit on when someone can be designated as a beneficiary.

To learn more about 529 plans, I encourage you to read IRS publication 970 or go to the http://www.savingforcollege.com website.

The focus of this chapter has been on the College Savings Account version of the 529, but you should know that there is another version of the 529 known as the Prepaid Tuition Program. Investopedia does a good job explaining the difference between these two types of 529s.

Prepaid Tuition Program

Under a prepaid tuition program, eligible expenses for a fixed period of time or a fixed number of credits are prepaid at an eligible educational institution. For example, an individual may make prepayments for two future semesters of college at today's cost. The prepayment guarantees the beneficiary two semesters, regardless of the cost in the future. This means that the program manager bears the risks of the investments. Contributions are limited to amounts necessary to pay the beneficiary's qualified education expenses.

> Unlike the assets in the college savings plan, which can be used to pay qualified expenses at any eligible educational institution, assets in a prepaid tuition program are usually used toward expenses at a predetermined educational institution, or an educational institution from a predetermined list. Should the beneficiary decide to attend an educational institution that is not included in the predetermined list, the current market value of the prepayments may not be sufficient to cover the cost of comparable tuition at the other educational institution. This means that the beneficiary may need to cover the difference out of pocket.

Let's end this chapter the same we started it, by reaffirming that a 529 is the best college savings vehicle for almost every American: "This is the best way to save for a child or grandchild's education, period, end of sentence," said Young Boozer, chairman of the College Savings Plans Network and state treasurer of Alabama, in Jessica Dickler's article.

When Tyrone found out about 529 college savings accounts, he was frustrated. He said to me, "This is great, but Alexandria is going to college in less than a year, so how much can my money actually compound?"

While it is true that it is better late than never with 529s, there is also no denying that the real power of 529s is their compound interest, and this takes time. If you're the parent of a newborn, a toddler, or an elementary school student, now is the best time to open a 529. Don't be discouraged if your child is older; I opened a 529 for Karis when she was a sophomore in high school.

151

What are the pros and cons of using a Roth IRA to pay for college?

According to Investopedia, here is the definition of a Roth IRA:

> Named for Delaware Senator William Roth and established by the Taxpayer Relief Act of 1997, a Roth IRA is an individual retirement plan (a type of qualified retirement plan) that bears many similarities to the traditional IRA. The biggest distinction between the two is how they're taxed. Since traditional IRAs contributions are made with pretax dollars, you pay income tax when you withdraw the money from the account during retirement. Conversely, Roth IRAs are funded with after-tax dollars; the contributions are not tax deductible (although you may be able to

take a tax credit of 10 to 50% of the contribution), depending on your income and life situation). But when you start withdrawing funds, these qualified distributions are tax free.

There are pros and cons to using a Roth IRA to pay for college.

Cons

- ✘ Most Americans are significantly behind where they should be with their retirement savings, and the numbers for blacks and Latino families are pretty abysmal. Any resources parents use from their retirement will increase their chances of struggling financially in retirement unless they have a nice nest egg socked away.
- ✘ Not everyone is eligible, because there are income caps on qualifying for a Roth. For 2017-18, for single filers it is $133K, and for married filing jointly it is $196K. The rates usually go up $1000 each year.
- ✘ Your IRA must have been established for five years.
- ✘ The major drawback by far, and the reason why it is generally not a good idea to use a Roth until your final year, is because whatever amount you use will be reported as income the following year on your FAFSA. Income increases your EFC significantly more than assets increase your EFC.
- ✘ There are caps on how much you can contribute every year. You can sock away up to $5500 a year for a Roth if you are under 50, and up to $6500 a year if you are over 50. With a 529 you would not have these limits imposed on you.

Pros

- ✓ I feel there is a place for using the Roth for the final two years of college, because it won't impact your financial aid. This is only something to consider if you have a lot of retirement money saved away. Now that the FAFSA is looking at Prior Prior year, your Roth IRA distribution will not be reported as income for the final year or the year before that. While it counts as income the following year on your FAFSA, there is no following year in your final two years, so the biggest downside to using a Roth is a non-factor. It is not an asset on the FAFSA because you used post-tax dollars to fund it. Tapping into a Roth is still nowhere near as good as using grants, scholarships, work, savings, and even the Stafford Loan, but compared to other options, using the Roth in the final year is something that may make sense, especially if you have saved a lot of money for your retirement. There is no Stafford Loan for retirement, so if your retirement savings are not where they should be, using the Roth loses a lot of its value, even for the final year.

- ✓ What if you get a scholarship? If you used a 529, you have to transfer the 529 to someone else, but with the Roth, you can save for retirement and wait and see if they get a scholarship and then decide if and how much to use.
- ✓ What if you decide you do not want to go to college? If you put all of your savings in a 529 then you have to transfer it to someone else, but if you have your money in a Roth, you can wait and see if you go to college, and then make the decision on if and how much of the Roth to use. The versatility of the Roth IRA is a very strong point in its favor.
- ✓ The five-year waiting period is not hard to achieve if you plan in advance.
- ✓ There are no age limitations when it comes to opening and establishing a Roth.

Conclusion: 529s overall are a better four-year strategy because the contributions and withdrawals are tax free, not to mention that there are tax breaks for 529s in two-thirds of the states. Assets are also more favorably viewed than income. 529s increase your assets, which will modestly impact your EFC. Still, there may be a place for the Roth IRA in paying for college in your final year in my opinion, if you can't pay for college with grants and scholarships, student and parent savings, work, or Stafford Loans.

A mom I worked with last year pulled money from her Roth, but she was a professional with a high income. She said, "I can't get time back for my child, and I have one shot at getting this right, but I can always make money." Her income was high; what worked for her may not be advisable for you.

152

DO SCHOOLS GIVE THE SAME AID AWARDS TO TRANSFER STUDENTS THAT THEY GIVE TO FRESHMAN APPLICANTS?

This depends on the school. Here's an example from Skidmore's website: "Skidmore College provides a limited number of transfer students need-based Skidmore grant awards each year. Your financial need is determined from data you provide on the CSS Profile application."

Don't miss the words "limited number." In other words, there are significant restrictions on the aid available for transfers.

Brown University was a school I highlighted as one of the few schools that offers no loans for students of modest income. Even this Ivy league school considers the ability to pay (need-aware admissions) in which transfer students they admit. Here is what their website says on this issue:

FINANCIAL AID POLICY FOR TRANSFER STUDENTS

> Transfer students are admitted to Brown under a need-aware Admission policy. Need-aware means that financial need will be taken into account in making the admission decision. To be considered for financial assistance at any time during their undergraduate years at Brown, students must apply for financial aid when they initially apply for admission as a transfer applicant. Students who do not apply for financial assistance with their initial admission application will not be considered for University Scholarship at any point during their undergraduate years at Brown, regardless of any changes in their family's financial situation.

TRANSFER STUDENTS CAN QUALIFY FOR MERIT AID

Here is what a November 16 *US News* article by Lynn O'Shaughnessy, titled, "Transfer Students: 8 Things You Need to Know," says about this:

> Seventy-seven percent of colleges reported that they provide merit scholarships to transfer students. 81 percent of small colleges, which have less than 3,000 students, report that they award merit scholarships to transfer students. In comparison, 66 percent of medium-sized schools and 67 percent of large schools offer merit awards.

This may be encouraging to you, but this means 33 percent of large schools give no merit aid to transfers, and there are many more schools who give aid, but it is a smaller amount of aid than a freshman student is eligible for.

There are a number of other financial matters that transfer students are going to need to handle. They are going to need to change their

FAFSA information. This means updating their FAFSA with the new six-digit code for their new school. They are also going to have to pay again for their CSS PROFILE information to go to their new school.

I have said several times that only 1 percent of the students I work with spend enough time on the college's websites of the schools they are considering. Well, this is one time that mistake is very costly. You have to know the transfer deadlines, because there are no standard deadlines from one school to the next. You also need to read about the application requirements and the financial aid policy.

Here are some more very helpful reminders about what transfer applicants need to think about from that same *US News* article:

> One of the most significant aspects in the financial aid process for transfer students concerns the management of government education loan information from the prior institution. Since your previous school will only report that you have left their institution to the United States Department of Education (via the National Student Loan Data System), it is important for you to communicate with all prior lenders that you are attending a new school. In order to qualify for deferment of payments on education loans based on your continued enrollment status, you must complete a loan deferment form, telling their former lenders that they are at a different institution. Failure to do this can result in loan payments becoming due while you are in school. Stay in very close contact with all your education lenders, private and government, as they both offer deferment options of some kind.

The article also addresses the issue of transfer school funding, and it talks about how some schools offer even less funding for spring enrollees:

> Some institutions may offer less college-based assistance to students transferring in the spring, relative to those planning the move in the fall. Some schools may not offer college funded grants/scholarships to transfer students at all! However, some schools offer very generous scholarship programs for transfer students.

Finally, as a transfer student, you should be very careful to weigh the number of credits you will receive from a particular institution against the total amount of aid offered. Plot out the amount of time it will take you to graduate, along with the aid offered to figure out the best financial fit. You might have to take an additional semester or year to fulfill requirements, so make sure to consider this when you're looking at financial aid packages. And remember, while scholarships generally require some minimum level of academic performance to be renewed from one year to the next, need-based grants can fluctuate annually with your family's financial situation.

Marsha is a new client of mine from New Jersey. She called me Sunday night to say her sister wants to hire me to help her son transfer from Michigan State because the out-of-state tuition is just not sustainable. I told Marsha, "I can do a single session with your sister, but I want to be very straightforward with you and let you know she has two significant challenges that will make getting aid challenging at most schools." First of all, Marsha's nephew is from Jamaica, and most schools give little to no aid for internationals. Secondly, he will also be a transfer student.

153

WHAT IS THE ROLE OF COLLEGE FINANCIAL AID CERTIFIED PLANNERS AND PAYING FOR COLLEGE?

Most people do not need a financial planner who specializes in the complex issues regarding the money and college. While most people don't need a tax accountant who is a college specialist, some people would be very well-served to hire someone with this level of technical expertise.

How will you know if you need a college financial aid planner? If your college coach cannot answer your questions about money, you probably would be advised to work with a college financial aid planning specialist.

Here are examples of the kinds of questions for which, even though I am a college coach, I recommend working with another college coach who is a certified financial specialist or a tax accountant who specializes in college:

- Anything involving trust fund planning
- Moving assets from an investment, like a 529 in the grandparent's name, to one in the parent or child's name
- Expertise about answering complex questions about the different 529 plans that all vary from state to state
- Working with annuities and their tax implications
- Detailed questions about UTMAs or UGMAs
- Tax planning and wealth management questions
- Setting up 401k, 403b, IRAs, SEP, SIMPLE, Keogh, profit sharing, pensions, and other retirement plans
- Advice for business owners and rental property owners about the tax implications of being a sole proprietorship, LLC, S Corp, or C Corp

I can answer basic questions about money, but if the question is too complex or outside my area of expertise, I will refer someone to an experienced college financial planning expert firm like Kal Chaney's Campus Consultants, Inc. (http://www.campusconsultants.com/) or Troy Onink's Stratagee (https://www.stratagee.com/)

I do not believe that you should have to hire a financial expert to review your FAFSA, even though many mistakes are made on the FAFSA. I believe this book is enough to help you with that, if you read the chapter on free help for the FAFSA, or the chapter on common mistakes people make with the FAFSA.

If you are applying to a school that requires the PROFILE, you may want to select a tax accountant who has real expertise with the PROFILE.

Two weeks ago, I was talking with Leticia, a new client's mom. I found out that Leticia has $100,000 saved in a 529 plan for her son to go to college. I was ecstatic. Most people who call me haven't put any significant savings away. The 529 plans all vary so much from state to state. Someday I may hire a college-focused certified financial planner who is a 529 plan specialist to start meeting with families who have younger kids to help them with long-range financial planning.

To appeal the right way, you must keep good records!

154

WHAT ADVICE DO YOU HAVE IF I WANT TO APPEAL THE AID AWARD I/OUR CHILD RECEIVED?

The first thing you should know is that college policies are all over the place when it comes to how they welcome financial aid appeals. Some colleges say they are not open to appeals, although this is quite rare. Other schools are very explicit about the fact that they encourage appeals.

Here are the four different sources of money you may target when appealing an aid award:

1. NUMERICAL-BASED MERIT APPEAL

This appeal says that you met the explicit criteria for merit money, but it was not awarded. In some cases, this can be the easiest appeal to win. For example, Mercer University accepts students through rolling admissions, and they learn of their aid awards in the fall if they apply in the fall. They have five tiers of merit aid ranging from $7500 to $20,000, and these merit offers are based on academic GPA and test scores, but if you keep taking the ACT or SAT and your scores go up, your merit award will be adjusted. They will count new test scores all the way up until May. A lot of schools use this model. Usually the revised merit offer will automatically be applied, but you are responsible for having your official scores sent to the school.

2. Competitor-Based Appeal

In this appeal, you are asking for a school to consider re-evaluating their aid offer in light of the fact that you received a more generous offer from a competitor. You should know that not only do most schools not match competitor offers, but they will be offended if you ask them to do this. Having said that, there are exceptions. According to a April 4, 2014, *New York Times* article, "Cornell instantly corrects itself if you've got higher need-based aid offers from other Ivy League schools or M.I.T., Duke, and Stanford; it will match that offer, no questions asked." The article says they instantly match, but they won't know what your other offers are unless you tell them.

So how do you not offend, but also not miss an opportunity? You can search the websites to see if their policy is clearly listed. You can also ask an admission counselor. If you ask, I recommend saying, "I am confused trying to understand how you evaluated my award totally differently from X school, and I am hoping you can help me to understand why the two awards are so different. Could you please explain it to me?" I do not want you to think this is going to work very often, but it absolutely can work sometimes. It will depend on how desirable of an applicant you are, how much money the school has, and what their policy is on these matters. A lot of schools that say they won't match a competitor offer will alter their offer, either matching or at least getting closer to the other offer, when you use this approach.

If the school you are appealing your offer to gives you a grant (need-based) and not a scholarship (merit-based) you would be advised to combine your appeal with the need-based appeal below by sharing any new information about your finances that was not disclosed.

You also need to know that even schools that are open to considering adjusting your award if you get a better offer will only do this if the school that gave you that award is seen as a peer institution by the school you are appealing to. Carnegie Mellon appears to be acting similarly, noting on its site that the university has "been open about our willingness to review financial aid awards to compete with certain private institutions for students admitted under the regular decision plan." Then it throws in this zinger: "Unlike most institutions, the university states these principles openly to those offered first-year admission under the regular decision plan."

Carnegie Mellon is much more likely to respond to an offer from MIT than they are to respond to an offer from University of Maryland, even though Maryland has a stupendous computer science program; CMU does not view them as a competitor. Don't expect a private school to respond to an offer from a public college, even a flagship school.

Policies vary from school to school. Here is what Victoria Romero, vice president for enrollment at Scripps College, says about appeals based on merit: "It is important for families to understand that financial aid packages are not subject to negotiation." She adds, seemingly for emphasis: "We award all merit aid at the time of admission and will not match another school's merit award."

3. Institutional Need-Based Appeal

This is where students are likely to have the most success, but only if they are appealing to a school that gives away a lot of their money based on financial need. Here is how that *New York Times* article I referenced describes this:

> Your best shot with an appeal will come from a change in your family's financial circumstances since you applied for aid. Possibilities include job loss or other reduction in income, new health expenses, death of a parent, and disability of a family member, nursing home costs, natural disasters, or parental credit woes that make borrowing impossible.

I'd like to add a few more unique financial situations in which a need-based appeal is often successful: parents are going back to college, changes in your financial picture due to divorce, a special needs child, your pay is mostly commission and you can document that this was an unusually high income year. These are all considered a special circumstance appeal.

I cannot emphasize how important it is that you heed the advice of Kelly O'Brien. When you make the appeal, Kelly O'Brien, the director of financial aid at Trinity College, suggests that it be written, quantified, and documented. I love it when students themselves do the appeal.

4. PELL GRANT APPEAL

This is another form of need-based appeal, but instead of the money coming from the college itself, the money is coming from the federal government. This is one of the easier appeals if you qualify. The Department of Education has empowered the financial aid staff at each school to make this determination. It isn't as hard for the school because it is not their money they are giving away, but from my experience, these financial aid officers are very ethical, and they know that abusing this privilege could result in them being terminated.

You can make this appeal if you have the same circumstances I described above in the institutional need-based appeal. The one additional category I have seen be very successful here is a new one. Now that Prior-Prior is here, the FAFSA is based on 2016 income for the 2018-2019 school year. However, if you have a child starting college in the fall of 2018, you have had to live off of 2017 and 2018 income and not 2016 income. A lot of schools that only take the FAFSA will be very sympathetic if your income is lower now than it was in the year your child started school or in the year prior to the year they started.

For schools that require the PROFILE, this will vary from school to school. Some schools will say, "If you can document that your income has gone down in the year child goes off to college or in the prior year, we will make an adjustment to your EFC." Other schools will stick to the income and assets on the year you submitted your PROFILE (also Prior-Prior year).

Here is how John Leach, Director of Financial Aid at Emory, explains why PROFILE schools are reluctant to do this. Leach says, "If you have the customary 2-4 percent raise you are not going to come back to us and say, 'I need to pay more because you based my EFC off of my Prior-Prior year, but my earnings went up.'" Leach adds, "If schools have to eat the cost only one way without getting an offset from more money when the income goes up, that is going to be a very expensive proposition for a college."

Remember, the FAFSA doesn't ask you about special circumstances like the PROFILE does, so you are going to have to write an appeal letter to the Financial Aid officer explaining this.

Financial aid appeals go by a lot of different names. Sometimes they are referred to as a "professional judgment review." Sometimes they are called a "special judgment," a "special circumstance," or a "financial aid appeal," but one thing that is a constant, no matter what it is called: you have to be very polite; you can't even give off a scintilla of entitlement; and it is best if the student is the initiator.

You may be wondering how successful these appeals are. The *New York Times* did some research in their article and here is what they learned:

> At Occidental, the financial aid office approved the appeals of one-third of the entire entering class (including those who did not apply for financial aid). Eugene Lang College at the New School reports a 57 percent success rate among all its students who have appealed. At Cornell and Sarah Lawrence, it's about 50 percent. Dartmouth would only say that it loosens the purse strings for a majority of the appeals, and it sympathized with those who curse the whole system, noting that the various formulas that most colleges use don't fully recognize the true cost of living for most families.

Of all types of appeals, the one I have been the most successful with has been the medical and dental expense appeal. I cannot emphasize how important it is that you keep detailed records of all of your medical and dental expenses. I am helping a student with an appeal right now and the financial aid officer has already told the family that the appeal is going to be approved, but they need to see all of the receipts. The student and parent I am working with are very honorable people--I believe them 100%--but they are having problems finding and assembling all of their receipts. Keep detailed records!

155

TELL ME 35 MYTHS ABOUT THE FINANCIAL AID PROCESS.

1. Most students can get a full ride to go to college for free.
2. Private scholarships are the key to making college affordable.
3. Billions of private scholarship dollars go unclaimed every year simply because no one applies for money that was just sitting there ready to be given away.
4. The higher the sticker price, the more likely a college will not be affordable.
5. Most students can go to college without any student loans.
6. Students should sign up for loans with the lowest initial interest rates.
7. Saving for college is not really worth it because you get punished for your savings.

8. Most colleges give their own money away mostly based on financial need.
9. Test scores are fading in their importance and therefore are not related to your aid package.
10. Colleges do not target rich students and bribe them with money disguised as a merit award.
11. Applying for the FAFSA in January is well before every state financial aid deadline.
12. There is nothing I can do about the expensive application fees.
13. If a college doesn't have very much money, it makes no sense to ask for my aid package to be re-evaluated.
14. The FAFSA doesn't give me a place to list my health care expenses, so I guess my health care expenses cannot lead to a stronger aid package for schools that only require the FAFSA.
15. Prior-Prior Year FAFSA prevents the prior year or the current year from having any basis on my aid award.
16. If my husband or my child's husband refuses to submit their financial aid information, I am sure that colleges will understand and not expect me to produce that.
17. Every college that requires the PROFILE requires the non-custodial parent application.
18. Filling out the FAFSA won't help me if I know we won't qualify for any financial aid.
19. The FAFSA is in the student's name, so they need to be the primary person to complete it.
20. If I am asked to verify my information on the FAFSA, the Department of Education must be suspicious that I did something unethical.
21. PLUS loans are federal loans, so they must be a good thing.
22. If I have a million dollars or more in retirement accounts, that is going to impact my eligibility for financial aid.
23. If I have a lot of equity in my primary home, a college is going to ask me to pay more for my child to go to college.
24. Most private scholarships go to students of color.
25. Applying to private scholarships that are under $1000 is a waste of time when there are so many larger ones out there to go after.
26. Expected Family Contribution (EFC) is how much I should expect to pay for college.

27. Coming up with the money for college is entirely the student's responsibility.
28. Cost of Attendance is usually lower than what I will actually pay for college.
29. If I move out of the house and start paying my own bills, I can apply to college as an independent student.
30. All colleges will accept my dual enrollment and give me college credit for it.
31. We have a lot of credit card debt and several auto loans, so I am sure schools will factor this into their aid award for my child.
32. I am wasting my time trying to play sports at a D3 school if I need a lot of aid, because they don't have athletic scholarships.
33. Meeting full demonstrated need is one of two things: 1) getting a full scholarship or 2) only being asked to pay what I feel that I can pay.
34. If a college is not need-blind, it must mean they don't have a heart for those students who can't afford to pay.
35. Being need-blind and meeting 100 percent of demonstrated need are the same thing

Angie Lyons is the Director of KIPP Through College in Metro Atlanta, and she is my boss. She called me into her office seven days ago and she said, "I want you to start doing overviews of the financial aid process starting with our ninth-grade parents." Then she said, "I need you to get it across to the parents that college isn't free; they are going to have to pay."

I was ecstatic that Angie asked me to do this, because I believe she is helping debunk one of the greatest myths out there: that someone is going to cover all of my costs and give students a full scholarship. It happens, but it is very rare. There is a second myth that is equally as pernicious: that a college knows your financial situation and certainly won't ask you to pay more than you think is reasonable.

156

How do I accept a Federal Student Loan?

There are several ways in which you may receive your aid award. You could receive it in the mail or you could receive in an email, but you probably are going to have an online portal on the college's website that you will use your username and password to access.

One thing I can't stress enough to students is that you have to get in the habit of checking your email daily. In addition to checking your email, you will have a place for messages in your online portal, and you need to check these messages regularly.

One of the biggest misconceptions I find that students and parents have is that they think they have to accept everything in the aid award. You don't! Of course you are going to accept the gift aid. Remember, gift aid is grants and scholarships. This is the free money that you will not have to repay. Grants are need-based aid awards and scholarships are merit-based aid awards, but I understand why this is confusing, because people often use the word scholarships to apply to both need-based awards and merit-based awards. You should also accept work-study if you received this. You are going to need the money, so work-study is very helpful, but in addition to this, there are a number of studies that show that students who have a job manage their time better. Having the extra structure in your day helps.

You are going to have to specifically indicate that you are accepting a loan. You also have the option of selecting a portion of the loan, but not *all* of the loan. The best loans are the federal subsidized loan, the federal unsubsidized loan, the Perkins loan (most schools don't offer this), and state loans. Sometimes schools have their own loans, and some of these are pretty good, but if you have read the chapters about PLUS loans and private loans, you know I am not a fan. If you read the chapter on how much loan debt you should incur, you know that you may not want to take out all of the unsubsidized loan money you are offered; it depends on your projected income based on your major.

Here is what the federal government's website (studentaid.gov) has to say about accepting your loans in your aid award:

> Read and follow the directions in the award letter. You might have to enter the amounts you're accepting in an online form and then submit the form. If you receive a paper award letter, you might have to sign it and mail it back to the school.

Accepting a loan listed in the award letter involves some additional steps, which vary depending on the type of loan you're receiving. Saying yes may be as simple as signing a promissory note.

You are going to have to go through loan counseling at studentloans.gov if you are accepting your federal loans. You only have to do this for the first year, but the tutorial is pretty comprehensive, and it takes about an hour. You should take this very seriously, because you want to understand the commitment you are making when you commit to a loan. You want to understand the repayment terms, loan consolidation, what happens if you default, etc. When you go through the online tutorial, you will be asked questions to make sure you comprehend what you are learning.

After you have completed the counseling, you will need to sign a Master Promissory Note (MPN). You will be able to use your FAFSA ID (aka FSA ID) to log in at studentloans.gov both for completing the loan counseling and for signing the MPN. The FSA ID is your official signature indicating that you are accepting the loan.

The money will go from the federal government to your student account at your school, and this happens quickly.

If there is a balance on your account, you can pay this off in one payment or set up payment plans.

Shinekwa is a student I worked with this year. Shinekwa and her parents liked my idea of having them cap their federal direct loans at $5000 per year, and if Shinekwa gets a 3.5 GPA or higher, her parents will pay $2500 of the $5000 loan. They also agreed to reject the PLUS loans, but in her aid award she received a $3500 subsidized loan, a $2000 unsubsidized loan and a $12,000 PLUS loan.

Shinekwa thought she had to accept all of these loans. I helped her log into her portal and showed her how she could accept the $3500 subsidized loan, change the $2000 in the unsubsidized loan to $1500, and just ignore the PLUS loan. Shinekwa was nervous about accidentally accepting the PLUS loan, but you can't get a PLUS loan without the parent applying for it, so she didn't have to worry about accidentally accepting it.

157

WHAT KINDS OF EXPENSES CAN PARENTS WHO HAVE CHILDREN IN COLLEGE POTENTIALLY CLAIM ON THEIR TAXES?

There are five potential tax deductions and two potential tax credits. I will touch on the deductions and do a deeper dive into the tax credits. Here is how the IRS Tax Benefits for Education Information Center explains the difference between a credit and a deduction: "A tax credit reduces the amount of income tax you may have to pay. A deduction reduces the amount of your income that is subject to tax, thus generally reducing the amount of tax you may have to pay."

1. **Interest paid on student loans:** Here is how Andrew Josuweit of *Forbes* describes this deduction in his excellent Feb 16, 2017, article, "4 Valuable Tax Breaks for College Students":

> If you are a student or a parent of a student and made payments on a qualifying student loan, you can deduct up to $2,500 of the interest you paid over the course of the year. And even if you made extra payments, you can deduct the extra interest you paid off.
> To qualify, you or a dependent must have paid interest on a student loan in 2016. Your filing status must be single or married filing jointly; if you file your taxes as married filing separately, you are not eligible for this deduction. Your income cannot exceed $80,000 if you're single or $160,000 if you're married. Loans that don't qualify include loans offered by a relative or friend or employer-offered loans.

2. If you take out a home equity loan to pay for college, you can deduct the interest.

3. **Tuition and Fees deduction:** You could potentially get a $4000 tax deduction here. Here is how Josuweit puts it:

> You can take the deduction if you are a student, spouse of a student, or if the student is your dependent. The expenses you deduct must be involved with higher education and cannot include living expenses like room and board. To be eligible, you must make under $80,000 if you're single or $160,000 if you are married and filing your taxes together. You can get the deduction even if you do not itemize your taxes.

4. **529 contributions.** Every state has its own rules and regulations for their own plans (see Chapter 150 on 529s). In Georgia, you can get a $2000 tax deduction, and in Pennsylvania you can get a whopping $14,000 state deduction. "Currently 32 states offer tax breaks for contributing to a 529 plan," says Joe Orsolini, a certified financial planner at College Aid Planners. "[And] some states offer the tax break for being in the 529 plan for as little as 5 business days."

5. **Student Interest Tax Deduction:** Here is how Josuweit explains this deduction: "If you are a student or a parent of a student and made payments on a qualifying student loan, you can deduct up to $2,500 of the

interest you paid over the course of the year. And even if you made extra payments, you can deduct the extra interest you paid off."

Now let's take a deeper dive into the two tax credits.

American opportunity tax credit (AOTC) can get you a $2500 tax credit. Here is how the IRS describes the AOTC:

> The American opportunity tax credit (AOTC) is a credit for qualified education expenses paid for an eligible student for the first four years of higher education. You can get a maximum annual credit of $2,500 per eligible student. If the credit brings the amount of tax you owe to zero, you can have 40 percent of any remaining amount of the credit (up to $1,000) refunded to you.
>
> The amount of the credit is 100 percent of the first $2,000 of qualified education expenses you paid for each eligible student and 25 percent of the next $2,000 of qualified education expenses you paid for that student. But, if the credit pays your tax down to zero, you can have 40 percent of the remaining amount of the credit (up to $1,000) refunded to you.

WHO IS AN ELIGIBLE STUDENT FOR AOTC?

To be eligible for AOTC, the student must:

- Be pursuing a degree or other recognized education credential
- Be enrolled at least half time (six credit hours) for at least one academic period beginning in the tax year
- Not have finished the first four years of higher education at the beginning of the tax year
- Not have claimed the AOTC or the former Hope credit for more than four tax years
- Not have a felony drug conviction at the end of the tax year

The other major tax credit that you need to know about is the Lifetime Learning Credit. Here is how the IRS describes this benefit:

> The Lifetime Learning Credit is for qualified tuition and related expenses paid for eligible students enrolled in an eligible educational institution. This credit can help pay for undergraduate, graduate and professional degree courses—including courses to acquire or improve job skills. There is no limit on the number of years you can claim the credit. It is worth up to $2,000 per tax return.

WHO CAN CLAIM THE LLC?

To claim a LLC, you must meet all three of the following:

1. You, your dependent, or a third party pay qualified education expenses for higher education
2. You, your dependent, or a third party pay the education expenses for an eligible student enrolled at an eligible educational institution
3. The eligible student is yourself, your spouse, or a dependent you listed on your tax return

When parents learn about these tax deductions and tax credits, they go crazy with exuberance, but let's pump the brakes a little. The government has a policy about not "doubling up," meaning that you cannot claim multiple education tax deductions, so you are going to have to pick and choose. Here is how the IRS phrases it:

Q16: Can I claim the tuition and fees tax deduction in addition to claiming the American opportunity tax credit?

> A. No. You cannot claim the tuition and fees tax deduction in the same taxable year that you claim the American opportunity tax credit or the Lifetime Learning credit. You must choose between taking an education tax credit or taking the deduction for tuition and fees. You also cannot claim the tuition and fees tax deduction if anyone else claims the American opportunity tax credit or the Lifetime

> Learning credit for you in the same taxable year. A tax deduction of up to $4,000 can be claimed for qualified tuition and fees paid. Although the credit will usually result in greater tax savings, taxpayers should calculate both the tax credit and the deduction on the tax return to see which is most beneficial.

I have clearly said that the tax credits are better than the tax deductions, and you now know you can only claim one of these per child per year, so how do you know whether to select the AOTC or the LLC? For ananswer to that question, I am turning to my second go-to guy (besides Mark Kantrowitz) when it comes to paying for college: Troy Onink, the *CEO of Stratagee.* In an excellent article titled, "Get $10,000 Per Child In College Tax Credits, Thanks To New Tax Deal," Onink tackles this question. The truth is, both the AOTC and the LLC have their advantages. Here are three advantages to each tax credit.

ADVANTAGES OF THE AOTC

1. Onink gets right to the point: "The American Opportunity Tax Credit (AOTC) is the logical choice for full-time undergraduates because it is by far the richest at up to $2,500 per eligible child, versus $2,000 for the Lifetime credit."
2. In case you think you may qualify for less aid, Onink addresses this as well:

> Since the AOTC reduces the federal income tax paid by parents (or whomever the taxpayer is), and therefore reduces the amount of tax allowances they have against their income in the aid formula, the credit would normally increase the student's expected family contribution and decrease the student's aid eligibility. However, the financial aid forms, the FAFSA and the CSS Profile, effectively "add back" the amount of the credit that parents claim on their tax return, thereby eliminating any negative impact on the student's potential need-based aid eligibility.

3. One final advantage to the AOTC comes from Josuweit: "But the LLC credit is not refundable; if the credit brings your tax liability to zero, you will not get any money back, unlike the AOTC." With the AOTC, you can get up to $1000 back as a tax refund, even if you have no tax liability, and don't forget, this is per child, per year. If you have three kids in college, in their first four years you can get $7500 back if you have the tax liability and $3000 if you don't have any liability.

ADVANTAGES OF THE LLC

Elyssa Kirkham answers this question in a February 14, 2017, article, "8 College Expenses That Are Tax-Deductible or Tax-Free." She says, "There is no limit on the number of years you can claim the lifetime learning credit, and the student is not required to be working toward a degree."

Onink points out another advantage to the LLC: "it is available for part-time and graduate study." The AOTC is only available for the first four years of undergraduate study.

Just yesterday, I met with Ms. Davis to talk about the AOTC and how she can get the credit for her daughter next year. She said, "Mr. Stucker, I never have $2500 in tax liability to claim." I told her that she is entitled to get a $1000 refund even if she doesn't have any tax liability, but then I had even better news for Ms. Davis: I told her she could file an amended return for the previous year and get a refund for her son, who is already in college.

158

HOW CAN I SAVE THOUSANDS OF DOLLARS THROUGH EXAMS AND CREATIVE COLLEGE PROGRAMS?

AP EXAMS

Getting a 3 on an AP score is considered passing. I tell my clients, “That’s nice, but what you really want is a ‘qualifying score.’” A qualifying score gets you college credit, and that can save you thousands of dollars.

Every college decides itself what score is a qualifying score. They decide this on a course-by-course basis. For selective schools, you will need a 4 or a 5 over 90 percent of the time to get credit. Colleges have plenty of experience seeing how students with various scores fare in their curriculum, and they use this information to determine whether a 3, 4, or 5 gets you credit. If there are 30 credits a year, and you get 15 college credits from AP courses, and you graduate one semester early, this could save you over $30,000 if you are paying full price at a private school. Even if you are getting financial aid and only paying $15,000 a year, that is still a $7500 savings.

INTERNATIONAL BACCALAUREATE EXAMS

The exact same principal applies to IB scores. Check the website for each school for each course and see if you need a 5, 6, or 7 in order to get college credit.

DUAL ENROLLMENT

One of the biggest changes in the last 15 years is the growth of dual enrollment programs. Here is how the Georgia Department of Education explains dual enrollment: "Dual Enrollment/Dual Credit courses provide opportunities for Georgia high school students to take college-level courses and earn concurrent credit toward a high school diploma and a college degree."

Once again, check the website of the colleges you are interested in to learn their dual enrollment policies. Both of my daughters graduated from Landmark Christian School and they both had around 20 dual enrollment college courses, but Karis went to Davidson, which had a policy that they will not double-count dual enrollment courses for both high school and college. Joy chose Valdosta State, and they counted Joy's college courses, allowing her to start college with two-thirds of her freshman credits already completed.

It is easier to get college credit from dual enrollment than it is from IB or AP courses, because you don't have to ace what can be a challenging exam.

ACCELERATED DEGREES

A growing trend some colleges are using to curtail the concerns about rising tuition is to allow students to get an accelerated degree. Here is what Wesleyan University says on their website about their three-year degree option:

Three-Year Option

> Students who graduate in six semesters (three years of normal course loads plus summer courses) may expect to save about 20 percent of the total cost of a Wesleyan education. The three-year option is not for everyone, but for those students who are able to declare their majors early, earn credit during Wesleyan summer sessions, and take advantage of the wealth of opportunities on campus, this more economical path to graduation can be of genuine interest. A maximum of two pre-matriculant credits (such as Advanced Placement, International Baccalaureate, or college credits earned during high school) may be applied toward an accelerated program. Students pursuing the three-year option will be held to all the graduation requirements for the Wesleyan bachelor of arts degree. Students considering this option should consult during their first year with Dean David Phillips to review policies and procedures.

Combined Degree Programs

Here is how Mercer's website describes these programs that are designed to take a year off of your payments and get you one year closer to earning money: A unique option for students interested in furthering their education at Mercer is the combined degree program, which allows students to earn both their bachelor's and master's degrees in just five years in the following:

Bachelor of Science in Engineering + Master of Science in Engineering

Bachelor of Business Administration + Master of Business Administration

Bachelor of Business Administration + Master of Accountancy

They also offer a 3 + 3 that allows you to get a BA and a law degree at Mercer in 3 years.

GUARANTEED SAVINGS FOR GRADUATE SCHOOL

We are going to stick with Mercer again here as our example because they have several other creative ways to save. One program they have rewards students who start their undergrad in business at Mercer and want to get an MBA at Mercer by giving them 30 percent off of their MBA if the following conditions are met:

- 32 semester hours completed at Mercer
- Overall 3.0 grade point average (GPA) at Mercer
- GPA for business core curriculum courses
- Earned grade C or better in ALL business courses taken at Mercer
- GPA in the Business Minor (in addition to an overall 3.0 GPA at Mercer)

CO-OP PROGRAMS

Here is how Georgia Tech describes its co-op program:

> The Georgia Tech Undergraduate Co-op Program is a five-year academic program designed to complement a student's formal education with paid practical work experience directly related to the student's academic major. It is available in all engineering majors. Co-ops give students the opportunity to combine the theories learned in class with paid practical experience related to their major.

According to the Georgia Tech website, "In Fall 2013, 1,713 undergraduate engineering students participated in the Co-op Program and their earnings were 10.24 million."

Co-op programs are very exciting. Check out Northeastern's co-op program. It is among the best in the country.

12 TUITION-FREE SCHOOLS

This list comes from a *US News* article published on September 13, 2016:

1. Alice Lloyd College: Residents of Kentucky, Ohio, Tennessee, Virginia and West Virginia. All students have work jobs.
2. Barclay College, Kansas: Students must live in the dorm to receive this tuition free offer from this Christian school.
3. Berea College, Kentucky: Students who work for ten hours can have their room and board and books covered, according to *US News.*
4. College of the Ozarks, Missouri: A 15-hour a week work job requirement is in place here.
5. Curtis Institute of Music, Philadelphia: For 90 years, this school has offered full tuition scholarships, but this school is for the serious and extremely talented musician.
6. Deep Springs College, California: This two-year school is only for men and they must work on the farm or the ranch. It is for the serious scholar. Every student I have known who has gone here has transferred to an extremely selective college.
7. United States Air Force, Colorado
8. United States Coast Guard, Connecticut
9. United States Merchant Marine Academy, New York
10. United States Military Academy, New York
11. United States Naval Academy, Maryland
12. Webb Institute, New York: Naval architecture and Marine engineering school.

All of the methods in this chapter won't just save you hundreds, but thousands, and in some cases, tens of thousands to hundreds of thousands.

A few years ago, I was touring Emory University and we had a very charismatic and engaging tour guide. At the end of the tour, one of the parents asked the tour guide what advice he had to share. The tour guide said, "Don't slack off just because you get admitted." He went on to say, "I am so glad that I kept studying hard on my AP exams. If you need to get a tutor, get a tutor. I got 4s and 5s on my AP exams and I started with a half a year of college credit, and am I ever glad that I didn't just go on a cruise after I got admitted to Emory."

159

WHAT ARE THE PROS AND CONS OF USING A HOME EQUITY LOAN OR A HELOC TO HELP ME TO PAY FOR COLLEGE?

If you read the two chapters on PLUS loans, you know I don't like PLUS loans, but what other options are there for parents? "Of the parents who borrowed money to pay for college last year, 75 percent took a Parent Plus loan, 17 percent tapped into their home's equity, and 8 percent borrowed a private education loan," according to a recent Sallie Mae Study.

This chapter will talk about the 17 percent who used Home Equity. The Sallie Mae survey found that, "On average, parents borrowed $7,406 through a home loan—an umbrella term that includes a home equity loan, a home equity line of credit known as a HELOC, cash-out refinance and a reverse mortgage, the survey found."

On August 9, 2016, in an article in *US News*, Farran Powell wrote about using home equity for college. Here is how she defined HELOC:

WHAT'S A HELOC?

"A HELOC is a type of home equity loan that allows borrowers to borrow a line of credit against the value of their home–it operates almost like credit card and usually has a floating interest rate."

The three big advantages to HELOCs are:

1. You can get lower interest rates than PLUS loans if you have reasonable credit. We are in a historically great time for low interest rates. You also don't have the high origination fee that the Parent PLUS loan has.

   "The lending environment has improved enough that some of the rates on home loans are more competitive over a PLUS loan," says Trish Gildea, senior financial planner at Summit Financial Corp in Burlington, Massachusetts, when comparing home loans with federal parent education loans.

2. You can borrow only the money you need, even if it's only $500. The downside with Home Equity loans is that you are usually will need to take out a larger loan. Here is what Trish Gildea says on this matter:

   > The vast majority of them gravitate toward the HELOC because of the flexibility ... A borrower can limit the amount to just what's needed under a HELOC compared with a home equity loan, which requires taking out a lump sum. The minimum amount for a home equity loan can range between $10,000 and $25,000 at lending institutions, home loan experts say.

3. Interest on the loans you take out is tax deductible.

Note: You should apply for a home equity loan or a HELOC after you have filed the FAFSA. If you have a lump sum of money sitting in your bank account because you are granted a loan or a line of credit, it will be labeled as an asset and it could reduce your eligibility for as much aid.

THE DISADVANTAGES TO TAPPING HOME EQUITY:

1) You are putting your home at risk if you default on this loan.
2) You don't get some of the government protections the PLUS offers, like flexible loan repayment options, discharge potential, and deferment options.

> While I was a student at Michigan State, I worked through the summers and I worked 27 hours a week, but finances were challenging for my family and I almost had to take a semester off after my sophomore year. Thanks to a $2000 gift from my Aunt Betty, and my mom and dad tapping into home equity, I was able to stay and graduate in 3.5 years.

You also need to realize that you normally will need at least 20 percent in home equity to take out loan, and a lot of experts believe you should have more than this: "I recommend 35 to 40 percent because you want to be conservative in case there's a drop in housing prices," says Jason Ting, senior vice president of wealth management at Merrill Lynch Wealth Management. "As long as clients understand the risk, it seems like a viable option."

I agree with Ting, but I am a "bottom line" kind of guy who watches my money, and the biggest reason why I like the HELOC more than the Parent PLUS loan is because of the money you will save in interest in this environment.

160

What can you tell me about the ROTC Scholarship?

From College Data's, "How to Qualify for ROTC Scholarships":

What Is ROTC?

The Reserve Officers' Training Corps is an officer training program for college students who commit to serve in the United States military after college. You can find schools that host and participate in an ROTC program on the recruitment websites of the Army, Navy, and Air Force, or by talking to your academic advisor. (Marine Corps cadets participate in the Navy ROTC. The United States Coast Guard does not offer ROTC.)

HOW CAN THE ROTC HELP PAY FOR COLLEGE?

ROTC cadets committed to serving in the military after college are eligible for scholarships covering the costs for tuition, fees, and textbooks for four years, plus a monthly stipend for personal expenses. If you have additional financial need, you are free to apply for regular financial aid and non-ROTC scholarships. If you leave the ROTC at the end of your freshman year, the ROTC will cover its share of your freshman expenses with no further obligation on your part.

HOW MANY STUDENTS RECEIVE THE ARMY ROTC SCHOLARSHIP?

From Deborah Ziff's *US News* article, "3 Myths About Army ROTC Scholarships for College":

> The Army ROTC – in addition to the Navy and Air Force ROTC programs – is one of the nation's biggest scholarship grantors. The Army ROTC alone provides $274 million in scholarship money to more than 13,000 students each year, according to the U.S. Army Cadet Command.

DOES A STUDENT WHO ENROLLS IN ROTC ON CAMPUS AUTOMATICALLY RECEIVE A FULL SCHOLARSHIP?

As the enrollment and recruiting officer for Army ROTC at the University of Massachusetts–Amherst, Travis Wright fields a lot of questions about the ROTC scholarship program. One of the biggest misunderstandings among families, he says, is that they assume if a student enrolls in ROTC, he or she will automatically receive a full scholarship.

"That's not the case," Wright says. "We do have scholarships that we offer out and those cover tuition and fees and some other things, but that is not a guarantee. It's a competitive process, just like receiving any other scholarship."

Some students complete ROTC programs—earning a commission as second lieutenant—without ever earning a scholarship.

WHAT ARE THE TWO WAYS A STUDENT CAN EARN THE ROTC SCHOLARSHIP?

Students can compete in the ROTC national competition while they are in high school, or they can compete when they are freshmen at a college and they join an ROTC program when they get to campus.

HOW CAN YOU QUALIFY FOR AN ROTC SCHOLARSHIP?

You are going to have to be a good student as determined by traditional indices like academic GPA and test scores to get the ROTC scholarship while you are in high school, and you are going to have to be physically fit.

From College Data:

The scholarship requirements vary slightly between the military branches, but basically you must meet the following criteria:

- Be a United States citizen
- Be at least 17 years of age
- Meet GPA requirements
- Meet SAT and/or ACT requirements
- Have a high school diploma
- Meet physical fitness standards

Here is what Tony Wolf of the University of Iowa says on this subject in "Get Money for College Through ROTC Programs":

> The majority of high school scholarship recipients are in the top 25 percent of their class, belong to an honor society, and participate in organizations or sports. Students should be working on building a résumé early in their high school career.

Are There Any Things You Can Do Besides Being a Good Student That Will Increase Your Chances of Receiving the Scholarship?

From College Data:

> Show your interest to your local military recruitment office as early as possible, preferably during your junior year of high school. Scholarships often go to students majoring in subjects that will be of value to the military, such as engineering, computer science, specific foreign languages, or nursing.

If You Receive the ROTC Scholarship What Is Your Obligation to the Military?

From College Data:

> The Army requires ROTC scholarship holders to serve eight years (four years of active duty and four years in the reserves.) The Navy requires four to five years of active duty. The Air Force requires four to six years of active duty and ten years for cadets trained as pilots.

Can You Be Called up to Service While You Are in College and Enrolled in the ROTC?

From Deborah Ziff, *US News,* quoting Tony Wolf and Travis Wright: "An ROTC cadet is considered nondeployable in the event that the United States. goes to war. That's the case even if the cadet is part of a National Guard unit that deploys," Wolf says. "If a student is in ROTC, he is just a student," Wright says. "Once he gets commissioned, then he belongs to Army, and yes, then he can be mobilized."

I've known Theresa since she was in the sixth grade, and she's always been very independent and hard-working. In high school, she rode the train 90 minutes each way in order to attend a quality school. She also worked 30 hours a week at a restaurant while maintaining a rigorous academic schedule. She didn't come from a family of means, but she realized in her sophomore year that ROTC could be her ticket to having college funded. She got very involved in the ROTC. I was so happy when Theresa told me she had been awarded a ROTC scholarship.

161

WHAT IS "AFFIRMATIVE ACTION FOR RICH KIDS"?

There are some powerful forces swirling beneath the surface that less than 1 percent of the people I have met know about. These forces are the invisible hands that influence many decisions that colleges make, and I want you to know about them.

I have discussed elsewhere in this book that state governments have cut back their allocation of funds to colleges, and the federal government has not kept up with the cost of inflation in their allocation. This has produced a financial crisis for colleges, causing them to change how they recruit and who they admit.

An article from the Center of Budget and Policy Priorities on August 18, 2016, titled, "State-by-State Fact Sheets: Higher Education Cuts Jeopardize Students' and States' Economic Future," shows how state appropriations have changed from 2008 to 2016 for each state.

Here are a few of the changes for eight states:

- Georgia: Per student funding down 20%
- Virginia: Per student funding down 22%
- Florida: Per student funding down 23%
- Pennsylvania: Per student funding down 33%
- South Carolina: Per student funding down 37%
- Louisiana: Per student funding down 39%
- Illinois: Per student funding down 54%
- Arizona: Per student funding down 56%

What is a state to do if they are losing hundreds of millions of dollars? They can use aggressive tuition hikes, and they do. They can prioritize out-of-state students who pay much more money, even if they are getting in-state money from taxpayers, and they do. They can prioritize students from China who pay extra international fees, and they do, but that still isn't enough, and they have to find a way to raise their tuition even higher, and they need to find people who are willing to pay for it.

An Inside Higher Education article titled, "Why American Colleges Are Becoming a Force of Inequality" states what Arizona did to counteract this 56 percent reduction in per-pupil funding: The University of Arizona raised its tuition 81 percent above inflation.

A large number of colleges have found they can follow a four-step blueprint to attract rich students who can afford to give them the money that the state is no longer giving them:

- Hike tuition costs up as high as possible
- Expand campus amenities from sports facilities to lavish dorms and student centers to gourmet food in an attempt to attract the wealthy and keep up with the Joneses
- Hire an enrollment management company like Noel-Levitz that will help them develop a data-driven strategy to target the wealthy with emails, direct mails, and campus events, where they choose to travel, and their facility's construction
- Give affluent families merit money (aka known as a tuition discount), because they need the money these families have to pay their bills.

Some of you may be thinking, "Mark, what is your proof?" A 2011 survey by Inside Higher Ed found that

> ... about 35 percent of admissions directors at 4-year institutions, particularly public colleges, had increased their efforts to target "full pay" students. Far from wanting to enroll more low-income students, colleges recruit more affluent ones who will pay full price to attend. A follow-up survey of college business officers found that the most common strategy to deal with financial challenges in the next few years was to "raise net tuition revenue." More than 7 in 10 college CFOs cited this answer.

Here is what Kim Clark said in her April 1, 2015, *TIME* magazine article, "Many Colleges Offer Affirmative Action for the Rich and Powerful":

> Investigators found that between 2005 and 2009, the University of Illinois admitted an estimated 800 underqualified students who were connected to politically powerful families ... The president of the University of Texas at Austin, Bill Powers, pressured his admissions officers to admit as many as 73 underqualified students from influential families in the last six years, a state investigation recently found.

In an August 18, 2014, *Forbes* article by Maggie McGrath called, "The Invisible Force Behind College Admissions," the author describes a gathering in downtown Chicago:

> ... a swath of the 1,500 top admissions and financial aid officials from 635 different schools who have gathered to set policies that determine which kids get into which college and how much money they'll receive. Cutting to the chase, Graber, a consultant (with Ruffalo Noel-Levitz enrollment management consulting company), launches by taking a poll: 'How many of you would say that the primary

> motivation for offering students merit scholarships is to reward academic achievement?' Not a single person raises his or her hand.

People pay the Noel-Levitz firm big bucks because of the data-driven approach it uses to help schools get more money from wealthy families. McGrath describes it as the "Enrollment & Revenue Management System." The model can instantly predict, for example, that if you offer a $5,500 grant to 100 students in a certain income range from Philadelphia's Main Line, only 24 percent are likely to enroll. But when you bump the offer up by $500, to $6,000, 48 percent are likely to come."

If you think Noel-Levitz has five or ten colleges paying for its services, here is how the *Forbes* article describes its influence: "Noel-Levitz has 220 full- and part-time staff and consults with 1,100 schools each year. Industry insiders estimate that its revenues top $35 million annually, but its influence over higher-education finance is several zeroes larger."

This firm and other competitors have schools signing up in droves because they know how to find money that schools desperately need. Here are a couple of examples McGrath shares:

> Aurora University in Illinois credits the firm with increasing retention by 10%, doubling out-of-state enrollment and growing net revenue from $7.7 million to $9.8 million. At Delaware State University, Noel-Levitz grew the applicant pool by 10%, increased its enrollment by 27%, upped its retention rate (the percentage of freshman who make it to sophomore year) by 6.5%, and increased net tuition revenue by $4 million.

Some colleges are using a different approach, paying international agents commission to find full-pay international students.

A lot of educators are extremely conflicted with these strategies.

This is what Donald Heller said in the *Hechlinger Report*: "It's a huge waste of billions of dollars nationally ... If the goal in the state is to increase the number of people getting college degrees, it doesn't do any good to subsidize students who are going to go to college anyways."

You can see a lot of regret, guilt, and the dilemma many educators are wrestling with in Stephen Burd's outstanding article "Merit Aid

Madness: How Ohio Colleges Started a Tuition Discount War for Wealthy Students That Has Now Spread Across the Country":

> Either a school offers tuition discounts to students from affluent families, or else those students (and the revenue they could provide) wind up going to other institutions that offer similar or more generous discounts.
> Today, these tuition discounts usually come in the guise of 'merit scholarships,' but often the students who get them are hardly the best and the brightest. For example, 10 percent of college admissions directors at four-year colleges (and nearly 20 percent of those at private liberal arts colleges) admit that they give affluent students a significant leg up in the admissions process—meaning that they are admitting affluent students with lower grades and test scores than other applicants. Indeed, nearly a fifth of all students receiving so-called merit scholarships have less than a B average, and a largely overlapping 19 percent have only mediocre SAT scores, according to a report by the National Center for Education Statistics.

Kenyon College resisted merit aid for a long time, but then they found they were losing applicants they needed, so they eventually joined the crowd. Now Kenyon finds that not only must it offer substantial aid to affluent students, but these students and their families have come to view such aid as an entitlement.

Georgia Nugent was the president at Kenyon until recently. She played a big role in implementing merit aid strategies while at Kenyon, but now she sees the problem this is creating, and she is speaking despite seeing "no easy way out. I just don't know how colleges are going to step off of that merry-go-round" (Burd).

When I explain this to students and parents I work with, they can get discouraged. The wealthy students feel as if I just diminished any acceptance offer or merit offer they may get, and the under-resourced students feel like the deck is doubly stacked against them.

I had a session two days ago with Evette, an under-resourced student I am working with. We are turning this knowledge of money into a positive by focusing on wealthy colleges that have the resources to give a great package, and we are looking at colleges who won't hold her income against her. I am also helping Evette to apply through QuestBridge, a program I cannot recommend more highly if you are a gifted and talented under-resourced student. QuestBridge has 39 incredible college partners, and they all love the program, so don't be discouraged if you are not wealthy.

You can learn more about Questbridge at https://www.questbridge.org/ QuestBridge places around 2500 low-income students a year through their match scholarship or through the regular decision process. Each school offers incredible aid to these students.

162

How can I save money through online courses?

Online education and hybrid education, which combines some classroom learning with some online learning, are here to stay. It is partly because of the convenience of learning from home, partly because of the worldwide access that the web provides to unparalleled resources, and partly because of the potential to save money.

Here is what a January 2012 article from learn.org titled, "10 Reasons Why Online College Courses Save You Money" says about the costs that you can save just by not having to commute:

> Driving to and from classes can be a real pain. With Internet classes, the longest commute you have to make is from your bed to your computer. You don't have to pay for gas, parking or any added fees to keep your car in good shape.

> Plus, you don't have to worry about other students mooching rides from you.

We have a tendency to think of college as an 18-year-old going off to live in a brick and mortar dorm, but more students are non-traditional students, older students pursuing a degree while they work, or adults who just want to enhance their skills or their intellectual curiosity by taking a few courses here and there. Here is how that Learn.org article addresses this:

> Taking classes in person means being some place at a set time. That also means that you have to restrict your work hours and schedule your job around schooling. In contrast, online courses often allow you to schedule schooling around your work instead. You can work longer, get more money and work more comfortable hours.

If you are taking online courses because you are trying to upgrade your skills for your job, there is a good chance that you can negotiate getting some help from your employer with these costs. Remember, you also have the $2000 Lifetime Learning Credit as a resource.

The website bestvalueschools.org took on this question by asking whether attending an online school is cheaper than a traditional college. Here is what they concluded about online schools:

> Colleges and universities that offer online degree programs typically will be cheaper than going to a traditional brick-and-mortar university for a variety of reasons. For many schools that solely specialize in offering online degrees, they have fewer expenses to incur. They usually do not have vast swaths of land, property, and buildings to manage. They do not have thousands of support staff and personnel to pay each month. This allows online colleges and universities to offer cheaper tuition rates compared to traditional brick-and-mortar colleges and universities. The average student will typically spend anywhere between $100 to $400 per credit hour. Also, students do not have costs associated with commuting to a college campus.

Believe it or not, there are some online courses that cost more than traditional courses if you are not factoring in staying on campus. Here is an excerpt from the website affordable-online-colleges.net that explains why this is true:

> Check out the online dual credit/enrollment opportunities offered by colleges that you are interested in attending. Some of these programs are very affordable and there is often scholarship money available. This can be a great way to show a college you are interested in them. It is a great way you can excel with their rigor.

WHY DO ONLINE CLASSES SOMETIMES COST MORE?

- Additional licensing
- Fees for technology-related services
- 55% outsource their server needs to a third party
- Support
- 98% of colleges offer a Help Desk and Tech Support for online students
- Training existing staff
- 43% of colleges require more than eight hours of training for distance education programs
- Hiring staff members who have special knowledge about distance education and technology skillsets
- Federal rules and regulation command a greater degree of administrative resources
- Student financial aid fraud
- State authorization
- Student authentication
- ADA compliance

In general, you will find more cost savings with online courses, and if you do your research, there are deals out there to be had, including some free courses.

My favorite source for researching online schools is http://www.guidetoonlineschools.com/

Here is how the website describes itself: "We've independently researched over 23,000 online degrees to find the top schools offering the lowest tuitions and the best outcomes for students." The website looks at over 1700 accredited schools, and they have thousands and thousands of student reviews.

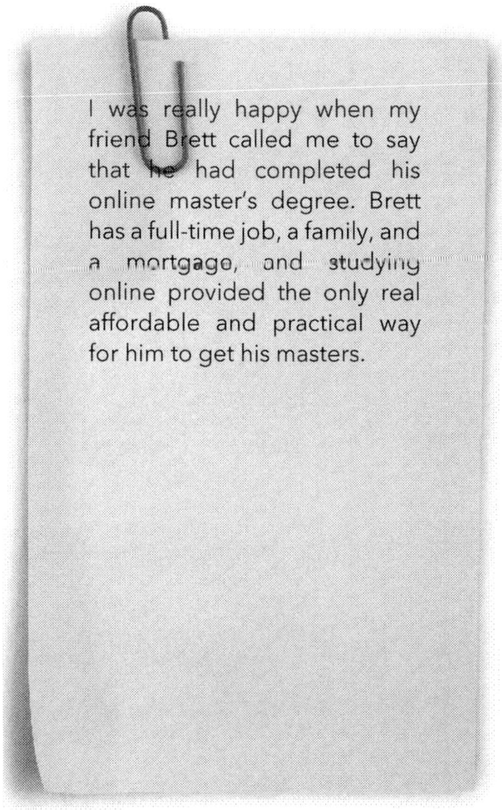

I was really happy when my friend Brett called me to say that he had completed his online master's degree. Brett has a full-time job, a family, and a mortgage, and studying online provided the only real affordable and practical way for him to get his masters.

Section 5

Staying in and Graduating

163

HOW CAN I SAVE OVER $100,000 MORE THAN MOST STUDENTS WHO ATTEND COLLEGE?

According to the United States Department of Education's National Center for Education Statistics (2017), *The Condition of Education 2017* (NCES 2017-144), Undergraduate Retention and Graduation Rates: The six-year graduation rate was 59 percent at public institutions, 66 percent at private nonprofit institutions, and 23 percent at private for-profit institutions.

Even though 41 percent of students who attend public colleges and 34 percent of students who attend private nonprofit colleges DO NOT graduate in six years, let's assume all students graduate in six years and you will still see where the $100,000 savings comes from.

Let's assume student A takes six years to graduate, and they pay $20,000 a year for college. This is a total of $120,000 they would pay for their degree. Let's say student B graduates in four years and pays

$20,000 a year to graduate; this would be a total of $80,000 spent to get their degree.

You may be thinking, "Mark, your math is wrong; the difference between $120,000 and $80,000 is $40,000, not $100,000. You are $60,000 off."

Economists have a term they call opportunity cost. Here is how Investopedia defines opportunity cost:

> Opportunity cost refers to a benefit that a person could have received, but gave up to take another course of action. Stated differently, an opportunity cost represents an alternative given up when a decision is made. This cost is, therefore, most relevant for two mutually exclusive events. In investing, it is the difference in return between a chosen investment and one that is necessarily passed up.

In other words, to really compare apples and apples between student A and student B, you have to factor in that in the two years student B was not in school (because they graduated in four years), they were working and making money. Let's assume they made $30,000 a year for those two additional years student A was in school. Now you get the $100,000 in savings: $20,000 saved in year five of college for student A + $20,000 saved in year six of college when student A was in college plus $30,000 in earnings in year five when student A was in college +$30,000 in year six when student A was in college=$100,000.

In reality, this $100,000 savings is an extremely conservative estimate for three reasons:

1) Around 40 percent of college students are not even graduating in six years.
2) The average family pays more than $20,000 for a year of college.
3) The average first-year wages for a college grad is more than $30,000.

Section 5 of *171 Answers* is next. In that section, we will take seven chapters to talk about what you can do to graduate in four years and not six, seven, or worse yet, not graduate at all.

I had lost touch with my friend Raymond. He lives almost 1000 miles away from me, but we got together recently. I knew he had started nursing school and took courses year after year and never graduated, but we had never really talked about it until now. The thing he said that stood out to me was, "I just finished paying off my loans." Raymond was 48 years old when he told me this.

164

WHY IS IT SO IMPORTANT TO SELECT THE RIGHT FRIENDS IN COLLEGE?

I have been determined to understand why some students graduate from college and others drop out. In my opinion, over 90 percent of the time when a student doesn't graduate, it is because of one of the following three reasons:

1) Inability to find a supportive community of people they like and can relate to
2) Financial challenges
3) A lack of discipline, lack of self-advocacy, and/or lack of self-confidence

The eight chapters in this section will cover eight actions students can take to ensure they graduate from college in four years. There will always be people who double major, are in co-op programs, or go part-time and take longer, but those are unique situations.

In 1998, researcher and author Judy Harris published *The Nurture Assumption: Why Children Turn Out The Way They Do.* The book argued that peers have noticeably more impact on teenage behavior than parents do. Who you spend time with will greatly determine how you behave. Here is how the Bible puts this in the Old Testament: "Walk with the wise and become wise, for the companion of fools suffers harm" (Psalm 13:20-NIV). If that wasn't convincing, here is how the Bible puts it in the New Testament: "Do not be misled, bad company corrupts good character" (I Corinthians 15:33-NIV).

Early today, I got together with Courtney, a student I worked with who just graduated from Vanderbilt. I wanted to hear more about how her final year went. Courtney said, "When you are at Vanderbilt, you are surrounded by such high achievers. Some are trying to get into medical school, while others are focusing on landing internships and jobs, but everyone takes their academics seriously; it can't help but rub off on you when you are around so many academically-driven students."

My older daughter Karis was able to get her younger sister to join her in an eight-week Christian leadership training program this summer for college students, run by Campus Outreach. My wife Anitra and I saw so much spiritual growth from Joy in her Christian faith. I talked to Joy about this and she said, "I look up to students I met this summer from the University of North Carolina at Greensboro, like Brooklyn and Erica. They were my friends this summer, but they were almost like mentors to me."

We dropped off Joy at Valdosta State and I wanted to say something profound to her before I gave her a parting hug and kiss, knowing she was about to be a college freshman. We were in a rush because after Joy checked into her room we went and got her favorite food, crab, at a local seafood restaurant. Joy had to be back in her dorm for a 7:00 p.m. meeting.

Before she ran into the meeting, I hugged her and kissed her and said, "Show me your friends and I'll show you your future, Joy; I am praying you will pick friends like Erica, Brooklyn, and Karis." I knew her peer group was going to be critical, so I made those my parting words.

It is important to pick the right friends and establish academic accountability

165

WHY IS IT SO IMPORTANT TO ESTABLISH ACADEMIC ACCOUNTABILITY?

If we are honest with ourselves, we all have lapses of discipline, and we need others to keep us in check or we are going to go off course. For example, Weight Watchers and Jenny Craig took off because of the need for accountability. Have you ever noticed when you are on the freeway and all of a sudden the traffic slows down? For drivers, just seeing a police officer is enough to curtail the speed of the traffic.

The same principle applies to academics. When I worked at the Westtown School, we had several very effective ways to change the behavior of a student who was struggling academically. One thing we did was start a group called SNID. SNID is an acronym for Saturday Night In-House Detention. When other students were at restaurants or the movies or a sporting event, the students who didn't handle their business academically were in a classroom with a teacher doing homework on

Saturday night. This was so effective that one teacher came up with another idea, SMOD. SMOD was an acronym for Sunday Morning Only Detention. It was similar to SNID, but it was on Sunday instead of Saturday.

Some colleges have academic accountability built into their structure. Karis's instructors at Davidson College make it very clear that it is not okay for you to skip class, and because Davidson classes are small, they'll notice if you don't show up.

Stanford researchers recently highlighted one school that applies a peer accountability program—Life Academy of Health and Bioscience in Oakland. The school is known for its low dropout rate and high number of graduates who persist through college for at least four years. This is from Zaidee Stavely's article in Mindshift (blog), published July 2, 2015.

I was talking to a leader at a large college in Georgia. He said to me, "Kennesaw State has a higher graduation rate than we have because they have implemented some creative programs to hold their freshmen accountable to getting off to a good start."

These ideas are great when they are initiated by the college, but you recall my words that being a self-advocate is one of the keys to graduating. What can you do if no such programs are in place?

Karis took a hard math and a hard science course last semester, but she was really smart in her approach. She knew that Chelsea, her best friend at Davidson, was disciplined, and she was good at math and science. They intentionally took the same math and science class, and Karis told me she could count on Chelsea to say, "Karis, let's get together and review the material before our tests."

My friend Dave and I grew up together, and Dave was always a high achiever. He graduated from Princeton for his undergrad, and he got his MD from Harvard. I was talking to Dave about his Princeton experience, and he said, "What helped at Princeton is a bunch of students would get together and study the difficult material in groups." Dave and his friends understood the importance of picking the right friends, but they also knew how to create academic accountability to ensure success.

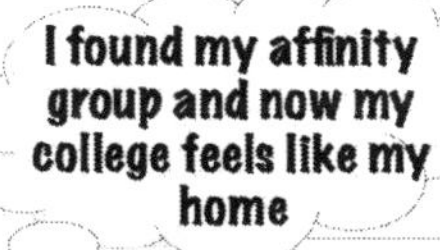

166

WHAT CAN YOU TELL ME ABOUT THE POWER AND VALUE OF AFFINITY GROUPS?

The PBS NewsHour ran a special titled *Why Poor Students Drop Out Even When Financial Aid Covers the Cost.* In the show, they quote research done by Anthony P. Carnevale and Jeff Strode showing that "when wealthy students and poor students have the same SAT scores, wealthy students have an 84% graduation rate and poor students have a 44% graduation rate." This is stunning, considering the fact that the wealthy students almost assuredly have their test scores inflated by top-notch test prep.

David Laude, Senior Vice Provost University of Texas, left teaching after decades to do something about this problem. When Laude was asked in the PBS special why there is a graduation gap, He replied by saying that when it comes to the poor students, "they don't feel they fit in." Laude, with support from the University of Texas started the "University Leadership Network" (http://student-success.utexas.edu/uln). A June 2, 2017, article in the school newspaper titled, "University Leadership Network Graduates Inaugural Class," describes how the graduation rate was up by 75 percent.

Yesterday I sat in on an information session at KIPP from the University of Pennsylvania. Kim Lopez, Associate Director of Admissions, was giving the presentation. She shared how UPenn has a 99 percent retention rate overall, and a 98 percent retention rate for students of color. These numbers are stupendous, 98 percent!!! That is 49 out of 50. Penn understands that if students are going to feel at home, they are going to have to support and celebrate differences to help students feel like they belong at Penn. Penn has six cultural centers for Intercultural, Black, Latina, Pan-Asian, Women, and LGBT students. (http://www.admissions.upenn.edu/life-at-penn/our-diverse-community/cultural-resource-centers). The truth is that everyone (not only the poor) needs to feel like they fit in.

Each center is staffed with people who are dedicated to helping students feel at home, find people like themselves, and feel great about their identity. A lot of people resent these groups, feeling they balkanize a community, but in reality, they diminish attrition and bolster self-confidence. The Posse Foundation, Inc., is another example of a group that has used affinity groups in a powerful way. According to https://www.possefoundation.org, Posse students persist and graduate at a 90 percent rate.

Here is what Meredith Kolodner said in a *New York Times* article on April 6, 2017, titled, "6 Reasons You May Not Graduate on Time (and What to do About It)":

> Some students slowly disengage because they never really feel part of a college community. Social isolation and depression can affect academic progress, especially for students living away from home for the first time. Studies have found that students who don't become involved in campus life, whether through friendship networks, clubs or sports, are more likely to drop out.

One of the reasons Karis selected Davidson College was the Christian affinity groups that they had. A lot of the academically-rigorous liberal arts schools Karis considered didn't have strong Christian groups, and that was very important to Karis. She got involved in Campus Outreach and was very active, and it made Davidson feel like home. Karis also wanted black Greek life. Even though she didn't pledge, she said to me, "Black Greek life is so much fun that I can't imagine not having it on campus."

167

HOW CAN I TAP INTO MY CAMPUS'S MOST VALUABLE RESOURCES?

Affinity groups are only one of the many resources that colleges have on campus to help students get to the graduation line. Colleges that have high graduation rates either have an Academic Success Center or they provide the services that Academic Success Centers provide. I am talking about things like tutoring, help with time management, writing support with papers, mentoring, money management, etc.

Georgia Tech's Center for Academic Success provides the following workshops:

- How to Develop Grit and Resiliency
- A Guide to STEM Study Strategies
- Whether to Drop or Not to Drop a Class

- ℵ I'm Late, I'm Late, I'm Always Late: Dealing with Procrastination
- ℵ Dealing with Academic Stress
- ℵ Prioritizing Study Tasks For Finals
- ℵ Study Smarter, Not Harder
- ℵ How to Form and Work in A Study Group

Opportunities abound, but you have to be a self-initiator. You have to have enough self-confidence to believe you can do the work.

There are resources available to help you with your health, like fitness centers and dieticians. There are counseling resources to help you if you are struggling with depression or another emotional or mental challenge. There are officers of multicultural or minority affairs to help students of color with special programming and mentoring, and to provide counseling and support for students of color. There are TRIO programs for under-resourced students. There are eating clubs, sororities, and fraternities by interest, and more to help students feel that all-important sense of belonging.

There are many services provided by the Office of International Studies. Here is the mission statement of Michigan State University's Office from the university's website:

MISSION STATEMENT

The mission of the Office for International Students and Scholars (OISS) is to provide support to Michigan State University's international students, scholars and families.

Services include:

- ℵ Advising on and facilitating compliance with United States immigration regulations.
- ℵ Conducting orientations and other special programming that help international students and scholars integrate into and adjust to the academic, cultural and social life of MSU.
- ℵ Serving as a liaison with United States government agencies, foreign embassies, sponsors, and educational foundations that support international students and scholars.

ℵ Contributing to the internationalization of MSU by providing opportunities for growth through cross-cultural interactions.

There are summer transition programs. There are freshman orientation programs. There are Living and Learning Communities where students can find like-minded peers and live with them. Here is how UCLA's website defines a Living and Learning Community:

> An initiative sponsored by Residential Life, it is a living-learning environment where students with similar interests live together and participate in programs that cater to their academic, social, and personal needs. Students living in these communities have the opportunity to partake in academic experiences with their peers and interact with faculty, enjoying the benefits of being part of a diverse community that shares scholarly interests.

The following link will take you to the 12 Living and Learning Communities that UCLA provides.

https://reslife.ucla.edu/livinglearning/

There are clubs and organizations designed to meet the interests and belonging needs of students. Some colleges have hundreds of these clubs, and every college I have ever known is open to adding new clubs if a student can show there is interest and if the club will be beneficial to the college.

We dedicated an entire chapter (Chapter 73) to talking about students with disabilities, and in that chapter we discussed the importance of the Disability Center. Then there is the all-important career center. Career centers are arguably the least-utilized resource that colleges provide. The last time I visited the University of Richmond, I was blown away by their Career Center, but I shouldn't have been, because colleges are pouring resources into these centers to help students with résumé writing, interview prep, internships, career fairs, job placement, etc. I tell students to visit the career center on their tours and ask them the tough questions. After all, you are going to college to learn, but you are also going to get a J-O-B.

I took 15 high-achieving KIPP students to tour Emory last week. After the tour and the information session, we met with Tim Fields, a real pro and a 12-year veteran of Emory's admission office, for a Q & A session. One student said, "Mr. Fields, does Emory provide opportunities for all of their students?"

I was doing cartwheels in my head about the way Tim answered the question. He said, "We have every imaginable opportunity here for you, but if you are struggling in a course, no one is knocking on your door saying you need to get to get a tutor. You need to get yourself out of bed and get a tutor. If you want to study abroad, you need to take the initiative on your own to get to the office of international and summer programs and learn about study abroad opportunities." Students who graduate tap into campus resources.

168

WHY SHOULD I TRY TO AVOID CHANGING COLLEGES?

Sometimes transferring is not only inevitable, it is prudent; other times, sticking it out is the advisable alternative. Some people will quibble with why Section 1 in this book begins by trying to identify the right major and career before you embark on your college search. They will say, "College is a time of exploration and discovery (which it is), and you are putting the cart before the horse." One reason why I advise taking so much time trying to identify where you want to study is because when you identify the area of interest and the right college up-front, it greatly increases your chances of graduating in four years.

When you transfer, it is very common for not all of your credits to transfer into courses that count toward your degree.

In Nika Anschuetz's December 16, 2015, article in *USA TODAY*, titled "Breaking the 4-Year Myth: Why Students Are Taking Longer to Graduate," the author discusses Complete College America, which is

> ... a non-profit organization that works with states to help close the college degree attainment gap, making it easier and more cost effective for students to pursue higher education. In their Nov. 2014 report, the group tackled the four-year graduation myth, stating most students at public universities don't graduate on time. For a non-flagship public university, only 19% of students graduate on time and even at flagship research public universities, the on-time graduation rate is only 36%. Only 50 of the more than 580 public four-year institutions have graduation rates above 50%. Thirty-seven percent of students transfer.

The problem with transferring is that it is very common for the credits that transfer to not count toward the department's degree requirements.

From Meredith Kolodner's article "6 Reasons You May Not Graduate in Time and What to Do About It," published on April 6, 2017, in the *New York Times*:

> Colleges and universities usually require 120 credits for a bachelor's degree, but students graduate with about 135, on average, according to data compiled by Complete College America, a nonprofit research and advocacy group.
> Some states' figures are even higher. Students at regional state colleges in New Mexico graduate with an average of 155 credits.
> One reason is the difficulty of transferring credits from another university or a community college. A third of students transfer at one point in their college careers. Nearly 40 percent of them get no credit for any of the courses they have completed and lose 27 credits on average—or about a year of school, according to a 2014 federal study.

Many colleges have developed articulation agreements to honor credits earned from other institutions. But often that isn't enough. A university may accept the credits, but the department of the student's major may not—and at most colleges, the decision rests with the department.

I was inquiring about Harvey, a student I once worked with, to see what he was up to because we hadn't communicated in a while. I asked Tracey, another college coach who knows Harvey better than I do. Tracey said, "Harvey left his first college and enrolled in a second college; he then left his second college to enroll in a third college. Harvey still hasn't graduated; he is in year seven." Don't let what happened to Harvey happen to you.

169

WHY IS IT SO IMPORTANT TO UTILIZE MY ADVISOR AND THEIR KNOWLEDGE?

Colleges are under more scrutiny to graduate the students they enroll. For decades, no one really questioned the value of college, but ever since the recession of 2008, colleges are being asked to prove their ROI by graduating students and delivering quality jobs.

Regular meetings with your advisor are imperative if you want to avoid five common mistakes that lead to either not graduating at all, or taking too long to graduate.

Problem #1

Falling into the "exploration" trap

According to an article on EAB, "5 Reasons–Other than Cost–That students don't graduate," "Communication has a lot to do with completion rates." After a rigid high school curriculum, the freedom to choose between thousands of course options can seem liberating for college freshmen—but can ultimately prevent students from graduating on time. Some students just start taking courses willy-nilly without thinking about whether they lead to fulfilling degree requirements.

Here is how *USA TODAY* put it in a December 2015 article by Nika Anschuetz:

> According to Dr. Bob Neuman, a former associate dean of academic advising at Marquette University, when students enter into college freshman year they often take a relaxed approach to college. "Students aren't sure what's going to happen to them once they start college," Neuman says. "They aren't thinking about how college should connect them with a career when they get out of college."

Problem #2

They don't create a four-year graduation plan.

When I was an advisor at Westtown School, I was responsible for creating a four-year plan with courses written in for each year. Sure, it changes as you learn more, but it keeps you from going wildly off course and it anchors you to completing in four years. Mapping out a four- year plan is invaluable.

Problem #3

The 12-Credit Fallacy: Take 15

From Meredith Kolodner's *New York Times* article:

> Most colleges define a full-time course load as 12 credits a semester, which is, not coincidentally, the ceiling for receiving the maximum Pell grant and most state financial aid. But degrees usually require 120 credits. Do the math—most students don't, and it's difficult to catch up: You need 15 credits a semester on average to get through in four years. "It shouldn't really surprise us, but it is remarkable how many students simply aren't made aware of what they need to do to graduate on time," said Rebecca Torstrick, assistant vice president for academic affairs at Indiana University.

Problem #4

They keep changing majors

It is unrealistic to expect a student to never change their major. How can an 18-year-old know exactly what they are going to major in when they are faced with so many choices? According to the government's own research, the National Center for Education Statistics, has found that almost 80 percent of students change majors. However if you take too long after matriculating to change majors, or if the change takes you in a totally different direction, it is likely to delay your graduation.

Problem #5

They don't schedule their courses wisely.

According to an article on EAB, "5 Reasons–Other than Cost–That students don't graduate," "Students overwhelmed by course choices often wait too long to take major requirements, only to discover those courses are full."

In some cases, it isn't the student's fault. Some courses that are required for graduation are offered infrequently. Other courses fill up so quickly when course registration opens that they are difficult to get into. In fact, this is such a serious problem that it is hard not to wonder if some colleges see this as a way to squeeze more money out of each student by having them stay on campus longer.

I followed up with Randy to see how his son Daniel was doing at the large state university that he was attending. Randy's gestures, his tone of voice, and his words indicated that he was frustrated, and so was his son Daniel. Randy said, "Daniel is trying to graduate with his engineering degree, and the courses that he needs are not available every time he tries to sign up for them."

The large state university Daniel attended had grown very quickly by merging with another school, and they weren't prepared to handle the growth. I had heard the same complaint about the same large state university from multiple people. The best way to handle this is to talk to your advisor about any courses that may be required for your major that are hard to get into. Your advisor should have some sagacious advice to help you.

170

HOW CAN I AVOID COMMON FINANCIAL PITFALLS?

I doubt anyone is surprised that one reason that explains why wealthy students graduate at a higher rate than poorer students is the disparity in family finances.

The National Student Clearinghouse's research says, "cost is the number one reason students fail to complete college in four years."

I was talking to my boss Angie Lyons at KIPP Through College in Atlanta about this section in my book about why students don't graduate. Angie said, "What reasons other than the money are you going to talk about?" In other words, she knew the correlation between a student not being able to afford college and a student dropping out of college.

I know what you are thinking: "What planet do you live on? Do you think I want to be in this financial bind?" I get it. Rarely in life are we able to completely avoid financial problems, but we can minimize them by being strategic and avoiding these expensive mistakes.

Mistake #1

Taking too long to graduate

According to_2013 data from the University of Texas at Austin, "students who graduate on time will spend 40 percent less than those who graduate in six years" (Anschuetz).

Mistake #2

Attending a dream college that was not affordable.

We addressed this subject in our chapters that discussed how much loan debt (Chapter 121) you should take out. We also addressed this in the cost questions we asked in the "Building Your College List" (Chapter 16) section. We also addressed it in our chapter about gapping. We had a chapter that showed you a method for learning what you can afford (Chapter 21) for college. Of course, this will vary from person to person. If you are attending an unaffordable college, you may survive a few years, but what about year five or six?

Mistake #3

Working too many hours

"This is the vicious cycle that comes from having so many bills. You have to work because you are in survival mode, but then your studies suffer. Students who are worried about debt sometimes work more and then reduce their course load," said Robert Kelchen, a professor of higher education at Seton Hall who studies student debt. "But by working instead of studying, they may find it more difficult to graduate on time" (Kolodner).

> About 40 percent of undergraduates work 30 hours a week or more, though a new study finds that more than 25 hours can get in the way of passing classes, especially for low-income students. Only 45 percent of students who work more than that are able to keep their grade-point averages above 3.0, according to the Georgetown University Center on Education and the Workforce. The percentage goes down as the hours go up (Kolodner).

Mistake #4

Out-of-control discretionary spending

This may be the six-dollars-a-day Starbucks habit that turns out to be $1200 a year. It could be eating out at restaurants at $20+ an outing when you are in drowning in debt. It could be spending sprees at the mall. This is why I tell students to use a financial software tool like Mint.com and create budgets in individual categories. This will help minimize your impulse purchases.

Mistake #5

Parent enablement

When Joy went off to college, she chipped in $50 and we spent $165 for her to get her hair the way she wanted it done, but after she had been at college for two weeks, she was calling to tell us that she had found an amazing person in her dorm who could do black girls' hair for only $50. She was calling to see if we would pay for her to get a touch up. We pumped the brakes on that so fast, she barely got the words out of her mouth. She knew she was supposed to sleep with her wrap for her hair to keep her style in good shape, and if she didn't do that, tough.

We told her, "Tap into your own savings or get a job, but we are not bankrolling your extravagance."

I know some people may think this is harsh, but I encourage you to watch the movie *Willy Wonka and the Chocolate Factory* and pay close attention to the character of Veruca Salt. You help your kids when you insist that they have skin in the game. Joy is no Veruca, and the reason for that is that we don't enable that attitude.

I have four presentations about Paying for College for four different groups of KIPP Metro Atlanta parents between September 12 and September 23. I am working on the presentation now. One thing I plan on doing in all four presentations is having the parents repeat: "I am not a bad parent because I tell my child that they cannot go to a college that is not affordable."

171

How can I develop the character to withstand life's storms?

I tell my students, "You are not going to go through four years of high school or college without having to deal with a significant storm in your life. I don't know if it will be an academic storm, a financial storm, a health-related storm, a family crisis, an emotional storm, a friendship storm (male or female), or a job storm, but take it to the bank: roaring thunder will be coupled with flashes of lightning in your life; the ominous clouds will be dark and the rain will be cascading down at some point in your four-year college experience. The question is: do you have the character to persevere?"

In the last 15 years, there have been some extremely encouraging developments in the world of education. There have been landmark books that have created educational epiphanies and changed what many schools value in education. There was Carol Dweck's *Growth Mindset,* Paul Tough's *How Children Succeed,* and Angela Duckwork's *Grit: The Power of Passion and Perseverance.* New research has shown how emotional intelligence helps predict academic performance. All of these outstanding books and white papers have put a premium on the value of character.

For the last 30 years, I have been fascinated by people who accomplish great things—movers and shakers who change the world. I have studied these "game changers" by reading biographies, watching documentaries, and just good old-fashioned people-watching. What I have focused my study on is what character traits these individuals have. I have looked at pastors, preachers, missionaries, entrepreneurs, athletes, businessmen, educators, civil rights leaders, and philanthropists.

I have noticed that highly accomplished individuals usually have 14 specific character traits, and when they don't have all 14 of them, they have at least 10 of them, and they usually have a few of these traits in exceptionally large doses.

Character traits highly accomplished individuals usually possess:

1. Being hard workers
2. Ability to build relationships well and get along with a wide range of people
3. Personal integrity
4. Grit and resiliency
5. Being lifetime learners
6. Ambition and motivation
7. Being self-advocates and initiators
8. Focus and discipline
9. Doing what they love
10. Doing what they are good at
11. Not afraid to take some risks
12. Having an optimistic worldview
13. Being kind and caring
14. Having faith in God

These same life skills are highly correlated with the character it takes to stay in and graduate from college when all hell is breaking loose around you.

Some of you are thinking, "You never said anything about a lack of academic ability as a reason for not graduating." No, I didn't. When a college accepts a student, that student has the ability to do the work more than 99 percent of the time. They may have to study two hours more a day than their peers, but if they are hungry enough, they will handle their business.

Lisa is a student of mine that a lot of people questioned. Her test scores were nowhere near the norms for the rigorous boarding school she attended, but I had known Lisa since she was 13; she had more drive, ambition, and discipline than almost all of her peers. Her work ethic was unparalleled. Lisa graduated from McGill University with honors, and then she went on to get a Masters degree from the London School of Economics.

Sherly is a student I recruited to Westtown from the New Jersey Seeds program, but I had moved to Atlanta by the time she graduated. I called her last Friday to get an update. Sherly told me how she was enrolled at TCNJ when one of those calamitous storms came into her life. She was told that her green card had expired and the full scholarship she was promised was being revoked, and she would have to reimburse TCNJ for thousands and thousands of dollars. Did Sherly quit? Absolutely not. She was resilient, self-motivated, and an initiator. She had to leave TCNJ, but she started working full-time as an intern in accounting while she simultaneously enrolled in Kean College. She wasn't afraid to take some risks, so she hired an attorney and won a settlement, and was reimbursed for the thousands she was overcharged. Sherly's work ethic, coupled with her love of learning, led her to be a full-time student while simultaneously working as a full-time accounting intern. Her optimistic world view kept her believing. Her relationship-building skills, combined with her personal integrity, led her accounting firm to say, "We don't normally hire graduates of Kean, but we are really impressed with you, and we want to offer you a full-time job in our firm." I asked Sherly, "Why did you select accounting?" She said, "It is something I am good at, and it is something I enjoy." It took Sherly six years to graduate, but her character led her to overcome her obstacles. If Sherly can graduate, so can you!

SECTION 6

RECOMMENDED RESOURCES

Mark's Most-Recommended College Admission Books

Books That Describe Colleges

Fiske Guide to Colleges 2018
Edward Fiske
July 11, 2017

The Best 382 Colleges, 2018 Edition (College Admissions Guides)
Princeton Review
August 1, 2017

Hidden Ivies, 3rd Edition: 63 of America's Top Liberal Arts Colleges and Universities
Howard Greene and Matthew W. Greene
August 17, 2016

Colleges That Change Lives: 40 Schools That Will Change the Way You Think About Colleges
Loren Pope and Hilary Masell Oswald
August 28, 2012

The Complete Book of Colleges, 2018 Edition (College Admissions Guides)
Princeton Review
July 4, 2017

America's Best Colleges for B Students
Tamra B. Orr and Gen Tanabe
July 4, 2017

A Review of Fifty Public University Honors Programs (Volume 1), 2nd Edition
John Willingham

The K&W Guide to Colleges for Students With Learning Differences, 13th Edition: 353 Schools With Programs of Services for Students With ADHD, ASD, or Learning Disabilities (College Admissions Guides)
Princeton Review

BOOKS THAT DESCRIBE COLLEGE MAJORS

Book of Majors 2018 (College Board Book of Majors)
July 3, 2017

The College Finder: Choose the School That's Right For You! 3d Edition
Steven R. Antonoff

BOOKS ABOUT PAYING FOR COLLEGE

The Forbes Guide to Paying For College
Jennifer Eum
July 30, 2014

The Scholarship System: 6 Simple Steps on How to Win Scholarships and Financial Aid
September 1, 2014

The Financial Aid Handbook, Revised Edition: Getting the Education You Want for the Price You Can Afford
May 15, 2017

Paying for College Without Going Broke, 2018 Edition: How to Pay Less for College (College Admission Guides)
Princeton Review and Kalman Chany

The Best Way to Save For College: A Complete Guide to 529 Plans 2015-2016, 11th Edition
Joseph F. Hurley

Filing the FAFSA, 2015-2016 Edition: The Edvisers Guide to Completing the Free Application for Federal Student Aid
Mark Kantrowitz and David Levy
December 16, 2014

Never Pay Retail for College: How Smart Parents Find the Right School for the Right Price
Beth V. Walker
March 14, 2017

The Ultimate Scholarship Book 2018: Billions of Dollars in Scholarships, Grants, and Prizes
Gen Tanabe
June 13 2017

TEST PREP HELP

The Official SAT Study Guide, 2018 Edition
The College Board

8 Practice Tests for the ACT: Includes 1,728 Practice Questions
Kaplan Test Prep

The Official Study Guide for ALL SAT Subject Tests, 2d Edition
The College Board

SAT Wars: The Case for Test-Optional College Admissions
Joseph A. Soares
April 12, 2013

A COMPREHENSIVE LOOK AT ALL PARTS OF THE APPLICATION PROCESS

College Admission: From Application to Acceptance, Step by Step

Robin Mamlet and Christine VanDeVelde
August 30, 2011

Admission Matters: What Students and Parents Need to Know About Getting Into College
Jon Reider and Sally P. Springer
May 1, 2017

COLLEGE ADMISSION ESSAY HELP

College Essay Essentials: A Step-by-Step Guide to Writing a Successful College Admissions Essay
Ethan Sawyer
July 1, 2016

Escape Essay Hell!: A Step-by-Step Guide to Writing Narrative College Application Essays
Janine Robinson
December 5, 2013

Conquering the College Admissions Essay in 10 Steps, Third Edition: Crafting a Winning Personal Statement
Alan Gelb
June 20, 2017

MISCELLANEOUS BOOKS

Where You Go is Not Who You'll Be: An Antidote to the College Admissions Mania
Frank Bruni
March 17, 2015

The GateKeepers: Inside the Admissions Process of a Premier College
Jacques Steinberg
July 29, 2003

College Rankings Exposed: The Art of Getting a Quality Education in the 21st Century
Paul Boyer
2003

Creating a Class: College Admissions and the Education of Elites
Mitchell L. Stevens
August 24, 2009

The Shape of the River
William G. Bowen Derek Bok
January 4, 2000

Paying for the Party: How College Maintains Inequality
Elizabeth A. Armstrong and Laura T. Hamilton
October 15, 2015

The Price of Admission: How America's Ruling Class Buys Its Way Into Elite Colleges—and Who Gets Left Outside the Gates
Daniel Golden
January 21, 2009

The Chosen: The Hidden History of Admission and Exclusion at Harvard, Yale, and Princeton
Jerome Karabel
September 8, 2006

Inside the College Gates: How Class and Culture Matter in Higher Education
Jenny M. Stuber
July 19, 2012

When Affirmative Action Was White: An Untold History of Racial Inequality in Twentieth-Century America
Ira Katznelson
August 17, 2006

Whither Opportunity?: Rising Inequality, Schools, and Children's Life Chances (Co-published with the Spencer Foundation)
Greg J. Duncan

Restoring Opportunity: The Crisis of Inequality and the Challenge For American Education
Greg J. Duncan

CHARACTER AND EDUCATION TO HELP YOU GRADUATE

Mindset: The New Psychology Success
Carol S. Dweck

Grit: The Power of Passion and Perseverance
Angel Duckworth

How Children Succeed: Grit, Curiosity, and the Hidden Power of Character
Paul Tough
September 4, 2012

HELP TRANSITIONING TO COLLEGE LIFE

The Naked Roommate: And 107 Other Issues You Might Run Into in College, 7th Edition
Harlan Cohen

MARK'S MOST-RECOMMENDED COLLEGE ADMISSION WEBSITES

The websites are listed alphabetically by their URL, not by my favorite to least favorite, so do check them all out!

Each college's own website!

1. http://www.act.org/
2. http://www.bestcollegesforblacks.com
3. https://bigfuture.collegeboard.org/?excmpid=VT-00061
4. https://www.bls.gov/ooh/
5. https://www.cappex.com/
6. http://www.chronicle.com/
7. http://www.city-data.com/
8. http://www.coalitionforcollegeaccess.org/
9. https://www.collegeboard.org/
10. http://collegecompletion.chronicle.com/
11. http://www.collegeconfidential.com/
12. https://collegecost.ed.gov/
13. http://www.collegedata.com/
14. http://www.collegexpress.com/
15. https://www.collegegreenlight.com/
16. http://college-insight.org/
17. http://collegemajors101.com/
18. http://www.collegeportraits.org
19. https://collegerealitycheck.com/en/
20. http://www.collegeresults.org/
21. https://collegescorecard.ed.gov/
22. https://www.collegeweeklive.com/
23. http://www.commonapp.org/
24. http://commonblackcollegeapp.com/
25. http://www.compassprep.com/blog/
26. https://www.ed.gov/
27. https://fafsa.gov/
28. http://www.fairtest.org/
29. https://www.fastweb.com
30. http://www.finaid.org/
31. http://www.guidetoonlineschools.com/

32. http://hbculifestyle.com/
33. https://www.hispanicoutlook.com/
34. https://www.insidehighered.com/
35. https://www.internationalstudent.com/
36. https://www.jbhe.com/
37. https://jlvcollegecounseling.com/
38. https://www.khanacademy.org/
39. https://myscholly.com
40. https://www.nacacnet.org/
41. https://www.nasfaa.org/
42. https://www.naviance.com/
43. http://www.ncaa.org/
44. https://nces.ed.gov/collegenavigator/
45. http://www.ncsasports.org/
46. https://www.niche.com/
47. http://www.parchment.com/
48. https://www.princetonreview.com
49. http://publicuniversityhonors.com/
50. https://www.questbridge.org/
51. http://www.road2college.com
52. http://www.savingforcollege.com/
53. https://www.scholarships.com/
54. http://smartcollegevisit.com/author/mmathews
55. https://studentaid.ed.gov/sa/
56. https://studentloanhero.com
57. https://studentloans.gov
58. http://www.thecollegesolution.com/
59. https://ticas.org/posd/home
60. https://www.unigo.com/
61. https://www.universalcollegeapp.com/
62. https://www.usnews.com/
63. https://web3.ncaa.org/ecwr3/
64. https://www.youniversitytv.com/category/college/
65. https://www.youtube.com/
66. https://www.youvisit.com/education/
67. https://www.wyzant.com

COLLEGE ACCESS ORGANIZATIONS FOR UNDER-RESOURCED STUDENTS

There are a lot of students who are at public schools where the teacher to student ratios for counselors are too high for them to get the individual attention they need. Other students have high school counselors that are not knowledgeable about the college process. The lower-income students who find themselves in this category may not be able to hire a private college coach. I wanted to provide a list of organizations that I am familiar with that can help. The descriptions below come directly from their own websites. Just because an organization is not listed that does not mean they don't do stellar work. It may mean their focus is not college counseling. It may mean they don't focus almost exclusively on under-resourced students. It may mean I just am not aware of their services. The 35 organizations listed below are known in admissions parlance as CBOs (Community-Based Organizations). These organizations are arranged alphabetically based on their websites.

http://advisingcorps.org/

College Advising Corps works to increase the number of first-generation college-going, low-income, and/or underrepresented students who apply, enter and complete college. We do this by placing recent college graduates from one of our partner universities as full-time college advisers in some of America's underserved high schools. In 2017-2018, our advisors will serve more than 600 high schools in 14 states. Advisors are in the Southeast, Mid-Atlantic, Northeast, Mid-Atlantic, Southwest, and the West.

http://www.beyond12.org/

One day, all students will have an opportunity to earn a college degree that provides them with meaningful economical and personal prospects. Beyond 12's mission is to dramatically increase the number of low-income, first-generation, and historically under-represented students who graduate from college.

http://www.buildingsteps.org/

We believe that where you come from does not determine where you can go. A college education changes a person's life. With a success rate of more than 80% of our graduates earning a college degree, we know we are propelling progress. Building STEPS works with Baltimore's brightest high school students, most of whom will be the first in their family to graduate from college, to unlock their potential. (Baltimore, MD)

http://cbo4success.org/

College Bound Opportunities (CBO) has been mentoring, motivating, and preparing under-served students from high schools in Highland Park (since 2007), Deerfield (2008), Lake Forest (2011), and Buffalo Grove (2017), and Cristo Rey St. Martin College Prep in Waukegan (2016) to attend and graduate from college.

https://www.chicagoscholars.org/

Chicago Scholars is transforming the leadership landscape of our city by resolving the fundamental barriers to success for academically driven, first generation college students from under-resourced communities. (Chicago)

http://www.collegeaccess.org/

Underrepresented students often must navigate the college pathway without adequate financial resources, guidance, or a strong college-going culture in their high schools. NCAN works to overcome these barriers so students can gain the postsecondary credentials they need to embark on successful careers and build America's future. (50 states)

http://collegeboundstl.org/

College Bound is a 7-9 year college preparation and success program. We are committed to staying with our students from the beginning of their sophomore year of high school until they have a college diploma in their hands and are on their way to finding a career of purpose. (St. Louis) http://www.collegefes.org/

College For Every Student is a global leader helping K-12 students from low-income rural and urban communities become college and career ready. CFES currently supports 25,000 students through partnerships with 200 rural and urban K-12 schools in (30 states and Ireland.)

http://collegeforward.org/

College Forward is an Austin-based nonprofit whose intensive, culturally-appropriate mentoring programs propel students from underserved backgrounds to collegiate success and remunerative careers. (Austin, TX)

https://www.collegegreenlight.com/

We connect first generation and underrepresented students to caring colleges, generous scholarships, and life-changing counselors and mentors. (50 states)

https://www.collegenowgc.org/

College Now's mission is to increase postsecondary educational attainment through college and career access advising, financial aid counseling, and scholarship and retention services. (Greater Cleveland, OH)

http://www.collegepossible.org/

College Possible is making college admission and success possible for low-income students through an intensive curriculum of coaching and support. (50 states)

http://collegespring.org/

CollegeSpring is dedicated to helping students from low-income backgrounds pursue the college educations they deserve. CollegeSpring serves students through partnerships with schools and community organizations in the San Francisco Bay Area, Southern California, and New York City, as well as in other communities across the country.

https://www.collegesuccessfoundation.org/

We provide a unique integrated system of supports and scholarships to inspire underserved low-income students to finish high school, graduate from college and succeed in life. (DC and Washington State)

https://collegetrack.org/

College Track recruits students from underserved communities and works continuously with them from the summer before ninth grade through college graduation. Our ten-year program removes the barriers that prevent students from earning their college degree by providing them with comprehensive academic support, leadership training, financial and college advising, and scholarships. We teach our students the skills necessary to succeed in college and beyond. (California, Colorado, Louisiana)

http://collegiatedirections.org/

The Scholars program isn't just about giving the kids the chance to go on to higher education. It's about getting them through their college years successfully, and giving them every tool they need to go out into the world and pursue the life of their dreams. (Maryland and DC)

https://edtrust.org/

Educational Trust are fierce advocates for the high academic achievement of all students—particularly those of color or living in poverty. (50 states)

http://eoschools.org/

Equal Opportunity Schools' mission is to ensure that all students have the opportunity to succeed in challenging high school courses. (23 states)

http://gotocollegenyc.org/

Throughout New York City there are African-American and Latino high school students from lower income families whose intellect, character, and academic achievement, in the face of poverty, is stunning. Go To College NYC was designed to find and support such students during and after the college admissions process, helping them break the cycle of poverty for children yet to come. (New York) https://imentor.org/

iMentor matches every student in our high schools with a committed college-educated mentor, equipped to guide that young person on their journey to college graduation. iMentor is expanding to serve more students in New York, Chicago, and the San Francisco Bay Area.

http://www.imfirst.org/

An online community celebrating first-generation college students and supporting those who will be. Hear inspiring stories and share your own, discover colleges that care about first-gen students, find answers to your questions about college, and receive guidance on the road to and through college. (National)

http://www.jkcf.org/scholarship-programs/college-scholarship/

The Jack Kent Cooke Foundation College Scholarship Program is an undergraduate scholarship program available to high-achieving high school seniors with financial need who seek to attend and graduate from the nation's best four-year colleges and universities. Selected from a nationwide pool of applicants, up to 40 students will become Jack Kent Cooke Scholars and have access to funding for up to four years for undergraduate studies. (50 states)

PODCASTS

Per Anika Madden: Your College Bound Kid is a podcast for parents and families everywhere who have (or will have) kids that aspire to go to—and most importantly, graduate—college. Co-hosted by Anika Madden and college admissions expert Mark Stucker, the show takes on a lively conversation between college coach and parent who share a common passion: to seal the cracks on families not understanding the admissions process. Every week, they'll share true stories and cover topics ranging from how to pay for college without going broke, building the right college list, getting accepted, and even choosing the right career.

Starting in 2018, the most pressing questions are answered. Fears are conquered. Find it on HandleItMom.com and you'll be able to download from your favorite podcast listening stations.

A SPECIAL OFFER FOR THOSE WHO PURCHASE 171 ANSWERS

For the last few years, the students I have worked with have had a tremendous experience getting excellent online test prep with a company called Test Innovators (https://testinnovators.com/). Test Innovators is the premier test prep company when it comes to helping students get into private middle schools and high schools, and they have now developed cutting-edge resources to help students prepare for college admission tests. I have gotten to know Edan Shahar, the founder of Test Innovators, and I have been so impressed with his company's cutting-edge technology, their unwavering commitment to customer service, and their commitment to providing affordable test prep to students of all incomes.

I was telling Edan about *171 Answers* and he said he wants to do something special for anyone who purchases this book. For anyone who has purchased *171 Answers,* Test Innovators will provide 10% off access to any of their online test prep platforms—just use the code 171ANSWERS at checkout to receive your discount.

FINAL THOUGHTS

I would love to hear from you! Here is my promise to you: If you send me an email at mark@schoolmatch4u.com, I will reply.

If *171 Answers* helped you, I would love to hear what chapters you found were the most helpful. Let me know how I can make *171 Answers* better in my next edition. If you would like for me to cover a subject I never covered in the book, communicate this. If something I said was confusing, please share this with me. If you are interested in me speaking to a group, let me know.

If you would like to receive more college information, go to 171answers.com and sign up for our blog. Once a month you will receive some free advice on college admissions and paying for college. The blog follows the same format as the book. We will have one article on colleges and majors, one on building your college list, one on getting accepted, one on paying for college without going broke, one on staying in and graduating, and one recommended resource a month.

If you feel like your school district, school, place of worship, or other organization you are affiliated with could benefit if your members had *171 Answers*, ask us about bulk-rate purchase opportunities.

Finally, I just want to thank you from the bottom of my heart for reading *171 Answers*. The most precious resource we have is our time. You invested your precious time to help yourself, help your child, or to improve the life of someone you are trying to assist, and that is something I am truly grateful for. Hope to hear from you!

With gratitude and sincerity

Mark

P.S. Remember, "It's not where you go, but it's what you do when you get there, and it's what you do when you get out of there that will determine your career opportunities."

Made in the USA
Columbia, SC
26 March 2019